CW01091167

Music and the Aesthetics of Modern

Essays

Music and the Aesthetics of Modernity

Essays

edited by
KAROL BERGER
& ANTHONY NEWCOMB

Isham Library Papers 6
Harvard Publications in Music 21
Harvard University Department of Music
2005

Distributed by Harvard University Press
Cambridge, Massachusetts, U.S.A. • London, England

Typesetting and printing by Puritan Press, Hollis, New Hampshire
Photograph of Reinhold Brinkmann by Jane Reed, Harvard News Office

Library of Congress Cataloging-in-Publication Data

Music and the aesthetics of modernity: essays /
edited by Karol Berger & Anthony Newcomb.— 1st ed.
   p. cm. — (Isham Library papers ; 6) (Harvard publications in music ; 21)
   Papers presented at a symposium held at the John Knowles Paine
Concert Hall of the Harvard Music Department, Nov. 9–11, 2001.
   "In honor of Reinhold Brinkmann"—T.p. verso.
   Includes bibliographical references and index.
   ISBN 0-9640317-2-8 (alk. paper)
   1. Music—Philosophy and aesthetics—Congresses. 2. Modernism
(Aesthetics)—Congresses. I. Berger, Karol, 1947– II. Newcomb, Anthony,
1943– III. Brinkmann, Reinhold, 1934– IV. Series.
  ML3845.M972 2005
  781.1'7—dc22
                       2004021410

For Reinhold Brinkmann—
scholar, teacher, friend

Contents

Part IV. The Anti-Hermeneutic Impulse:
Beyond Modernity or Beyond Modernism?

PREFACE

THE NOTION OF modernity, of an era in the history of the West distinct from antiquity and the Middle Ages, has been around for several centuries now and is common coin among historians of politics and economy, society and culture. It is therefore particularly striking and puzzling that it has not so far found much favor with music historians. Historians of European art music routinely acknowledge the existence of the early-twentieth-century modernism, but when it comes to recognizing features that so many historians associate with the larger concept of modernity, we prefer to talk variously of the Renaissance, Baroque, Classicism, or Romanticism.

One of the central reasons for this preference must undoubtedly be the wish of a relatively young, small academic discipline to establish its separate identity, and to study its object, art music in the West, as separate from other domains of culture. Hence, for at least a hundred years (since, say, Guido Adler), the story music historians most want to tell is the story of the internal evolution of music's stylistic means. To be sure, the names given the periods that emerge from telling a story of this sort (the Renaissance, etc.) are invariably borrowed from other, older disciplines, from art history in particular. But such borrowing is indicative of a largely unexamined belief in a common *Zeitgeist* underlying all cultural phenomena of an age (a spirit supposedly already well described by other historians and just waiting to receive its musical illustration), rather than of a genuine attempt to understand music at any given time as a component of a larger cultural configuration. In short, what has until now inhibited music historians from a serious engagement with the notion of modernity is our understandable but exaggerated tendency to maintain music's (and music history's) autonomy.

Conversely, the advantage of introducing the notion of modernity into the discourse of music history would be, precisely, that it would help to bring down the barriers that separate music from other cultural domains, and music history from other branches of history. The principal purpose of the present book is to encourage a debate over musical modernity, a debate that would consider the question whether, and to what extent, an examination of the history of European art music may enrich our picture of modernity, on the one hand, and whether our understanding of music's development may be transformed by insights into the nature of modernity provided by other historical disciplines.

It would be premature at this point to offer a systematic treatise that would investigate every aspect of the subject. A debate might be much more fruitfully encouraged at this early stage by bringing together a number of exploratory studies, which approach the subject from widely divergent perspectives and enter it at a number of widely divergent points. It is an exploratory ferment of this sort that we attempted to foster when we invited music historians of different generations, methodological orientations, and areas of expertise to participate in our volume. In addition, and precisely because the notion of modernity has been the subject of much discussion in other disciplines, we have also invited several literary scholars, several art historians, and a philosopher (almost all with strong musical interests) to offer examples of how issues raised by this notion might be approached in their respective domains. It should be noted that a number of contributors cross disciplinary boundaries to such an extent that it is no longer possible to assign their papers to a single specific field, which by itself is a demonstration of the potential fruitfulness of the approach encouraged here. Thus, for instance, music and film studies are intertwined in Abbate's essay, philosophy and music in the contribution by Goehr, and art and music in the papers by Bredekamp and Treitler, while Gumbrecht and Ryan go back and forth between literature and music.

It has already been mentioned that for most music historians, the modernism of the twentieth century was until recently the only appearance of the "modern" in music. The widely perceived recent decline, perhaps a demise even, of musical modernism makes it now possible to see the modernism of the twentieth century as a chapter in a much longer story, the story of musical modernity. It is this possibility that underlies many of the contributions to this volume, regardless of whether it is explicitly thematized as such, or treated as an implicit background of a specific exploration. It is this possibility, too, that explains why some of the contributions treat twentieth-century topics (Abbate, Burgard, Goehr, Kropfinger, Lewin, Painter, Ryan, Shreffler, Treitler), others reach back to the nineteenth (Newcomb) or even eighteenth century (Berger, Burnham, Danuser, Zerner), while still others range over many centuries, from the sixteenth to the twentieth (Bredekamp, Gumbrecht, Warnke).

Three motives in particular animate the collective project presented here. First and foremost, we wish to encourage a debate that would make room for the notion of modernity, and not only for the narrower concept of modernism, within the vocabulary of historians of Western art music. Second, we would like to facilitate such a debate by demonstrating and examining the eighteenth-century, and even earlier, roots of musical modernity. Third, for the same reason we would also like to explore the pre-modernist roots of modernism.

Part I brings together essays that explore the eighteenth-century origins of modernity. Once we shift our attention from the stylistic means of music to the aims these means were expected to serve, KAROL BERGER suggests, the changes music went through in the late eighteenth century will reveal their truly revolutionary, epoch-making character. The later eighteenth century, Berger claims, was a period when the dominant circular conception of musical time was demoted in favor of a linear one. By the end of the century, the central genres of the Viennese instrumental repertoire were based on the assumption that the temporal order in which musical events occurred was of the essence. But this assumption, largely taken for granted ever since, is not valid for much of the earlier, pre-modern music which favored temporal shapes that suggested circularity or infinity rather than an irreversible line connecting the past with the future. It was only in the later eighteenth century, in short, that "European art music began to take the flow of time from the past to the future seriously."

This revolution in the shape of musical time allowed musicians, in turn, to reflect in their works the new conception of historical time that came to dominate the self-understanding of European educated classes by the late eighteenth century. From Mircea Eliade in 1949 to Reinhart Koselleck in 1979 and Marcel Gauchet in 1985, historians have been repeatedly suggesting that, while traditional societies embraced a circular conception of time, the moderns live in the irreversible time of history, replacing the security of cyclical returns with an exhilarating vision of endless creativity and linear progress. It is this vision that modern music could celebrate thanks to its "new found ability to embody the experience of linear time ..."

In one of only two essays without an explicit reference to music (the other being Burgard's), the art historian MARTIN WARNKE investigates the evolution of graphic representations of military formations from the sixteenth to the twentieth century. (The results of the investigation resonate suggestively with the central role attributed to the arrow of linear time in the self-understanding of the moderns in Berger's essay.) In sixteenth- and seventeenth-century military manuals, Warnke shows, military formations were represented in an abstract fashion, independent of any specific place and time. By the mid-eighteenth century, Frederick the Great began to acknowledge the significance of the specific topography of the battlefield. A century later, arrows were added to represent the dimension of time, lines of action, and these have dominated representations of the battlefield ever since.

Similarly to Berger, SCOTT BURNHAM also emphasizes the essential modernity of late-eighteenth-century music. Burnham's interest lies with those passages in Mozart that reveal and explore "the interior realm of consciousness," and he offers detailed and subtle readings of a number of such passages. In passages of this sort, he argues, Mozart not only turns away from the objective external world toward subjectivity itself, but also "reflects a fundamentally ironic and melancholic condition of modern, post-Enlightenment self-consciousness."

HENRI ZERNER, in turn, examines the notion of style put forward in Buffon's 1753 *Discours du style*. Where his predecessors held that style had to be appropriate to the subject matter of the discourse, for Buffon style served to capture the individuality of the speaker, a radical change of perspective which Zerner, an art historian, finds to resonate with such modern formalist ideas as the "significant form." Moreover, Zerner demonstrates Buffon's dependence on a 1741 *Essai* by Père André whose understanding of style strikingly anticipated the Romantic notion that music, because of its expressive power and immediacy, should serve as a model for other arts. The question with which Zerner leaves off, namely, the question of how should we relate these anticipations to later cultural developments, might serve as a transition point to the second part of our volume.

The essays in Part II explore the pre-modernist roots of modernism. In fact, HERMANN DANUSER's paper bridges Parts I and II, being concerned with the pre-modernist roots of modernism and with locating specific roots in the later eighteenth century. The comic meta-operas (operas about opera) of the period, Danuser shows, contributed through their self-reflexivity to the development of musical modernity and can be fruitfully compared to the intensely self-conscious avant-garde musical theater of the twentieth century. (Burnham, too, identified the abandonment of "naïve" immediacy in favor of "sentimental" self-consciousness as a characteristically modern phenomenon.) This would correct the historiography of musical modernism that either focuses exclusively on twentieth-century developments, or at best invokes the precursory role of Wagner or the German Romantics, but rarely if ever looks back to the period that preceded the French Revolution. It would also correct the narrow Adornian understanding of musical modernism exclusively in terms of the development of compositional means (the putative "objective tendency" of the "musical material" to become ever more complex), and bring aesthetic, intellectual, and social issues into play, making visible again such characteristically modern phenomena as the self-reflexivity of the late operas of Richard Strauss.

HORST BREDEKAMP examines critically the sources of John Cage's interest, from 1949 on, in chance operations and in silence. Going beyond the composer's own explanations that these sources lay in Zen Buddhism and *I Ching*, Bredekamp, an art historian, traces two lines of transmission. First, he outlines an artistic theory and practice of chance images with roots in antiquity and with interchanges between Europe and China since the seventeenth century, and he identifies Marcel Duchamp as the conduit through which this tradition became operative in Cage's own practice. Second, he brings out the German Weimar- and Nazi-era filters through which both Zen Buddhism and *I Ching* became known to Cage. This in turn allows him to bring out the authoritarian implications of Cage's seemingly apolitical aesthetics: "the one who creates an area of chances is the master of everything which is possible."

Various aspects of modernism are explored in the papers of Part III. ANTHONY NEWCOMB investigates German mid- and late-nineteenth-century attitudes to the practice of quoting from and alluding to the thematic material of a recent composer. He comes up with an unexpected conclusion that until at least around 1860 quoting or alluding was universally frowned upon, considered an infringement of the principal modern artistic value of originality. Only in the later part of the nineteenth century, and only gradually, did the view still current today that this might be something positive—a gesture of homage, or a source of a meaningful engagement with the tradition—begin to emerge, and this in conservative circles eager to counteract the high premium that the New German school put on originality. Newcomb's study complicates the received wisdom considerably: the practices of quoting and alluding, so central to modernism, originate, in his reconstruction, in a conservative reaction against an earlier stage of musical modernity.

In his contribution, DAVID LEWIN (1933–2003) argues that it is only from today's post-modernist standpoint that we can fully appreciate the modernism of Gustav Mahler's music. With great analytical subtlety, Lewin demonstrates, on a number of specific examples, how Mahler's harmonic usages, deceptively traditional and diatonic, seemingly regressing back from the advanced positions reached by Wagner and his successors, point in fact toward the practices of today's minimalists.

The following three essays investigate various ways in which advanced music and radical politics interacted during the past century. KAREN PAINTER offers a richly documented corrective to the view that new music and socialist politics were necessarily in conflict during the years between the two World Wars. Drawing on writings of many composers and critics in Germany and Austria, Painter argues that modernist music and social-democratic politics were often intertwined in unexpected ways.

The aesthetic and political significance of Arnold Schoenberg's setting of Lord Byron's "Ode to Napoleon" is the subject of JUDITH L. RYAN's essay. Ryan, a literary scholar, relates Schoenberg's methods to those of Bertold Brecht, showing how the composer aims at an estrangement effect preventing the listeners from being emotionally swept away. The modernist privileging of complex reflection that would keep unrestrained emotion in check, she argues, was a natural stance in the age of charismatic tyrants.

Like Painter and Ryan (and like Bredekamp, earlier in the book), ANNE C. SHREFFLER is particularly concerned with the intersections between modernist music and politics in the age of struggles between the liberal and totalitarian forms of democracy. Shreffler joins a growing number of scholars who investigate the impact of the Cold War on avant-garde serialism in Europe and the U.S.A. in the 1950s. While it is easy to see why an avant-garde composer of the period might wish to distance himself from Nazi and Soviet aesthetics, she points out, it is much less easy to make the connection between the music and politics specific to individual works. Her case study, the sponsorship of Igor Stravinsky's *Threni* at the 1958 Venice Biennale by the U.S.-funded Congress for Cultural Freedom, attempts to do just that, to connect the notes with the political context.

Against the theorists of post-modernism, KLAUS KROPFINGER is concerned with demonstrating, on a number of concrete examples drawn from the avant-garde music of the past half century, that modernist consciousness remains alive and well. For the past two hundred years, linear time has been incorporated into the modern composer's understanding of his own historical position: in a characteristic dialectic of actuality and survival, the idea of progress, the wish to make it new, is a prerequisite for the creation of enduring masterpieces. This basic structure of self-understanding, Kropfinger thinks, remains intact even today.

In marked contrast to Kropfinger, LEO TREITLER takes post-modernism seriously and attempts a delicate balancing act between the claims of modernism and post-modernism. On the one hand, as befits a historicist, he urges us to see modernism through the modernists' own eyes, rather than through the eyes of their predecessors or successors. At the same time, however, he adopts a characteristically playful, collage-like post-modern tone to urge us to see modernism as a musical embodiment of, and reaction to, its socio-political context. Thus, like Shreffler, he suggests that Stravinsky can be seen as a Cold-War figure—hardly the way Stravinsky saw himself.

What the last two essays of Part III have in common is the willingness to subject verbal texts to formal analysis and draw from such analysis far-reaching interpretative conclusions. PETER J. BURGARD takes the apparent simplicity of language and plot in Franz Kafka's "Das Urteil" at its face value and delivers a starkly literal, formalist reading of the story, attributing what he takes to be its comic effect to its structure. He then brings Nietzsche and Freud to bear on his analysis, which allows him to see the story as a "critique of phallic discourse."

LYDIA GOEHR interprets and compares two twentieth-century philosophers with deep interest in music, Adorno and Wittgenstein, as modernist figures. A philosopher, she locates the core of modernism in formalism, and argues that, like music, philosophy can reveal truth through form. She intertwines themes of literal exile and home-seeking, as well as the metaphorically exiling and home-seeking activity of philosophy, and relates philosophy to both humor and music—all dynamically shaped and driven toward significant endings and all, she thinks, crucially dependent on performance.

Part IV, finally, presents two essays that explore perspectives reaching beyond modernism, and perhaps even beyond modernity itself, and question the hermeneutic impulse that, the authors claim, animates much of the modern project.

In an important programmatic statement, the literary scholar HANS ULRICH GUMBRECHT contrasts as two ideal types a culture that aims at the "production of presence" (in the real time and space of the participants) and one concerned with the "production of meaning" (located in an imaginary time and space, different from the real time and space in which the participants are placed). While pre-modern European culture was interested primarily in the production of presence, he claims, since the seventeenth century, European modernity has privileged the production of meaning. (Like Berger, Gumbrecht stresses the reversibility of pre-modern time, and irreversibility of modern time.) Moreover, Gumbrecht's ideal types allow him to interpret the crisis of representation in the high modernism of the early twentieth century as an attempt to leave the culture of meaning behind and move back toward the culture of presence.

What this model suggests is that the hermeneutic imperative that the humanities take for granted should be questioned: if not every culture is a meaning culture, the interpretation of meaning cannot be seen as the only natural aim of research. And in particular, the humanities will have to resist the hermeneutic impulse if they are to catch up with high modernism.

There is a nice irony in the spectacle of a literary scholar urging musicologists concerned with opera in particular to worry less about the librettos and their meaning and more about the music's sonic, physical presence. But beyond that, Gumbrecht's argument has interesting implications for understanding the position of music within modernity: if modernity privileges the production of meaning and high modernism the production of presence, it would follow that music, which since its emancipation from language in the late eighteenth century has exhibited considerable discomfort with the culture of meaning, has entered its own high-modernist phase a good century earlier than other arts.

With her characteristic love of paradox and virtuosity, CAROLYN ABBATE deploys formidable hermeneutic resources to interpret the use of music in Josef von Sternberg's 1931 film, *Dishonored*, as an argument against hermeneutics. Abbate puts forward two claims. First, she thinks that the desire to interpret, to spell out the meanings supposedly encoded in the music, to cross over from the medium of music to that of language, is quintessentially modernist (here she differs from Gumbrecht), because of the modernists' well-documented interest in abolishing the borderlines separating various artistic media. Second, this desire, she affirms, has disquieting, morbid, nightmarish aspects and should be resisted. To be sure, Abbate does distinguish the completely unacceptable, to her, "low hermeneutics" that "sees social meanings as inscribed in musical texts at the moment of their creation, remaining legible in semi-permanent ways thereafter," and the less disreputable "soft hermeneutics" that "acknowledges that nothing is immanent in the work, that music unleashes associations in the listening subject, which may correspond in part to the historically pedigreed reactions of some hypothetical past listener …" But even this soft hermeneutics does not escape her strictures. For one thing, there is no essential difference between the two hermeneutics, she thinks, and for another, "soft inevitably shades into low."

The problem with the hermeneutic impulse is that it diverts the attention from what music truly is, a real, presently sounding, performed event, to something else, an inaudible abstraction, the ideal work as a medium of access to meanings, to a metaphysical Other. But it is not a resistance to metaphysics that ultimately motivates Abbate's doubts. "Low hermeneutics," she persuasively claims, changes the experience of music into a kind of mechanical cryptography, thus eliminating all freedom and life. But "soft hermeneutics" is no less insidious: if music has "a legible connection to the world," it "could have the power to create us, ... to engender our actions or beliefs, to commit murder." (The idea that, by the same token, music would also have the power to motivate us to do good does not enter Abbate's moral calculation.) The ultimate motivation of Abbate's anti-hermeneutic impulse is thus ethical. Real music in live performance, improvisatory and free from slavish obedience to the score, celebrates human freedom that exists in "a narrow corridor between spiritual automatism, in which one follows a script ..., and caprice or chaotic irresponsibility ..."

The issues raised by Abbate's essay are of central importance to the humanities and one can expect that her text will generate much discussion within musicology and neighboring disciplines. There will be those who will want to argue that the anti-hermeneutic impulse itself is a quintessentially modernist phenomenon: from Duchamp through Cage and beyond, painters and musicians in the twentieth century have expended tremendous effort to arrest the movement from the objects they make toward a meaning, to make sure that, in Frank Stella's words, "what you see is what you see" (and hear). Thus, it may well be that, far from representing a move beyond modernism, the anti-hermeneutic impulse deserves a serious consideration and interpretation as a characteristic strand within high modernism. There will also be others who (while wholeheartedly agreeing with Abbate that naïve, neo-Kretzschmarian low hermeneutics should be resisted) will point out that all efforts to make sure that "what you see is what you see" thus far have ended in failure, and hence that soft hermeneutics may be inescapable. They might even use Abbate's own text in support of their claim: what is the conclusion that live performance celebrates freedom, after all, if not an exercise in hermeneutics?

If this preface ends with a question, this is only appropriate for a book of essays, explorations designed to open up rather than close the inquiry. But before we end altogether, it is our pleasant duty to acknowledge Lesley Bannatyne, who managed the publication of this volume with great competence and grace, and our two indefatigable editorial assistants, Martin Deasy and Arman Schwartz. We are also grateful to several people in and associated with the Harvard University Department of Music: William Bares, Aaron Berkowitz, Gary Duehr, Robert Hasegawa, Jonathan Kregor, Christina Linklater, Jesse Rodin, and Jonathan Wild.

This book had its origin in a conference, co-directed by Karol Berger and Lewis Lockwood, at the Harvard University Music Department on 9–11 November 2001. The editors' aim, however, has not been to offer a conference report, but rather a book that can stand on its own. Hence neither the list of the contributors to this volume, nor the contents of their contributions, correspond exactly to those of the conference. One thing remains unchanged: the conference was designed to honor Professor Reinhold Brinkmann, and so is the present volume. Together with the authors, we offer it to Reinhold with the hope that it will not displease him.

Karol Berger
Anthony Newcomb

The Eighteenth-Century Origins of Modernity

Time's Arrow and the Advent of Musical Modernity

KAROL BERGER

I.

THE GENERATION OF Europeans whose memories reached back from the period after the fall of Napoleon to the days of the *ancien régime* shared the sense of having lived through the most profound upheaval and transformation in human history. This sense is the thread running through Chateaubriand's *Mémoires d'outre-tombe*, where it found its perhaps most unforgettable expression. "The old men of former times," wrote Chateaubriand in 1822,

> were less unhappy and less isolated than those of today: if, by lingering on earth, they had lost their friends, little else had changed around them; they were strangers to youth, but not to society. Nowadays, a straggler in this life has witnessed the death, not only of men, but also of ideas: principles, customs, tastes, pleasures, sorrows, opinions, none of these resembles what he used to know. He belongs to a different race from the human species among which he ends his days.[1]

In a preface of 1833, the leitmotif got its most pithy formulation: "... I've seen the beginning and the end of a world ...."[2] Chateaubriand was hardly alone. In an article originally published in *Heidelberger Jahrbücher* in the winter of 1817–18, Hegel talked of "... the last twenty-five years, possibly the richest that world history has had, and for us the most instructive, because it is to them that our world and our ideas belong."[3] Nearly two centuries later, and in spite of the seemingly still more profound disruptions Europe experienced after 1914, these thoughts, whether expressed with Hegel's sobriety or voiced in Chateaubriand's sonorous tone of somber melancholy, still ring true.

Ernst Robert Curtius opens and closes his 1948 meditation on *European Literature and the Latin Middle Ages* with some thoughts on the temporal shape and limits of his subject.[4] The development of European literature, he thinks, is marked by two caesuras. The first was "the fallow period of decline which extended from 425 to 775" and separated the ancient from the medieval world.[5] The second caesura is where we still find ourselves: "A new period of decline begins in the nineteenth century and reaches the dimensions of catastrophe in the twentieth."[6] Elsewhere we learn that the beginning of this new period can be dated back to around 1750.[7] Here Curtius follows the English historian G. M. Trevelyan who, in his *English Social History* of 1944, proposed to see the medieval period as extending into the eighteenth century, until the Industrial Revolution which "changed human life more than did the Renaissance and the Reformation."[8] (This notion of the "long Middle Ages" extending until the Industrial Revolution, by the way, is still alive in Jacques Le Goff's 1985 book on *L'imaginaire médiéval.*[9]) Similarly, for Curtius, "a break with the more than millennial European literary tradition also makes its appearance in England about 1750."[10] And elsewhere: "The middle of the eighteenth century witnessed not only the beginnings of that great economic change which is termed the Industrial Revolution. It saw also the first powerful revolt against cultural tradition, which is marked by Rousseau."[11]

Curtius cannot quite make up his mind as to how the times that followed antiquity should be called. "But does it make sense to call the period from 400 to 1750 the 'Middle Ages'?" he asks. "Obviously not."[12] But elsewhere he affirms that "medieval forms of life subsist until about 1750, to put it roughly."[13] Ultimately, "we need not bother to find a name for this period. But if we try to consider it as a cultural unit, we may get a better understanding of our past."[14] As for the times that followed, "historians in times to come will presumably set our age down as the 'Period of Technique,'" although Curtius is as aware as anyone that it is customary to call the age the "Modern Period."[15] Again, we need not bother with the name. What matters is the underlying vision of the shape of historical time.

Of the two caesuras that mark the development of European literature, the more recent one is also the more important, profound, and catastrophic. In spite of the interregnum that separated the ancient and medieval worlds, those two worlds maintained an underlying continuity: "... the substance of antique culture was never destroyed."[16] If "the bases of Western thought are classical antiquity and Christianity, ... the lesson of the Middle Ages is reverent reception and faithful transmission of a precious deposit,"[17] so that the continuity of the tradition from its "founding hero," Homer, to its "last universal author," Goethe, is maintained.[18] For the modernity of the last two centuries, by contrast, the "break with the more than millennial European literary tradition" is not only defining, but threatens to be definitive (though, of course, one cannot know that for sure):

> The nineteenth century produced a type of writer who championed revolutionary ideas and revolutionary poetry. That is a feature which betrays an age of disintegration, to use the formula of Toynbee. It may amount to what he called "a refusal of mimesis." But the equilibrium of culture will be preserved only if those disrupting forces are balanced by new ways of stating and adapting the legacy which has been entrusted to us by the past.[19]

Curtius explicitly opposed his dark vision of modernity to the inherited optimistic notion of progress: "The decisive change that the nineteenth and twentieth centuries have brought about in the world was accomplished through industry and technique—both of which were at first hailed as 'progress' but are now manifestly powers of destruction as well."[20] Thus he wanted to distance himself from those who saw the "Modern Period" beginning around 1500, because "to assume that a period begins shortly before or shortly after 1500 depends upon also admitting, at least tacitly, that the Modern Period, up to 1914, was a realization of progress—in the direction of enlightenment and democracy (England and France) and in the direction of the national state (Germany and Italy). This belief in progress was refuted by the world wars of the twentieth century."[21]

It is understandable that in the late 1940s this dark vision of modernity was widely shared, as was the view that the origins of the recent European collapse reach back into the eighteenth century (think of Adorno and Horkheimer, or, for that matter, of Heidegger, figures seemingly as distant politically from Curtius and from one another as can be). Whether we still find this pessimism persuasive today, after half a century of undeniable progress, is a question that need not detain us here. What matters and survives intact, whether we give it a dark, bright, or neutral coloring, is the belief that something fundamental and decisive happened in the late-eighteenth century, that history, and not only the history of literature, then took a decisive new turn, more decisive and new than any taken earlier, a turn marked by the beginning of the unprecedented and more or less constantly accelerating economic growth fuelled by the new science and technology, and by the revolutions in America and France. Whether we are optimists or pessimists, whether we like our world or abhor it, we still locate its origins in the political, economic, social, and cultural developments of the late-eighteenth century. It is then that our modernity was born.

II.

This sense that the late-eighteenth century marks the arrival of modernity may be a commonplace among political, economic, social, cultural, literary, and art historians, but, with the significant exception of those influenced by Adorno, it is not widely shared by music historians.[22] Unlike the much narrower notion of early-twentieth-century musical modernism, modernity is not a concept that figures often in our vocabulary, and on the rare occasions when it does, the birth of modern music is located around 1600 rather than around 1750 or 1800. In this vein, Leo Schrade called Monteverdi the "creator of modern music" in his 1950 book on the composer, and an important current journal, *Early Music History*, identifies its scope in the subtitle as *Studies in Medieval and Early Modern Music* thus suggesting that the post-medieval music is "early modern." But, in any case, this is exceptional: in the standard usage of our music history texts, to say nothing of our concert life, twentieth-century modernism is the only "modern" music there is.

To be sure, we do commonly recognize that an important stylistic change occurred some time around, roughly speaking, the middle of the eighteenth century, when the "Baroque" was replaced by the "Classical" style. But we do not claim that this change was different in kind, more fundamental, let alone catastrophic, than the stylistic revolution that preceded it and transformed the "Renaissance" into the "Baroque" style. And while we often do agree with Friedrich Blume who did not consider the next stylistic transition, that between the "Classical" and "Romantic" styles, to be in the same league, and who proposed to talk of a single "Classic-Romantic" period (on the grounds that no truly fundamental changes in compositional technique occurred between, say, 1740 and 1907), we certainly do not see the mid-eighteenth-century revolution as more thoroughgoing than the one effected by Schoenberg and Stravinsky around the time of the Great War; quite the contrary.

For a sense of the exceptional, epoch-making character of late-eighteenth-century musical innovations, we need to go back to the second decade of the nineteenth century, to E.T.A. Hoffmann's landmark essays on "Beethoven's Instrumental Music" and on "Old and New Church Music."[23] Hoffmann would probably not object to Blume's notion of a single Classic-Romantic period, since for him the two terms do not contradict one another: Haydn, Mozart, and Beethoven are all Romantics, and they are also the new music's classic authors, its Homers and Virgils. More importantly, their "new art, whose earliest beginnings can be traced only to the middle of the eighteenth century,"[24] is also identified as "modern" (Mozart and Haydn are "the creators of modern instrumental music"[25]) and a gulf separates it from the music of their predecessors. That earlier, pre-modern music was a mimetic art, like painting or poetry with which it was often combined. It imitated something specific and definite: the emotion of the subject who delivered the text. What defined the new music was its separation from language and hence from the mimesis of anything definite, anything in particular. The new music's "only subject-matter," Hoffmann famously declared, "is infinity." "All precise feelings" of earlier music were left behind in favor of "an inexpressible longing." [26]

What accounts for this difference of vision? Why can Hoffmann see an epochal break, nothing less than the birth of musical modernity, where we see no more than one stylistic renovation among many? In part, obviously, because we are aware of the later developments that Hoffmann could not know and our understanding of these later developments colors our interpretation of what happened in the eighteenth century. (At mid-twentieth century, one tended to attribute to the undermining of tonal and metric framework fifty years earlier the fundamental importance which made all preceding changes in music history look pale by comparison. Today we are more inclined to see the Schoenbergian and Stravinskian expressionisms as contingent stylistic developments rather than inevitable revolutions and hence are more likely to consider them as episodes within a longer story.) Less obviously perhaps, we tend to concentrate exclusively on stylistic matters, on compositional means. The essentials of the mid-eighteenth-century innovations lie, for us, in the demotion of thorough-bass from its central role in composition to the margins of performance practice, in the emancipation of instrumental music, and in the development of formal thinking based on the interplay between tonal planning and thematic argumentation. Hoffmann was as aware of these technical innovations as we are, but he did not put them at the center of the story he was telling. Decisive for him was not the renovation of compositional means, but the change of aims these means were expected to serve. His emphasis was on the "subject-matter," the content, of music, on the new ambition to embody in music the infinite totality and longing, rather than any definite emotions. The means employed to satisfy this ambition were of secondary importance.

How would the evolution of music during the eighteenth century begin to look to us if we took the methodological cue from Hoffmann and thought of it primarily in terms of aims rather than in terms of means? This is precisely what I would like to explore now. For Hoffmann, what was essential about modern music was what might be termed, with a nod to Curtius and Toynbee, the "refusal of mimesis." While I do think that Hoffmann put his finger on a centrally important point here, this will not be my subject. Instead, I would like to concentrate on a change in the shape of musical time, on the demotion of what might be called, this time with a nod to Stephen Jay Gould, "time's cycle" in favor of "time's arrow."[27] (Thus, I would be indirectly responding to the challenge recently issued by Reinhold Brinkmann in his wide-ranging essay on "Die Zeit der *Eroica*" where he reproached musicology for neglecting the subject of the radical temporalization of all domains of knowledge around 1800.[28])

III.

It was one of the effects of Scott Burnham's book on *Beethoven Hero* to have reminded us to what extent the expectations and values of all those brought up in the European art music tradition continue to be informed by the assumptions derived from the key works of Beethoven's heroic style, not the least among them the Fifth Symphony.[29] The particular assumption I am interested in here, however, goes beyond the confines of the heroic style and underlies virtually all of the classical Viennese instrumental repertory which was for Hoffmann the paradigm of musical modernity. The assumption is, simply, that in music the temporal order in which the events occur always matters.

There can be little doubt that, indeed, it does matter in the Viennese sonata-genres. The disposition of events in a sonata (or a string quartet, a symphony, a concerto), the temporal order in which they appear, is of the essence: to tamper with it is to drastically change, or destroy, the meaning of the work. The temporal positions of the main and second subjects, or of the exposition and recapitulation, cannot be swapped at will. If one is to experience such works with understanding, one has to register, however dimly, that the material being developed has been exposed earlier, or that what is being now recapitulated has already been heard in some form before. The interpolation of the Scherzo material in the Finale of the Fifth Symphony does not make much sense unless one is aware of its having made an earlier appearance.

This much is obvious. What is less obvious is that not all music works this way. The Viennese classics have shaped our musical expectations and values to such an extent that these values inform any music we encounter. A characteristic example of how widespread is this assumption that all music must be necessarily and essentially temporal, that the disposition of events in time always matters in music, is provided by Carolyn Abbate's argument against the plot-centered, as opposed to narrator-centered, understanding of what is a musical narrative: since all music is temporal, Abbate argues, that is, since it always has a "plot" (a temporal arrangement of events), it is all "narrative," and hence the application of the term relative to music is redundant.[30] But it is precisely this assumption of the primacy of the temporal disposition of events that is invalid for music written a mere half century before the Viennese classics.

I take it to be the main virtue of Laurence Dreyfus's illuminating book on *Bach and the Patterns of Invention* to have demonstrated this particular point on a whole range of Bach's instrumental genres.[31] Whether he composed a two-part invention, a fugue, or a concerto movement, what mattered to Bach first and foremost, Dreyfus repeatedly and persuasively shows, was the finding of a melodic-contrapuntal-harmonic material capable of interesting transformations and figuring out what these transformations were. The "invention" of a piece, in the terminology Dreyfus borrows from the rhetoric, was precisely the sum total of the material and its transformations. Since all of these could not be presented at once in actual sounding music, they had to be somehow ordered in time, one after another. But this temporal "disposition" was a matter of relative indifference: one found a suitable order in full awareness that other arrangements might do equally well. The central interest, for the composer, performer, and listener alike, lay not in the disposition, but in the invention. (And, I might add, it was the invention that required most talent, skill, and ingenuity; the disposition was a fairly easy matter by comparison.)

Take the very first, C major, fugue in the first of Bach's two sets of preludes and fugues for *The Well-Tempered Keyboard* (Ex. 1).[32] Like every fugue in the sets, it begins by presenting its melodic subject successively once in each voice, either on the first or on the fifth scale degree of the tonic key. What follows, in this, and, again, every fugue, is a series of demonstrations of what can be done contrapuntally with the subject. Here, there are seven such demonstra-

Example 1

Example 1 (continued)

tions, each designed to show how the subject can be combined with itself in imitation. A majority of these demonstrations involve the subject's statement on the first scale degree and an answer on the fifth scale degree, whether in the tonic or in some other key. And many are designed to show the possibilities of imitating at a given interval and temporal distance, with the answer either above or below the statement, that is, in invertible counterpoint.

It is striking how few transpositions Bach chooses to use. Most of the demonstrations appear untransposed in C major or its relative, A minor.

Demonstrations two and six are the only ones to be transposed, and these minimally, up a fifth. A trek through many different keys is clearly not on Bach's mind here. The tonal plan, in fact, is simplicity itself: areas of tonal stasis in the tonic key at the beginning (mm. 1^1–10^2) and the end (mm. 24^1–27^4) frame two areas of tonal motion, the first one from the tonic to the relative minor (mm. 10^3–14^1), the second from the tonic through the secondary dominant and the dominant back to the tonic (mm. 14^1–24^1).

When the thematic events are considered along with the tonal plan, the overall form emerges: the exposition (mm. 1^1–7^1) and the coda (mm. 24^1–27^4), both in the tonic key, frame two sets of demonstrations, one (mm. 7^1–14^1) beginning in the tonic key and ending in the relative minor, the other (mm. 14^1–24^1) beginning and ending in the tonic. The overall proportions are elegantly symmetrical, without any beat-counting pedantry.

The fugue is the product of three distinct operations. First, one needs to invent the subject and figure out what can be done with it contrapuntally; that is, one needs to produce the essential components of the exposition and a set of demonstrations. Second, one needs to decide upon a logical tonal framework or plan for the piece. And third, one needs to fit the exposition and the demonstrations into this framework, which may force one to transpose some of the demonstrations and to inflect chromatically some notes within them. The first and second operations can be performed in any order one wishes: none is logically prior, that is, none presupposes the other. The third operation, obviously, has to follow the other two. All three operations are essential: we would not have a fugue without them. Thanks to them we do get something reasonably close to a fugue, but additional, less essential, operations are needed to complete the work: counterpoints can be added in voices not occupied by the subject; gaps between the demonstrations, if there are any, need to be filled; cadences composed and ornamented; the whole performed.

The first two operations, it has just been said, are both essential, and neither is the prerequisite for the other. But their logical parity does not mean that they have equal weight in the process of composition, nor that they are equally important to the listening and understanding of the fugue. A rather basic level of musical literacy suffices for anyone who wants to devise interesting and elegant tonal plans. The invention of subjects capable of many interesting and varied contrapuntal treatments requires an incomparably higher level of skill and imagination. And what is true for the composer is also true for anyone who wants to understand the work. For the listener, the focus of interest in a fugue is on the subject and what is being done with it contrapuntally. A logical tonal plan into which the succeeding demonstrations are fitted is rather taken for granted and hardly registered at all.

It is something of a bonus that we have an independent confirmation that this is how Bach himself viewed the matter, how the composer listened. We read in the celebrated passage from a 1774 letter that Bach's second son and most substantial pupil, Carl Philipp Emanuel, wrote to his father's first biographer, Johann Nikolaus Forkel: "When he listened to a rich and many-voiced fugue, he could soon say, after the first entries of the subjects, what contrapuntal devices it would be possible to apply, and which of them the composer by rights ought to apply, and on such occasions, when I was standing next to him, and he had voiced his surmises to me, he would joyfully nudge me when his expectations were fulfilled."[33]

In short, what truly matters in a fugue is our first operation: the invention of the subject and its contrapuntal treatment in a series of demonstrations. The second and third operations, the devising of a tonal plan and the disposition of the demonstrations in a series that fits the plan, are of less importance. Now, the crucial difference between the results of operations two and three, on the one hand, and the results of operation one, on the other (between the "disposition" and the "invention," in Dreyfus's rhetorical terms), is that the former are essentially temporal, while the latter is not. In a tonal plan, temporality is of the essence: the temporal order in which the stable and unstable tonal areas, keys, and chords follow one another matters and cannot be disregarded. It is not so with the demonstrations. They have to be presented in some temporal order, of course, but there is nothing essential or necessary about any specific order chosen for presenting them, apart from the tonal plan. They are a temporally unordered set. The fugue is a genre in which the atemporal and temporal layers are combined, but it is the atemporal one that focuses the attention of the composer, player, and listener.

My claim, now, is that within the next half century this order of priorities will be reversed. For the Viennese classics, the temporal disposition of the events will be of the essence. To realize how profound a change this is, try a simple thought experiment. When one listens with understanding to a sonata movement by Haydn, Mozart, or Beethoven, one is always aware where within the movement one is, what has happened since the beginning, and what must still come before the movement can end. Most importantly, one can anticipate the moment when the piece will end long in advance. This is not what happens when one listens with understanding to a Bach fugue. One does not really care how much longer the piece will go on. In fact, more often than not, Bach has to go out of his way to announce the ending emphatically a few measures ahead, so that it does not come completely unexpected. Unlike in a sonata, in a fugue one is usually not aware of where within the piece one is, and even when one becomes vaguely aware of where one is, this does not much matter, because the understanding of what goes on at any given moment does not depend on such an awareness (as it emphatically does in a sonata movement). And this contrast is not just due to our comparing two different genres, sonata and fugue. The same contrast obtains when you think of Bach and Mozart concerto movements: in a Mozart concerto movement, the moment of the ending can, and is, anticipated almost from the beginning; in a concerto movement by Bach, it is not, and cannot be, anticipated until the final ritornello gets underway. In a Bach concerto movement, the meaning of any given event does not essentially depend on its temporal position within the movement. One needs to recognize that a given segment belongs to a ritornello, but it does not much matter whether the ritornello in question is the second, third, or fourth one (and, in fact, one does not know in advance how many ritornelli to expect). In a Mozart movement, one does not understand an event unless one knows where in the temporal order it occurs. The point Dahlhaus once made with regard to Beethoven's *Tempest* sonata (that "the theme is not so much the object of a musical discourse as a mere substrate of a process which imparts meaning to the music by providing that substrate with formal functions") is valid with regard to the music of the Viennese classics in general.[34]

IV.

What I am suggesting, in short, is that in the later-eighteenth century, European art music began to take the flow of time from the past to the future seriously. Until then, music was simply "in time," it "took time," its successive events had to be somehow arranged one after another, but the distinction between past and future, between "earlier" and "later," did not much matter to the way it was experienced and understood. From then on, music also made time's arrow, the experience of linear time, its essential subject matter. It could no longer be experienced with understanding, unless one became aware of the temporal ordering of the events.

In 1949, almost simultaneously with Curtius's, another book appeared which put the resources of erudition at the service of illuminating not only the past, but also, at least indirectly, the European present: Mircea Eliade's *The Myth of the Eternal Return*.[35] For much of the duration of human adventure, Eliade argued, traditional societies, from the most archaic to the present-day

European agrarian ones, lived in "cosmos" rather than "history"; that is, they embraced a circular rather than a linear conception of time. In these traditional societies, a profane action or object submerged in the incessant flow of time of the real world could acquire a value and meaning only if it was related to something other than itself, to something in another world, in a transcendent eternal sacred reality. Everything of value and importance was originally revealed to humanity by gods. Human actions acquired meaning only in so far as they repeated these mythical models. And the effect of such imitation of archetypes was the abolition of time. It suspended the profane time and activated the sacred eternity: ". . . in so far as an act (or an object) acquires a certain reality through the repetition of certain paradigmatic gestures, . . . there is an implicit abolition of profane time, of duration, of 'history.' . . ."[36] Not every object, and not everything one did, was meaningful, of course; much of experience was submerged in the meaningless, profane time. But at essential periods, ritual lifted the participants from this meaningless flow of "history" and deposited them on the lap of the meaningful, unchanging, eternal "cosmos."

The time of history is irreversible, its future always different from the past. It is the devouring, destroying time, the bearer of change and death. Interest in, and positive evaluation of, this sort of time as the product of an individual and free creativity which brings forth the new and unprecedented is a relatively recent phenomenon, and it defines modernity with its vision of infinite, linear progress. Traditional societies did what they could to hold such time at bay, abhorring the freedom and novelty of history and craving instead the immortality, repetitiveness, and permanence of nature. Their time was not linear and irreversible, but cyclical, marked by periodic returns and repetitions. The model for this sort of time was the cycle of seasons, each year repeating the cosmogonic act and regenerating life in the eternal return to the moment of birth. Thus the cyclical cosmic time annuls time's irreversibility, refuses history, allows an escape from the meaninglessness of the incessant change of profane reality.

The Hebrew discovery that irreversible history could have its intrinsic value since it revealed God's successive interventions into the affairs of humanity constituted an essential step on the way to modernity. In Messianism, time was no longer periodically renewed. Rather, its regeneration was expected to occur only once. In Christianity, the course of human history from the initial Fall through the Incarnation to the final Redemption was irreversible. But also Messianism only tolerated, rather than embraced, history and awaited its ending and the final regeneration of the eternal order. History merely separated the two eternities. Moreover, traces of the archaic vision of the eternal cyclical return survived even in Christianity, in the liturgical year with its periodic repetitions of the Nativity, Passion, and Resurrection. Thus the nominally Christian agrarian populations of Europe could continue to live by the cosmic cyclical rhythms of nature, even as the secular elites embraced the irreversible time of history, the vision of infinite linear progress generated by free human creativity.

We need not be detained here by the political subtext of Eliade's theory. It is understandable that, at mid-twentieth century, those European intellectuals who, like Curtius or Eliade, found the modernist vision of historical progress, whether in its liberal or Marxist version, discredited, would search for a traditionalist or even archaic escape from the terrors of history (the paradigmatic case is that of later Heidegger). It is not Eliade's motivation that interests me here, but simply his reading of what constitutes the difference between the modern and traditional societies. And similar readings have been developed, independently of Eliade, by more recent historians. Here are two particularly telling cases.

In his 1985 book, *The Disenchantment of the World: a Political History of Religion*, Marcel Gauchet argues that modern social order differs radically from all previous ones on account of our attitude to time and change.[37] Gauchet's world history has three stages: first, for dozens of millennia, the primitive societies that preceded the emergence of the state, their politics dominated by religion; then, the rise of the state ca. 3000 BC in Mesopotamia and Egypt, and five millennia of religion dominated by politics; and finally, our modernity, where religion has been excluded from the political domain and relegated to the margins of private life. "Somewhere around 1700," writes Gauchet, "the deepest-ever fracture in history occurred, namely, the establishment of human becoming in a logic and mode diametrically opposite to what it had been from time immemorial."[38] Where our ancestors aimed at securing their identity by submitting to an inherited order and avoiding change, we, on the contrary, embrace change and favor individual creation, including self-creation.

Gauchet's understanding of primitive, pre-political societies is strikingly similar to Eliade's. These are societies in which religion appears in its purest form and determines all social order: "... the real kernel of religious attitudes and thought lies in accepting the *external as the originating source and the unchangeable as law*."[39] Whatever has meaning and value had already happened in the mythical primordial past, when our world was established by beings different in kind from us, the gods, heroes, ancestors. Our role is to preserve and perpetuate this inheritance by repeating the founding events, by regularly coming back to them in ritual and thus regenerating the world. The temporal orientation is toward the past, and the shape of time is cyclical, governed by periodic returns. "The essence of the religious act lies wholly in this antihistorical frame of mind."[40] European peasant societies preserved traces of this attitude until as recently as a hundred years ago.

The five millennia since the emergence of the state are, in Gauchet's scheme, something of a halfway house between prehistory and modernity. The sacred past that legislates for the profane present is now no longer beyond reach. The rulers act in the name of the gods who can be entreated and whose will can be interpreted. A slow, imperceptible transition from a social order wholly received from the gods to one wholly willed by humans takes place. In this sense, the great world religions, Christianity above all, are less perfect religions than the archaic ones; they are stages along the way in which humans gradually took over the responsibility for themselves, for their meanings and laws, away from the gods.

At the end of this transition, in the eighteenth century, the modern social order appears, completely emancipated from any dependency on the beyond, autonomous in its political power relationships, in its economic and technological relationship with nature, and in its intellectual understanding of the world. The world no longer seems to us to be unalterable; rather, it is something for us to make and remake. The passivity and static dependency of our ancestors has been replaced by our dynamic, self-sufficient activism. The original temporal orientation toward the past is now reversed: ". . . a society no longer externally determined is a society which must necessarily turn completely toward the future. The future is the obligatory temporal orientation, legitimacy converted into time, of a society containing its own ordering principle. The age of religion was also the reign of a certain legitimate temporality, basically that of the past where pure primeval religion was mixed up with the indivisible dictatorship of origins. . . . From now on, there is no legitimate obligation to renew what used to be, but rather one to create what does not yet exist and what ought to happen."[41] For Gauchet, no less than for Eliade, it is definitive of modernity that it embraces change and abandons cyclical time for linear time.

The change of the shape of time with the advent of modernity is also the subject of an important 1979 collection of essays by Reinhard Koselleck entitled *Futures Past: On the Semantics of Historical Time*.[42] Koselleck's conclusions, too, are reminiscent of Eliade's, although, unlike Eliade and Gauchet, he is not interested here in the distant archaic past and contrasts modernity only with its immediate predecessor. (Koselleck's view of what happened before 1500 is offered in a more recent collection, *Zeitschichten*, where he stresses the ever-shorter duration of the three fundamental phases of human history.[43] The first phase, extending from ten million to six thousand years ago, a phase in which natural conditions dominated human existence, was marked by such milestones as the appearance of the first documented tools two million years ago, and of the first men-killing weapons and self-reflective art thirty thousand years ago, and the introduction of agriculture and domestication of animals twelve thousand years ago. The second phase, which lasted until about two hundred years ago, was one of humanity gradually mastering the natural determinants of its existence, developing high cultures on the basis of previous achievements. And the present, third phase is one of acceleration and globalization shaped by science, technology, and industry.) Between 1500 and 1800, Koselleck argues, a transformation occurred in the way in which Europeans imagined the shape of historical time. In pre-modern European societies, the experience of history was based on repeatability. The future held nothing truly novel, it was bound to come back, in cyclical fashion, to a state known from the past. The ancient doctrine long in force held that, just as nature went forever through its annual cycle of seasons, political human-ity constantly recycled a small number of possible constitutions. Modernity detached the future from the past. Modernity, *Neuzeit*, was to be also *neue Zeit*. Well before the French Revolution, the eighteenth-century philosophy of progress, fueled by the new experience of scientific, technological, and eco-nomic growth, held the possibility of a radically new future characterized by two features: first, precisely its novelty; and second, its accelerating rate of speed. The Revolution itself helped to spread widely this transformation of the way historical time was experienced and imagined. Time's circle had been straightened into an arrow, and that arrow traveled ever faster.

My claim, then, is that just as this new experience and image of historical time emerged, musicians too dropped the predominantly circular model of time in favor of a predominantly linear one. This is not a claim about causal-ity; I do not presume to explain why music changed the way it did, certainly not by invoking some mysterious workings of the *Zeitgeist*. Rather than wor-rying about the causes of the change, let us just register the structural homol-ogy between the shapes of the historical and musical times, and note its con-sequences. Perhaps the causes and the consequences are not too far apart in cases like this one: if one thinks along the lines suggested by Hoffmann, new musical means are adopted to realize new aims.

Hegel famously claimed that art "only fulfils its supreme task when it has placed itself in the same sphere as religion and philosophy, and when it is simply one way of bringing to our minds and expressing the *Divine*, the deepest interests of mankind, and the most comprehensive truths of the spirit," albeit by means specific to it, that is, by embodying these truths in sensuous images.[44] Modern music's newfound ability to embody the experience of linear time made it into a suitable vehicle for bringing to the minds of its contemporaries some of their deepest interests. Definitive of modernity are narratives of secular universal history, whether conceived in liberal terms of progressive continuity, or in egalitarian terms of revolutionary breakthrough. Once the transcendent divine has been brought down to earth and made immanent in the historical march of mankind toward a utopian future, those composers who were at all interested in such themes found ready means to capture them in their musical narratives.

Mozart has shown how this might be done in the transition from the dark archaic minor to the bright modern major of the trial scene in *The Magic Flute*, and in the general trajectory of the opera from darkness and confusion to light and clarity (a trajectory commonly read, from the early 1790s on, as a political allegory of the recent events in France; in our own time, Jean Starobinski sees in the opera an embodiment of "the solar myth of the Revolution").[45] Beethoven's translation of such progressions into purely instrumental terms in his Fifth Symphony provided music with one of its most beloved "archetypal plots" for more than a century. (It was against this optimistic plot that the pessimistic anti-archetype, identified by Reinhold Brinkmann with a phrase borrowed from Thomas Mann's *Doktor Faustus* as "the taking back of the Ninth," defined itself.[46]) It is only proper that the Fifth served as the main focus of Hoffmann's interpretation of musical modernity. That he was not fully taken in by its triumphalism, that he found its insistent vehemence to be ultimately self-undermining, is a tribute to his uncannily sensitive musical and historical antennae. But whether confident, hesitant, or self-defeating, symphonic narratives of this sort were simply not possible before the advent of musical modernity with its emphasis on the experience of linear time.

Notes

1 François-René de Chateaubriand, *Mémoires d'outre-tombe*, Bk. 9, Ch. 10, trans. Robert Baldick, *The Memoirs of Chateaubriand* (New York: Alfred A. Knopf, 1961), 174.

2 *The Memoirs of Chateaubriand*, xxi.

3 G. W. F. Hegel, "Proceedings of the Estates Assembly in the Kingdom of Württemberg 1815–1816," *Political Writings*, trans. T. M. Knox (Oxford: Clarendon Press, 1964), 282.

4 Ernst Robert Curtius, *European Literature and the Latin Middle Ages*, trans. Willard R. Trask (New York: Harper & Row, 1963), 19–24, 585–96.

5 Ibid., 20.

6 Ibid., 20.

7 Ibid., 23–24, 587.

8 Ibid., 24.

9 Jacques Le Goff, *L'imaginaire médiéval* (Paris: Gallimard, 1985).

10 Curtius, *European Literature and the Latin Middle Ages*, 24.

11 Ibid., 587. Cf. Hans Robert Jauss, "Der literarische Prozess des Modernismus von Rousseau bis Adorno," in Reinhart Herzog and Reinhart Koselleck, eds., *Epochenschwelle und Epochenbewußtsein* (Munich, 1987), 243–68, who similarly locates the origins of modernism in the mid-eighteenth century.

12 Curtius, *European Literature and the Latin Middle Ages*, 24.

13 Ibid., 587.

14 Ibid., 587.

15 Ibid., 23.

16 Ibid., 20.

17 Ibid., 594–95.

18 Ibid., 16.

19 Ibid., 595.

20 Ibid., 23.

21 Ibid., 23.

22 See, e.g., Daniel K. L. Chua, *Absolute Music and the Construction of Meaning* (Cambridge: Cambridge University Press, 1999).

23 E.T.A. Hoffmann, *Musical Writings: Kreisleriana, The Poet and the Composer, Music Criticism*, ed. David Charlton, trans. Martyn Clarke (Cambridge: Cambridge University Press, 1989), 96–103, 351–76.

24 Hoffmann, "Old and New Church Music," *Musical Writings*, 372.

25 Hoffmann, "Beethoven's Instrumental Music," *Musical Writings*, 97.

26 Hoffmann, "Beethoven's Instrumental Music," *Musical Writings*, 96.

27 Stephen Jay Gould, *Time's Arrow, Time's Cycle: Myth and Metaphor in the Discovery of Geological Time* (Cambridge: Harvard University Press, 1987).

28 Reinhold Brinkmann, "Die Zeit der *Eroica*," in Richard Klein, Eckehard Kiem, and Wolfram Ette, eds., *Musik in der Zeit, Zeit in der Musik* (Weilerswist: Velbrück Wissenschaft, 2000), 198, n. 40.

29 Scott Burnham, *Beethoven Hero* (Princeton: Princeton University Press, 1995).

30 Carolyn Abbate, *Unsung Voices: Opera and Musical Narrative in the Nineteenth Century* (Princeton: Princeton University Press, 1991), 21–29.

31 Laurence Dreyfus, *Bach and the Patterns of Invention* (Cambridge: Harvard University Press, 1996).

32 For Dreyfus's own analysis, somewhat different from mine, see his *Bach and the Patterns of Invention*, 150–55.

33 Hans T. David and Arthur Mendel, eds., rev. Christoph Wolff, *The New Bach Reader: A Life of Johann Sebastian Bach in Letters and Documents* (New York: W. W. Norton & Company, 1998), 397.

34 Carl Dahlhaus, *Nineteenth-Century Music*, trans. J. Bradford Robinson (Berkeley: University of California Press, 1989), 15.

35 Mircea Eliade, *The Myth of the Eternal Return*, trans. Willard R. Trask (New York: Pantheon Books, 1954).

36 Ibid., 35.

37 Marcel Gauchet, *The Disenchantment of the World: a Political History of Religion*, trans. Oscar Burge (Princeton: Princeton University Press, 1997).

38 Ibid., 162.

39 Ibid., 28.

40 Ibid., 25.

41 Ibid., 176–77.

42 Reinhard Koselleck, *Futures Past: On the Semantics of Historical Time*, trans. Keith Tribe (Cambridge: The MIT Press, 1985).

43 Reinhart Koselleck, *Zeitschichten. Studien zur Historik. Mit einem Beitrag von Hans-Georg Gadamer* (Frankfurt am Main: Suhrkamp Verlag, 2000), 78–96.

44 G. W. F. Hegel, *Aesthetics: Lectures on Fine Art*, trans. T. M. Knox, 1 (Oxford: Clarendon Press, 1975), 7.

45 Jean Starobinski, *1789: The Emblems of Reason*, trans. Barbara Bray (Cambridge: The MIT Press, 1988), 43. See also my "Beyond Language. 30 September 1791: Emanuel Schikaneder's *Die Zauberflöte*, with music by Wolfgang Amadé Mozart, is premiered at the Theater auf der Wieden in Vienna," in David E. Wellbery, ed.,

The New History of German Literature (Cambridge: Harvard University Press, 2004) 445–50.

46 Reinhold Brinkmann, *Late Idyll: The Second Symphony of Johannes Brahms,* trans. Peter Palmer (Cambridge: Harvard University Press, 1995), 220–26.

Spatial Graphics

MARTIN WARNKE

FLIPPING THROUGH THE pages of treatises on military theory from the six-teenth and seventeenth centuries, we frequently find images of troops that al-most appear to be removed from time and space. In the manual of Johann Ja-kob Wallhausen (Fig. 1) dating from 1616, the troops seem to be distributed in the landscape like building blocks.[1] In the foreground one discovers a natural landscape with hills, valleys, shrubbery, and a river; in the background there are mountains, where on the highest peaks castles have been placed. However, the countryside containing the military formations, the *tercios* with the lances, does not appear to have any effect on the formal arrangement of the troops: the wings of the military formations are composed of long rectangular blocks between which groups of three and four as well as more compact double col-umns have taken position parallel to one another. In the interstices the officers or commanders and their personnel are in action. The army presents itself totally in the sense of an *ars militaria* for which it is of particular importance that the military formations take shape in a geometrical order that appears as pre-established. In the military primer of Antonio Valperga published in 1653 an ideal "fronte di Battaglia" is represented (Fig. 2), in which case the highest aim apparently is to achieve an appealing ornament of squares and framing columns, causing the whole pattern to spread itself across the ground like the drawing of a butterfly.[2] This lacks all topographic features—it is framed in the front and background by populated hills covered with vegetation. On the field, however, every kind of scenic formation is excluded. Yet I wish to show another, topographically differentiated, campaign plan. Taken from the writings of Wilhelm Dilich, dating from 1689 (Fig. 3), the countryside is subtly characterized as being hilly without this situation, causing any of the front lines to run crookedly or a square formation to become distorted.[3]

Figure 1. Armed forces according to J.J. Wallhausen, 1616

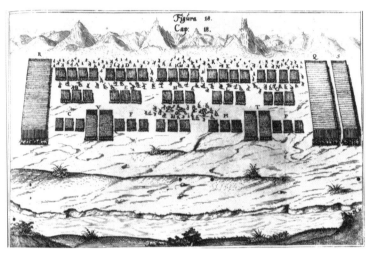

Figure 2. Order of the battle according to A.M. Valperga 1653

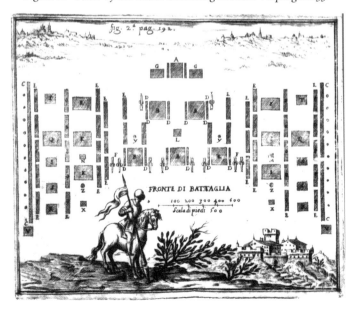

Figure 3. Order of the battle according to W. Dilich 1689

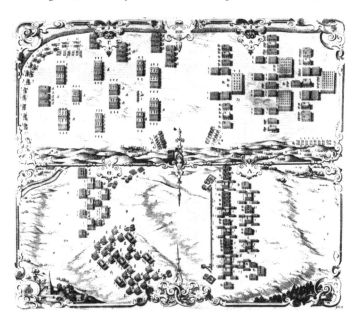

One may be certain that in practice these armed forces were indeed fully capable of taking into account the local circumstances; in the graphic representation, however, an intact formation has been presented and any natural irregularity has been neutralized as if the whole terrain were a parade ground. Even when, for instance, the formation of the Christian and Turkish Armada in the Battle of Lepanto was to be rendered (Fig. 4), the surging waves had no chance to disrupt or even to merely irritate the geometrical figures in which the rows of ships were facing each other. [4] In this instance, as in the case of field formations à la Dilich, the factors of time and space are completely missing; the formations stand motionless opposite one another, as if caught up in the ornamental patterns. It is difficult to imagine that some of the elements of this pattern might detach themselves from their ornamental context to destroy the enemy patterns—it is a fixed formation. In the Museum of Military History in Vienna a hand-colored pen-and-ink drawing (Fig. 5) is to be found depicting the Imperial battle formation near Lützen where on November 14, 1632, King Gustav Adolf was confronted. It shows that even in a pressured military situation it was impossible to express oneself in drawings in a manner diverging from the mode of depiction used in the military textbooks of the time.[5] The drawing was either produced by Wallhausen himself or on his behalf to serve Imperial Field Marshal Pappenheim as a basis for intervening in the battle. The regiments are standing in Dutch formation, that is, distributed in a relatively flat symmetrical fashion, with identical wings right and left, under exclusion of all topographical data as if they were suspended in air like swarms of motionless birds. Pappenheim was then probably supposed only to gain an overview regarding the points where this pre-established formation might be threatened during the battle in order to be able to intervene precisely at these specific places.

Figure 4. Order of the naval battle of Lepanto

Figure 5. The order of the battle of the imperial forces in Lützen, according to
an anonymous drawing, 1632. Vienna, Heeresgeschichtliches Museum

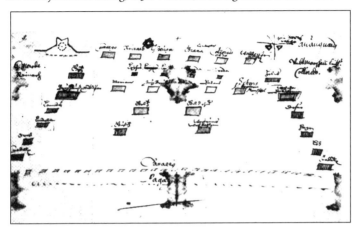

Figure 6. Drawing by Frederic II of the "Schiefen Schlachtordnung," 1746.
Berlin, Prussian Geheimes Staatsarchiv

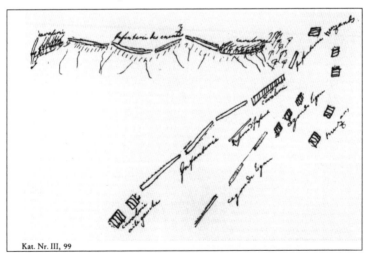

If one compares this with the famous "Schiefe Schlachtformation"
("asymmetrical battle formation") Frederick the Great personally outlined in
a document now in the Prussian Geheimes Staatsarchiv (Fig. 6), then one
immediately recognizes a novel quality emerging here. Frederick disregards
the symmetrical, balanced battle formation. Initially he deploys his men as
the enemy troops are lined up—cavalry on the wings, infantry front in the
middle. The formation becomes asymmetrical through the fact that he rein-

forces or, as he puts it, "masks"[6] the right wing through a "segonde ligne" from the back.[7] Frederick himself describes the plan as follows: "The objective is to deny the enemy one wing, while reinforcing the other wing destined for combat. The latter then attacks an enemy wing with full force, namely on the flank. An army of 100,000 men seized on the flank can be conquered by 30,000 men since the battle is then quickly resolved. See the plan."[8] The whole point of these tactics obviously consists of the fact that the king has no qualms about employing an irregular formation pattern and finds an asymmetrical battle plan adequate.

The courage to operate with an "asymmetrical formation" is apparently linked with the willingness to acknowledge the supremacy of the landscape. A sketch that Frederick the Great produced concerning the attack on Baumgarten in the First Silesian War in 1741 (Fig. 7) shows how the troops have taken up their position in the mountain valleys;[9] their formation follows from the topographical prerequisites. According to Frederick, what particularly distinguishes the Austrians at present "is the art of consistently choosing for their positions an advantageous site and making much better use of the local obstacles for deploying their troops than in the past."[10] For him this results in the following: "Thus, my first rule is focused on the choice of the terrain." "Weak armies must seek mountainous and deeply fissured areas; since here each segment of the terrain is limited and a superiority in number does not place the enemy at an advantage (...) We should never have succeeded in the battle of Soor (1745) had we not been assisted by the terrain."[11] Frederick admits that his victory was not gained due to the braveness of his troops but due to the topographical circumstances.

*Figure 7. Drawing by Frederic II of the raid near Baumgarten, 1741.
Berlin, Prussian Geheimes Staatsarchiv*

Kat. Nr. II, 43 a

*Figure 8. Order of the battle of the Brigade Roeder in June 1864 near
Ulkebüll according to Fontane, 1866*

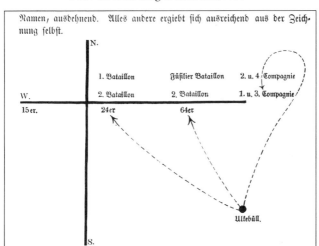

I will refrain from describing the further phases in the development of this scheme of representation following the French Revolution and will instead confine myself to some references to Gerneral Carl von Clausewitz's book *Vom Kriege* ("On War"), published after his death in 1831, in which he writes about the "geometrical, i.e., spatial element": "In the theory of positions and warfare [their] angles and lines rule like legislators who have the task of deciding the dispute,"[12] while, according to Clausewitz, chance itself, the individual moral force, can render such prerequisites invalid.[13] Clausewitz introduces new elements into the game—ethics, patriotism, the desire for freedom, and an ideological impetus—all of which can also neutralize topographical circumstances.[14] In Theodore Fontane's report on the Second German-Danish War of Schleswig-Holstein in 1863/64, for example, this potential is not yet recognizable. Occasionally Fontane adds to his reports diagrams that he introduces as follows: "Until we move on to a description of the individual actions, we will try to give the reader an orientation in the succeeding drawing (Fig. 8) that in result will make it easier for him to understand the combat manœuvres. The horizontal line renders the Prussian deployment; the vertical line is the route that leads from Arnkiel-Oere over Rönhof and Kjär to Sonderburg; where both lines cross, Kjär is located, toward the right and left sides are its row of houses (. . .) everything else is sufficiently revealed by the drawing itself."[15] This is exemplified by the fact that the Danes commanded three (unsuccessful) "strikes" (as Fontane puts it) from their headquarters at

Ulkebüll against the advancing Prussians: one passing by the outermost left flank of the Prussians in the east in order to then return and attack them from the rear; a second strike directly within the village of Kjär; and, finally, a third strike between the two positions mentioned. Although Fontane speaks of the "great force of the attack," being under the impression that it was "the most violent battle during the whole war,"[16] this is not at all revealed by the schematic drawing. The columns' movements are traced in delicately-sketched lines, almost as if these were ballet instructions.

It would hardly have surprised me to note at least a tendency toward a fundamentally new development of this type of war graphics in the First World War. However, the findings are not as unequivocal as one might suspect, even when taking into account that my survey of materials cannot be conclusive. I will show here only a few of the battle schemes from the memoirs of Erich Ludendorff published in 1919. Basically, all of the battle plans rendered here are designed in the same manner as the plan for the double battle at the Aisne and in Champagne northeast of Reims in spring, 1917 (Fig. 9)[17], where, on a normal geographical map, the deployment of the German front line is shown with thick lines. The former line deployment is depicted in a complete black line, the new line deployment after the French attack visualized in a broken black line highlighted by short, bold arrows. In comparison to the previous examples' graphic representation, these are actual novelties: in Fontane's case the lines of action already had arrowheads. Now, however, a new kind of dynamic enters the design of the arrow as well, introducing into the graphic rendering of the battle scenario a temporal and spatial quality. Through the duplicate deployment of the front line, one is not only provided with a topographical and spatial description but is also informed through the arrows of the energetic inevitability of the military strike. The same thing is revealed in the plan of the defensive battle between Soissons and Reims in July 1918 (Fig. 10)[18], where the brunt of the French attack is now illustrated through a thick sequence of what one might call "arrow shots." In this sense the enemy attacks are not distinguished from the German attacks. The not-so-highly-successful German counteroffensive in late March/early April in 1918 at Armentières and in the vicinity of Kemmel (Fig. 11)[19] is established by the very same arrows (the established front is marked by a broken line) that had also characterized the enemy strikes. These arrows that are supposed to represent visually the quick campaign of the German-Austrian troops in Serbia and Russia (Fig. 12)[20] at the end of the year 1915 are slightly longer; they do not, however, actually display a higher level of aggressive energy since the shafts are slightly curved and the tips have a blunter shape. Not only the more expressive graphic stroke but also the employment of arrows (which also play a role in Russian art and propaganda at this time) are elements that again subordinate the topographical prerequisites.

Figure 9.   Order of the battle on the Aisne in
Spring 1917 according to Ludendorff

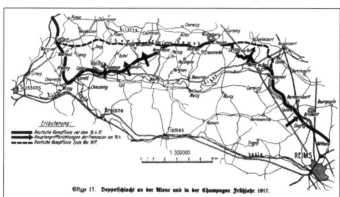

Figure 10. Order of the battle of Soisson and Reims in July 1918 according to Ludendorff

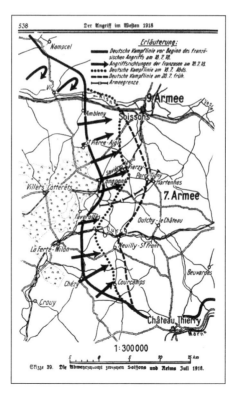

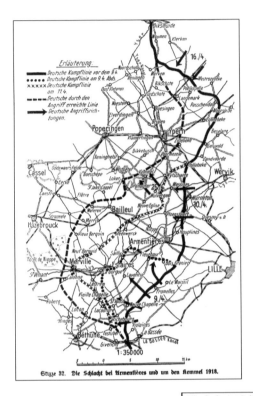

Figure 11. Order of the battle of Armentières and around the Kemmel, 1918, according to Ludendorff

Figure 12. Movements of the German, Austrian-Hungarian, and Bulgarian armed forces during the campaign in Serbia, 1915, according to Ludendorff

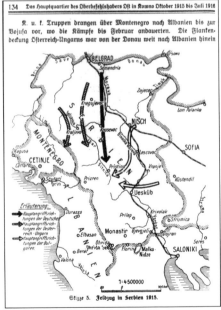

In the Second World War this approach is fully developed into the type of graphic rendition one might call "spatial" illustration. A battle plan for the battle of Charkow (Fig. 13)[21] which the supreme commanders of the Wehrmacht presented to the public in May, 1942, shows that geographical conditions almost disappear from the illustration in favor of forceful graphical elements that highlight the sections of the German front and their advances. Now arrows of varying thickness are employed which indicate direct or swerving movements of the military formations. The infantry is characterized by arrows of varying strength, while the advances of the tank division are characterized by long arrows whose rhythmical interior pattern apparently is designated to signal the sudden and inexorable advance. This type of map is no longer merely a source of information but, above all, a visual presentation designed to suggest that this march led inevitably to victory. In cases where the war map is openly used as propaganda material, this becomes even more obvious: In his brochure "Der Krieg 1939/1941 in Karten" ("The War of 1939/1941 in Maps")[22], published in Munich in 1942, Giselher Wirsing used maps of the Wehrmacht. He claimed to have employed colors merely to

Figure 13. Order of the battle of Charkow, 1942

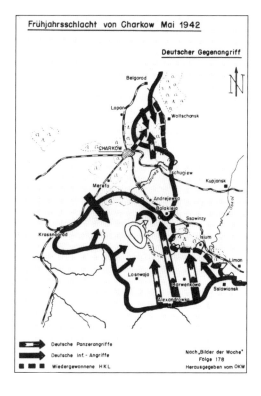

make this material more distinctive, while the color red stood for the German troops. Here the Polish campaign in 1939 is schematically depicted (Fig. 14) as if many-headed snakes gradually invaded the Polish territory up to the previously agreed German-Russian border, without much fuss and meeting no resistance, while at the same time the allied Russian troops were more timidly penetrating into the territory conceded to them. This can fundamentally change just a few pages further on: the Russian policy of annexation and aggression in 1939/40 is expressed in the form of fork-like green groups of arrows (Fig. 15) which appear as a terrible threat to the German Reich. The tongued thrust of this expansion spontaneously arouses the urge to react in a corresponding fashion. A German leaflet that was dropped on French soldiers in May, 1940, attempts to reveal (Fig. 16)[23] the pressure which England found itself under, particularly through the conquest of Norway and Denmark in April of 1940: from the coasts of the occupied countries arrows proceed up to the English East coast, the distances in kilometers respectively having been added to them. The swiftness of the arrows, being suggestively implied, makes the distances insignificant. Space is conquered, it is implied, by the power of the will. Giselher Wirsing elaborates this graphic idea further on the jacket of his brochure (Fig. 17). From the Norwegian and French coasts swarms of arrows radiate and spread across England, as if erasing the island from the map. These arrows form a grid over England almost like a coat of chain-mail, while, on both sides of the arrows over England, larger and more expansive trifurcated arrows aim to reach across the Atlantic. What appears like a ballistic utopia is transformed on the total Eastern front into a densely-drawn, parallel grid front of arrows whose tips penetrate deeply and bloodily into the vast expanse of the country. Topographical or other obstacles no longer matter since space is now subject to will.[24]

The development of a vocabulary of emotive, expressively charged denotative signs for the depiction of battle might also be shown, as I imagine, in a purely statistical graphic diagram. In this connection I would like to show one more flagrant example from the book mentioned above by Wirsing. Under the title "Die blockierte Insel" ("The Blocked Island") England is shown (p. 46) (Fig. 18), surrounded from three directions by powerful streams of arrows. The streams indicate the quantity of food that England must import in order to feed its population. Red bars superimposed on these black streams show where the German armed forces can stop these supply movements. Even totally disregarding the data concerning food requirements, the viewer cannot help but see the island kingdom slowly expire in a stranglehold—space as victim of will.

Figure 14. Schematic description of the campaign against Poland in 1939 according to Giselher Wirsing, 1942

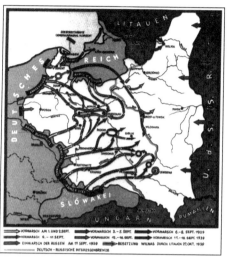

Figure 15. Schematic description of "Moscow's grasp at the West" according to Giselher Wirsing, 1942

Figure 16. A German leaflet for French soldiers in May, 1940

Figure 17. Cover of Giselher Wirsing's book, "Der Krieg 1939/41 in Karten," 1942

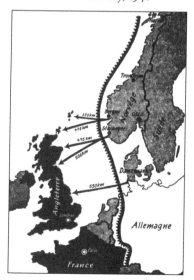

Of course the phenomena which I have only briefly sketched here may be explained from various other points of departure as well. I do not, however, wish to further undertake such an attempt in this context, since I would be quite content if I should have accomplished addressing a question and problem on the basis of material which, to my knowledge, has not yet been an object of study for any scientific discipline.

Figure 18. Schematic description of the nourishment-blockade, which German troops brought about against England, according to Giselher Wirsing, 1942

Notes

1 Johann Jakob Wallhausen, *Manuale Militare oder Kriegs Manual* (Frankfurt am Main, 1616), 2. For the development in general, see Volker Schmidtchen, *Kriegswesen im späten Mittelalter: Technik, Taktik, Theorie,* (Weinheim: Acta Humaniora, 1990).

2 Antonio Maurizio Valperga, *Essercitio Militare* (Naples, 1653), 192.

3 Wilhelm Dilich, *Hochvernünfftig gegründet- und auffgerichtete, in gewisse Classe eingetheilte . . . Kriegs-Schule* (Frankfurt am Main, 1689), 100.

4 *Mercklicher Schiffstreit und Schlachtordnung bey der christlichen und Türckischen Armada,* illustrated in Wolfgang Harms, 4 of *Deutsche illustrierte Flugblätter des 16. und 17. Jahrhunderts* (Munich: Kraus, 1987).

5 See the exhibition catalogue, *Wittelsbach und Bayern* (Munich: Hirmer, 1980), 2, no. 696.

6 See *Ausgewählte Werke,* ed. Gustav Berthold Volz (Berlin: R. Hobbing, 1916), 1, 273.

7 Ibid., 273. For the drawing, see the exhibition catalogue *Friedrich der Große* (Berlin: 1986), no. 3, 99.

8 Ibid., 255.

9 See exhibition catalogue *Friedrich der Große,* no. 2, 43a.

10 *Ausgewählte Werke* (see no. 6), 295.

11 Ibid., 254

12 General Carl von Clausewitz, *Vom Kriege* (Bonn: Dummler, 1952), 301.

13 Apart from what the French meanwhile call "terrain" and Clausewitz defines as "Gegend und Boden" ("area and ground"), he distinguishes between natural phenomena (mountains, forests, marshes, or lakes) and cultural phenomena within a landscape (canals, ditches, or fences). He states that people's armies prefer the open countryside because here their mass power can unfold, whereas their opponents prefer an unwieldy terrain because it serves to disperse and isolate the national army. The comments on "domination" or "elevation" are particularly instructive: this conveys "a sense of superiority and security for the person who is positioned on the mountain edge and discovers his enemy below and a sense of weakness and anxiety for the person who is below. Perhaps this total impression is even stronger than it should be . . . Perhaps it thus goes beyond the truth; in this case this effect of the imagination must be viewed as a new element though which the effect of extreme elevation is increased," *Vom Kriege,* 318. Clausewitz, however, also draws a conclusion which then becomes important. For him these advantages of the terrain are "nothing but a dead instrument, a mere quality that must realize itself upon an object. This strike and this blow, this object, this quantity is the victorious battle, only this truly counts . . .", 9. Nothing distinguishes these indications of action from the paths

that Fontane sketches for the reconnaissance units on July 1, leading from Hobro in a northerly direction toward the Limpfjord (Fig. 8), of which only one unity had to withstand a "more serious engagement," 334.

14 For him the "völkische Geist des Heeres (Enthusiamus, fanatischer Eifer, Glaube, Meinung)" causes one of the "bedeutendsten moralischen Kräfte im Kriege" (*Vom Kriege*, 254ff).

15 Theodor Fontane, *Der Schleswig-Holsteinsche Krieg im Jahre 1864* (Berlin: Verlag der Königlichen Geheimen Ober-Hofbuchdruckerei, 1866), 328.

16 Ibid., 331.

17 Erich Ludendorff, *Meine Kriegs-Erinnerungen 1914–1918* (Berlin: 1919), 336.

18 Ibid., 538.

19 Ibid., 486.

20 Ibid., 134.

21 Friedrich Dettmer, Otto Jaus, and Helmut Tolkmitt, *Die 44. Infanterie-Division* (Friedberg: Podzun-Pallas-Verlag, 1979), 87.

22 See Giselher Wirsing, "Der Krieg 1939/41 in Karten" (Munich: Knorr and Hirth, 1942). See also Janusz Piekalkiewicz, *Die Schlacht um Moskau* (Herrsching, 1989), 103.

23 Klaus Kirchner, *Flugblätter aus Deutschland 1939/1940* (Erlangen: Verlag D+C, 1982), no. 163.

24 Wirsing, *Der Krieg 1939/41 in Karten*, 46.

On the Beautiful in Mozart

SCOTT BURNHAM

In the beginning of the slow movement from Mozart's Piano Concerto in C major, K. 467, music of placid and effortless beauty takes a turn into some other realm and then comes back to the business of thematic convention and closure. The bass line arrives on C at m. 11 and then freezes there for the next six measures, while the harmony does not resolve the A♭ of m. 10 to an expected G or A♮, but holds to it, thus seeming to become entrapped in the minor mode. During the ensuing six-measure interpolation, the upper voice descends from D♭ to F through a series of expressive leaps. This descent is counterpoised by the more stepwise and sinuous ascent of an inner voice, sonorously scored in octaves for bassoon and second violins and marked by dissonant suspensions on each downbeat. The pedal point in the bass holds the passage in a state of suspension, the upper-voice descent keeps it directed, the general rise of dissonance gives it an increasingly otherworldly sound—and then the bass finally moves off its C and steps down to A, just as the upper voice gets to F, arriving together at m. 17 on the first downbeat in quite some time that is absolutely consonant. This first-inversion tonic sonority has a limpid, daylight clarity not unlike the easing of a fever, and the theme soon arrives at its appointed periodic cadence. When the piano soloist then takes up this theme in m. 23, we hear a much more normative and undisturbed 6 + 6 period (with a one-measure introductory vamp). But this would-be normality cannot mask what we heard first: the theme, with its center expanded and its periodic gravity suspended, with its revelation of a strange, new world emanating from within the phrase.[1] This world disturbs

Mozart's beautiful surface with an even more transfixing beauty, a captivating and terrible beauty.

Passages like this may well have moved E.T.A. Hoffmann to exclaim: "Mozart leads us deep into the realm of the spirits. Dread lies all about us yet withholds its torments and becomes more an intimation of infinity . . ."[2] In saying this, Hoffmann was eager to claim Mozart as a Romantic artist. His reference to intimation [*Ahnung*] suggests that he recognized a liminal element in Mozart's music, a sense of being on the threshold of some other state of mind. And he often referred to this other state as the realm of the spirits.

Hoffmann's realm of the spirits is arguably the interior realm of consciousness, increasingly recognized around 1800 to hold both exalted inspirations and unspeakable terrors, transcendence and madness, a deep and uncharted space within each of us, a space fearlessly explored by the artist and cravenly shunned by the philistine. For Hoffmann, Mozart announces the first glimmers of this kind of consciousness by composing music that makes this newly conceived interior space resonate—and this is what makes Mozart a Romantic artist.

Mozart's music frequently stages moments like the one described above, passages that arise as inspired interpolations in the middle of a phrase and that seem to signal the emergence of a higher—or deeper—consciousness, passages that have been felt to brush the listener with what Rudolph Otto called "primal numinous awe."[3] In what follows, I will listen to passages from a number of Mozart's slow movements, in order to explore this effect of beautiful intimation that is somehow both transcendent and inward.[4] I will suggest that Mozart's music, in staging these intimations, reflects a fundamentally ironic and melancholic condition of modern, post-Enlightenment self-consciousness. And because such passages seem eternally renewable, their undiminished effect always available, they can be heard to underwrite, and to be sustained by, the cultural mandate of rehearing music that has held sway from the age of the Romantics to the present day. But before speculating about ways we might relate this special dimension of Mozart's beautiful music to the construction of modern subjectivity, we must first attempt to characterize the general nature and effect of Mozart's musical beauty.

I. The Sound of Mozart

That Mozart composed the most beautiful music we can know is an article of faith among listeners and critics of Mozart's music. And like other articles of faith, it is rarely if ever held up to scrutiny. Most musically trained critics are content simply to acknowledge the sheer beauty of this music as they move on to more tractable topics. A luminous exception to this can be found in Maynard Solomon's recent biography of Mozart, in which two entire chapters are given over to a psychoanalytical interpretation of the beautiful in Mozart's music. And there are brilliant aperçus about the beauty of this music that sparkle throughout the writings of Charles Rosen.[5] But for most others, those in the rank and file of academia as well as millions of music-loving civilians, the beauty of Mozart's music is simply taken for granted as a happy boon, one of the few things in life that do not need to be questioned or examined but only enjoyed. The beautiful in Mozart has even been commodified in recent years in the form of the so-called "Mozart effect," a kind of spiritual balm that enhances the growth of house plants, increases the intelligence of children about to take tests, and generally leads the troubled modern mind to a semblance of serenity.[6]

The beautiful in Mozart stands apart, untouched by human hands. What creates this effect? Consider the opening bars of the Adagio from the Clarinet Concerto, often held up as an example of pellucid beauty. There is nothing the least bit exotic in the first two phrases (mm. 1–16). Harmonically, melodically, and rhythmically, everything is transparent and straightforward: simple harmonies (tonic and dominant), simple melody, slow harmonic rhythm. And yet there is a force at work that holds this texture together in beautiful suspension, a focal energy that creates a sense of apartness and special integrity. Note first the warmly cohesive, floating quality of the accompanying string sonority: the pedal tone in the viola keeps it sustained, while the murmuring figures in the violins lend it a gentle animation—the contrary motion of their figuration facilitates independence as well as moderation. In Mozart's instrumentation, every part has a satisfying role to play; every part sounds (this is one of the reasons that his music is never labored but always buoyant). Consider the bass line, which works in tandem with the harmonic rhythm: its brief nudges on the dominant give the texture just enough push to keep it floating, but not so much as to force anything. That the dominant falls on the downbeat and not on the preceding upbeat subtly undermines the downbeat as an arrival and contributes to the effect of a floating, suspended tonic. Meanwhile, the clarinet melody of the first phrase calmly opens more space, each subphrase becoming more varied in shape and intervallic content (the penultimate snippet contains the intervals P4, m7, P5, and M6). This intervallic intensification works in conjunction with the overall harmonic trajectory of the passage, contributing to a gentle surge of energy that brings about a cadence on the dominant. Repeating the entire phrase with the wind instruments adds a broad infusion of fresh sonority, amplifying this intimate utterance in the same way that a strong breeze transforms the stillness of a forest.

The energy of this entire passage is largely focused on maintaining its sonorous envelope, on enforcing a special centeredness that—like a spinning space station—seems to create its own artificial gravity, apart from the temporal pull of functional syntax. The passage hums with the pleasing tension of holding everything in such exquisite suspension. This effect of suspending mundane musical reality—and doing so with the most transparent elements of that reality—fosters a special awareness in the listener, creating the condition for intimation, creating an expectant and yet relaxed state of mind. And then (mm. 17–24), as if gathering and channeling the atmospheric energy of this opening, the music in this third phrase moves into a charged sequence, with three rising stations, each heard as an intensification, followed by an elaborate four-measure descent that both recovers the space opened in the slow ascending sequence and answers the move to the dominant in the first long phrase. And then *this* entire phrase is again repeated and ratified by the winds (mm. 25–32).

Perhaps the single most beautiful number in all of Mozart's operas is the farewell trio "Soave sia il vento" from *Così fan tutte* (Act I, no. 10). Here Mozart's characters find themselves suspended within some supra-personal emotional dimension well beyond the puppet-stage confines of their comic misery. Like the Adagio from the Clarinet Concerto, "Soave sia il vento" creates its effect of beautiful suspension through simple harmonies, a slow harmonic rhythm, and murmuring string figures. The mere sound of its opening seems to transport us to the threshold of an enchanted realm. And again like the Adagio from the concerto, the opening of the trio soon gives way to an intensified passage featuring winds, the subdominant harmony, and a newly swelling melodic line.

With examples like these in our ears, it is not hard to see why Mozart's music is often described as if it exists in a unique and isolated state of grace. Thus Maynard Solomon suggests that "what may be most unusual in [some of the superlatively beautiful passages in Mozart] is their wholeness, their encapsulated sense of completion, their inherent resistance to forward motion because they have already approached a state of perfection . . ."[7] And thus the theologian Karl Barth wistfully asks: "Could it be that the characteristic basic 'sound' of . . . Mozart—not to be confused with the sound of any other—is in fact the primal sound of music absolutely?"[8] To entertain such a view is perforce to regard all other musics as corrupt, fallen—exiled from Mozart's timeless grace. Yet rather than claim some sort of prelapsarian innocence for Mozart, Barth positions the composer at the other end of the history of human perfectibility, investing the composer with creative omniscience, and thus lending a note of divine authority to his role as the creator of music's primal sound. "Knowing all, Mozart creates music from a mysterious center . . ." And the all-knowing being at the center does not remain indifferent to the great circumferential struggle of good and evil. Mozart's music knows and acknowledges both darkness and light, and yet always achieves a "consoling turn," in which "the light rises and the shadows fall."[9]

Though a theologian such as Barth may be well placed to hear the beauty of Mozart's music as a source of goodness and consolation, other critics hear it as ultimately exercising a subtle subversive force. "Trouble in Paradise" is the title of one of Solomon's chapters on the beautiful on Mozart, and in a later chapter he discusses "[t]he strange, the terrible, the uncanny, and the deadly aspects of beauty" in Mozart's music.[10] He goes on to claim that these more sinister strands of Mozart's beauty "are interwoven with its erotic implication," thus echoing Charles Rosen's sense that "What is most extraordinary about Mozart's style is the combination of physical delight—a sensuous play of sonority, and indulgence in the most luscious harmonic sequences—with a purity and economy of line and form that render the seduction all the more efficient." Rosen sums up this line of thought with his own seductive point: Mozart subversively corrupts sentimental values by rendering his "supreme expressions of suffering and terror . . . shockingly voluptuous."[11] Barth, Solomon, and Rosen all assume a constitutive contrast in Mozart's music between darkness and light, or sensuousness and purity, a contrast that results, for Solomon, in a beautiful suffusion of opposites.[12] Solomon's notion of "suffusion" indicates that Mozart's beauty is not simply a kind of balanced musical chiaroscuro, light and shadow profiling each other with pleasing clarity. Solomon's suffusion, Barth's omniscience, and Rosen's subversion all suggest the presence of a special dimension, a realm that transcends simple combination or juxtaposition. And the full effect of Mozart's beauty transcends simplicity itself: one of the astonishing things about the quality of beauty in Mozart's music is that it is often intensified, heightened, at just those moments when it appears to leave simplicity and innocence behind—it paradoxically finds a kind of superadded grace in the very loss of grace. The first, best way to get at this aspect of the beautiful in Mozart is to hear some dissonance.

II. Dissonance and Consciousness

Dissonance in Mozart is rarely routine, and though it is often extreme, it is never ugly or shrill.[13] In fact, Mozartean dissonance sometimes creates un-

heard-of sounds, plaintive and yet pleasantly thrilling, strange and yet exquisite. We have already encountered one such dissonance. At the climax of
the otherworldly interpolation in the theme from the Piano Concerto (m. 15)
Mozart introduces an extraordinary combination of pitches: from the bass
up we hear C, B, f, bb¹, ab². The wide-open spacing of this sonority attenuates
the fact that it contains a cluster of pitch classes a half-step apart (C, B, Bb). If
you were to remove the Bb, you would hear a fairly common configuration: a
vii7 over a tonic pedal. But by adding the Bb as a cross relation to the B♮ at the
same time that the B♮ is sounding against the C, Mozart has transformed and
elevated a common dissonant configuration into something *unerhört*, something even more dissonant and yet strangely beautiful, mournfully sonorous.

A perhaps even more extraordinary example of uniquely Mozartean dissonance can be heard in the slow movement of his String Quintet in Eb major,
K. 614. In m. 79, within a lengthy middle section in Eb, the untroubled gavotte
figure from the movement's Bb-major opening suddenly finds an unheard-of
dissonance. With the onset of this special dissonance, Mozart's simple gavotte
now seems to be speaking in tongues. To create this effect, he introduces dis-
sonantly juxtaposed pairs of sixths (he overlays the Bb/G with C/Ab). There
is no dissonance quite like this in anyone's glossary.[14] It is not simply a combination of tonic and dominant, though it has elements of that. Nor is it an
orthodox thirteenth-chord (with added ninth), because the Ab sounds above
the G. With the C, and the juxtaposed sixths, Mozart achieves a strikingly
dissonant yet sonorously bell-like sonority, as if finding a spectral resonance
from some other dimension.[15]

Mozart's single most famous dissonance is surely the first note of the first
violin in the slow introduction to his String Quartet in C, K. 465, known forever afterward as the "Dissonance" Quartet. As a pitch class, the first violin's
A♮ would seem impossibly gauche, appearing as it does after the successive
entrances of C, Ab, and Eb in the other strings. But the *mise en scène* of this
impossible dissonance is utterly captivating: as if in a séance, a mysterious
and solemn invocation in the lower strings summons the ghostly A♮, a sonic
apparition from on high that glides only gradually into the known, corporeal
world as the upper note of a turn figure. One attends this séance time and
again, one knows exactly what will happen and when, and yet Mozart's dissonant apparition never misses its effect—its quality of intimation seems ever
renewable, eternally fresh.

Such dissonance seems to signal a preternatural presence; it does not
leave us longing for consonant resolution, nor does it leave us shattered and
overwhelmed. Rather it leaves us brushed with awe. This is dissonance as in-

timation, and it is a new kind of dissonance. It is not simply marked as the absence of consonance, as the audible need to resolve. It is not, in other words, dissonance for the sake of consonance but dissonance for the sake of dissonance. It is thus dissonance as a kind of *surplus*. There is an available analogy to the onset of ironic self-consciousness, for just as dissonance can be heard here as surplus, so too can self-consciousness be conceived as a surplus to simple consciousness. The burr of dissonance, like the burr of consciousness, suggests an added dimension.[16]

George Santayana closed his lectures on beauty, delivered over a century ago, with this sentence: "Beauty is a pledge of the possible conformity between the soul and nature, and consequently a ground of faith in the supremacy of the good."[17] In other words, beauty tells us we belong; the perception of beauty is a form of well-being, in which existence needs no apology. Mozart's beautiful dissonance is a special inversion of Santayana's beauty—one that seems to answer to the ironic pain of consciousness. This is beauty through which consciousness is heard to be in exquisite disharmony with nature. The word "dissonance" itself, as a Latinate compound of the inseparable prefix *dis* and the present participle *sonans*, denotes a "sounding apart." Precisely *not* in harmony with nature but aware of standing apart from nature—this is the gift and the curse of consciousness in an age of irony, allowing us to conceive of nature as a redemptive force even while exiling us from that force.

Friedrich Schiller theorized about his age's drift toward self-conscious art in his 1796 essay "On Naïve and Sentimental Poetry." Naïve poets, such as Homer and Shakespeare, were able to represent a finite reality to perfection; sentimental poets, the moderns, attempt but imperfectly to represent an infinite reality. No longer comfortably at home in the real world, their art reaches for the ungraspable. With his beautiful dissonance, Mozart brings sentimental self-consciousness to naïve grace, intimates the ungraspable with perfectly grasped musical language. This is why the great Mozart authority Hermann Abert refused to understand Mozart as either naïve or sentimental but rather as both at the same time.[18]

And with this we touch upon the originary impulse of the modern construction of self, that point at which Enlightenment rationality creates the space for an irrational Romanticism to emerge, an individual and interior space.[19] Mozart, poised at the crossroads of the Enlightenment and Romanticism, offers ironic intimations at once revelatory and resigned, redemptive and melancholy. We hear the sound of these intimations as beautiful. The awe we experience in perceiving them is not overwhelming, not in the sublime manner. Rather we find ourselves always poised on the hair-raising threshold of some other order of reality. Where is that otherness to be found?

III. The Move Inward

The renowned British music critic Donald Francis Tovey, borrowing a phrase from Horace, often referred to "purple patches" in the music of Mozart and others (usually Haydn and Schubert).[20] These purple patches are deeply colored, richly expressive passages, and they almost always involve a move into tonal regions on the flat side of the prevailing key center, the subdominant side. Moves to the sharp side of a key, the dominant side, involve an increase of tension and a sense of moving out of that key. Explorations of the flat side of a key seem rather to move within the key, to speak of its inner depths. This is partially because the flat side is the side of the minor mode, through which the major mode can be expressively enriched without even changing its key center. The parallel minor mode can thus sound as a latent expressive realm within any given major key. And because the tonic harmony can be said to contain the subdominant harmony within it as a kind of nether projection from the tonic note, the subdominant harmony itself can be heard as a sign of interiority. (The traditional "amen" cadence is as good an illustration of this as any: while the final tonic continues to sound in the voices of the congregation, the subdominant opens up a space beneath and within that tonic, and "amen" is given the kind of musical support that allows it to arise like a ratification swelling up from deep within.)

As a classic example of a Mozartean purple patch, consider mm. 37–48 from the slow movement of the G minor Symphony, K. 550. A transparent phrase in B♭ major plunges into its flat side, only to emerge in a luminously exultant cadence. This comes on like a sudden infusion of divine afflatus, transforming an unpretentious phrase into something that seethes with emotional depth and experience. Because this interpolation expands from the middle of the phrase, and because it has recourse to the flat side of the key center, it is made to sound as if emanating from within.

Another example, mm. 55–64 from the slow movement of the G minor String Quintet, K. 516, finds depths within depths. In this passage, Mozart will bring us back to a thoroughly transformed E♭ major after an extended and multidimensional exploration of its flat side. At measure 56 the scene darkens suddenly, with a series of expressive melodic descents in E♭ minor, answered by sobs in the viola. Then this somber procession is stilled as the music plunges deeper yet into the flat side, now finding the rare light of C♭ major, written enharmonically in the cello as B major. As the G♭s persist in the upper violin, the texture moves chromatically to the dominant of E♭ minor. And then a miracle ensues. Mozart simply allows his cadence to resolve back to E♭ major, but that key and its treatment now sound impossibly poignant. No major third ever sounded so extraordinary as the G in the first violin, heard after all those G♭s. And now we hear those melodic descents from a few moments before, as well as that earlier section's active accompanimental commotion, but both are transfigured into a major-mode texture that seems to smile through tears, that is somehow both world-weary and suffused with hope. This is an astonishing emotional effect, one that would be rivaled only by Schubert.

Mozart does not always need to plunge so deeply into the flat side to achieve an effect of emotional ballast. Sometimes the diatonic subdominant harmony can itself work in this way. At the outset of the slow movement from the "Jupiter" Symphony (mm. 1–11), notice how Mozart withholds the subdominant until the second big phrase, and how the movement only finds its feet (or, rather, finds its bass line) at the point of its entry. Later in the movement (mm. 28–39), Mozart again exploits the latent expressivity of the subdominant. Some untroubled phrases in C major are followed by a circle of fifths progression that leads to the subdominant and the makings of a cadence. But before closing the circuit, Mozart interrupts the cadence with a repetition of the circle of fifths. And this time around, the subdominant (F) finds its own subdominant (B♭) with a two-stage bass descent by thirds (from F through D to B♭). The effect is one of taking increasingly deeper breaths, filling an increasingly expansive inner space—and then the bass line climbs, step by step, back up into the daylight of C major.

Mozart never reaches for these effects; like much else in his music, they seem to arise without strain, as if eternally available. This is another reason why they sound like revelations of an interior state rather than something achieved by moving out of oneself (as they might sound in Beethoven). And as we have heard, these passages are somehow both richly emotional and archly ultramundane, somehow both personal and otherworldly. As such they seem to emanate from an interiorized sense of self, but one that also functions as a locus of transcendence. With this crucial tension between the deeply personal and the transcendently supra-personal we are verging on the realm of what some have called post-Kantian subjectivity.

IV. Unveiling the Grail

The occluded core of this modern construction of subjectivity is the noumenon, the opposite number of the phenomenon in Kant's transcendental analytic, the supersensible thing-in-itself, forever unavailable to human cognition. For Gary Tomlinson, "the advent of the noumenon . . . signals the fixing of a modern relation between the subject and the supersensible. Unperceived realms ... now have been introjected into the forms of subjective knowledge."[21] Karol Berger has noted the connection between "the Kantian noumenal realm of the thing-in-itself, a realm utterly unknowable" and E.T.A. Hoffmann's "infinite realm of the spirits."[22] Implicit in Hoffmann (and later explicit in Schopenhauer) is the idea that music, like no other medium, "gives voice to this noumenal realm."[23] Music was also heard at this time to give voice to an increasingly interiorized sense of self. As Hegel put it, for example: "The proper task of music is to vivify some content or other in the sphere of subjective inner life."[24]

Losing faith in the ability to connect with, to harmonize with, or even to understand external reality, modern subjectivity moves inward, gaining an interior realm. The world is then reconceived in terms of the self, and the self begins to peer out at reality as if looking out a window. This type of relation to reality constitutes the subjective warrant of much Romantic art, literature, and music, and is perhaps nowhere so directly conjured as in Romantic landscape painting: the famous *Rückenfigur* in so many of Caspar David Friedrich's paintings appears as an iconic sign of this experience. In Mozart's music we can hear intimations of this new, interiorized self, still deeply suffused with a sense of what has been lost, namely, the transparent and innocent harmony of Enlightenment faith (a harmony encapsulated in Alexander Pope's freeze-dried assertion: whatever is, is right). But to lose that innocence is to find a new kind of beauty, the melancholy beauty of ironic intimation, the sound of the unreachable noumenon.

This crystallization of beauty with the loss of innocence, lingering in the aura of so much of Mozart's later instrumental music, becomes more explicitly grounded in *Così fan tutte*.[25] There the main characters are disabused of their idealized view of love and fidelity to the accompaniment of astonishingly beautiful music. The audience witnessing the ignoble deceit practiced upon the women by their male lovers also observes the demise of the cherished equation of truth and beauty, for, as Mary Hunter argues, numbers featuring remarkable musical beauty serve to frame the plot's central deceit.[26] And something closely related to this same crystallization informs the many *sotto voce* "*sorpresa*" scenes in Mozart's other operas, where, after some shocking discovery, the action freezes in a moment of surpassing musical beauty, marking the loss of certainty by making audible the awe of transformed consciousness.

Mozart's music intimates this ironic state of consciousness by staging suspended moments of revelatory beauty, moments whose preternatural second sight is made possible by the presence of a threshold that can never be crossed, the threshold created by modern subjectivity. With this threshold, consciousness becomes an exclusionary inner space created in contradistinction to the outside world, defining the outside world: to be inside is to know of an outside. Mozart's beautiful moments make this space resonate as an interior realm, activating its divination of a remote transcendence. This is how the deeply emotional can at the same time sound otherworldly. Moments granting sonic presence to such a precarious confederation cannot last, but they can be renewed. For Mozart's music is music to be reheard: the listening experience lives and lives again to anticipate and then savor such moments.

The beautiful intimations we have been listening for in Mozart's music are ever renewable. As such, they offer a model of musical experience in the modern age, for the cultural practice of rehearing music continues to be sustained on the wager that what music offers us is ever renewable. We stage Western art music the way Mozart stages *his* special moments. This is because music remains our *noumenon*, the *Ding an sich* we are always in the business of approaching. We routinely try to ground Western art music in other discourse systems, because we still tend to think of this music as a profound, even oracular, utterance from a wordless transcendental realm, as something that needs to be grounded even while we reassure ourselves that it can never be. (For once music is grounded, the lights will come on in the magic theater, and the show will be over.) Mozart more than anyone taught us to rehear music as if unveiling the Grail.

And the spell has not yet been broken. For even on the post-modern frontier, where the once-infinite depths of the modern self have been compressed and flattened into an infinitely crowded surface, where the magic theater stands empty, a *Kinderspiel* from the childhood of modernity—even in *this* landscape, it is hard to imagine reaching a standpoint from which Mozart's music would not register as beautiful and as noumenal. Despite the harrowing destruction of so many cherished fantasies—from Mozart's age to our own, from the terror of 1793 to the terror of 2001—it seems we can still find ourselves exquisitely suspended in the sound of Mozart, still find ourselves haunted by his uncanny intimations. What Mozart offers to modernity is the sound of the loss of innocence, the ever renewable loss of innocence. That such a sound is beautiful has nothing to do with Mozart and everything to do with us.

Notes

1 Charles Rosen has claimed that "No composer was a greater master of the expansion of the center of a phrase than Mozart . . ." See Rosen, *The Classical Style:
   Haydn, Mozart, Beethoven* (New York: Norton, 1971; 1997), 88.

2 E.T.A. Hoffmann, review of Beethoven's Fifth Symphony, in *E .T. A. Hoffmann's
   Musical Writings: Kreisleriana, The Poet and the Composer, Music Criticism*, ed.
   David Charlton, trans. Martyn Clarke (Cambridge: Cambridge University Press,
   1989), 237–8.

3 Rudolph Otto, *The Idea of the Holy: an Inquiry into the Non-Rational Factor in
   the Idea of the Divine and Its Relation to the Rational*, tr. John W. Harvey (Oxford: Oxford University Press, 1923; 1973), 126. Otto's phrase first came to my
   attention in Richard A. Etlin's book *In Defense of Humanism: Value in the Arts
   and Letters* (Cambridge, MA: Harvard University Press, 1996), 154.

4 Why the exclusive focus on slow movements? As the "contemplative" center of a
   multi-movement sonata, slow movements make for an obvious place to begin a
   study of the effect of beautiful intimation in Mozart's music. Maynard Solomon
   also emphasizes the expressive centrality and interiority of Mozart's slow movements. See Solomon, *Mozart: A Life* (New York: Harper Collins, 1995), 206. For
   a different approach, see Adorno's essay "Schöne Stellen," in which he selects
   three examples of Mozartean beauty from the second-theme groups of first-
   movement allegros (from K. 465, K. 542, and K. 526). Adorno, "Schöne Stellen,"
   in *Musikalische Schriften* (Frankfurt: Suhrkamp, 1984), 5, 704–06. Special thanks
   to Reinhold Brinkmann for making me aware of Adorno's essay.

5 Solomon, *Mozart*, ch. 12 and 24. For Rosen, see especially *The Classical Style*; and
   "Radical, Conventional Mozart," in *Critical Entertainments: Music Old and New*
   (Cambridge, MA: Harvard University Press, 2000), 85–104.

6 Don Campbell, *The Mozart Effect: Tapping the Power of Music to Heal the Body,
   Strengthen the Mind, and Unlock the Creative Spirit* (New York: Avon Books,
   1997).

7 Solomon, *Mozart*, 375.

8 Karl Barth, *Wolfgang Amadeus Mozart*, trans. Clarence K. Pott (Grand Rapids,
   MI: William B. Eerdmans Publishing Company, 1986), 28. The original German-
   language version of Barth's monograph was published in 1956 by Theologischer
   Verlag Zurich.

9 Barth, 53–56. See also Karol Berger's musicologically-informed elaboration
   of this view, specifically in regard to Mozart's piano concertos, in "The First-
   Movement Punctuation Form in Mozart's Piano Concertos," in Neal Zaslaw, ed.,
   Mozart's Piano Concertos: Text, Context, Interpretation (Ann Arbor: University
   of Michigan Press, 1996), 254–6.

10 Solomon, *Mozart*, 379.

11 Rosen, *Classical Style*, 324–5.

12 Solomon, *Mozart*, 379.

13 Though it can be violent and disturbing. When I first presented this paper, Robert Levin and Anthony Newcomb independently reminded me of the dissonant violence within the slow movement of Mozart's Piano Sonata in F, K. 533 (bars 59–72).

14 Mark DeVoto lists it as an example of a "mordantly dissonant" appoggiatura chord in his expanded revision of Walter Piston's harmony textbook. See Piston, *Harmony*, 5th ed., rev. and exp. by Mark DeVoto (New York: Norton, 1987), 520.

15 The bell-like core of this sonority is formed by the pitches B♭, C, and G.

16 Maynard Solomon, in one of his chapters on Mozart's beautiful music, speaks of the "excruciating, surplus quality that transforms loveliness into ecstasy, grace into sublimity, pleasure into rapture." Solomon, *Mozart*, 363.

17 George Santayana, *The Sense of Beauty: Being the Outline of Aesthetic Theory* (New York: Dover Publications, 1955), 164.

18 Hermann Abert, *W. A. Mozart, Zweiter Teil: 1783–1791*, 7th ed. (Leipzig: Breitkopf & Härtel, 1956), 14.

19 For a stimulating treatment of Mozart as a transitional figure between the Enlightenment focus on object and the Romantic focus on subject, see Denis Donoghue, "Approaching Mozart," in James M. Morris, ed., *On Mozart* (Cambridge: Cambridge University Press, 1994), 33–35. Marshall Brown and Rose Rosengard Subotnik have also written illuminating essays on Mozart's music and various aspects of Romantic consciousness. See Brown, "Mozart and After: The Revolution in Musical Consciousness," *Critical Inquiry* 7, 4 (Summer 1981), 689–706; and Subotnik, "Evidence of a Critical Worldview in Mozart's Last Three Symphonies," in her book *Developing Variations: Style and Ideology in Western Music* (Minneapolis: University of Minnesota Press, 1991), 98–111.

20 For the original context of "purple patches," see Horace, *Ars Poetica*, lines 14–16, in which Horace deplores the tendency of poets to pad their works by cobbling together ill-assorted purple patches of descriptive splendor.

21 Gary Tomlinson, *Metaphysical Song: An Essay on Opera* (Princeton: Princeton University Press, 1999), 77.

22 Karol Berger, *A Theory of Art* (New York: Oxford University Press, 2000), 136.

23 Ibid.

24 Cited in Berger, *A Theory of Art*, 208. From G. W. F. Hegel, *Aesthetics: Lectures on Fine Art*, 2 vols., trans. T. M. Knox (Oxford: Oxford University Press, 1975), 902.

25 I have explored this idea at much greater length in "Mozart's *felix culpa*: *Così fan tutte* and the Irony of Beauty," *Musical Quarterly* 78, 1 (Spring 1994), 77–98.

26 Hunter also traces the existence of a Viennese opera buffa convention calling for a specific type of musical beauty (one that shares elements with what I referred

to above as "the sound of Mozart"). This convention is often employed as a sign of liminal interiority, as in Hunter's telling example from Haydn's *Il Mondo della Luna*. See Mary Hunter, *The Culture of Opera Buffa in Mozart's Vienna: A Poetics of Entertainment* (Princeton: Princeton University Press, 1999), 285–296.

A propos of Buffon's *Discours du style*

HENRI ZERNER

BUFFON'S *Discours du style*, "Discourse on Style" as it is generally known, is still very famous today, at least in France, but it is rarely read (most of the friends I asked had never actually read it).[1] There is, however, one phrase in it that has become proverbial. It is usually quoted as "Le style c'est l'homme," "style is the man." The actual quotation, whose meaning depends on the context in the *Discours*, is "le style est l'homme même," "style is the man himself." Although the proverbial phrase alters the original slightly, the gist of it does not falsify Buffon's meaning. It affirms with extraordinary vigor that style is tied to the writer's individuality. Today the idea seems obvious, and the phrase sounds, I am afraid, like a well-turned platitude, so thoroughly has its message been assimilated. What I propose here is that when Buffon wrote it, in 1753, it was a bold innovation, and also that in the context of the *Discours*, Buffon's concept of style is more complex than the familiar formula suggests.

A few words about the author and the circumstances that surrounded the *Discours*. Georges Louis Leclerc, comte de Buffon, is famous as one of the *philosophes* along with Voltaire, Montesquieu, Condillac, and others; in other words, a major figure of the Enlightenment. He is generally considered one of the founders of modern zoology, but he also had important roles in the formation of evolutionism, paleontology, and geology. He was exceptionally vain, particularly about his writing. In 1753 he was elected to the *Académie française*. This institution, founded by Richelieu in 1634, comprised forty members; it was established as the watchdog of the French language. Appointment was for life. When a member was elected and took his seat he had

53

to deliver a speech or *discours de réception*; he was expected to devote some time to praising the institution itself and its history, the king, and above all to give a eulogy of his defunct predecessor. By the mid-eighteenth century the *Académie* had fallen into the habit of electing members for their prominence in society rather than their literary accomplishments. Buffon's discourse is unusual. Although shorter than most, it is a sustained treatment of a real topic; on the other hand, it does away with the conventional eulogies (except of the king, in a short paragraph at the end). His predecessor, a prelate of no great distinction, is only mentioned briefly and in the final sentence is not even named.[2] By choosing to give an ambitious aesthetic dissertation Buffon made it clear that he took his immortality seriously; that, while he was famous as a scientist, he was taking his seat as a writer: "Books that are well written will be the only ones that will be passed on to posterity: the quantity of information, the singularity of facts, even the novelty of discoveries do not secure immortality...."[3]

There was not that much discussion of style before Buffon; it was not a very important concept in aesthetics before the late-eighteenth century. But, when one finds discussions of style, it is almost always a matter of decorum. That is, it is a matter of the appropriateness of the way something is expressed to the subject that is under discussion: of the form to the content. This is still very much the case in the long article on style in the *Encyclopédie* of Diderot, published several years after Buffon's *Discours*. It was written by the Chevalier de Jaucour who defines style as "the manner of expressing one's thoughts orally, or in writing, the words being chosen and arranged according to the laws of harmony and number, in relation to the elevation or simplicity of the subject treated. The result is the Style."[4] It is perfectly clear that for him style is a matter of decorum. His ideas still come right out of the rhetoric of Quintilian. And, like the Roman rhetorician, he distinguishes three styles: the elevated style, the low style, and the medium or moderate style. Jaucour elaborates further, giving a number of styles appropriate for specific kinds of subject matter: the pastoral, lyric poetry, and so forth, each kind of writing, that is, each domain of discourse having its own style. All this has to do with what is being said and never with who says it, with the author. In an earlier volume of the *Encyclopédie*, under "*Genre* de style," Voltaire also attached style indissolubly to genre: "since the kind of execution that an artist must use, depends on the objects he treats. Since the genre of Poussin is not that of Teniers, nor the architecture of a temple, the same as an ordinary house, nor the music of a tragic opera the same as that of an opera buffa, consequently each genre of writing, has its own style in prose as well as in verse."[5] It is true that Poussin

and Teniers are named, but they do not appear as individual authors; they appear as representatives of the specific genres in which each excelled: Poussin
as the paragon of history painting and Teniers as the ultimate representative
of genre painting, that is, the painting of daily life. In other words, the two
represent high and low style. It has nothing to do with their individuality as
authors. The only place where one might find the term "style" as a distinctive
characteristic of an individual is in the discourse of connoisseurship, and only
in passing as a substitute for the more usual term "manner."

Buffon is very original, then, I might say revolutionary, in the way he dis-
engages style from content and firmly associates it with the individual author,
the man: "le style c'est l'homme." When one looks at the *Discours* a little more
closely and tries to see more specifically what it is that Buffon means by style,
one is somewhat surprised. His point of departure is that having a good style
is to write well. But this according to him is a matter of thoughts rather than
words. Here is how the topic of style is introduced: "Style is nothing but the
order and movement that one gives to one's thoughts."[6] And he will stress
that again later on: "To write well, is at once to think well, to feel well, and
to express oneself well. It is to have, all at once, wit, soul, and taste . . . it is
only ideas that constitute the substance of the style. The harmony of words
is secondary."[7] Buffon breaks with the rhetorical view of style still sustained
by Jaucour, which sees it as a harmony of words: ". . . this harmony of words
constitutes neither the substance nor the tone of the style and is often found
in writings empty of ideas."[8] You will have noticed a new move here, which is
to differentiate between the substance and the tone of style.

In disengaging style from content, Buffon did not altogether discard the
appropriateness of style to substance—the notion of decorum; he did not
turn his back on Quintilian. This is in fact what he meant by the "tone" of the
style as opposed to its substance. Here is his definition of "tone": "The tone
is nothing but the appropriateness of the style to the nature of the topic. It
should never be forced. It will rise naturally from the substance of the subject . . . ."[9] In other words, decorum is part of the style, but it is not the whole
thing, and not necessarily the most important part.

It is time now to return to the passage where we find the proverbial phrase,
the crucial passage where he attaches style to the person. "Well-written works
are the only ones that will be transmitted to posterity: the mass of information, the singularity of facts, even the novelty of discoveries, are no reliable
assurance of immortality. If the works that contain them are only concerned
with minor matters, if they are tastelessly written without nobility and without genius, they will perish, because information, facts and discoveries can be

easily lifted, taken away and even improved upon when put to use by more able hands. These things are outside of man, style is the man himself: style, therefore, cannot be taken away, nor transferred, nor altered: if it is elevated, noble and sublime, the author will be admired in all times . . . ." At this point, when you might think that Buffon has reached the end of his argument, having argued that the distinctive form of expression of the individual is what will keep his writings alive, he pushes on with what seems to me the most striking and surprising move of the whole discourse. The sentence continues: "because only truth is durable, and even eternal. And a beautiful style is such only through the infinite number of truths it presents. All the intellectual beauties it contains, all the relations of which it is constituted, are so many truths that are as useful, and perhaps more precious for the human mind, than those that might comprise the matter under discussion."[10] What exactly Buffon means may not be absolutely clear, but there is no question that the idea of placing the truth value in the style rather than in the subject or substance of the discourse, and suggesting that this truth value might be more precious to humanity than the substance itself seems remarkably consonant with modern ideas. Indeed, is it not reminiscent of the concept of "significant form," the rallying motto of a certain formalism?

To recapitulate, we see Buffon making three important moves: the first is to separate style from its traditional relation to subject matter and decorum; the second is to define style not as the arrangement of words, but the concatenation of ideas, that is, a sort of necessity in the order and succession of ideas; the third, finally, is to suggest that what is most important in a piece of writing, its main contribution, what one might call its human meaning, is attached to its style.

Buffon did not make all this up *ex nihilo*, and I believe that his singular understanding of style had a point of departure in a text rarely cited today, although it may be more familiar to musicologists than others, because its aesthetic ideas give a large place to music. Yves Marie de L'Isle André (1675–1764), known as le Père André, published his *Essai sur le beau* in 1741, twelve years before Buffon wrote his *Discours*.[11] André, unlike most writers on aesthetics before Buffon, has a sustained discussion of style, to which he attaches great importance. The author distinguishes three elements in discourse: "expression, *tour* [by which André seems to mean the formal devices of language, the use of tropes] and style; expression renders our thought [it seems to correspond to what linguists call denotation], *tour* gives it a particular form, and style develops it in order to show it under the various lights that it requires in relation to our purpose."[12] Each of these aspects has its particular kind of beauty. Not surprisingly, the main beauty related to expression is clarity. "*Tour,*" that is, the particular way you choose to present an idea, can be more or less explicit or more or less elusive, giving the reader/auditor the pleasure of filling in the gaps. When he comes to discuss the specific beauty of style, André gives a definition. This is a complex and unusual idea of style and one that clearly anticipates Buffon's and probably inspired it. André was particularly interested in music and his concept of style is based on a musical simile. "I call style," he writes, "a certain succession of thoughts and *tours* which is so sustained within a single work, that all its parts seem like the strokes of the same brush; or, if we think of discourse as a kind of natural music, a certain arrangement of words which, together, constitute chords, the result of which is a harmony agreeable to the ear."[13]

For all his originality, and the extent of his apparent contribution to Buffon's thought, André does not arrive at what is Buffon's most memorable contribution, to detach style from decorum and attach it to "the man," that is, to make it an expression of the author.

On the other hand, Buffon did not retain the particular value that André put on the emotional power of music with clear pre-romantic sensibility: ". . . can one doubt that style, as we have defined it, is somehow the soul of discourse, its attraction and its charm, which sustains the attention of the mind by the succession of the materials that it ties together, by the natural link of the various turns of phrase that it attaches to them, by the sweetness of the harmony with which it strikes our ear and through it our heart which, from an invincible impression of nature, loves harmony everywhere, not only in music, but in all kinds of composition."[14] Here André already anticipates the idea that music, because it moves us so directly and so powerfully in a way that appears to be natural rather than conventional, is the model of all the arts, an idea that was going to be very inspiring throughout the nineteenth century, ending with Walter Pater's famous saying and Symbolist theory.

In addition, I would like to discuss briefly another remarkable text by Buffon, one which he did not publish himself. It was found in his papers, and it is not clear exactly when it was written. The original editor believed it was written at the very end of Buffon's life, but I think it more likely that it represents the notes he took when he was working on the *Discours*.[15] Here he distinguishes "painting" from "describing," painting being understood metaphorically, since what he discusses is what makes good writing.

> To paint, and to describe, are two different things. One only requires
> eyes, the other demands genius. Although they both aim to the same

goal, they cannot go together. Description presents all the parts of its object, successively, and coldly. The more detailed it is, the less of an effect it makes. Painting, on the contrary, first capturing only the most salient features, preserves the imprint of the object and gives it life. To describe well, it is sufficient to see coldly. But, in order to paint, one must use all the senses. To see, to hear, to touch, to feel, these are as many aspects that the author must render through the energetic expressions. He must combine the finesse of colors with the vigor of the brush. He must nuance, condense or fuse the colors together. In brief, he must shape a living whole of which description can only present dead and separate parts. [16]

Here again, I am convinced that Buffon's point of departure was André, who distinguished ordinary writers from great geniuses in the following terms: "The ones only sketch them in [the things they are discussing], the others paint them; the former know at most how to describe them, the latter engrave them deep in our heart through the turn of imagination and feeling with which they enliven them."[17] Buffon, however, goes further than his model (if indeed I am right about his dependence on André) because he introduces the idea of synesthesia, which will play such an important role in Romantic and Symbolist aesthetics. These manuscript notes were published in 1860 and then again in 1885, at a time when Buffon's synthetic view of writing and his call for synesthesia must have found strong echoes.[18]

In a sense, this recourse to synesthesia is understandable from a rationalist, Enlightenment philosopher who is attempting to give an account of the emotional effect of great writing and hence needs to find some explanations based on the senses. Similarly, it is clear that while Buffon does see style as an individual trait, this is compatible in the context of the *Discours* with a classicizing understanding of composition and other aspects of traditional rhetoric. The interesting question is how such ideas, which arose rather surprisingly and more or less marginally at one time, will become central later. Or, put another way, how do we relate these texts to later cultural and artistic developments? It is clear that the excerpting of a formula like "style is the man" gave it great resonance in the future, while the integrity of the entire text betrays complex ties with an earlier aesthetic, and with a contemporaneous culture.

Figure 1. *Frantisek Kupka,* Piano Keys, *1909.*
© 2004 Artists Rights Society (ARS), New York/ADAGP, Paris.
Photograph © National Gallery in Prague, 2004.

Notes

1   *Discours prononcé à l'académie française par M. de Buffon, le jour de sa réception.*
    There are innumerable editions of this text. I have used the text from *Oeuvres*
    philosophiques de Buffon, ed. Jean Piveteau (Paris: P.U.F., 1954). I have kept the
    original spelling.

2   This lack of decorum was noted at the time. In a draft of the speech that was
    submitted for approval, the final sentence read: "But it is for you, Gentlemen, to
    praise a prelate who was as noteworthy in the Church as you made him note-
    worthy in literature." ("Mais c'est à vous, Messieurs, à qui il est réservé de louer
    un prélat aussi considérable dans l'Eglise que vous l'avez rendu considérable
    dans les lettres.") *Oeuvres philosophiques de Buffon*, 509. This must have seemed
    too implicitly sarcastic to be tolerated.

3   Ibid., 503. "Les ouvrages bien écrits sont les seuls qui passeront à la postérité:
    la quantité des connoissances, la singularité des faits, la nouveauté même des
    découvertes ne sont pas de sûrs garans de l'immortalité . . . ."

4   *Encyclopédie, ou, Dictionnaire raisonné des sciences, des arts et des métiers*, ed.
    Denis Diderot, 15 (Neuchâtel, 1765), 551.

5   *Encyclopédie*, 7 (1757), 594–95. Voltaire notes that insofar as an author has a set
    style it is only a defect. "Remarquons ici qu'un auteur qui s'est fait un *genre* de
    style, peut rarement le changer quand il change d'objet. [He then gives exam-
    ples in La Fontaine and Benserade.] La perfection consisterait à savoir assortir
    toûjours (*sic*) son style à la matière qu'on traite; mais qui peut être le maître de
    son habitude, & ployer à son gré son génie?"

6   *Discours*, 500. "Le style n'est que l'ordre & le mouvement qu'on met dans ses
    pensées."

7   Loc. cit., "Bien écrire, c'est tout-à-la-fois bien penser, bien sentir & bien rendre,
    c'est avoir en même temps de l'esprit, de l'ame & du goût; . . . Les idées seules
    forment le fond du style, l'harmonie des paroles n'en est que l'accessoire."

8   Ibid., 503. ". . . cette harmonie de mots ne fait ni le fond, ni le ton du style, & se
    trouve souvent dans des écrits vides d'idée."

9   Ibid., 503. "Le ton n'est que la conveance du style à la nature du sujet; il ne doit
    jamais être forcé; il naîtra naturellement du fond même de la chose . . ."

10 Loc. cit., "Les ouvrages bien écrits sont les seuls qui passeront à la postérité:
    la quantité des connoissances, la singularité des faits, la nouveauté même des
    découvertes ne sont pas de sûrs garans de l'immortalité; si les ouvrages qui les
    contiennent ne roulent que sur de petits objets, s'ils sont écrits sans goût, sans
    noblesse et sans génie, ils périront, parce que les connoissances, les faits & les dé-
    couvertes s'enlèvent aisément, se transportent, & gagnent même à être mises en
    oeuvre par des mains plus habiles. Ces choses sont hors de l'homme, le style est
    l'homme même: le style ne peut donc ni s'enlever, ni se transporter, si s'altérer:
    s'il est élevé, noble, sublime, l'auteur sera également admiré dans tous les temps;

car il n'y a que la vérité qui soit durable & même éternelle. Or un beau style n'est tel en effet que par le nombre infini de vérités qu'il présente. Toutes les beautés intellectuelles qui s'y trouvent, tous les rapports dont il est composé, sont autant de vérités aussi utiles, & peut-être plus précieuses pour l'esprit humain, que celles qui peuvent faire le fond du sujet."

11 André, Yves-Marie, *Essai sur le beau* (Paris: Guérin, 1741). This first edition is anonymous. I have used the text in *Oeuvres philosophique du père André: avec une introduction sur sa vie et ses ouvrages, tirée de sa correspondance inédite*, ed. Victor Cousin (Paris: Charpentier, 1843). The author himself published a new edition at the end of his life in 1763, which is enlarged by the addition of six more discourses (the first only had four). The text of the parts published in 1741 is unchanged except for the modernization of spelling and punctuation. There were editions of the *Essai* in 1824, 1827, 1838, and 1856, which shows its sustained interest for the nineteenth century.

12 Op. cit., 53–54: ". . . je distingue dans le corps du discours trois choses qui en sont comme les éléments: l'expression, le tour et le style; l'expression, qui rend notre pensée; le tour, qui lui donne une cerrtaine forme; et le style, qui la développe pour la mettre dans les différents jours qu'elle demande par rapport à notre dessein."

13 Ibid., 57: "J'appelle style une certaine suite d'expressions et de tours tellement soutenue dans le cours d'un ouvrage, que toutes ses parties ne semblent être que les traits d'un même pinceau; ou, si nous considérons le discours comme une espèce de musique naturelle, un certain arrangement de paroles qui forment ensemble des accords, d'où il résulte à l'oreille une harmonie agréable: c'est l'idée que nous en donnent les maîtres de l'art."

14 Ibid., 57–58: "Cependant, Messieurs, peut-on douter que le style, tel que nous l'avons défini, ne soit en quelque sorte l'âme du discours, l'attrait et le charme, qui soutient l'attention de l'esprit par la suite des matières qu'il enchaîne ensemble, par la liaison naturelle des tours differents dont il les assortit, par la douceur de l'hamonie dont il nous frappe l'oreille, et par là le coeur, qui, par une impression invincible de la nature, aime partout les accords, non-seulement dans la musique, mais en tout genre de composition."

15 Charles Bruneau, who prepared the text for the Piteveau edition (see n. 1) also believed this text to precede the final writing of the *Discours*. The text is reprinted in *Oeuvres philosophiques*, 510–11.

16 Buffon, *Oeuvres philosophiques*, 510. "Peindre ou décrire sont deux choses différentes: l'une ne suppose que des yeux, l'autre exige du génie. Quoique toutes les deux tendent au même but, elles ne peuvent aller ensemble. La description présente successivement et froidement toutes les parties de l'objet; plus elle est détaillée, moins elle fait d'effet. La peinture au contraire, ne saisissant d'abord que les traits les plus saillants, garde l'empreinte de l'objet et lui donne de la vie. Pour bien décrire il suffit de voir froidement; mais pour peindre, il faut l'emploi de tous les sens. Voir, entendre, palper, sentir, ce sont autant de caractères que

l'auteur doit sentir et rendre par des traits énergiques. Il doit joindre la finesse des couleurs à la vigueur du pinceau, les nuancer, les condenser, ou les fondre; former enfin un ensemble vivant, dont la description ne peut présenter que des parties mortes et détachées."

The Pre-Modernist Roots of Modernism

The Textualization of the Context:
Comic Strategies in Meta-Operas of the
Eighteenth and Twentieth Centuries

HERMANN DANUSER

IN THE HISTORY of literature, the crucial relevance of comic strategies for the development of literary modernity has never been ignored. The contributions to the aesthetics of modernity made by the great novelists—from Cervantes through Sterne, Diderot, Jean Paul, and later writers—are too obvious for the historiography of modernist literature to be overlooked. This is particularly true of the category of self-referentiality, which developed largely within the traditions of the comic novel and the play within a play. The role of the comic in the development of musical modernity, however, has rarely been addressed.[1] I will try to elucidate some of its aspects, focusing on the genre of opera and more specifically on those operas that deal with opera, that is operas on opera, or, as one could also say, meta-operas, that branch of the *commedia per musica* that thematizes the world of opera itself.

In so doing, I wish also to revise the historiography of the avant-garde in light of what one might call an early history of musical modernism, demonstrating a specific reflexivity as the significant contribution of meta-operas to the aesthetics of modernity. By focusing either on the Western avant-garde in the twentieth century[2] or on earlier developments such as the German Romantics,[3] Wagner,[4] and the *fin de siècle* around 1900,[5] the historiography of musical modernism so far has not attended to phenomena prior to the French Revolution. My aim, however, will not be just to expand the reign of modernism by suggesting a specious historical continuity of the meta-opera from the eighteenth through the twentieth centuries. Rather, it will be to re-consider the special development of musical modernism in the broader realm of tendencies that, more often than not, appear first in other fields before they begin to influence music.[6] Renouncing any historiography, however sketchy, of meta-opera, I intentionally pass over the nineteenth century, although several important aspects of the genre survived into that primary age of aesthetic autonomy or even made their first appearance then.

A few sharply contrasting examples—very few indeed, as the focus here is on prominent, general features of the meta-opera—will suffice to underscore the differences between works from the eighteenth and twentieth centuries as well as to indicate some common points of view. As a foundation for this comparison of barely comparable works—three traditional, one avant-garde—I will ground my approach in musicological text theory; more specifically, in the relations between the categories "text" and "context," as indicated by the title of this essay.[7] After some introductory remarks about comic self-reflexivity and the idea of modernism, I will combine historical reconstruction with a phenomenological outline of meta-opera's most central aspects, touching first on *agon* as a type of social and artistic competition, then on the process of pragmatic and self-reflective textualization, and lastly on open form as a species of context art. I will conclude with reflections on aesthetic reversals and the question of power.

I. Introduction: Comic Self-Reflexivity and the Idea of Modernism

In theories of musical modernism, or of aesthetic modernity in music, aspects of the musical material have been—and still are—in the forefront of the critical discourse. According to the theory put forward by Theodor W. Adorno in his epochal *Philosophie der neuen Musik* (1949), the musical material follows a kind of objective tendency to become more and more complex by respecting a "canon of forbidden procedures" [*Kanon des Verbotenen*]. The development of high modernism in the second half of the twentieth century, especially in the two decades before the appearance of post-modernism in the 1970s, took this tenet as a basis, and exponents of a "new complexity" around the composer Bryan Ferneyhough still do today.

But modernity is not just an acoustic category established by structural procedures of composition centered on such catchwords as "complexity" and "innovation." It is also an intellectual category in the field of aesthetics. We must therefore supplement the musical dimension—insofar as it can be grasped acoustically—with an intellectual dimension that is not necessarily audible in any obvious way. A good case in point is the later œuvre of Richard

Strauss.[8] The standard opinion that this composer, after having completed *Elektra* (1909), had abandoned a truly modernist aesthetics proves to be short-sighted if we take into account the reflexive quality of his music. In *Capriccio*, Strauss's last opera, a "Conversation Piece for Music," reflective strategies replace any aesthetics of shock by converting seemingly old material into something truly new. It does this through a dramaturgical structure that has been described by Harald Fricke under the rubric of "paradoxical iteration," for which he cites the mythical Uroboros ("tail devourer") as a symbol: "As the plot unfolds, the characters invent precisely that opera with precisely those characters that they already play. The operatic snake bites its own tail." [9]

In an essay that is fundamental to our theme, Fricke opposes the more harmless normal case of graded iteration to paradoxical iteration. He subdivides graded iteration into infinite and recursive iteration. Fricke thus offers the most complete terminological overview ever given of the phenomenon of artistic self-reflection, as well as a bibliography of further literature in the principal European languages. The linguistic distinguishing marks are word compounds that begin with "ipso," "selbst," "auto," or "meta." As he sees it, his own conceptual distinctions based on iteration enlarge on the concept of "potentialization" first developed by early German Romantics. In this respect, he follows Lucien Dällenbach who turned André Gide's graphic phrase "*mise en abyme*" into a term of literary criticism.[10]

To understand a possible musical modernism in the eighteenth century, a conceptual dichotomy made by Jürgen Habermas may be helpful, the distinction between aesthetic and social dimensions of the modern.[11] Until recently, scholars have focused mainly on an aesthetic dimension grounded in the structural complexities of Johann Sebastian Bach's music. However, if one tries to cover the social dimension of the modernist process as well—a dimension manifest in the age of Enlightenment—one may well focus more on Bach's Italian contemporary Giovanni Battista Pergolesi. The new simplicity of Pergolesi's music was not just a major and well-known source for the development of the Viennese classical style that, as James Webster has argued, might be conceived as the advent of the modern in music history.[12] It was also, through its impact on the genre of opera buffa, crucial for the development of meta-opera's modernism as it is discussed here. Thus, I argue that the history of musical modernity should be re-evaluated in terms drawn from the eighteenth century and I do not center this argument on Bach (though he was a touchstone of complexity and a primary source for modern developments), but rather on the self-reflective quality that comic strategies made manifest in meta-operas of that time.

In a study of greater breadth than is possible here, it would be necessary to attend to the artistic work-concepts that arose in the seventeenth, rather than in the eighteenth century. For example, Miguel de Cervantes' novel *El ingenioso hidalgo Don Quijote de la Mancha* (published in two parts in 1605 and 1615) marks a true epochal milestone in the development of modernity. According to Dostoyevsky, there is nothing deeper or stronger in the world than this work.[13] With such works in mind, one could reflect on the possible prehistory of the categories of quotation and intertextuality, categories developed in the post-modern thought of the recent past. This could be linked to other work-concepts, such as that manifested by *La comédie de chansons* (Paris 1640). In the preface ("Avertissement aux Lecteurs"), one reads:

> It is a comedy in which there is not a single word that is not [from] a verse or a couplet of some chanson. One must esteem the agreeable invention and the subtle artifice involved in arranging things so well that a ridiculous chanson often responds to one of the most serious, and an old to a new. And even though the entire subject is nothing but buffoonery, one must admire the links and the meetings where one often finds what one does not expect.... Who would prevent us from believing that even having ingeniously interlaced low and popular talk, this agreeable concatenation renders it much more estimable? For the most beautiful *airs de cour* are mixed in this place with the *vaudevilles*; it is as if one had mixed gold and straw in order to make a work more exquisite.... So we have good reason to call our piece LA COMEDIE DE CHANSONS, unique in its genre. If the chansons are variously dismembered, that makes them more ingenious of artifice, and it is best when one says but a verse from each.[14]

But what, in fact, are comic strategies? It would make no sense to decide in advance which elements of a theoretical history that encompasses a time span of no less than two-and-a-half thousand years are most relevant in our context.[15] However, I wish to underline first the connection between the comic self-reflectivity and the aesthetics of modernity, a connection obviously basic for our task.

If, in a two-level structure, the comic presents a person, an action, or a situation in contrast to given norms (of human personality, action, or social situation), the listener, spectator, or reader recognizes the discrepancy between the two levels and thereby transforms the aesthetic experience from an immediate to a reflective one. We all know this structure from the circus.

When a clown opens a huge suitcase and takes from it a hardly visible violino piccolissimo, or when he holds in his hand a small box and pulls out a nearly endless strip of paper, the contradiction between form and content causes us to laugh. A quasi-universal mediation between our sensual experience, the objects, and the signs reflects a tendency towards modernity and its complex structures that force us to renounce any possible naiveté, any quasi-natural immediacy. A man who falls in love with a woman would not confess, "I love you," but would nowadays rather say, "I know that in the given situation one would expect me to say to you I love you." Such complexity (alas!) tends to be a sign of a "modern" condition of life.

For our present purposes the concept of "text" might be identified with the musical "work" and its performance (and it should be kept in mind that the genre of opera does not seem at first glance to offer the best opportunities for a text-theoretical study). Literary theorists have distinguished four different meanings of "context": 1) intratextual context (the relationship of one part of a text to other parts of the same text); 2) infratextual context (the relationship of a part of a text to the whole); 3) intertextual context (the relationship of a text or section to a class of texts or to other texts or sections); and 4) extratextual context (the relationship of a text to non-textual factors).[16] Here, I wish to concentrate on the third and fourth aspects: the connection of several works within a larger concept of "genre," or the connection between the pragmatic presuppositions or external circumstances and the artifact itself. The third aspect (intertextuality) opens up a wide field of relations between a given work and others of a similar kind that in their totality form a musical, or musico-dramatic, "genre," in our case more specifically, the meta-opera as a sub-genre of the opera buffa in and since the eighteenth century,[17] as well as a sub-genre of avant-garde art in the twentieth century. The fourth aspect deals with the fact that composition, performance, and reception form an extratextual context that necessarily belongs to a musical work, but to the pragmatic prerequisites rather than to the aesthetic object itself. All these dimensions radically change their status in meta-operas. One might even define these as works that extend the category of text to the last two mentioned aspects of context, the intertextual and the extratextual context, and thus textualize their contexts.

In the eighteenth century, the context of a work was defined by a well-established generic frame, in our case the opera buffa and its parodistic form.[18] In the twentieth-century avant-garde, however, the context of a text, that is, the surrounding factors of a musical work, have become completely uncertain and extremely volatile with the consequence that a clearly established framework no longer serves as reference for factors that become the text, that is, that become artistically relevant. The difference between functioning within a generic tradition and functioning in isolation marks an important difference between the types of context textualized in the eighteenth and the twentieth centuries: while in the eighteenth century the inter- and extratextual contexts textualized in meta-operas referred to a thriving contemporary art and its generic frame, the opera buffa, of which they formed a part, in the twentieth century the contexts textualized in meta-operas referred to both inter- and extratextual contexts, to elements of the older opera used as source material, and to the culture of the avant-garde in which they formed a series of isolated works.

II. Agon *as Social and Artistic Competition*

Among the many aspects of inter- and extratextual contexts that become textualized in the meta-melodrama since the early eighteenth century, I should like to mention first the human relationships between the persons involved in opera outside the aesthetic time of a work's performance, that is, their social roles within the institution as a prerequisite of the artistic roles they play within a work's dramaturgy. There, of course, competition plays a major role, and indeed, the *paragone* between artists trying to find the pattern of excellence is a very old theme in music history as well. When he planned an event for one of the long winter evenings in 1786 that honored a visiting delegation from the Netherlands, Emperor Joseph II, as is well known, organized a competition between a German and an Italian musical comedy in the orangerie of the Schönbrunn palace in Vienna: *Der Schauspieldirektor*, a "Komödie mit Musik" in one act, with a libretto by Gottlieb Stephanie the Younger and music by W. A. Mozart (K. 486), versus *Prima la musica, poi le parole*, with a libretto by Giambattista Casti and music by Antonio Salieri. Contrary to today's rankings as epitomized by Peter Shaffer's play and Milos Forman's film *Amadeus*, that evening's prize went to Salieri.

In *Der Schauspieldirektor*, a short piece combining spoken and sung parts and including two female singers who both claim "*Ich* bin die erste Sängerin" (*I* am the prima donna), comic self-referentiality is constituted through the textualization of the paratext[19] as both performers sing musical tempo marks: Madame Herz "Adagio," and Mademoiselle Silberklang "Allegro." Tempo indications, and dynamics (as in Monsieur Vogelsang's attempted mediation), belong so undisputedly to the performance marks of a score that to hear such words sung on the level of the poetic text inevitably creates a comic effect, despite the tautological parallelism of singing the words "Adagio" slowly and "Allegro" quickly.

To understand the agonal music-theatrical disposition, the "Terzett" (no. 3) is especially illuminating. Here, the singers (presented only individually up to this point—Madame Herz in an "Arietta" [no. 1] and Mademoiselle Silberklang in a "Rondo" [no. 2]) confront each other directly. Mozart's compositional strategy synthesizes the opposites into a higher unity, but of course at the same time subtly subverts this harmony so that an ambiguity between conflict and reconciliation is palpable as an aesthetic signature. While the levels of text and music should be differentiated, both contribute in close conjunction to the aesthetic effect of the ensemble. At the discursive level of textual semantics, as represented within the libretto, one finds a tripartite progression. First, each of the two singers pretends to be primary ("I am the prima donna"); next, they move toward the mediating position of Monsieur Vogelsang ("I rescind my demand" / "I rescind mine as well"); finally, they renew their earlier antagonism with new conviction ("I am the prima donna"). The music simultaneously supports and reconfigures this movement. Rather than essentialize the opposites, a basic principle of Mozart's style sublates them in a higher harmony that preserves the interwoven opposites and their tension with each other. To this end, the trio is divided into four sections of differing tempos.

Section 1 (mm. 1–89): Arranged agonally in the trio (Tempo I, "Allegro assai"), it modulates from the tonic B♭ major to the dominant F major. Prolonged after m. 62 as the new tonic, it creates a space for the first open exchange of blows. At this point, the two women present the same text in alternation with each other and with increasing virulence (mm. 62–73). In the following passage, the music modulates in an analogous fashion to the parallel minor, G minor (with a general pause in m. 89).

Section 2 (mm. 90–112): Still organized agonally but giving up the trio structure, the dramaturgy now splits temporally into two contrary phases. The first phase (Madame Herz: *Adagio*, mm. 90–97) introduces a contrast in tempo; the second (Mademoiselle Silberklang: *Allegro assai*, m. 98–112) restores the initial tempo. As the two women sing no text other than the tempo designations assigned to their passages, a humorous situation arises (as mentioned above): song has made itself independent. Musically, both phases are organized as vocal exercises, the first in a lyrical, slow style with an expansive coloratura, and the second in a highly virtuosic, dramatic style with aimlessly meandering chains of triplets. A means (vocal technique) is ostentatiously raised to an end. However, a self-reflexive trait raises the comic effect above that of a mere transposition of means and ends. The music emancipates itself from dramatic intention and becomes music about music. Within the

Example 1. W. A. Mozart, Der Schauspieldirektor, Nr. 3 "Terzett"
(mm. 158–174), vocal parts and bass

parodistic scenes, it becomes autonomous and displays itself in its quality as independent sound, a quality that Richard Wagner later criticized as song made an end in itself and that Rudolf Kolisch censured as the artistic perversion of ideal string sound into a "religion" of "beautiful tone."[20] Tonally, this second section is structured as an instable, cadential intermezzo. To prepare the structural return to the tonic (B♭ major) at the beginning of the next section, it features the subdominant E♭ major in the *Adagio* and the tonic B♭ with a half-cadence close in the *Allegro assai*. The ends of the subsections thus produce a cadential movement from E♭ to F to B♭.

Section 3 (mm. 113–145): Tonally, if not thematically or textually, the sense of an ending governs this return to the tonic B♭ major. The paired antagonists reconcile themselves musically for the sake of a higher unity. The text supports this action, as it signals accord. All trace of contrariety has vanished from this section, which is structured according to the model of a love duet. It stages harmony musically, at first through a canonic structure (with the unison as the interval of imitation), and then in a free trio, often with soaring euphonic parallel lines.

Of course, Mozart's music wholly transcends the aforementioned tripartite structure of the libretto in this section as well. In a later subsection based on recurrent cadential confirmations (mm. 137–147), lines of text sung as asides (after m. 138: "I am the prima donna!") alternate with loud pledges of harmony, revealing the accord between the two women as an empty illusion. Declarations to the audience and speech within the dialogue diverge. The orchestral accompaniment graces this aesthetic-semiotic ambiguity (one only possible in music theater) so gently that the music seems to constitute itself as a metaphysical principle of the world, able to lead the polarities of reality—the *agon* of societal and artistic life—into a higher sphere of unity.

Section 4 (mm. 146–174): This music-theatrical principle returns triumphantly at the end of the trio (see Ex. 1). Referring back to the dramaturgical-antagonistic structure of mm. 62ff. (section 1)—the two singers exchange the same lines of text as well as their repeated phrases—the fight for primacy is woven together as a totality in which the fight between two artists is both intensified and reduced to an almost irrelevant part of a dynamic whole. Finally, Monsieur Vogelsang intensifies the self-referential dimension of the text even further by animating a veritable verbal arsenal of performance directives ("piano, pianissimo, calando, mancando, diminuendo, decrescendo. . .") into a witty amplification of the fruitless attempts at pacification.

Mozart's music thus transcends any ephemeral dimension and constitutes far deeper effects by the sublime tranquillity of the *concordia discors*—a symbol of an aesthetically purified human life. The antagonistic women and the mediating man form an ensemble that creates a perfect harmony, a special achievement of opera buffa. A double character of antagonism and harmony, relevant for the musical comedy through Rossini, thus transforms the dramatic competition into a higher, musically constituted balance.

Expanding this scheme, as shown by the ambition of two singers to the single role of the prima donna, and highlighting the tensions between the different functional roles necessary for the realization of an operatic work, the musical dramaturgy of *Prima la musica, poi le parole*, a "Divertimento teatrale" in one act, is based on two competing pairs: a musician (*il maestro di cappella*) and a poet (*il poeta*), as well as an opera-seria prima donna (Donna Eleonora) and an opera-buffa singer (Tonina). The social competition between individuals is put into an artistic perspective through two antagonisms: a structural one between music and poetry, the basic elements of opera, and a generic one between two kinds of opera, the seria and the buffa. Three strategies may be mentioned.

First, playing with authorship, the auto-referential integration of the real as a fictive author in the work, is a technique with a long tradition in literature. Its example can be found in Jean Paul's *Flegeljahre*, where a person with the name Jean Paul Friedrich Richter is introduced as the author of a biography of Gottwalt Peter Harnisch with the title "Flegeljahre," as stipulated by the testament of a certain van der Kabel whose former name was Friedrich Richter, that is, Jean Paul's own official name (Johann Paul Friedrich Richter), a biography that will be the novel.[21] In Salieri's *Prima la musica*, the prima donna Donna Eleonora is supposed to rehearse "Pensieri funesti" ("dark thoughts"), a "first cavatina by Salieri," a fictitious piece of music within music. This is analogous to the evocation of fictive authorship within real authorship, while in fact it is Salieri's parody of the entrance aria from Giuseppe Sarti's opera *Giulio Sabino*.[22] The interplay between the real and the fictive author—both bear the very same name, Salieri—creates an effect similar to the interchange between reality and fantasy that is an essential part of the comic tradition in dramatic works as well, from *La vida es sueño* (Calderón de la Barca) through *Così è, se vi pare* (Luigi Pirandello).

Second, is the rejection of the classicist doctrine that musical genres have to be stylistically pure, a systematic fusion of divergent artistic principles, in this case the intertwining of seria and buffa principles. As later in Hofmannsthal and Strauss's *Ariadne auf Naxos*, the seemingly artless poetics, of course, proves to be all the more refined, complex, and modern. According to the artistic doctrine of the age, the task formulated in the third scene of *Prima la musica* with regard to the two female singers (Maestro: "Ma l'una è buffa, l'altra è seria: or come / Potrem metterle insieme?" / Poeta: "Eh! Veramente / Facil non è"[23]) could not be fulfilled: a work had to be either buffa or seria; a combination of both in one single work could only have produced a barbarous monstrosity. Yet the seemingly absurd proved to be a rich source of dramaturgical fantasy, and—through the transgression of boundaries—of a reflective, or self-referential, comic art. At the end, in the seventh scene, buffa and seria indeed are combined, when—an idea far away from any responsible art—two arias merge into a single one, as we will see more closely later on. It is a meta-poetic piece of music.

Third, context in the sense of a work's genesis is included within the work-text, thus becoming textualized. While the combination of two separate genres refers to stylistic problems, the production of the work itself (writing the libretto, composing the musical score, rehearsing with the singers, using stuttering and misspelling) shows the pragmatic dimension as a basis for comic effects in this meta-opera. Before our times of political correctness, in a tradition stemming from Theophrast, human deficiencies served as a source of humor, albeit at the expense of the disabled.[24] In the case of *Prima la musica*, spelling and misspelling while rehearsing vocal parts produces an astonishing range of effects, from traditional faults to avant-garde-like "phonetic poetry" (*Lautpoesie*). In the third scene, misunderstandings prevail between the poet and the musician, the former's word "costato" (chest) being transcribed by the latter into his score as "castrato." In the sixth scene, Tonina's tale of her different operatic roles degenerates into a linguistic free-for-all, a chaotic confusion, using stuttering as a comic device (as later on by Thomas Mann in well-known passages of his novels *Doktor Faustus* and *Felix Krull*[25]). By such means, the process of studying or rehearsing musical structures becomes part of the text, the incompleteness part of a totality, the fragment—in a truly modern sense—part of the comic whole.

The second and third strategies are intermingled in the work. Musical structures are first introduced in their genesis (the act of composition), then presented by the two adversarial artists in individual performances, and finally (as a *telos*) contrapuntally superimposed on each other as a simultaneity. If the structural antagonism in the *Schauspieldirektor* is quite straightforward, it is more involved in *Prima la musica, poi le parole*. The title of the work produces its own reception history. In the first instance, it implies that it is not the libretto, as was normally the case in the eighteenth century, but rather the music that is composed first and that the poet has to hew his words to its phrases. The title thus indicates primarily a temporal relationship (*prima-*

poi), and secondarily, or at least only as a subtext, an aesthetic hierarchy of values (primary-secondary). However, the agonal relationship of text vs. music—later so important—already glimmers here.[26]

The aesthetic presentation *in* a work of the genesis *of* a work offers the possibility of recapitulating musical material in different contexts. One of Tonina's buffo segments recurs not less than four times over the course of the work, each time in a new dramatic and musical context (see Ex. 2a–d).

After the poet has rejected two suggestions by the Kapellmeister to use pre-existent music for the artistic objective set before them (Scene iii), he proves more amenable to a third suggestion ("Questa potrebbe andare"[27])(see Ex. 2a). Scene iv portrays the maestro at work at the compositional realization of this melodic material, alternating constantly between sketching the vocal part and questioning himself, though with less criticism than incessant self-congratulation (see Ex. 2b). In No. 12 (part of the seventh and last scene), Tonina (the soubrette) wishes to perform this piece, written for her, but is immediately interrupted by Eleonora and the two men (see Ex. 2c). Only in the finale (No. 13), the only time that all four characters sing an ensemble together, does she sing her part, not as a solo but rather as the second voice in a quartet (see Ex. 2d).

Example 2a. Salieri, Prima la musica, poi le parole, *scene iii,*
Recitative before Nr. 7 (mm. 134–136), Piano-vocal score

Example 2b. Salieri, Prima la musica, poi le parole, *scene iv, Nr. 8 (mm. 1–3)*

Example 2c. Salieri, Prima la musica, poi le parole, *scene vii, Nr. 12 (mm. 4–6)*

Example 2d. Salieri, Prima la musica, poi le parole,
scene vii, Nr. 13 Finale (mm. 1–3)

There is an analogue in the part of Donna Eleonora, the opera-seria hero-ine, that is inserted in this conclusion. To compose her music in Scene iii (No. 7), the maestro accompanies himself, sings isolated vocal lines to test them, and then writes them down as a piece, once again in alternation with his own self-congratulatory remarks and with the poet's interjections.[28] As with the case of Tonina's piece, it is this piece, then, that is integrated into the ensemble of the finale (No. 13) as its highest voice.

If *Schauspieldirektor* presents the antagonism of two singers aiming at the same goal, *Prima la musica* thematizes a distinction between two vocal types and maintains it almost until the end. The first section of the finale (mm. 1–32, *Allegro moderato*, in $\frac{4}{4}$) raises this tension to a dramaturgical climax through its contrapuntal structure. As in Mozart's work, though with much simpler music, the next section (mm. 33–122, *Andante maestoso*, in $\frac{2}{4}$) sublates the differentiation of types to produce a *lieto fine*. And after the poet, long so skeptical, finally concedes that an opera can be produced in four days, the singers present a homophonic quartet in an even faster tempo directly to the public (mm. 123–261, *Allegro*, in $\frac{2}{4}$). It is the speech *ad spectatores* typical of the genre. The last remains of *agon* are sublated in the frenetic activity of operatic hubbub proper to a finale.

III. Pragmatic and Self-Reflective Textualization

The title page of the libretto to *L'opera seria* is oxymoronic, a *commedia per musica* in three acts by Ranieri Calzabigi with music by Florian Leopold Gassmann, first performed in Vienna in 1769 (and staged again by René Jacobs in Schwetzingen in 1994 and subsequently in Berlin—a performance that, with a duration of four hours, nearly reached Wagnerian proportions).[29] In this work two dimensions of context, the pragmatic and the self-reflective, merge in a way that truly puts *L'opera seria* into the early history of aesthetic musical modernism despite the fact that, stylistically, the work is no more "progressive" than the level of composition reached for instance by the young W. A. Mozart at that time.

The double list of characters, one for the comedy *L'opera seria*, the other for the opera seria *L'Oranzebe*, mirrors the basic idea of this work. On the side of the "comedy" with its parodistic names we see the scheme of the pieces by Salieri and Mozart expanded: we have first, an impresario whose name (Fallito) proves to be a self-fulfilling prophecy; second, a poet (Delirio) and a maestro di cappella (Sospiro); and third, a broader list of singers—the prima donna (Stonatrilla), the seconda donna (Smorfiosa), the primo uomo (Ritornello) and the secondo uomo (Porporina, a castrato's part in a female role). In addition to these functional roles there are, fourth, dancers, in particular the choreographer (Passagallo); fifth, three "mothers" of the female singers, natural or fictive mothers serving as their protettori, promoting agents of their respective protégées; and finally sixth, a "coro di popolo" representing the public's critical reception. All these roles or exemplifications of an operatic production since the eighteenth century are situated in a generic frame of references, as is shown by the large number of works centered around figures such as "the maestro di capella,"[30] "the impresario,"[31] or even the "mothers" who became immortal through Donizetti's *Le convenienze teatrali* (today known as *Viva la Mamma!*). On the other side, the list encompasses the forces required for the performance of the fictitious "opera seria" *L'Oranzebe*, a monumental drama of early orientalism, a "kind of baroque *Aida*," in the words of René Jacobs.[32]

This double list of characters tells us in advance that *L'opera seria* follows a strategy different from any normal opera with a plot, characters, and a musical dramaturgy. The pragmatic conditions of an operatic work—including, among others, the authors of its text, the various forces responsible for the actual performance, and a public that supports the production—all these different but constitutive factors of the extratextual context of a work are transformed, through a comic strategy, into layers of the work-text itself. Sospiro's hate-filled tirade against the impresario is a systematic attack on the whole institution of opera, an attack comparable to those implicit in avant-garde works of the twentieth century. Aimed at all the spokes of the operatic machine, the tirade leads to the final chorus of the work: "Yes, but first let us swear eternal hate to these perfidious tyrants, the impresarios, who govern us with such a heavy hand, both for us and for the others who will come after us—composers, dancers, poets, conductors, players, designers, pages, lighting technicians, stage hands, supers, carpenters, machinists, metal workers, copyists."[33]

Opera as an artistic and social institution thus forms the subject of *L'opera seria*. Its mimesis refers to operatic mimesis through pragmatic self-reflection of the genesis and failed performance of *L'Oranzebe* (see Fig. 1).[34] The first act shows the preparation for the production at an early stage when the hired singers appear one by one in the house of the impresario while the librettist and the composer, confronted with conflicting wishes (the impresario demands cuts, the singers want their roles to be longer), still struggle to get the work's text finished. The second act shows the dress rehearsal in an ambience of artistic deficiency and selfish ambition, the production, marred by opposite forces, still far away from any state of near-perfection. And the third act is supposed to represent the performance of *L'Oranzebe*, but after a short while—the sinfonia, a triumph march and three arias (from Ritornello, Smorfiosa, and Stonatrilla)—the angry public intervenes and brings the parodistically distorted performance to a stop, even before the singer of the title role can appear on stage. After that, in a scene that, playing behind the stage within the interior sphere of the dressing rooms, superbly applies the dramaturgical idea of textualizing context to the category of theatrical space, the mothers, having extended the *agon* between the singers to the substitute-level of protettori and having consoled their protégées, all unite in their fury against the fraudulent impresario.

Figure 1. Calzabigi, L'opera seria, Mutazioni di scene
(Facsimile from the printed libretto of, n.p. [=6])

M U T A Z I O N I

DI SCENE.

N ELLA C OMEDIA.

ATTO I.   Camera con Tavolino e Sedie
in Cafa dell' Imprefario.
Veftibulo nella fteffa Cafa.

ATTO II.   Galleria grande in Cafa dell'
Imprefario con Cimbalo e fe-
die; Tavolino con fopra Ca-
lamajo e Candelieri.

NELL' OPERA SERIA.

ATTO III. Gran piazza d'Agra Capitale
dell' Indoftan , adorna d'Archi,
e 'Trofei; difpofta a celebra-
re il Trionfo di Nafercano.

NELLA COMEDIA.

Corridore che forma la comunicazione a'
Camerini deftinati a fpogliarfi , e
veftirfi i Virtuofi.

L' Azione della Comedia è in ogni Cit-
tà , ove fi fanno Opere in Mufica.

AT-

The survey of *Mutazioni di scene* shows the circular movement from comedy to opera seria and back again to comedy (in the second part of the third act). According to "A' Lettori," the preface to the libretto,[35] only *L'Oranzebe*, the "opera seria," is located at a specific place (in Agra, the famous Indian capital), while the action of the "comedia" is situated "everywhere and nowhere," wherever opera is played.

As in some works by Shakespeare (for example, the comedy *A Midsummer Night's Dream* with Pyramus and Thisbe, or the tragedy *Hamlet* with the murder of Gonzago), a dizzy, *mise-en-abîme*-like complexity becomes evident in a multitude of references. In *L'opera seria*, there are three dimensions of "role" or "character," all bearing different names: first, the official name and personality of the singer that performs in actual productions of the work; second, the professional name of the singer as made evident by parodying her or his vocal class (the tenor "Ritornello" in his professional role as primo uomo); and third, the name and role within the fictive opera seria *L'Oranzebe* (Ritornello in the role of the victorious general Nasercano). While, according to an older view of operatic aesthetics, vocal art consisted solely in shaping the specific role or character within the performed work, in a newer view, singers mediate between their operatic roles and their own social-artistic personalities. By playing with the multiple identities of each singer—as social person, professional person, and operatic role—the dramaturgy of this meta-opera becomes extremely complicated, in particular if we additionally take into account the vastly pluralistic identity within each of these three categories. The comic strategies in *L'opera seria* form a structural totality, none of the instances of the pragmatic, or extratextual, context of art, as mentioned earlier, being left out from the process of textualization: the artistic authors poet and composer; the singer and the dancer as the performing artists who enact the textual score into aesthetic reality; the institutional author, that is, the producer as impresario who assumes not only the ultimate artistic responsibility, but also takes the financial risks (and reaps the potential benefits); the promoting agents, the "mothers"; and finally the public itself, the body of collective reception, as critical authority.

In the third act, Stonatrilla, in her role as the jealous Rossanara addressing the captivated Indian princess Saebe, sings a parody of a seria aria, a piece marred by endless repetitions that ensure an artistic failure. The reaction by the public that is included as "coro di popolo" is therefore not a provocation; rather, it seems completely justified. Its "susurro" and "strepito" produce an acoustic chaos, a concert of noises long before Russolo's "art of noises." Alas, Gassmann did not set this *coro di popolo* to music. Calzabigi's libretto antici-

Figure 2. Calzabigi, L'opera seria, Libretto, Act. III, scene iii (end, Stronatrilla's aria as Rossanara) and scene iv (beginning, Coro di popolo) [62-63 recte, notated in pencil: 61-62]

Sm. da "Non negarmi pietà , che non m'
Soc.   avanza
 "Se tu non me l' accordi altra spe-
     ranza,
Sto da Rof, "Nò; se a te non toglie il Fato
 "Quel bell' occhio lusinghiero ;
 "Non lo puoi chiamar fevero ,
 "Non è vero - il tuo timor.
 "Chi ogni core a suo piacere
 "Può far misero , o felice,
 "Sarà (credo) vincitrice
 "Del suo stesso vincitor. (*Parte.*)

S C E N A   IV.

RITORNELLO da NASERCANO,
SMORFIOSA da SAEBE, e POR-
PORINA da RANA.

Sm. da Sac. **R**ossanara è gelosa ,
 " Spera mio cor.)
Porp.daRan." (Tutto sin' or mi giova.)
Rit.da Naf. " (Del mio bene il sospetto
 " Corrasi a dileguar.) (*va per*
      partire.)
Porp.daRan." Che pensi amico? (*lo trattiene.*)
 " Lo sai, t'attende il Re L'ora
    preferitta
 '· D' offrirti ad Oranzebbe è gia
     vicina.
Rit da Naf." (Che trionfo crudel!) Vieni, o
 Regina. (*parte con Saebe, e*
  col seguito.)

CORO di POPOLO.
Dentro: via. Già la tenda :
    Giù, giù.
Oh che libbro! Oh che Musica!
   Uh! uh!

All' intuonar del Coro accompagnato da susurro , e
strepito fuggono dentro la Scena tutti. Sospiro
ch'era al Cimbalo scappa per sotto il Teatro.
Viene abbassato il tendone ; e calmato il rumore
esce davanti al tendone medesimo Passagallo,

Paf. Riveriti Signori ,
 Noi colpa non abbiamo. Se comandano
 Vedere il primo ballo, fra' mezz'ora
 Possiamo esser vestiti.

CORO di POPOLO.
 Il Ballo fuora.
Paf. I miei Balli son tanti miracoli;
 Oh grand' Uomo! Dovrete gridar.
 Tutti gli altri Maestri più celebri
 Che dell' arte son come gli Oracoli
 Sotto gamba li posso pigliar.
 Mi richiede per feste, e spettacoli
 Francia, Svezia, Inghilterra, e
    Moscovia:
 A Turino, a Venezia, a Cracovia
 Monti d'oro mi vogliono dar.
 Ne' balli è ridicolo
 Volere un perchè:
 D' azione , o invenzione
 Bisogno non v'è.
 Ci voglion Coupè, Brizè, Balancè,
   D 5   Chaf·

pates two entrances for the *coro di popolo* (see Fig. 2), which lead dramaturgi-cally into the ensemble finale. (The second entrance, however, repeats the first interlaced between the recitative and aria sung by Passagallo: "I miei balli son tanti miracoli.") In the score in the Austrian National Library in Vienna,[36] one finds only the verbal direction "Coro di Popolo" between Papagallo's recitative and aria without any precise instructions as to how it should be musically or scenically realized.[37] At present, one can only speculate as to why Gassmann did not set this "*coro di popolo*" to music, or why, if he did, the music did not make it into the score.

Nonetheless, by using a chorus to suggest the intervention of the public, the librettist Calzabigi seems to have pointed the way to a musical resolution. There is, however, a gap between dramaturgical and musical modernity in this work. Even though the librettist included them in the work conception, "susurro" and "strepito" were still strictly foreign to the circle of potential mu-sical textuality. As "noises," they belonged to the dramaturgical but not to the musical creative means in the strict sense. Only in the early twentieth century, when Luigi Russolo systematized the world of noises for musical use,[38] did "noise and sound composition" become one strand of musical modernism, and an important one at that. The scenic effect seems all the more drastic, then, when all the interpreters of *L'Oranzebe* flee the stage. Mentioned only in the stage directions, the departure of the Kapellmeister (who directed from the harpsichord) seems almost to recall Mauricio Kagel's *Entführung im Konzertsaal*, in which the "abduction" of the conductor from the performance is part of the performance.

Something similar happens in the penultimate scene of Strauss's *Capriccio*, where the prompter, Monsieur Taupe ("mole") appears as an operatic character on stage, as well as in market-place scenes from Marco Marazzoli and Virgilio Mazzocchi's *Chi soffre speri* (1637 und 1639)[39] to Gaetano Donizetti's *L'elisir d'amore* (1832). In all such instances, the moment materials from outside the work enter into the work, they are incorporated into the work-text itself.[40] These comic procedures contribute to a fundamental self-relativization of the artwork, for the work's postulated dramatic and aesthetic closure is shown to be illusory and conditioned many times over.[41] The category of the work is not, however, thereby destroyed. On the contrary, within the framework of an aesthetics of modernity, it survives triumphant.

IV. Open Form as Context-Art

With Richard Strauss, meta-opera as a self-reflective strand of musical modernism (*Ariadne auf Naxos* combines seria and buffa principles, and *Capriccio* again stages the conflict between poet and composer as artistic creators of opera) reached well into the twentieth century. Instead of addressing this well-known operatic tradition, I should like, however, to consider now the textualization of extratextual contexts by the artistic avant-garde. In the wake of Marcel Duchamp's ready-made revolution in the years around 1914 (in 1917, for instance, Duchamp declared an object of everyday life as "low" as an urinal to be, to represent, or provocatively to replace a work of art by giving it the title *Fountain* and by signing it with "R.[ichart] Mutt 1917"[42]), important steps in the history of avant-garde art progressively resulted from a textualization of formerly extratextual, or contextual, elements. In 1913, Duchamp could still ask, "Is it possible to create works that are not artworks?"[43] Given that the de-auratized ready-mades received an aura through a process of reception, he later recognized an operative, apparently unavoidable dialectic between the attempted destruction of the aura and the creation of art. "The fact that [the ready-mades] are now viewed with the same awe as art objects probably means that I have not been able to solve the problem of the attempt to over-come art completely."[44]

As more and more contexts were brought into the realm of art, boundar-ies between art, architecture, life, science, and politics were blurred. Art theory recorded these tendencies under labels such as "context art,"[45] "action art," or "Ausstellungskunst."[46] As early as 1972, Daniel Buren stated that the object of the exhibition was no longer the work of art, but rather the exhibition itself as a work of art.[47] The pilgrimage to art exhibitions, so frequent in our days, is a reaction to the almost universal availability of art provided by rapidly growing means of technical production and reproduction that deny works of art the quality of uniqueness they had enjoyed in their original functions during centuries.

In response, the textualization of the context appears to be one of the pos-sible answers to the ubiquity of technologically-reproduced music. In order to allow non-substitutable experiences, events have been created at very spe-cial places and at very special times, as for instance the Metamusik-Festival in West Berlin's New National Gallery in the 1970s, or the "Europäischer Musik-monat Basel" in November 2001 that presented well-attended concerts in a newly-built "Paul Sacher Halle," designed by the famous architects Herzog & de Meuron and dismantled immediately after the end of the "Musikmonat." In today's music culture, trends celebrating a cult of "presence" attribute spe-cial relevance to contextual surroundings for unique aesthetic experiences.[48]

In twentieth-century avant-garde music, the textualization of the context in "instrumental theater," "phonetic composition," or, more recently, "sound sculpture"[49] referred to acoustic as well as visual elements. As mentioned earlier, acoustic textualization increasingly involved elements that in former times and in different cultures were strictly excluded from the sphere of "art music," in particular noises of all kinds. The emancipation of noise involved to some degree the transfer of acoustic materials from everyday life into the newly defined sphere of musical material. In a parallel move, the visual di-mension of music's production, emancipated within what was called "instru-mental theater," reached its extremes in books such as John Cage's *Notations* or Dieter Schnebel's *Mono—Musik zum Lesen*, where this pragmatic prere-quisite of music appeared to be transformed into the aesthetic realm. I should like to exemplify now with Mauricio Kagel's *Staatstheater* how far, through the years around 1970, avant-garde textualization of newly defined, or newly discovered, elements of former contexts became a driving force for the inno-vation of musical material.[50]

This work, composed between 1967 and 1970 as a commission by Rolf

Liebermann for the Hamburg State Opera and premiered in 1971, reflects the historical high point of the West European avant-garde.[51] In *Staatstheater*, the textualization of the context has become absolute, destroying the very category it was supposed to support, namely, text. The score of this "scenic composition" ("Szenische Komposition," as its subtitle reads) no longer represents a "text," a structure of interconnected, intertwined elements (remembering the Latin word "textus"), but rather an "open work of art" (Umberto Eco[52]) which leaves the shaping of the actual musical form to the performers' choice.

Figure 3. Kagel, Staatstheater, *Table of contents (from the printed score)*

> *repertoire,* szenisches konzertstück . . . .
> *einspielungen,* musik für lautsprecher . .
> *ensemble,* für sechzehn stimmen . . . . .
> *debüt,* für sechzig stimmen . . . .
> *saison,* sing-spiel in 65 bildern . . . .
> *spielplan,* instrumentalmusik in aktion . . .
> *kontra* → *danse,* ballett für nicht-tänzer .
> *freifahrt,* gleitende kammermusik . . . . . .
> *parkett,* konzertante massenszenen . . . .

The table of contents from the printed score shows the nine different sections of *Staatstheater* in one of the many possible arrangements. Only "repertory," if included at all, holds an obligatory position at the beginning of the work. The table shows the order chosen by Kagel himself for the printed score, which as a bound book does not allow such diversity of orderings.[53]

The very institution ("State Theater") reveals its manifold inner structure as far as the context for operatic production is concerned (in contrast to more intrinsic elements of context). Terms as different as "repertory," "ensemble," "debut," "season," "program," and "orchestra" all belong to the institutional sphere in its full pragmatic sense. But Kagel would not be Kagel if these dimensions of extrinsic context were not transformed into most fantastic audiovisual sceneries, into a surreal world of its own. The titles show context, this royal path of avant-gardist aesthetics, radically universalized. The single elements, or sections, are no longer supposed to form a textual coherence. While the context has become ubiquitous it is left entirely to the creative fantasy of the performers to shape a text from elements that categorically defy aesthetic cohesion.

As a true multi-medialist, Kagel is a paradigm of the multi-dimensional artist. An exclusive aesthetic is not his thing. Even though he has long forsworn the pathos of progress typical of the avant-garde, he walks as an avant-gardist along paths of inclusion, beyond a totalizing grasp for a type of *Gesamtkunstwerk*. As a sophist, skeptic, and philosopher, Kagel well knows that a totalizing worldview and aesthetics contradict the idea of an aesthetic modernism. Rather, only a splintered cosmos pulverized to atoms can be adequate to it.

Rather than resting on a solidly fixed basis, Kagel's basic artistic idea changes in constant reciprocity with contrary, if not even contradictory, counterforces: first, between the spiritual (which reveals a material exterior) and the material (which hints at traits of something spiritual, however constituted); second, between visual components (which liberate unimagined and even unimaginable acoustic implications) and acoustic mechanisms (whose scenic visuality is integrated into a multi-media play); third, between elements subordinated to musical codes (elements whose energies, transcending the accepted canons of rules, Kagel liberates through isolation) and forces that lie beyond the musical codes (forces integrated through their contextualization in *Staatstheater* into a music-theatrical coherence that had never yet been conceived as a possibility). In this respect, the textualization of the context points to the essence of these quite various strategies of particularization and recontextualization of all the phemonena that Kagel, with his overflowing, inexhaustible artistic fantasy creates as a possibility of the world: of the world sonority, of the world view, and of irony. It is the responsibility of the interpreter to create a modern text from this material, to create a real world through a scenic realization. The score offers the possibility of infinitely various textualizations by isolating (that is, decontextualizing) extremely heterogenous contexts and by opening them up to interpretive manipulation through a reconfiguration of the text.

To attempt to reconstruct the principles of this superabundant Kagelesque world of scenic composition (which is music theater in the double sense of acoustic-optic intermediality) would be to try to square the circle. Nevertheless, one can illustrate some of its characteristics with a few scenes, without any claim at universal applicability.[54]

Kagel is always fascinated by the ingenious inventiveness of the instrument maker. In "Armgeige" ("arm violin," 29, see Fig. 4) from "repertory," as in "Mundplatte/Mundtrommeln" ("mouthplate/mouthdrum"), the language artist reads the composite word in an unusual way: he reverses the metaphoricization and surprises the audience through a literal reading. While the normal violin uses the words "da braccio" (arm violin) to distinguish it from "da gamba" (leg viol), here the human arm itself (outfitted with a double-bass endpin) constitutes the body of the instrument.

Figure 4. Kagel, Staatstheater, *"Armgeige" ("arm-violin")*
from "repertory," score, 29

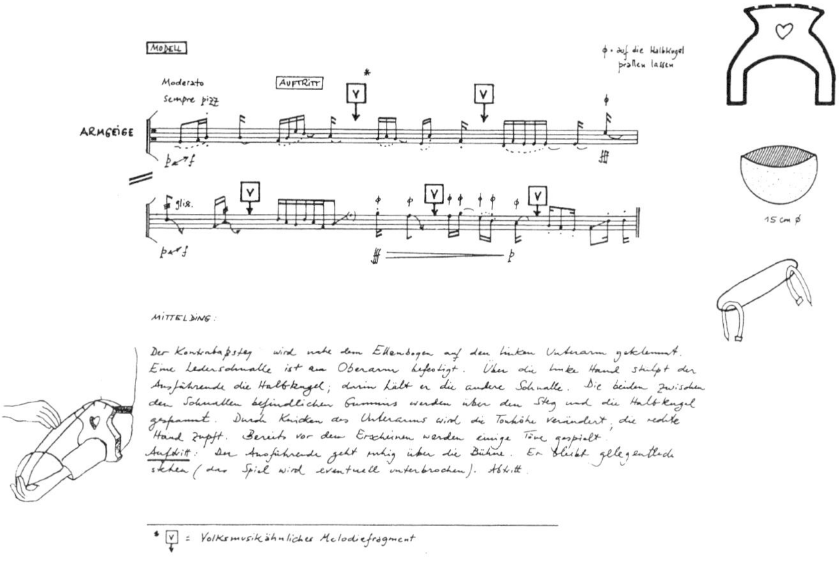

In "Schallplatte" ("record," literally "sound plate," see Fig. 5), again in repertory (46), the work with media is recontextualized in the "scenic composition." The medium itself is no longer the support for a musical sequence of sounds, but rather itself becomes the subject of the action: a *medium in abstracto*. Scratches on record grooves bring forth the acoustically perceptible. Born from an aesthetic of ugliness, the noise of scratches, at least before the rap age, is hated by all users of record players because it indicates the damage or even destruction of the music captured on the record. Here, Kagel's idea reminds one of the piece *Piano Activities* by the American composer Philip Corner. Corner staged the destruction of a piano as a happening during the Wiesbaden "Fluxus" Festival in 1962.[55] The context becomes the text, just as the means (the medium of the record) become the end.

In "season" (a "Singspiel in 65 scenes"), the optical visual opulence unfolds in a particularly diverse manner and is comparable to that of Kagel's Lieder opera *Aus Deutschland*. The frequently black humor of "season" (also celebrated in the "Sonic Fable on Two Stages" *Bestiarium*) manifests itself in the scene "Hearse" (280), as it is accompanied by the titular word "Volksfest" ("people's festival"). Linked self-referentially to the institution of the state theater, the black humor is also found in the scene "swan-wagon" (256, see

Figure 5. Kagel, Staatstheater, *"Schallplatte"* ("record")
from "repertory," score, 46

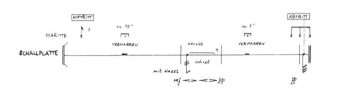

Figure 6. Kagel, Staatstheater, *"Schwan-Wagen"* ("swan-wagon")
from "season," score, 256

Fig. 6), whose subtitle "the Next" alludes to the *Lohengrin* joke, "When does the next swan leave?"

In all of these cases, individual actions can or should be included or left out at will. Usually, their sequence is left free to the choice of the interpreter, as is the choice and succession of the nine main parts of *Staatstheater*. Individual sequences can also be superimposed on each other. The process of musical formation as textualization is flexible and the responsibility for it is delegated to the interpreters. As little as Kagel's splintered universe allows a coherent text to be created, the artistic idea of the work blazes brightly in the details.

In contrast to *L'opera seria* with its reference to "L'Oranzebe," the title *Staatstheater* indicates an institution, not a musical genre. Kagel's reference is, of course, deeply ironic: "State Theater" not only alludes self-referentially to German opera houses as state institutions,[56] but bears a political subtext as well, insofar as contemporary political life—I assume, not only in Germany—has many theatrical or aesthetic dimensions.[57]

V. Epilogue: Aesthetic Reversal and the Question of Power

Comic effects often result from a reversal of given conditions into their opposites; part of what since antiquity has been called "parody."[58] Structures that are not given facts, as is the case in traditionally organized societies, but are transmitted only as norms may be, and are open to changes. But the temporal reversal of given structures in a carnevalesque culture of laughter (Bakhtin[59]) was since ancient times, and still is, also bound to preserve those very societal structures by showing "otherness" as an exception. Upsetting the norms of societal life for a precisely defined time span once a year served and still serves to conserve these very norms. Considering the inherent ambiguity in this area, it is difficult to decide when and under which conditions laughter had a long-term stabilizing, or destabilizing, effect on the hierarchical structures of societies.

Comic strategies, by inverting given structures, are important tools for modernist aesthetics as well. They set free an enormous power of creative fantasy because by liberating societal norms, they contribute to a loosening of artistic norms. This is the case in the early history of modernism during the seventeenth and eighteenth centuries as well as, and in particular, in the later avant-garde, where the transgression of given social rules and artistic procedures based on acts of reversal often revealed comic features, at least when seen from a distance.

In comedy, the reversal of power structures provides an aesthetic pleasure comparable to catharsis in tragedy. Regardless of the level of society a person occupies, men and women normally take pleasure in seeing, hearing, and feeling the norms of everyday life questioned, collapsed, and inverted into their opposites through aesthetic liberation.

The power structures questioned by musical comedies in the eighteenth century included the grand narratives of social hierarchy, gender, and art[60]: first, the hierarchical structure of society—the relation between "master" and "slave" (to use the terms of Hegel's *Phänomenologie des Geistes*)—as dealt with in such works as Pergolesi's "Intermezzo" *La serva padrona*; second, the traditional gender hierarchy between dominating man and dominated woman, as dealt with in such works as Galuppi's *Il mondo alla roversa ossia Le donne che comandano*; and third, opera as a cultural institution, including its generic structure, as dealt with in such works as Gassmann's *L'opera seria*. The outcome of the reversal in each of the three works is a different one. In Pergolesi, the female servant not only behaves as a mistress, but confirms her new status through marriage. In Galuppi, well before the age of feminism, the rebellious power of women submits again in the end to male domination. In Gassmann, the catastrophic failure of a "seria" performance turns into an ultimate success of comic opera: the earlier hierarchy of the intermezzo genre framed by a seria work is reversed into a buffa work framing a kind of seria intermezzo.

Reversal is also a central category in Mauricio Kagel. In a general sense, it is a part of Kagel's surrealist heritage that incessantly strives to subvert given structures. We see its relevance throughout Kagel's œuvre, in the case of *Staatstheater*, for instance, in the cute "Ballet for Non-Dancers." It is a means to create new art, but for this immigrant to Germany from South America it is a political category, too. Kagel never separates the artistic from the political sphere, nor the political from the artistic one. And their dialectical connection is perfectly manifest in works like *Mare nostrum* with the subtitle: *Discovery, Participation, and Conversion of the Mediterranean by an Amazonian Tribe*[61] and in the "epic radio play" *The Reversal of America*,[62] two works belonging to different genres, but both superbly concretizing the idea of reversal.[63]

The very idea of comic strategies in meta-operas obviously underwent deep changes between the pre-revolutionary, aesthetically pre-autonomous eighteenth century to the post-revolutionary, and aesthetically post-autonomous twentieth century. We certainly may also discern profound differences between the political impact those strategies were intended to have, or did have, in these two eras. As meta-operas belonged to a partly aristocratic culture of laughter in the eighteenth century, they were considered to be a factor that stabilized society.[64] On the other hand, as meta-operas formed part of a bourgeois or semi-bourgeois subculture in the twentieth century, the ideology of the avant-garde assigned to these "works" a destabilizing or even a revolutionary effect on their respective societies. Historical retrospection, however, shows in both cases a different picture. In the twentieth century, the revolutionary potentials of avant-garde art—and its often comically perceived earnest strategies of provocative contextualization—were heavily exaggerated. In the eighteenth century, by contrast, the possibly destabilizing impact of comic reversals on societies may have been greatly underestimated. After all, the *coro di popolo* of the French Revolution that took place only twenty years after the production of *L'opera seria* still resonates today.

Translated by Keith Chapin

Notes

1 See, for example, Benet Casablancas, *El humor en la música: broma, parodía e ironía. un ensayo* (Kassel und Berlin: Reichenberger, 2000).

2 See, for example, Paul Griffiths, *A Concise History of Modern Music from Debussy to Boulez*, (London: Thames and Hudson, 1978); Robert P. Morgan, *Twentieth-Century Music: A History of Musical Style in Modern Europe and America*, (New York: Norton, 1991); Hermann Danuser, *Die Musik des 20. Jahrhunderts*, Neues Handbuch der Musikwissenschaft, no. 7 (Laaber: Laaber, 1992).

3 The literature on this subject includes, among others, John Daverio, *Nineteenth-Century Music and the German Romantic Ideology* (New York: Schirmer-Macmillan 1993), and Charles Rosen, *The Romantic Generation* (Cambridge, MA: Harvard University Press, 1995).

4 See, for example, *Richard Wagner. Konstrukteur der Moderne*, ed. Claus-Steffen Mahnkopf (Stuttgart: Klett-Cotta, 1999); *Von Wagner zum Wagnérisme. Musik, Literatur, Kunst, Politik*, ed. Annegret Fauser and Manuela Schwartz (Leipzig: Leipziger Universitätsverlag, 1999); *Zukunftsbilder. Richard Wagners Revolution und ihre Folgen in Kunst und Politik*, ed. Hermann Danuser and Herfried Münkler, (Schliengen: Argus, 2002).

5 Carl Dahlhaus, *Die Musik des 19. Jahrhunderts*, (Wiesbaden: Athenaions 1980), 279–285.

6 See the summary of self-referential structures in Harald Fricke, "Oper in der Oper. Potenzierung, Ipsoreflexion, Mis en abyme," in *Fiori musicologici. Studi in onore di Luigi Ferdinando Tagliavini nella recorrenza del suo LXX compleanno*, ed. François Seydoux in cooperation with Giuliano Castellani and Axel Leuthold (Bologna: Patron, 2001), 221–245.

7 On the category "text" and its many usages see *Musik als Text. Bericht über den Internationalen Kongreß der Gesellschaft für Musikforschung Freiburg im Breisgau 1993*, ed. Hermann Danuser and Tobias Plebuch, 2 vols. (Kassel: Bärenreiter, 1998).

8 See *Richard Strauss und die Moderne. Bericht über das Internationale Symposium München, 21. bis 23. Juli 1999*, ed. Bernd Edelmann, Birgit Lodes, and Reinhold Schlötterer (Berlin: Henschel, 2001).

9 Fricke, "Oper in der Oper," 244.

10 Ibid., 219–236. Cf. Lucien Dällenbach, *Le récit spéculaire : contribution à l'etude de la mise en abyme* (Paris: Éditions du Seuil, 1977). A colleague of Fricke's on the faculty of the University of Fribourg, Victor C. Stoichita, is moreover the author of several central monographs on the theory of art, including *L'instauration du tableau. Métapeinture à l'aube des temps modernes* (Paris: Kliensieck, 1993), translated into English as *The Self-aware Image: An Insight into Early Modern Meta-painting* (Cambridge: Cambridge University Press, 1997).

11 Jürgen Habermas, "Die Moderne—ein unvollendetes Projekt," in *Die Zeit*, 19 September 1981, 47–48. Jürgen Habermas, *Die Moderne – ein unvollendetes Projekt* (1980), in *Kleine politische Schriften (I–IV)*, (Frankfurt am Main: Suhrkamp, 1981), 444–464.

12 James Webster, "Between Enlightenment and Romanticism in Music History: 'First Viennese Modernism' and the Delayed Nineteenth Century," in *19th-Century Music* 25, no. 2–3 (Fall/Spring 2001) and "Die 'Erste Wiener Moderne' als historiographische Alternative zur 'Wiener Klassik'" in *Wiener Klassik: Ein musikgeschichtlicher Begriff in Diskussion*, papers presented at a conference, held 11–12 November, 2000, in Vienna, Austria (Vienna: Böhlau, 2002).

13 Cited in Mikhail Bakhtin, *Probleme der Poetik Dostoevskijs*, translated into German by Adelheid Schramm from the 2nd, rev. ed. [*Problemy poetiki Dostoevskogo*, Moskva 1963] (Munich: Carl Hanser, 1971), 143.

14 Cited in the printed libretto (Paris 1640) found in the Bavarian State Library in Munich, 1–4.

15 See the article "Komödie," in *Der neue Pauly. Enzyklopädie der Antike*, ed. Hubert Cancik and Helmuth Schneider, 6 (Stuttgart und Weimar: Metzler, 1999), Columns 692–704; "Komik, Komisch," "Komödie," in *Reallexikon der deutschen Literaturwissenschaft*, ed. Harald Fricke, 3 vols. (Berlin: de Gruyter, 1997), 2, 289–294, 309–313; "Komödie," in *Metzler Literatur Lexikon. Begriffe und Definitionen*, ed. Günther and Irmgard Schweikle, 2nd rev. ed., (Stuttgart: Metzler, 1990), 245–248. All of these articles include extensive bibliographies.

16 See Lutz Danneberg, "Kontext" in *Reallexikon der deutschen Literaturwissenschaft*, ed. Harald Fricke, 2 (Berlin and New York: de Gruyter, 2000), 335–337, here 333–334. For a comprehensive overview on the state of musicological research on text and contexts, see the "Begriffsregister zur Textkategorie" (Register

of Concepts associeted with the Category "Text") compiled by Tobias R. Klein for the Freiburg congress report *Musik als Text*, 1, 443–454. In the essay "The Art of Contextualization: Specificity in Musicology" (*The Musical Quarterly*, in press), I have discussed the musicological applications of the four meanings of "context" discussed by literary theorists.

17 See the list of works in Harald Fricke, "Oper in der Oper," 236–243. An important special case of the meta-opera that also plays a role in this essay has been discussed by Thomas Betzwieser, "Komponisten als Opernfiguren. Musikalische Werkgenese auf der Bühne," in *Studien zur Musikgeschichte. Eine Festschrift für Ludwig Finscher*, ed. Annegrit Laubenthal with the help of Kara Kusan-Windweh (Kassel: Bärenreiter, 1995), 511–522. A list of the relevant works can be found on 513. A select few further sources and references are as follows: the anthology *La cantante e l'impresario e altri metamelodrammi*, ed. Francesca Savoia and Roberto De Simone (Genoa: Müller-Speiser, 1988); Jürgen Maehder, "'A queste piccolezze il pubblico non bada': Librettisten und Komponisten als Zielscheibe der Opernparodie," in *Die lustige Person auf der Bühne*, 1, ed. Peter Csobádi et. al. (Anif: Müller-Speiser, 1994), 237–254; Manuela Hager, "Die Opernprobe als Theateraufführung: Eine Studie zum Libretto im Wien des 18. Jahrhunderts," in *Oper als Text*, ed. Albert Gier (Heidelberg: Winter, 1986), 101–124.

18 See especially Mary Hunter, *The Culture of Opera Buffa in Mozart's Vienna: A Poetics of Entertainment* (Princeton, NJ: Princeton University Press, 1999).

19 On the category of the paratext, see Gérard Genette, *Palimpsestes: La littérature au second degré* (Paris: Éditions du Seuil, 1982).

20 Richard Wagner, *Oper und Drama*, ed. Klaus Kropfinger (Stuttgart: Philipp Reclam, 1984), 23–122; "Über Schauspieler und Sänger," in *Späte Schriften zur Dramaturgie der Oper*, ed. Egon Voss (Stuttgart: Philipp Reclam, 1996), 41–130. Rudolf Kolisch, "Religion der Streicher," in *Zur Theorie der Aufführung. Ein Gespräch mit Berthold Türcke (Musik-Konzepte 29/30)* (Munich: edition text + kritik, 1983), 113–119.

21 See the first two chapters of the "First Little Volume" of *Flegeljahre—eine Biographie*, "Nr. 1 Bleiglanz. Testament—das Weinhaus" and "Nr. 2 Katzensilber aus Tühringen. J.P.F.R.s Brief an den Stadtrat," in Jean Paul, *Siebenkäs, Flegeljahre*, ed. Gustav Lohmann (Munich: Carl Hanser, 1959), 571–586.

22 Giuseppe Sarti, *Giulio Sabino, Dramma per musica*. [score], Reprinted Vienna 1782, Bologna: Forni, 1969 (*Bibliotheca musica Boloniensis* 4; 128); Antonio Salieri, *Prima la musica, poi le parole, Divertimento teatrale in einem Akt von Giambattista Casti*, German edition edited by Josef Heinzelmann, piano-vocal score by Friedrich Wanek, Mainz: Schott 1972 (Edition Schott 6547), Cavatina Nr. 2, 36ff. In addition to Josef Heinzelmann's article on Salieri's *Prima la musica, poi le parole* (1786) in *Pipers Enzyklopädie des Musiktheaters*, ed. Carl Dahlhaus and Sieghart Döhring, 5 (Munich and Zurich: Piper, 1994), 534–536, see the analysis by Thomas Betzwieser in "Komponisten als Opernfiguren," 515–516. Betzwieser also sketches an analysis of the compositional and rehearsal

situation of Molière and Lully's comédie-ballet *Le Bourgeois gentilhomme,* an early example of a self-referential structure in seventeenth-century musical theater. It built on corresponding tendencies in spoken theater, such as in Molière's own independent works.

23 Antonio Salieri, *Prima la musica, poi le parole,* piano-vocal score, 75–76.

24 Volker Klotz has placed the end of such factors of laughter somewhat earlier. In addition to the "liberated laughter about the immoderate phalluses in the comedies and satyr plays of antiquity," "the comical quality of flatulence and bodily excretions is historically over, at least officially, even as it continues under the surface. Blind, deaf, and crippled persons who helplessly entangle themselves in normal, everyday activities are a fixed part of comedy until the early eighteenth century." Klotz, *Bürgerliches Lachtheater: Komödie, Posse, Schwank, Operette* (Munich and Vienna: Carl Hanser, 1984), 12.

25 See Thomas Mann, *Doktor Faustus: Das Leben des deutschen Tonsetzers Adrian Leverkühn erzählt von einem Freunde* (Frankfurt am Main: S. Fischer 31–36. Tausend, 1976), Ch. 8, 69–96, here 69–74; *Bekenntnisse des Hochstaplers Felix Krull: Der Memoiren erster Teil* (Frankfurt am Main: S. Fischer 47–51. Tausend, 1974), Ch. 5, 86–108, here 102–104.

26 It is palpably manifest in, for example, the conflict between Kapellmeister Sospiro and the poet Deliro in Act II, Scene i of Calzabigi and Gassmann's *L'opera seria.*

27 Scene iii, mm. 136–137, piano reduction 78, continuation of Ex. 2a.

28 Cf. *Prima la musica, poi le parole,* piano reduction 81ff.

29 The printed libretto of *L'opera seria*—by Ranieri di Calzabigi, though he is not named therein—that accompanied the Viennese premiere of 1769 (Library of Congress, Schatz 3623) is reprinted as a facsimile in Howard Mayer Brown, ed., *Italian Opera: 1640–1770,* 15, Italian Opera Librettos: 1640–1770 (New York and London: Garland, 1984). The *coro di popolo* is in Act III, Scene iv (unpaginated). Cf. René Jacobs, "Theater auf dem Theater. Florian Leopold Gaßmanns Opernsatire," in *Programmheft der Staatsoper Unter den Linden zur Aufführung von* L'opera seria *im Rahmen der Wochen der Alten Musik, am 30. Januar 1996 in Berlin,* 13–14, here 14. See also Jennifer Anne Griesbach, *Calzabigi and Gassmann's "L'opera seria",* University of California at Berkeley, PhD, 2000.

30 Among many examples, Domenico Cimarosa's "Intermezzo giocoso" *Il maestro di cappella* is perhaps the best known. While composition produces the stilted music in Mozart's *A Musical Joke* (the village musicians' sextet, K. 522), here the interpreters produce the catastrophe of the musical event. Artistic miscalculation, intentional failure, and the processual imperfection of all learning are elements that link the eighteenth century with the most recent avant-garde in many ways—such as with the aesthetic of Dieter Schnebel.

31 The character of the impresario who unites all disputants in their hatred of him at the end of *L'opera seria* was frequently a central figure in meta-operas af-

ter Pietro Metastasio's "Intermezzo" *L'impresario delle Canarie* (1724). Another example is Domenico Cimarosa's oft-performed "Farsa" *L'impresario in angustie* (text by Giuseppe Maria Diodati, premiere in 1786 in Naples). Cf. Silke Leopold, "Domenico Cimarosa: *L'impresario in angustie*," in *Pipers Enzyklopädie des Musiktheaters*, ed. Carl Dahlhaus and Sieghart Döhring, 1 (Munich and Zurich: Piper, 1986), 590–592.

32 René Jacobs, "Theater auf dem Theater: Florian Leopold Gaßmanns Opernsatire," 14.

33 "Sì, ma prima giuriamo, / E per noi, e per gli altri che verranno / Musici, Ballerini, / E Poeti, e Maestri, e Sonatori, / Ingegneri, e Pittori, / Suggeritori, Affittapalchi, e Sarti, / Paggi, Smoccolalumi, Tirascene, / Comparse, Legnajoli, Macchinisti, / E Magnani, e Coposti: a questi perfidi / Tiranni d'Impresarj, / Che sì fiero governo / Fanno sempre di noi, un odio eterno." Quoted from the unpaginated Viennese libretto, fourth-to-last page.

34 The central historical and systematic significance of parallels in literature and spoken theater for the genesis of the meta-opera is obvious. The many examples, among them works of contemporary literature, include Günter Grass' "German tragedy" *Die Plebejer proben den Aufstand* (*The Plebians Rehearse a Revolution*, premiered in Berlin in 1966). I thank David Lewin for alerting me to this four-act play.

35 Ibid., n.p. [=3].

36 ms. 17775. Cf. the edition by Eric Weimer in the Garland series "Italian opera 1640–1770", 89, New York: Garland, 1982, unpaginated "Preface," [=5].

37 *L'opera seria*, score, n.p. [=474].

38 Luigi Russolo, *L'arte dei rumori* (Milano: Editione Futuriste di "Poesia," 1916); French edition, *L'art des bruits*, ed. Giovanni Lista (Lausanne: L'âge d'homme, 1975).

39 The libretto of *Chi soffre speri* is from Giulio Rospigliosi. The author thanks Stewart Reiner, University of Cape Town (South Africa), for bringing this work to his attention.

40 See Günter Saße, "Das Spiel mit der Rampe: Zum Verhältnis von Bühnenwirklichkeit und Zuschauerwirklichkeit im Theater der Moderne," in *Deutsche Vierteljahrsschrift für Literaturwissenschaft und Geistesgeschichte* 61 (1987), 733–754.

41 Dieter Henrich has stressed the significance of the part which has given the arts the "character of modernity." See Dieter Henrich, "Kunst und Kunstphilosophie der Gegenwart (Überlegungen mit Rücksicht auf Hegel)," in *Immanente Ästhetik - Ästhetische Reflexion: Lyrik als Paradigma der Moderne. Kolloquium Köln 1964*, ed. Wolfgang Iser (München: Wilhelm Fink, 1966), 11–32, here 15 and 27.

42 The object, sent by Duchamp to an exhibition by the "Society of Independent Artists" in New York, was destroyed. What remains is a photograph made by

Alfred Stieglitz, New York 1917. Decades later (1950), Duchamp made a replica of the urinal.

43 *The Essential Writings of Marcel Duchamp*, ed. Michel Sanouillet and Elmer Peterson (London: Thames and Hudson, 1975), 74.

44 Cited in Herbert Molderings, *Marcel Duchamp: Parawissenschaft, das Ephemere und der Skeptizismus* (Frankfurt am Main: Campus Verlag, 1987), 99. I wish to thank Jörg Zimmermann (Mainz) for this information about the visual arts.

45 See *Kontext Kunst*, ed. Pete Wiebel (Cologne: DuMont, 1994).

46 By this term I do not mean the tendencies since the eighteenth century reconstructed by the Swiss art historian Oskar Bätschmann, *Ausstellungskünstler: Kult und Karriere im modernen Kunstsystem*, (Cologne: DuMont, 1997), but rather a most recent tendency discussed by Kerstin Stremmel in her article "Metropolis oder das Netz: Wo findet die Gegenwartskunst statt?" in *Neue Zürcher Zeitung* 131, June 2001, 56.

47 Op. cit.

48 Cf. Hans Ulrich Gumbrecht, *Production of Presence: What Meaning Cannot Convey* (Stanford: Stanford University Press, 2004); cf. also Gumbrecht's contribution to this volume.

49 On this point, see my *Die Musik des 20. Jahrhunderts*, 373–392; see also *Klangkunst. Tönende Objekte und klingende Räume*, ed. Helga de la Motte-Haber (Laaber: Laaber, 1999).

50 Because in the musical avant-garde intertextual relations between works created by different artists, although evident in many cases, no longer form a generic structure of poietic and aesthetic norms, I will concentrate exclusively on *Staatstheater* and not consider other works of avant-garde music theater, such as Henri Pousseur's *Votre Faust* (libretto by Michel Butor), John Cage's *Europeras*, or Luciano Berio's *Opera*.

51 It is paralleled, by the way, by Reinhold Brinkmann's pathbreaking studies of Schoenberg and Eisler. See his *Arnold Schönberg: Drei Klavierstücke op. 11: Studien zur frühen Atonalität bei Schönberg* (Wiesbaden: Steiner, 1969); "Schönberg und George: Interpretation eines Liedes," in *Archiv für Musikwissenschaft* 26 (1969), 1–28; "Kompositorische Maßnahmen Eislers," in *Über Musik und Politik*, ed. Rudolf Stephan (Mainz: Schott, 1971), 9–22.

52 Umberto Eco, *Opera aperta: Forma e indeterminazione nelle poetiche contemporanee* (Milano: Bompiani, 1976).

53 See also Werner Klüppelholz, *Mauricio Kagel, 1970–1980* (Cologne: DuMont, 1981), 30–42.

54 Mauricio Kagel, *Staatstheater*, Scenic Composition, 1967–70, Vienna: Universal Edition no. 15197.

55 See the photograph of this performance of *Piano Activities* in my *Die Musik des 20. Jahrhunderts*, 298.

56 The city of Hamburg (Freie und Hansestadt Hamburg) is also a "state," a "Bundesland," in the Federal Republic of Germany.

57 See Herfried Münkler, "Politik als Theater: Die Inszenierung der Politik nach den Vorgaben der Kunst" in *Zukunftsbilder* (see endnote 4), 274–288.

58 See "Parody," in *Princeton Encyclopedia of Poetry and Poetics*, ed. Alex Preminger, Enlarged Edition, (Princeton, NJ: Princeton University Press, 1974), 600–602.

59 See Mikhail Bakhtin, *Probleme der Poetik Dostoevskijs*, translated by Adelheid Schramm from the 2nd rev. Russian ed. [*Problemy poetiki Dostoevskogo*, Moskow 1963], (Munich: Carl Hanser, 1971), 113–202, v.a. 136ff., and *Rabelais und seine Welt: Volkskultur als Gegenkultur* (Frankfurt am Main: Suhrkamp, 1987). On this point, see also Hans Ulrich Gumbrecht, "Literarische Gegenwelten. Karnevalskultur und die Epochenschwelle vom Spätmittelalter zur Renaissance," in *Literatur in der Gesellschaft des Spätmittelalters* (Heidelberg: Winter, 1980), 95–144.

60 Cf. Mary Hunter, *The Culture of Opera Buffa in Mozart's Vienna*, Ch. 2 ("Opera Buffa's Conservative Frameworks," 52–70) and Ch. 3 ("Opera Buffa's Social Reversals," 71–92).

61 The original title of this work is *Mare nostrum. Entdeckung, Befriedung und Konversion des Mittelmeerraumes durch einen Stamm aus Amazonien.*

62 *Die Umkehrung Amerikas.* Episches Hörspiel (1976).

63 Werner Klüppelholz, *Sprache als Musik: Studien zur Vokalkomposition bei Karlheinz Stockhausen, Hans G. Helms, Mauricio Kagel, Dieter Schnebel und György Ligeti* (Saarbrücken: Pfau, 1995). See also Kagel's own essay "Die Umkehrung Amerikas," in *Darmstädter Beiträge zur Neuen Musik*, no. 16, (Mainz: Schott, 1976) and Werner Klüppelholz, "Die Umkehrung Amerikas. Episches Hörspiel," in *Mauricio Kagel. 1970–1980* (Cologne: DuMont, 1981), 133–138.

64 This is Mary Hunter's thesis. In her monograph on the Viennese culture of opera buffa in the second half of the eighteenth century, she speaks of the "conservative framework" of this genre within which the hierarchical order is restored after a disturbance to the hierarchy. Cf. Mary Hunter, *The Culture of Opera Buffa in Mozart's Vienna*, 58–70.

John Cage and the Principle of Chance

HORST BREDEKAMP

I. The Eastern Myth

JOHN CAGE SAW his piece, 4'33", premiered in 1952, as his most important work, and still recently it has been valued as "one of the milestones of music in the twentieth century."[1] It is divided into three periods of silence which add up to four minutes and thirty-three seconds. The unexpected silence was to activate the listeners' senses to the noise which they themselves and the ambiance produced by chance. Chance, created through silence, became the enigmatic term of Cage's concept of liberating music from notes, instruments, structures and orders: from itself.

Cage defined this step as an unprecedented breakthrough, inspired by Eastern philosophy, namely Zen Buddhism. Only rarely, as in an interview given at the end of his life, did he confirm that "much of what happened in music since 1950 was a reaction to developments in the visual arts,"[2] and that "in twentieth century art each composer depended on a painter."[3] This is of course an exaggeration; as Paul Klee and others show, it could be turned around.

But the statements offer an insight into Cage himself. "Each composer" is obviously a *pluralis majestatis* in reverse. The plural overemphasizes what with respect to his own person Cage always denied. When being asked if, for example, Marcel Duchamp's chance operations had an impact on his development of chance music, he answered: "My use of chance operations came out of contact with *I Ching*, the ancient Chinese oracle which uses chance operations to obtain the answer to a question." After the interviewer insisted, "Did you know about Duchamp's use [of chance] at that time?" the response avoided a clear answer: "Not particularly. I knew about the *I Ching*. It was *I Ching* that I saw one day as a possible way of writing music."[4]

As has been pointed out, it is rather impossible that Cage did not know about Duchamp's chance operations like the *Stoppages-Etalon* from 1913,[5] as it is almost certain that via Erik Satie he was familiar with the Parisian group "Les incohérents," which in the 1880s produced not only white and black monochrome paintings but also a piece of absolute silence.[6] But when the interviewer insisted, "Do you know of any other visual artist using chance operations?" Cage finally neutralized the question with the answer: "I don't really know."[7]

Many scholars have thus tried in vain to figure out in what way and through which influence Cage developed his theory and practice of chance in the years 1949–1951.[8] On the contrary, I will try to show that Cage's rupture was not as clear-cut as it might seem at first glance. Instead, his principles of chance and silence are embedded in a long-standing tradition of artistic chance theory and chance images.

II. Chance in Art Theory

The theory of chance images goes back to antiquity, mainly to Pliny, who had put the effect of chance images into a kind of *paragone* between nature and art.[9] The first Renaissance concept stems from Alberti: "Those [who were inclined to express and represent (. . .) the bodies brought forth by nature] would at times observe in tree trunks, clumps of earth, or other objects of this sort certain outlines (*lineamenta*) which through some light changes could be made to resemble a natural shape. They thereupon took thought and tried, by adding away here and there, to render the resemblance complete."[10] It is, as Horst Woldemar Janson put it, the first modern formula of the "spontaneous discovery of representational meanings in changing formations."[11]

From Pliny's *Natural History* and the overwhelming description of the protean image-generation of clouds in Lucretius' *De rerum natura*[12] comes the articulation of nature as an almost absolute artist who is able to forge the figure of a tiny horseman in the sky, as painted in the *Sebastian* of Andrea Mantegna. In his *Triumph of Virtue* Mantegna has shaped two silhouettes in another formation of clouds.[13]

The unparalleled formula of an endless play of veiling the chance production in seemingly artificial creations stems from Torquato Tasso, who in *Gerusalemme liberata* described the fiction of a garden, as if he had Mantegna's natural architecture in mind: "Art seems like nature, which for her own delight / laughingly imitates her imitator."[14]

It has long been overlooked that cabinets of curiosities of the sixteenth and seventeenth centuries played together with gardens as chance rooms. They provided an alternative to the mechanics of the strict pragmatics of utilitarianism. Francis Bacon imagined such "a goodly huge cabinet, wherein whatsoever the hand of man by exquisite art or engine hath made in rare stuff, form, or motion; whatsoever singularity *chance* and the shuffle of things hath produced; whatsoever Nature hath wrought in things that want life and may be kept."[15] Even Leibniz, when he proposed a *Kunstkammer* for Hannover, played with this idea when he regarded the mountains of the Harz and their minerals and fossils as "nothing else than a wonderful show-place, where nature seemingly is quarrelling with art."[16] In these formations he saw chance creations of a playful nature.

In full consciousness of this tradition Alexander Cozens in the eighteenth century developed a method to use accidental ink blots on paper for the imagination of the movements of the brush, and then putting a transparent paper over the sheet and copying everything that seemed natural. Rightly so, he defined his landscapes as "a production of chance, with a small degree of design."[17] As Ernst Gombrich has suggested, from here a line could be drawn to Justinus Kerner's "Klecksographien" from the middle of the nineteenth century, and thence to Hermann Rorschach's ink-spot tests.[18]

Twentieth-century Dadaism and Surrealism brought the triumph of Alberti's chance images. Marcel Duchamp is named too often in this context; Hans Arp may be even more important, as he stuck to the principle of chance over a period of four decades. Having arranged his compositions after the position of four strings of different length that he let fall to the ground in 1915, he claimed his creations being "arranged according to the laws of chance."[19] And still in 1960 Arp stated: "*Chance* in the art of our time is not at all an accident, but a gift from the muses."[20]

It should have become clear that the iconography of *chance* was meant to represent a principle of a nature creating endless protean metamorphoses. The artist thus had to play with the playfulness of nature in an even more playful way.

III. The Chinese-European Tradition

Directed against this line of tradition, Cage stated in countless writings and interviews that his turn to chance had by no means to do with the Western, but with the Eastern tradition as developed by Zen Buddhism.

In one of his articles on chance images Janson quotes the creation method of the *i-p'in* artists, who would become drunk, spatter ink onto the surface of the painting, stamp on it and smear it with feet and hands and in the same moment brush it while laughing, then shape landscapes out of it "with the suddenness of Creation. It was exactly like the cunning of a God."[21] Not a single sheet of these young Jackson Pollocks has survived, but creations that resemble the theoretical frame of chance exist in various styles.[22]

It is of specific importance that since the seventeenth century there had been a remarkable interchange of the concept of chance images between China and Europe. In one of the most influential books ever written on China, *China illustrata*, published in 1667 by the German Jesuit Athanasius Kircher, there are a number of pictures which illustrate rootworks which Kircher meant to be chance pieces of nature.[23] And in the mountains of China he saw gigantic chance sculptures of Nature like the so-called "Idolum" on the top of the hill and the silhouette of a head on the right side of it.[24] Even more impressive is his explanation of the Chinese signs of writing as abstractions of natural phenomena of chance. One of the illustrations shows fish which in their movements shape letters and signs of the Chinese scripture.[25] Through Kircher, European art-theory of chance and Chinese iconography were combined.

IV. Mystification of Chance

Even Cage's strongest argument in support of the Eastern roots of his concept of chance music, the book *I Ching*, had in a similar way gone through a European filter. Cage did not get the book before 1950, when the German version of 1923 had been translated into English and when the composer Christian Wolff gave it to him. The book is a product of the Weimar Republic's Orientalism, enriched by a foreword by C.G. Jung in which he exposed an extremely hierarchical view of *I Ching*.[26]

Also, the influence of the Japanese Zen Buddhist Daisetz Teirato Suzuki on Cage was not purely Eastern. With a certain pride, Cage underlined instead, that his concept of chance was not founded in a European tradition at all: "since the forties and through study with Suzuki of the Philosophy of Zen Buddhism, I got the music as a means of changing the mind . . . [and as] an activity of sounds in which the artist found a way to let the sounds be themselves."[27]

This picture is again a product of self-mystification, which recently was demystified with some disturbing results.[28] Cage's often-repeated statement, that it was "of great luck" that he was able to participate in the seminars of Suzuki in the late forties,[29] veils the fact that he did not get to know Suzuki before 1952, after he had taken decisive steps towards the practice and theory of chance, after he had met Pierre Boulez in Paris in 1949, and after he wrote his *Sixteen Dances* (1950), which employed the principles of chance, and *Music of Changes* (1951), a composition which had been produced through playing dice on the hexagram of the *I Ching*.[30]

In addition, Cage never mentioned the historical and political framework of Suzuki's philosophy. Suzuki belonged to the extreme-right Kyoto school, which had a network of connections to the Weimar Republic and Nazi Germany. Among others, Keiji Nishitani, a friend and later successor of Suzuki, studied with Martin Heidegger between 1936 and 1939.[31] For Suzuki and others the reign of chance was the tool of wiping out the individual in the name of absolute superior powers. Chance in this ambiance played a role in the cult of dying for authority, ending in the Kamikaze pilots.[32]

V. Chance and Authority

Against this previously-veiled background, Cage's theory of chance receives a new framework. Cage, like most of the listeners of Suzuki's New York lectures, was surely not particularly interested in the political implications of Suzuki's philosophy, but when he took over elements of Suzuki's Zen Buddhism in order to strengthen, mystify, and at the same time popularize the concept of chance which he had developed before, a kind of systematic doublefoldedness was at work, which he was never able to escape. Absolute chance cannot work without absolute order as its opposite, and the one who creates an area of chances is the master of everything which is possible.[33]

Surely, never has a composer focused the audience on his personality as strongly as John Cage did in his *4'33"*. The effect of the unexpected silence was that conscious and subconscious thoughts became oriented towards the creator of this piece. And through the rigid measurement of time it became perhaps the most authoritarian piece of music ever written. The freedom of performing a regular song or a symphony under normal conditions is of course not very large, but it exists, since absolute time is modified by the audience's perception of time. *4'33"* instead, by measuring three parts of silence in seconds, is extremely restricted, and in its "pedantic clarity"[34] it overrules the audience's perception of time.[35]

It is not at all by chance that the *tabula rasa* of Cage's composition remains deeply grounded in the tradition of the artist as second God. Whether it be the blank *tabula* in Raphael's *Madonna di Foligno*, Robert Fludd's seventeenth-century black field into which God is implanting the creation;[36] the white field into which Otto van Veen, teacher of Rubens, put the "A" as a creation of God;[37] or the empty canvas in Diego da Saavedra's 1640 book on the education of a coming ruler:[38] emptiness is always the tool of a sovereign, as it is finally also in Robert Rauschenberg's "White Paintings" from 1951, which inspired Cage to produce his silent *4'33"*.[39] They all play their role of framing an initial, thus sublime creation.

VI. Conclusion

I have assimilated my rather short iconography of chance to the subject, and my choice of examples was rather arbitrary. This is exactly the crux of the matter. I wanted to demonstrate that chance is only one face of a Janus head whose obverse face is total control. In art theory, this authority was, and is, nature in its various emanations. As Cage installed chance, he could not escape the majestic aura of the art of nature, but tried to emulate it quite consciously: "I found, that it is the responsibility of the artist to imitate the effects of nature."[40] This might be what Theodor W. Adorno had in mind when he criticized Cage for his "nature mysticism."[41] Anti-authoritarianism and absolute order are bound together; as in art theory, so in music, and perhaps in politics as well.

There is no doubt that Cage played a most charismatic and fruitful role in the loosening of a stiff and cramped music culture. As a public figure and innovator he will keep a dominant role in music history. But it should not have been overlooked that his orientalism was the veil under which he could hide his European roots as well as his foundation in the art theory of chance images and their bifold political impact.

Cage's personal drama lies in the fact that Schoenberg forced him to dedicate his life to music. As he followed Schoenberg's advice, he had to omit his theoretical roots in the visual arts, in contrast to his wonderfully documented capacity as an orientalizing painter.[42] For a historian the word "if" is forbidden, and thus I do not argue that if Cage had not met Schoenberg, the twentieth century would have lost a prophet, but would have gained a superb and less mystifying painter. This conclusion, as I said, I do not bring forward seriously, but just as a product of a historical *chance* game, which would allow us to reverse Cage's statement cited at the beginning: "In twentieth century art each painter depended on a composer."

Notes

1   Eric de Visscher, "Die Künstlergruppe 'Les Incohérents' und die Vorgeschichte zu *4'33"*," in *John Cage: Anarchic Harmony*, ed. Stefan Schädler and Walter Zimmermann (Frankfurt am Main: Schott, 1992), 71.

2   *John Cage im Gespräch*, ed. Richard Kostelanetz (DuMont, 1989), 137; cf. Günter Seubold, "Verdinglichter Zufall, Verräumlichte Zeit, Weiße Stille. John Cage oder Wie man dem Gefängnis westlicher Musik durch östliche Anleihen entgehen will und dabei doch nur den endgültigen Sieg der abendländlischen Bild- und Präsenz-Ästhetik über die sich zu befreien suchende Musik erringt," in *Mythos Cage*, ed. Claus-Steffen Mahnkopf (Hofheim: Wolke, 1999), 172.

3   *John Cage im Gespräch*, 139.

4   *Musicage: Cage Muses on Words, Art, Music*, ed. John Retallack (Hanover, NH: University Press of New England for Wesleyan University Press, 1996), 153.

5   Ian Pepper, "John Cage und der Jargon des Nichts," in *Mythos Cage*, 14.

6   Visscher, "Die Künstlergruppe," 73f.

7   *Musicage*, 154.

8   Ian Pepper, "From the 'Aesthetics of Indifference' to 'Negative Aesthetics': John Cage and Germany 1958–1972," in *October* 82 (1997): 31f.

9   Horst Woldemar Janson, "Chance Images," in *Dictionary of the History of Ideas*, ed. Philip Wiener (New York: Scribner, 1973), 1, 340–342.

10 Leone Battista Alberti, *De Statua De Pictura Elementa Picturae*, ed. Oskar Bätschmann and Christoph Schäublin (Darmstadt, 2000) 142; quoted in Horst Woldemar Janson, "The 'Image Made by Chance' in Renaissance Thought," in *De Artibus Opuscula XL: Essays in Honor of Erwin Panofsky*, ed. Millard Meiss (New York: New York University Press, 1961), 254.

11 Janson, "The 'Image Made by Chance,'" 254.

12 Pliny, *Naturalis Historiae.*, II, lxi; Titus Lucretius Carus, IV, 129ff.

13 Janson, *Chance Images*, 346f.

14 Stimi (sì misto il culto è col negletto)
Sol naturali e gli ornamenti e i siti.
Di natura arte par, che per diletto
L'imitatrice sua scherzando imiti.
(Tasso, *Gerusalemme liberata*, 16, 10.)

15 Francis Bacon, *Gesta Grayorum*, in *Works*, ed. James Spedding, Robert Leslie Ellis and Douglas Denon Heath (London: Longman, 1862), 8, 335.

16 "Maßen der Harz an sich selbst nichts anderes als ein wunderbarer Schauplatz, alda die Natur mit der Kunst gleichsam streitet." Gottfried Wilhelm Leibniz, *Sämtliche Schriften und Briefe*, ed. Preussische (later Deutsche) Akademie der Wissenschaften zu Berlin (Berlin, 1923), I, III, Nr.17, 17.

17   Alexander Cozens, quoted in Janson, "The 'Image Made by Chance'," 264.

18   Ernst Gombrich, *Kunst und Illusion* (Cologne: Phaidon, 1967), 129 and 213ff.

19   Quoted by Janson, *Chance Images*, 352.

20   "Der 'Zufall' in der Kunst unserer Zeit ist nichts zufälliges, sondern ein Geschenk der Musen." Jean Arp, "Die Musen und der Zufall," in *Zufall als Prinzip: Spielwelt, Methode und System der Kunst des 20. Jahrhunderts*, ed. Bernhard Holeczek and Lida von Mengden, exhibition catalogue (Heidelberg, 1992), 120. For the context see Austin Clarkson, "The Intent of the Musical Moment," in *Writings through John Cage's Music, Poetry, and Art*, ed. David B. Bernstein and Christopher Hatch (Chicago and London: The University of Chicago Press, 2001), 97f.

21   Janson, *Chance Images*, 352f.

22   Sheng-Ching Chang, *Natur und Landschaft. Der Einfluss von Athansasius Kirchers "China Illustrata" auf die europäische Kunst* (Berlin: Dietrich Reimer Verlag, 2003), 35ff. See also the following notes.

23   Athanasius Kircher, *China monumentis, qvà sacris qvà profanis, nec non variis naturae artis spectaculis, aliarumque rerum memorabilium argumentis illustrata* (Amsterdam, 1667), 165.

24   Kircher, 172.

25   Kircher, 232.

26   Pepper, "John Cage und der Jargon des Nichts," 13f. The most precise analysis of this moment and of the Jungian influence in general is given by Dörte Schmidt, in "Die Geburt des Flugzeugs: Cage, *I Ching* und C.G. Jung," in *Das Andere: Eine Spurensuche in der Musikgeschichte des 19. und 20. Jahrhunderts*, ed. Annette Kreutziger-Herr (Frankfurt am Main: Peter Lang, 1998), 353–366.

27   Cage, in George J. Leonard, *Into the Light of Things* (Chicago: The University of Chicago Press, 1994), 147.

28   Martin Erdmann, *Untersuchungen zum Gesamtwerk von John Cage* (PhD diss., Rheinische Friedrich-Wilhelms-Universität Bonn, 1992), 23–37; Schmidt, 355f.

29   John Cage, "Eine autobiographische Skizze," in *John Cage: Anarchic Harmony*, 25.

30   Cage, 1991; cf. Stefan Schädler, "John Cage und der Zufall in der Musik," in *Zufall als Prinzip. Spielwelt, Methode und System in der Kunst des 20.Jahrhunderts*, ed. Bernhard Holeczek and Lida von Mengden, exhibition catalogue (Heidelberg: 1992), 65–74, 70f.

31   Pepper, "John Cage und der Jargon des Nichts," 20.

32   Ibid., 23f.

33   Ibid., 21.

34   Ibid., 15.

35   Peter Cox, "Über John Cage," in *Mythos Cage*, 52.

36   Robert Fludd, *Utriusque cosmi maioris scilicet et minoris metaphysica, physica atque technica historia* (Oppenheim, 1617), 26.

37   Otto van Veen, *Physicae et Theologiae Conclusiones* (Orsellis, 1621), 5.

38   Horst Bredekamp, *The Lure of Antiquity and the Cult of the Machine: The Kunstkammer and the Evolution of Nature, Art and Technology* (Princeton: Princeton University Press, 1995), 112.

39   John Cage, *Silence* (Middletown, CT: Wesleyan University Press, 1973), 63. cf. Cage, "Eine autobiographische Skizze," 26f.

40   Cage, "Eine autobiographische Skizze," 24.

41   Theodor W. Adorno, *Schwierigkeiten beim Komponieren*, in *Gesammelte Schriften*, ed. Walter Benjamin (Frankfurt am Main: Suhrkamp, 1972), 17:270f.; cf. Pepper, "From the 'Aesthetics of Indifference' to 'Negative Aesthetics'," 38.

42   *Kunst als Grenzbeschreitung: John Cage und die Moderne*, ed. Ulrich Bischoff, exhibition catalogue (Düsseldorf, 1992).

Aspects of Modernism

The Hunt for Reminiscences in Nineteenth-Century Germany

ANTHONY NEWCOMB

Mais notre héritage est écrasant. L'homme moderne, comme il est
appauvri par l'excès même de ses richesses. . . . Nos trésors nous
accablent et nous étourdissent.

—Paul Valéry, *Le Problème des musées* (1923)

INCREASING ATTENTION HAS been paid in the musicological literature over
the past thirty years or so to the subject of musical borrowing.[1] My hope with
this essay is to sharpen the vocabulary and criteria with which we talk about
this phenomenon. My concern is not primarily to discuss the status of individual instances, although it was my wondering over the status of a possible
Beethoven quotation in Schumann's Second Symphony and *Fantasie*, op. 17
that initially led me to pursue the question. I will return to this example briefly in conclusion. My concern is also not to discuss a taxonomy of the various
possible kinds of musical borrowings, although I will want to insist that the
two categories of quotation and allusion must be intentional in order to count
as such. My main concern here is a historical one. It is with the attitude toward
the issue of the originality of one's thematic material—of one's prominently
placed melodic themes or motives—in the German-speaking musical culture
of the mid- and late-nineteenth century. My thesis, which has several parts, is
this: In the earlier part of this period, ca. 1830–1860, and to some extent for

the rest of the century, quotation, or even similarity of melodic material (that is, allusion) to music of the recent past by another composer (as opposed to self-quotation) and coming from the art music tradition, was not viewed as we now tend to view it—as a source of aesthetic meaning and as a gesture of homage and emulation to older music of the growing musical canon.

This view of melodic quotation or allusion, widespread in our age, simply did not exist as a concept at that time. Or, to be more circumspect, I have found so far no written evidence of the existence of that concept in this culture. I propose that this concept came into currency across the latter part of the nineteenth century. The concept gained gradual acceptance across this period, but this acceptance was by no means universal, even by 1900. The change to gradual acceptance of the new concept began around 1860 with conservative critics and journals—for example, Adolf Schubring,[2] Selmar Bagge's *Leipziger Allgemeine musikalische Zeitung* in the 1860s,[3] and eventually Hermann Kretzschmar in the *Grenzboten* in the 1880s.[4] It began with those critics partly, I propose, as a reaction against the stress on originality, novelty, and a break with tradition, which was seen as characteristic of the other, *neudeutsche* school. Previous to the 1860s, and to some extent throughout the century, thematic or motivic material—again, in the sense of *melodic* material—was seen as the primary locus of originality and of *Erfindungskraft*, which was the mark of the truly great musician-composer. Allegations of quotation or even similarity in this area were always seen as accusations and as a negative element—as something against which one had to defend the composer and the piece.

Before moving to some examples in evidence of this thesis, I will propose some reasons why this issue was such a concern and problem for musical culture in German-speaking lands of the post-Napoleonic era. A primary reason was the change in the concept of the musical work, a change discussed by many recent historians,[5] and in particular the rapid growth of the concept of the musical *Meisterwerk*—individual, highly distinctive [*unverwechselbar*], and made for the ages. Other separate but intimately connected reasons would be: the growth of the public concert series; the growth of the musical canon of concert pieces; the growth of print culture in general and especially for the preservation and diffusion of these canonic works; and the relation of the composer to his audience via the anonymity of the commercial publisher and the marketplace—in short, the rise of the modern musical world. All of these matters placed a premium on originality and distinctiveness as a way of establishing and distinguishing a composer's individual voice or style in this culture and this marketplace. Finally, I would cite the widespread concern with *Epigonalität* in the whole German artistic culture of the time after the death of Beethoven, Hegel, and Goethe, a concern most famously represented by Karl Immermann's novel *Die Epigonen*, begun in the 1820s and finally published in 1836.[6]

At the risk of redundancy, I want to emphasize several points. First, that the matter of similarity with past pieces of the tradition was in fact a burning concern in the 1840s and 1850s. Second, that it was *not* viewed—from my experience I would say it was *never* viewed at this time—as a positive element, as an explicit and intentional reference meant as a source of meaning. Under this heading, I will at least raise the questions of conscious intention on the part of the composer, of the operations of musical memory, and of when a similarity might be understood as a quotation or allusion. Third, that the stress on originality was located in melodic invention (as opposed, for example, to formal modeling, harmonic vocabulary, rhythmic novelty, instrumentation). Fourth, that there was increasing impatience on the part of professionals with the widespread tendency to melodic reminiscence hunting, and that it was especially associated with amateurs and "dilettantes." Fifth, that the attitude does seem to have begun gradually to change in the 1860s to a more approving one and one closer to that of the twentieth century, especially among more conservative critics, but that this change was by no means universal, even by 1900.

That the musical world of mid-nineteenth-century Germany was preoccupied with the issue of originality will be no surprise to those who have occupied themselves with the period. What I was not prepared for was the thoroughness and subtlety with which some commentators around 1850 analyzed the issue of reference to music of the recent past.

The issue seems first to have been raised, for musical journalism at least, in an article headed "Ueber Reminiscenzenjägerei" and signed "R." in the *Allgemeine musikalische Zeitung* (hereinafter *AMZ*) of 18 August 1847 (Vol. 49, cols. 561–66). (The author claims that the issue "to our knowledge has not been previously subjected to a closer examination," "bisher, so viel uns bekannt ist, einer näheren Prüfung nicht unterworfen ist.") Particularly strong in this initial version is the impatience with what had become, he says, a "*Mode*," and with the fact that it was pursued mainly by dilettantes. Our author offers as explanation for this latter point the need on the part of those who cannot easily take in and understand new musical experiences to latch on to a detail which is somewhat familiar, which is similar to what they already know. In making allegations of melodic reminiscence, however, they do the

composer "the gravest injustice" and the result is "to subtract something from
the value of the composition." Our author also stresses the primacy of thematic material ("We look for the independence or originality of a composer
first in the invention of musical ideas," which phrase he has earlier equated
with "Melodien").[7] And he skirts what one might call the issue of conscious
versus unconscious similarity. Not all asserted similarities are "untrue," but
he would attribute to them a different meaning. "One can easily find similarities between two ideas [Gedanken], for even the most gifted of composers
will be affected by external impressions, but his worth, his independence will
not always suffer therefrom."[8] I take the phrase "external impressions" to be
a reference to the experience of other music and the matter of unconscious
memory. He goes on to make what I will call the historical argument—that is,
the argument concerning the increasingly large cultural store of music from
the past. "Everything that the world of dilettantes justly admires as individual
and characteristic in this or that composer has for a long time been able to be
found as an isolated instance in previously existing pieces of music, often in
scarcely different positions and contexts."[9] All of these matters will re-appear
in later considerations of the same issue, with new emphases and sometimes
with new elements added.

I would like to highlight a few excerpts from three other striking examples of these later considerations. "Ueber musikalische Reminiscenzen" by
the young composer Wilhelm Herzberg, which appeared in the *Neue Berliner
Musikzeitung*, I, 353–55 (27 October 1847), is the next consideration of the issue that I have found, and it may be a direct response to the *AMZ* article.[10]
Herzberg insists that a genuine reminiscence can only be of a distinctive, concrete *Gestalt*. "This concrete *Gestalt* is melody, the inspired physiognomy of
music. The more individual is its formation, the more striking will be each
allusion to it and the more it indicates deliberate intention."[11] Important here
is the insistence on melody, on distinctiveness, and on intention. Herzberg
goes on to give an example of a commonplace passage that we should not be
surprised to find "in the same version in Zumsteeg and Mendelssohn and in
addition in a third and fourth composer, without one's having to think of a
reminiscence . . . It will not be easy for anyone to make an allusion, conscious
or not, to a genuinely individual melody without that allusion sooner or later
being recognized as such and avenged. To be sure, in the case of a conscious
allusion, there are enough ways of concealing, of covering up by rhythmic
variations, different keys, careful insertions, and many other clever operations.
The countenance of the original will shine forth ironically through all such
fortifications as a warning to everyone for all time that the individual [me-

lodic idea] must be honored and left untouched."[12] Striking here is the idea of the danger involved in trying to reuse or disguise a strong idea. It will always shine forth and have its revenge. Note that the idea of the positive use of such distinctive melodic ideas from the past is simply not present. And note that, since the re-use, or re-appearance, of commonplace turns of melody cannot be called a reminiscence, it would seem that for Herzberg in 1847, true musical reminiscences are, if not impossible, at least dangerous and to be avoided.

An article headed "Ueber Plagiate und Reminiscenzen" in the *Berliner Musik-Zeitung Echo* of Feb. 18, 1855 (Vol. V, Nr. 7, 49–51, 58–60) and signed "—f." makes similar points. What do we understand by this word Reminiscence? the author asks. "A striking similarity, which a musical passage has with another, more or less well known and in any case previously composed passage, especially with respect to melody." It has become the passion of "small minds, after they have stumbled around in music for a bit," to hunt for these. "Thus out of short-sighted musical erudition a real system of intimidation has been widely cultivated, which has eventually, like some sick obsession, gotten completely out of hand, such that people, sometimes with passionate anger, hunt for every melodic similarity that has found its way into [the works of] new composers, more or less unconsciously, from the works of their predecessors."[13] Yes, he goes on, some "artrascals" ("*Kunstspitzbuben*") do put out potpourris of the ideas of others. But we have gone too far with this *Reminiscenzenjägerei*. It has made life very difficult for many blossoming talents, even squelched them (for fear of such similarities being found and censured). And it has given birth to a literature of the worst sort, which has not only not enriched us, it has left us much the worse off. He then goes into the, for the time, typical historical defense of his thesis, citing Lasso, J. S. Bach, Stradella, Gluck and Handel, Mozart and Gluck and Cimarosa, and many others as examples of "how often these composers surprisingly agree in the use of frequently used favorite turns of phrase or from time to time even in complete melodies."[14] The need, he says, is to decide on some principles that can determine intellectual property in some lasting way.

Again we have the stress on melodic material and on the need for distinctiveness as opposed to "frequently used favorite turns of phrase." Striking is the vehemence of his impatience with the phenomenon, the linking of it with dilettantish people who want to show their own knowledge, and the idea that it may be clogging the compositional flow of some younger composers, out of the fear that some unconscious borrowing may be discovered and censured. As a further example of the first two characteristics I might quote a passage from Selmar Bagge's conservative *Leipziger allgemeine musikalische*

Zeitung of 1866: "One talks a great deal about epigonism, and not so long ago one even counted masters such as Mendelssohn and Schumann among the epigones . . . This kind of talk tells us nothing, and the whole line of talk comes from dilettantes who find only similarities everywhere and who have no understanding for the exceptional and the unusual—or at least they arrive at such an understanding only after considerable time."[15]

A final example in this set of particularly focused examinations of the problem comes from Leopold August Zellner, who was, for me at least, the most exciting discovery in my rambles through some musical journals of the 1840s through the early 1860s. Zellner, born 23 September 1823, was a virtuoso harmonium player (forgive the seeming paradox) and composer of masses, oratorios, and chamber pieces, who took over Simon Sechter's place as teacher of thoroughbass and counterpoint at the Vienna Conservatory in 1868. He began his career as music reviewer with the *Ostdeutsche Post* around 1850, then founded and edited the variously named *Wiener Blätter für Musik [Theater u. Kunst]* in 1855, retaining its editorship until taking the post at the Conservatory. He was the declared defender of Liszt and Rubinstein as composers and the explicit antagonist of Hanslick on the Viennese music-critical scene. He had the distinction in this world of music journalism of publishing extensive analytical reviews, with numerous and lengthy musical examples. Zellner himself is an interesting critic-analyst and worthy of a separate study. It was a dust-up with Hanslick in 1855 that provoked his reflections on musical thievery in one of his first issues and led finally to his lead article "Ueber Plagiate" of 27 November 1855 (Vol. I, Nr. 86).

At issue initially was Hanslick's review of 29 March 1855 of a concert by Anton Rubinstein, in which he remarked on a new "Waltz" by Rubinstein, "the theme of which unfortunately had already previously been invented by R. Schumann and used in his 'Carnaval.' . . . We can attribute to the inventiveness [Erfindung] of the composer neither sustained strength nor real originality."[16]

Zellner shot back in his lead editorial of 3 April 1855. We may expect this kind of thing from small musical minds, he said. "It must strike us as sad, however, when we see that a respected, 'aesthetically' cultivated Viennese critic bases his judgment on such quotations, and cites [Ernst] Kossak [founder in 1851 of the *Berliner Echo*] as critical authority."[17] (Hanslick had quoted a rather offensive and derogatory comment by Kossak on Rubinstein's compositions in general later in the same review). He then prints the presumed passage from *Carnaval* and what he calls the "incriminated [inkriminirte] passage from Rubinstein's 'Waltz'" (see Fig. 1). He continues, "thus it will be clear to anyone, even the layman inexperienced in musical notation, alone from the

Figure 1

und hierauf die inkriminirte Stelle aus Rubinstein's „Walzer"

simple comparison of the *outward appearance of the two melodic figures* [emphasis in original], that here there can be no question of a similarity of the themes. The course of the harmony shows some partial agreement, but how many thousand times must this progression already have been used! If one speaks of reminiscences, only a close agreement of the melodic idea can be meant, not one of harmony, which forms more or less only the outer garment or the support for the melody, which, as one will admit, was the first to exist in most if not all musical ideas. If one were to take this point of view as a point of departure [that is, the mistaken one attributed to Hanslick] one would have to see Mendelssohn's E-major Andante from the G-minor Piano Concerto as a competent plagiarism of Grétry, and the Finale of the same work as a clear borrowing from Weber's *Konzertstück*. If we go down this path in our critical judgments, the entire musical literature can easily be reduced to a couple of dozen original works."[18]

One may not now agree with his emphasis on melody and his underestimation of harmonic originality. One may even find this a bit disingenuous from one who would soon become the stubborn and detailed defender of Liszt's compositions of the mid 1850s. But it was characteristic of the time, which believed that originality and *Erfindungskraft* and—to use one of our current terms to which "—f" of the *Echo* comes close—intellectual property rights rested in melodic material.

Zellner returned to the subject in his lead article *Ueber Plagiate* of November, which begins, "Why is it that we hear so often and so readily complaints about borrowings? Above all because one needs only the slightest musical ability and the slightest intellectual effort for such declarations." It takes only a superficial acquaintance with earlier compositions, he claims, to find "passages that one composition has in common with another." It would be a matter of no importance if this "constant outcry about thievery would remain just a kind of superficial gossip." But, he asserts, the deeper problem here is that it stifles many good creations and causes many young composers to seek after melodic novelty, and the public to judge a piece only by the novelty of its [thematic] details. He again makes the historical argument: think of all the agreement in details in the music written across the past 300 years: "well-known passages can easily be found in the most original of composers and new passages in the most superficial."[19] Even this vigorous defender of the Liszt-Wagner school is ready to admit thematic concurrences across the broadening span of music history. But he sees them as irrelevant details, and he never sees them as an essential and intentional part of the meaning of a piece, or as something even potentially positive.

Herzberg's 1847 article for the *Neue Berliner Musikzeitung* is in many ways the most detailed and nuanced treatment of the issue, and I would like to call attention to a few further points in his article before releasing these lead witnesses. Like Zellner, Herzberg claims that harmony "is in and of itself common property" ("Gemeingut"), unless the chord or the progression is extremely unusual. The same is true for rhythm and for figuration, unless the latter begins to shade over into the realm of melody. He is unique in analyzing the relationship of *Manier* and *Eklecticismus* to *Reminiscenz*. *Manier* is that which, "too feeble in its own content, arises from a rigid imitation of a character or style. Its essence lies in the one-sided reminiscence of a foreign form." As examples he cites Pleyel, Vanhal, Winter, Zumsteeg, Danzi. Eclecticism is that in which "the available treasures, the various stages of stylistic development appear in isolation as something remembered, that which does not come into being as truly possessed elements working for the unity of the style. Thereby the reminiscence comes especially strongly to the fore, both in the whole and in details, often with unmistakable intentionality." He illustrates this with a fabric-based metaphor and gives Meyerbeer as his example. His counterexample is Mendelssohn, "who, standing in the midst of the wealth of historical memory, has built for himself out of this an [individual] character and therefore unjustly is called an eclectic by many."[20]

Part of Herzberg's closing section is an explicit consideration, unique in the articles I have looked at, of the role of memory in the matter of melodic *Erfindung*. The truly original composer (what he calls *das Genie*) has a deep musical memory, which participates in the creation of new material. But with the genius, this is not the "mechanical putting together of remembered material, but rather an unintentional arousal, quite independent of the will, and an association of existing thoughts and elements in interaction," which are shaped with the energy of genius into new shapes. "The genius, in the grip, in the joy of creation, has no time to stop and ask repeatedly whether this or that has existed previously."[21]

I understand this last as Herzberg's wrestling with the problem of what both "—f" and Zellner had seen as the stifling effect on younger composers of this worry about censure for similarity of melodic material with art music of the past. Herzberg is the first that I have seen to talk explicitly about the unconscious role of memory in producing unintentional similarities of material, though he is careful to insist on the reshaping role of the true creator.

Echoing this last point, one can find several examples of composers' explicit displeasure at having similarities in their melodic material pointed out to them, and the concomitant, at least implicit connection of these unconscious similarities with memory. Johann Leopold Ebner, writing in 1858, recounts that, when Schubert some forty years before played his recently composed song "Die Forelle" to his circle of friends, one of them exclaimed, "Good Heavens, Schubert, you got that out of 'Coriolan.'" Schubert saw this at once, says Ebner, and wanted to destroy the song, but his friends prevented him.[22] This may be apocryphal, but it does at least point out Ebner's belief in the mid 1850s that such behavior on Schubert's part, which he claimed to remember vividly, would have been natural and appropriate.

Schumann himself commented in at least one striking instance on what he can only understand as an unintentional slip of memory, which allowed an apparent borrowing of thematic material to damage a movement he otherwise liked by a composer that he generally admired. In a review from 1842 of the String Quartet op. 6, no. 1 by Johannes Verhulst, he remarked, "The last movement begins with the last [movement] of the 'heroic' symphony almost literally. Did this slip by the composer unnoticed? If not, why did he let it stay? Soon however an idea of his own [*ein eigener Gedanke*] pops up . . ."[23]

Natalie Bauer-Lechner in 1900 recounts that Mahler, speaking of the Trio of the second movement of the First Symphony, lamented that "everyone will label me a thief and unoriginal because of the two opening bars, in which my memory deserted me and which recall a symphony of Bruckner that is very well known in Vienna."[24] She also recounts that Mahler was annoyed by "similarities" ("dass ihn zwei Anklänge darin ärgern") to a symphony by Brahms and to a piano concerto by Beethoven that had unwittingly been woven into the fabric of the first movement of his Fourth Symphony and that he had noticed too late to remove them.[25] Based on papers of Bauer-Lechner in his own Mahler archive, Henry-Louis de La Grange reports that Mahler told the young Zemlinsky that his opera *Es war einmal* was "so full of resemblances and plagiarisms" that "Zemlinsky must have a very bad memory if he was not able to avoid them."[26] Paul Thissen observes "that the use of previous material is not necessarily intentionally motivated is shown by Mahler's efforts to avoid such *Anklänge*," and he cites Richard Specht's 1913 biography of Mahler in support of the same point.[27] Specht wrote that ". . . it was moving with what naive concern [Mahler] could ask if in a certain phrase [*Wendung*] there was really an *Anklang* to another piece to be found."

Egon Voss dismisses the alleged quotations of Wagner in the original version of Bruckner's Third Symphony as "eine Legende, ein Mythos" started by Göllerich as late as 1936. I need not go into his arguments here for dismissing the entire "myth," but his conclusion is worth quoting. "As a composer Bruckner was self-conscious enough to recognize these similarities as dependencies and thus as weaknesses."[28] The passages are not found in the 1877 and 1889 versions of the symphony.

But Mahler and Bruckner were, of course, more of the *neudeutscher Schule* than not, where emphasis was placed on departure and separation from the past. Not so Brahms. The issue of Brahms and allusion is the aspect of this question that has received the most attention in the recent literature, especially in the thorough and thoughtful dissertation of 1989 by Kenneth Hull.[29] Hull's care and thoughtfulness require him to do a delicate dance around the question of intentionality on the part of the composer, which is explicitly required by literary theorists for any claim of allusion or quotation.[30] This dance is made necessary by the several documented instances in which Brahms denied or ridiculed the significance of thematic resemblances, including one letter to Otto Dessoff in which Brahms declares that "one of the dumbest chapters of dumb people is the one of reminiscences."[31] (Relevant passages from the correspondence with Dessoff, not to my knowledge previously examined in the literature about quotation and allusion, are presented and translated in the Appendix to this essay.)[32] Hull finally has to rest his case for allusions "not on documentary or biographical evidence, but on the inherent plausibility of any allusive interpretation," which seems to me to move over toward a kind of intertextuality not dependent on authorial intention or even on what Linda Hutcheon calls the original "enunciative context" of the work itself.[33]

To take but one striking instance from 1889: one can only surmise what was the reason for Brahms's removal from the second version of his Piano Trio op. 8

of what Hermann Kretzschmar in his long article of 1884 for *Die Grenzboten* heard as a quotation of a passage from Beethoven's *An die ferne Geliebte* (the same passage that Schumann was supposed by later writers to have quoted in his opp. 17 and 61, and that had directed my attention to this question in the first place). Kretzschmar found no cause for censure in this reminiscence. In fact his attitude toward what he calls this "*Umspielung*" is virtually that of later twentieth-century critics. "The last period of Beethoven has had, without a doubt, a great deal of influence on the form and on the content of the early works of Brahms. The thinking and planning of the young Brahms seem to have orbited around the genius of the master as around a sun. In one work, the Trio Opus 8, in many respects very interesting, this cult finds a genuinely moving expression. The second theme in its last movement, so beautifully introduced by the cello, is an explicit play on the main melody from Beethoven's 'Liederkreis to the distant beloved'—the same melody that, at the end of the work, sets the words of the dedication 'please accept these, then, these songs.' One encounters this sort of symbolic use of significant melodies in the compositions of Brahms right up to the most recent times."[34] I would also note here that Kretzschmar, obviously fond of finding such thematic interrelationships, makes no mention of an intermediate reference to Schumann, either to Opus 17 or Opus 61, or to any connection of the theme with Clara.[35]

Brahms's friend and admirer Adolf Schubring, in the articles of 1862–66 on Brahms to which Walter Frisch has called our attention,[36] is the first critic that I have encountered to assert a whole series of specific thematic *Anklänge an die alten Meistern*, if without Kretzschmar's open-armed acceptance, at least without generally implying that they are worthy of censure. (His examples are taken from Brahms' two Serenades and his First Piano Concerto.) Brahms, in his gently mocking reply, seems clearly to call into question Schubring's extremely diligent, almost Rudolf Réti-like finding of interrelationships between themes and motives both within and without Brahms's movements and pieces. In his letter of 1869 to Schubring at the end of Schubring's series, he chides him ironically for his zeal in finding thematic similarities, in that he had supposedly failed to discover the "political allusions in my Requiem . . . 'Gott erhalte' right at the beginning—even in 1866."[37]

But even Schubring criticizes the second Scherzo of Opus 11 for its thematic reminiscences. The aesthetic motto of the Schumann school was "neuer Inhalt in altbewährter Form," he says. But here the *Inhalt* was 100 years old. Haydn and Beethoven's D-major Symphony did it better, he says. In fact, Hanslick in his review of Opus 11 for the Viennese *Presse* of 10 December 1862 had found this similarity so clear as to suggest that the movement be dropped.[38] In a similar vein the critic Carl van Noorden had recommended in a review of 1861 that this "Beethoven'schen Scherzo" be dropped because of the close similarity of its thematic material, and Selmar Bagge in a review of 1862 had said that one should fault Brahms in that "he had let this work be *printed* or even performed, without first removing the most striking reminiscences."[39] The long review by van Noorden of Brahms's Sextet, Opus 18 is full of the same concern, but from the opposite side. Van Noorden praises Brahms particularly "because he does not recognizably borrow from any of his predecessors or does not indulge in any epigonen-like eclecticism so characteristic of our time, and because he does not let himself settle rigidly and self-sufficiently into one, perhaps even original, style of mood and expression, but rather because a genuine artistic inspiration leads him to individual and distinctive musical ideas."[40] Still, he must criticize Brahms on one detail. "Disturbing to us were the passing resemblances on page sixty-one [of the original Simrock score] to the first movement of the Pastoral Symphony. Reminiscences of this kind, as unintentionally as they may come to the surface, must and can be avoided by every composer." [41]

My combing through this material has made me much more sensitive to the words commentators use and what they actually claim. Schubring and van Noorden talk of "Anklänge," and Schubring claims that various themes "erinnern [an]" other specific themes, or that the *Hauptmotiv* of the Scherzo of Opus 16 is "verwandt" with that of the Finale of the Beethoven's Eighth Symphony. Similar concern with precise vocabulary now makes me realize that I was not correct in claiming in an article of 1984 that Wasielewski in the revised third edition from 1880 of his Schumann biography had "explicitly recognized" an "allusion" to Beethoven's Opus 98 in the Finale of Schumann's Opus 61.[42] What Wasielewski says is this: "It is very worthy of notice how one and the same motive is used by various masters, without one's speaking thereby of a plagiarism."[43] He then quotes a bit of the Beethoven passage, the "Andante" of Mendelssohn's *Lobgesang*, and a Haydn Piano Trio.[44] He is in fact making what I have called above the historical argument also made by all of the critics quoted above (that other composers have used the same or similar "turns of phrase"), but without claiming an intentional allusion, or even an unconscious failure of memory. His care to defend Schumann from any accusation of *Plagiat* is, of course, revealing of his continuing concern. But he does not hesitate to comment on the kinship he has noticed. He simply does not call it an intentional quotation or allusion. And he does not attribute biographical meaning to it or connect it to Opus 17. This from one who was close to Schumann and his circle.

To take just one more example, almost at random: David Brodbeck claims "a most telling allusion" in the third movement (Scherzo) of Brahms's A-major Piano Quartet, op. 26, and he gives as evidence a passage from a letter from Clara Schumann to Brahms of 15 July 1861. But what Clara says there is that the passage reminds her of a passage (the second theme, mm. 46ff.) in Robert's String Quartet, op. 41, no. 3. She quotes a brief passage, then goes on, "not exactly melodically but in layout and mood" (translation from Brodbeck). What she has said is that it reminds her of the passage from Robert's piece: "Das 2. Motiv erinnerte mich sehr an eine Stelle in Roberts Streichquartett." She attributes to this fact no intentional allusion on Brahms's part, nor is there any evidence that Brahms took it that way. Likewise Brodbeck's assertion that "when, a few months later, [Joseph] Joachim was sent the score, he too noted a parallel between the same two themes" and that this supports the idea of allusion here—this assertion is not borne out by what Joachim says in his letter of 15 October 1861. He remarks on the "afterbeats in the Scherzo [and here he writes one measure of a syncopated accompaniment in eighth notes to the theme], which will necessarily prove unpractical in performance. Already in the first movement of the Schumann A-major Quartet, whose tempo is nevertheless much slower, it sounds uncomfortable. But what a whole, unified, and successful impression the Scherzo makes [otherwise]. It reminds one sometimes of late Beethoven, so concentrated is the structure, and so individual the melodic turns of phrase."[45] Thus he is not claiming allusion or quotation at all, or even reference to the Schumann quartet. If any hint of this sort is made, it is that the movement reminds him of late Beethoven in its general style. But his specific remark about the melodic material of the piece is just the opposite. He uses the word *eigentümlich*, which one often sees to praise independence and individuality of melodic material.[46]

I cannot pass over this issue without mentioning that I continue to doubt that the passage in Schumann's Opus 17 as well is a conscious allusion or quotation. Wasielewski, who was close to Schumann in his later life, never mentions it, nor do Robert and Clara in their considerable correspondence about the piece at the time of the creation of Opus 17. The first to do so is Hermann Abert in the second edition of 1910 of his short book on Schumann. Building on the destination of the never-published first version of the piece for the Beethoven monument in Bonn, he claims that "at the end . . . Schumann again evoked Beethoven's 'ferne Geliebte,' who had already appeared in m. 14."[47] In a letter to Clara of 9 June 1839 about the first movement of the piece, Robert did quote the "Melodie" that "gefällt mir am meisten darin," but this was not the supposed Beethoven quote. It was the right-hand melody of mm. 65–67, something in the area of but not identical with the main closing subject of the initial section of the movement, whose transformation in the coda to the movement results in the supposed Beethoven reference.[48]

Incidentally, I would admit that, whether or not this reference was part of the conscious and intentional content of that piece for Schumann or for its listeners and performers in the first decades of its existence, it is part of the content of the piece for many of its listeners and performers today. It is, I believe, important to separate these two issues and to identify what audience we are talking about and when, in discussing allusiveness from the point of view of the listener—for example, in such phrases as "we cannot help hearing . . ."; or "the reference to . . . is obvious."

I would also want to separate the actual quotation of specific melodic-thematic material—which this is claimed to be, I gather, and which is claimed to be intentional—from the issue of less thematically identical allusion, which is still, I would think, claimed to be intentional in, say, the articles by Schubring quoted above. And I would separate both of these categories from similarities which are unconscious surfacings from the musical memory (for example, the Mahler examples, the examples brought forward by Dessoff—see the Appendix to this essay—and the one Schumann found in Verhulst). I would finally separate all of these categories from general formal and structural modelings on admired pieces. All of these in turn should be clearly separated, in our claims about them at least, from passages brought together by later critics without any claim that they had any influence on the genesis of the later passages in which they hear similarities to earlier ones.[49] I believe that clear structural modelings of the sort pointed out in an oft-cited article by Charles Rosen some twenty years ago—and also approvingly by a number of the reviewers of 1840–60 that I have read—were in fact a sanctioned part of the musical culture of the mid-nineteenth century.[50] But I also must conclude that literal quotation of, or even too close similarity to, the thematic material of a piece from the art music tradition of the recent past was not something that was viewed positively in the mid-nineteenth century, and that our current concept of this practice as a positive part of the intentional meaning of the piece was not a concept that was part of the public musical culture of the time.

With this, I come to what many readers have doubtless been expecting: the issue of allusion (not quotation) in the Finale of Brahms's First Symphony. I believe that the allusion *is* there, which means, in my vocabulary, that it was intentional. This case is quite different from, for example, the putative quotations in Opus 8. First, the passage in the First Symphony does not quote Beethoven's or anyone else's melodic material. The allusion is made more by style and by the formal position, similar to that of a famous place in a very famous work. One might call it an instance of formal anti-modeling (no use of chorus, or voices, or words). Second, the allusion in the First Symphony is to an iconic piece of the same public (sub)genre—the monumental symphony, as opposed to the lighter, more divertimento- or serenade-like symphony— and to a piece with which Brahms's long-awaited first symphony would immediately be compared. All of this is different from the case in the op. 8 Trio (or Schumann's Opus 17).

Brahms's alleged conversational comment on the Finale of the Symphony, transmitted by Kalbeck, seems to recognize the existence of an allusion.[51] What I would highlight is the (perhaps typical) courage and stubbornness with which Brahms flies in the face of cultural prejudice with this allusion—a gesture in an extremely public genre and in a piece and in a place in that piece that was laden with significance for that culture and that genre. This background simply adds weight to the full cultural meaning of this gesture, a meaning that Reinhold Brinkmann has laid out for us richly and eloquently and without a hint of the exaggeration that mars some studies of allusion and influence.[52] I would add only that I interpret the second part of Brahms's reported remark ("and still more noteworthy is that every ass hears that right away") as reflecting his annoyance with *Reminiscenz jägerei* in general and with the shallow way in which the dilettante culture that habitually indulged in it would doubtless understand—or misunderstand—what he had done and what it meant.[53] He was in his First Symphony, I believe, alluding—by exception, quite publicly and in the sense that we now tend to view such allusions, namely as a meaningful reference to a piece from the tradition in which he worked and a piece against which, even in opposition to which, his own piece should be understood. But he also realized that the habits of the musical culture of which he was part meant that his gesture would be criticized and misinterpreted.

Appendix

Brahms's exchange with Otto Dessoff in June 1878—cf. *Brahms: Briefwechsel*, Vol. 16, ed. Carl Krebs (Deutsche Brahms-Gesellschaft, 1922), 174–93.

In letters of earlier 1878, Dessoff (b. 1835) joyously reported that he had begun to compose. He mentioned in particular a string quartet, which he would like

to send to Brahms for his comments and advice. The letters directly involved
in the exchange over the quartet (I would assume this is the F-major Quartet
op. 7 of Dessoff, which I have not yet been able to consult) are numbers 58, 59,
60, 65, and 66 in the Krebs edition. Only letters 58 and 60 are dated (5 June
1878 and 19 June 1878 respectively).

In letter 58, Dessoff worries that the first movement of his quartet, "which
came into being as a recalling of the mood of the first movement of your Second Symphony, may finally contain direct reminiscences, and so I will wait
until the Symphony appears [in printed form], (which by the way has taken
already long enough) to at least be reassured about this."[54]

Brahms answers in letter 59, "but there are certainly no allusions to my
Second in your Quartet—I would have noticed them."[55]

In dated letter 60 of 19 June, Dessoff assents, "The famous undemanding
quartet [the reference is to a phrase Brahms had used in undated letter 59]
I will now indeed allow to be printed, since you have assured me about its
reminiscencelessness, and since I believe I can read from your words that you,
even if you don't give any specific advice, consider it to be good enough. Do
you have any objections to my dedicating it to you? *You should answer this
absolutely freely!*"[56]

Brahms accepted the dedication in letter 61, dated simply "Juni 78," and
continues, "I wanted to convince you of the absence of reminiscence, but Simrock has still printed off no further scores [of the Second Symphony]."[57]

The matter seems to have continued to gnaw at Dessoff's conscience, since
it surfaces again in the undated letter 65. The date of letters 65 and 66 is still
in question in my mind. Kalbeck (I, 191) claims 66 (Brahms's reply) is from
July 1878. This repeats his claim on page 152 about July, and makes me suspect
that 1888 on page 152 is a simple typographical misprint of 1878. I also wonder
that letters 62 and 66 in the edition of the correspondence supposedly bear
the same postmark but make no reference to one another. In letter 65 Dessoff
replies, "No, that you didn't notice them is in the realm of the unbelievable!
Or is my conscience so sensitive that it judges even where the plaintiff himself
not only fails to complain, but, as it seems, does not even know that something has been taken from him? Just look at the accompanying notepaper and
then say whether or not I am right."[58] (He wrote out a brief quote from mm.
361–64 of the first movement of the Brahms.) He then recounted the quick
creation of his quartet around the turn of the year, after having heard (at least
part of) Brahms's Symphony from Brahms in September of 1877. "That I now
should have retained in my memory a variant in the closing section of your
exposition is seemingly impossible, for even your most popular bits do not

easily stick in the memory, how much less so phrases torn out of context; and yet there it is. Now I had read over your piece 3 times and I noticed nothing, and today at 6 in the morning I sit with my coffee and read it again and come to the passage; I think I'm about to have a stroke, because I wanted to send the Quartet today to the printer. Now I ask you to tell me honestly, whether there isn't still a similarity there."[59]

He complained that he would like to change his passage, but he can't bring himself to do it. "You will probably laugh over my reminiscence hunting; but after I have had the misfortune that the first of [my] four songs ('Mein Falk hat sich verflogen') begins exactly like a song of Jensen, which I have never heard or seen in my life, and even, to be more precise, in the same key and tempo and for two whole measures, so would it be extremely embarrassing if a similar thing happened to me again, especially if I were conscious of it. . . . In addition, the public and the critics fix on a similarity, however superficial it may be, with such enthusiasm and delight, and that spoils completely even the tiny bit of pleasure there may be."[60]

Brahms answered (letter 66, also undated but postmarked Pörtschach am See 26.6.78) with the passage quoted by Kalbeck. "Please don't do anything stupid. One of the stupidest practices of stupid people is that of [proclaiming] reminiscences. The little passage of mine in question, as excellent as all the rest may be, is really absolutely negligible. Your passage is, on the other hand, of an enchantingly warm, beautiful, and natural expressiveness. Don't spoil anything; don't touch a thing. You are not often able to express yourself so beautifully—indeed you are only now beginning to speak easily and freely. Indeed, I would have said nothing and afterwards would have taken for myself the ownerless goods. You should not change a note of it. In the end, of course, you know that I have stolen, and much worse. The reminiscence from Volkmann is not worth mentioning. This ornamental bit existed long before Volkmann was born. That didn't in the slightest prevent him from making from it once again a very attractive piece."[61]

Notes

1 For such a general taxonomy we have thoughtful and ongoing studies, led principally by Peter Burkholder. See especially "The Uses of Existing Music: Musical Borrowing as a Field," *MLA Notes* 50/3 (1994), 851–70.

2 Walter Frisch, "Brahms and Schubring: Musical Criticism and Politics at Mid-Century," *19th-Century Music* 7 (1984), 271–81.

3 Rebecca Grotjahn, *Die Sinfonie im deutschen Kulturgebiet 1850 bis 1875* (Sinzig: Studio, 1998), 21 and 254ff.

4 Hermann Kretzschmar, *Gesammelte Aufsätze über Musik* (Leipzig: Fr. Wilh. Grunow, 1910), "Johannes Brahms," 151–207, esp. 158 and 181, article reprinted from *Die Grenzboten* of 1884.

5 See Peter Burkholder, "Museum Pieces: the Historicist Mainstream in Music of the Last Hundred Years," *Journal of Musicology* 2 (1983), 115–34 and Lydia Goehr, *The Imaginary Museum of Musical Works* (Oxford: Oxford University Press, 1992), especially ch. 6.

6 See Matthias Wiegandt, *Vergessene Symphonik? Studien zu Joachim Raff, Carl Reinecke und zum Problem der Epigonalität in der Musik* (Sinzig: Studio, 1997), esp. 9–34, "Epigonalität—ein problematischer Begriff."

7 "Die Selbständigkeit oder Originalität eines Componisten suchen wir zunächst in Erfindung der musikalischen Gedanken."

8 "Aenlichkeiten zweier Gedanken können sich sehr / leicht finden, denn selbst der begabteste Componist wird äusseren Eindrücken unterworfen sein, doch wird nicht immer deshalb der Werth, die Selbständigkeit des Einen darunter leiden."

9 "Alles das, was sie [die Dilettantenwelt] an diesen oder jenen Componisten selbständige, als eigentümlich mit Recht bewundert, finde sich schon längst in vonhandenen Musikstücken vereinzelt, oft kaum in andere Stellung und Verbindung."

10 Herzberg died at the age of 28 early the next month of a fall from a horse. Cf. the obituary by Flodoard Geyer on page 396 of the same volume of the *Neue Berliner Musikzeitung*. He was, says Geyer, a richly talented young artist who had so far composed sonatas for piano duet, songs, and character pieces for piano.

11 "Diese concrete Gestalt ist die *Melodie*, die beseelte Physognomie der Musik. Je eigenthümlicher sie gestaltet ist, desto mehr wird jedes Anklingen an sie auffallen und auf eine Absichtlichkeit hinweisen."

12 "bei Zumsteeg und Mendelssohn in derselben Fassung noch bei einem Dritten und Vierten vorkäme ohne dass man an eine Reminiscenz dabei zu denken habe . . . An eine wahrhaft eigenthümliche Melodie wird nicht leicht Jemand, bewusst oder nicht, einen Anklang haben, der nicht früher oder später als solcher erkannt und gerächt würde. Es giebt zwar beim bewussten Anklang genug Mittel zu bedecken, zu bemänteln, durch rhythmische Verschiebungen, fremde Tonarten, vorsichtige Einführungen, durch manche andere schlaue Operation: das Antlitz des Originales wird dennoch hinter allen Verschanzungen ironisch hervorsehen und Allen für alle Zeit eine Mahnung sein, das Eigenthümliche in Ehren zu halten und unangetastet zu lassen."

13 "Eine auffallende Aehnlichkeit, welcher ein musikalischer Satz, besonders in melodischer Beziehung, mit einem schon mehr oder minder bekannten, überhaupt schon früher verfassten, hat . . . kleineren Geister . . . nachdem sie etwas

in der Musik herumgehaust haben . . . So ist denn von Seiten kurzsichtiger, musikalischer Gelehrsamkeit ein wahres Abschreckungssystem weidlich cultivirt worden, welches endlich wie eine krankhafte Passion so überhand genommen, dass man seitdem, zum Theil mit wahrer Wuth, Jagd macht auf jegliche melodische Aehnlichkeit, welche sich bei neuen Componisten, mehr oder weniger unbewusst, in ihren Werken mit denen ihrer Vorgänger vorfindet," 49.

14 ". . . wie oft dieselben in häufiger gebrachten Lieblingswendungen oder in mitunter sogar vollständigen Melodieen merkwürdig übereinstimmen."

15 "Man spricht viel von Epigonenthum und es ist noch gar nicht so lange her, dass man selbst Meister wie Mendelssohn und Schumann zu den 'Epigonen' zählte. . . . Mit all dem ist nichts gesagt, und das ganze Gerede geht von Dilettanten aus, die überall nur die Ähnlichkeiten herausfinden, für das Besondere und Abweichende aber kein Verständnis haben, oder sehr spät dazu gelangen." 4 (1866), 290, "Aphorismen." Quoted in Matthias Wiegandt, *Vergessene Symphonik? Studien zu Joachim Raff, Carl Reinecke und zum Problem der Epigonalität in der Musik* (Sinzig: Studio, 1997), 23.

16 ". . . dessen Thema nur leider früher schon von R. Schumann erfunden und in dessen 'Carnaval' aufgenommen worden ist. . . . Der Erfindung des Componisten können wir weder nachhaltige Kraft, noch echte Originalität zuerkennen." Eduard Hanslick, *Sämtliche Schriften. Historisch-kritische Ausgabe*, ed. Dietmar Strauss, I/3 (Vienna: Böhlau, 1995), 52.

17 ". . . traurig muss aber die Wahrnehmung berühren, wenn ein geachteter, 'ästhetisch' gebildeter Wiener Kritiker sein Urtheil auf solche Citate stützt, und Kossak als kritische Autorität anführt!"

18 ". . . so wird es Jedem, selbst der Notenschrift unkundigen Laien, allein schon aus dem einfachen Vergleiche der *äusserlichen Gestalt beider melodischen Figuren* [emphasis in original], klar werden, dass hier von einer Aehnlichkeit der Themen keine Rede sein kann. Der Zug der Harmonie zeigt wohl theilweise Uebereinstimmung, aber wie viele tausend Male mag diese Modulation schon gebraucht worden sein! Wenn man von Reminiscenzen spricht, kann doch wohl nur die Homogenie des melodischen Gedankens, nicht die der Harmonie gemeint sein, welche mehr oder weniger nur das Gewand, die Unterlage der Melodie bildet, die, wie man zugeben wird, in den meisten, wo nicht in allen Gestaltungen bereits vorhanden war. Wollte man von diesem Gesichtspunkte ausgehen, so müsste, um nur ein Beispiel anzuführen, Mendelssohn's E-dur-Andante aus dem G-moll-Klavierkonzerte als ein tüchtiges Plagiat Gretry's, das Finale derselben Komposition als greifbare Anlehnung an Weber's Konzertstück angesehen werden. Gehen wir auf diese Weise in's kritische Gericht, so würde sich die musikalische Literatur bequem auf ein paar Dutzend Originalwerke reduziren lassen."

19 "Woher kommt es, so oft und so leichtfertig über Entlehnungen klagen zu hören? Vor Allem daher, dass man zu solchem Ausspruche die geringste musikalische Fähigkeit und die geringste Geistesanstrengung nöthig hat . . . Züge, die eine Composition mit einer andern gemein hat . . . ewige Geschrei vom Dieb-

stahl ein blosses Hin- und Herreden bliebe . . . bekannte Sätze finden sich leicht bei den originellsten und neue bei den plattesten Componisten."

20 "zu schwach an eignem Geist, aus einer formellen Nachahmung eines Charakters, [oder] Styles hervorgegangen ist. Ihr Wesen ist es, in der einseitigen Reminiscenz der fremden Form zu leben . . . die vorhandenen Schätze, die verschiedenen Stufen der Entwickelung und Style in ihrer Vereinzelung als Erinnertes erscheinen, dass sie nicht als überwundene, zur Einheit des Styles verarbeitete Momente zur Erscheinung kommen. Dadurch tritt die Reminiscenz im Ganzen und Einzelnen hier besonders stark hervor, oft in unverkennbarer Absichtlichkeit . . . der mitten im Reichtum der geschichtlichen Erinnerung stehend, sich aus diesem heraus zum Charakter gebildet hat und deshalb mit Unrecht von Manchen Eklectiker genannt wird."

21 "Nicht die mechanische Zusammensetzung des Vorhandenen, die Reflexion wird hierbei wirken, sondern eine unabsichtliche, vom Willen unabhängige gegenseitige Erregung und Aneinanderreihung (Association) der vorhandenen Gedanken und Elemente . . . Das Genie, im Drange, in der Freude des Schaffens, hat nicht Zeit, erst lange zu fragen, ob dies oder jenes schon da gewesen."

22 *Schubert: Memoirs by his Friends*, ed. Otto Erich Deutsch (London: A. & C. Black, 1958), 47. "Himmel, Schubert, das hast du as dem 'Coriolan.' In der Ouvertüre jener Oper ist nämlich eine Stelle, die mit der Klavierbegleitung in der 'Forelle' Ähnlichkeit hat; sogleich fand dieses auch Schubert und wollte das Lied wieder vernichten, was wir aber nicht zuliessen und so jenes herrliche Lied vom Untergang retteten." *Schubert: Die Erinnerungen seiner Freunde*, ed. Otto Erich Deutsch (Leipzig: Brietkopf und Härtel, 1966), 55. Cited in Edward T. Cone, "Schubert's Beethoven," *The Musical Quarterly*, 46 (1970), 779.

23 (*Neue Zeitschrift für Musik*, v. 16, 1842/1. *Gesammelte Schriften*, 2, 76). "Der letzte Satz fängt mit dem letzten der 'heroischen' Sinfonie an, beinahe buchstäblich. Ist das dem Komponisten entgangen? Wenn nicht, warum liess er es stehen? Bald aber hüpft ein eigener Gedanke hervor; Cello und Bratsche fangen sich zu necken an, und das lustige Spiel geht hübsch vonstatten."

24 "Da werden mich alle wegen der zwei Anfangstakte, bei denen mich das Gedächtnis verliess und die eine in Wien sehr bekannte Symphonie Bruckners erinnern, als Dieb und unoriginellen Menschen verschreien!" Herbert Killian, *Gustav Mahler in den Erinnerungen von Natalie Bauer-Lechner* (Hamburg: K.D. Wagner, 1984), 173. Cited in Miriam K. Whaples, "Mahler and Schubert's A-minor Sonata, D. 784," *Music and Letters* 63 (1984), 261.

25 Ibid., 163–64. It is likely that Rosamund McGuinness ("Mahler und Brahms: Gedanken zu 'Reminiscenzen' in Mahlers Sinfonien," *Melos/NZ* 3 (1977), 222) has correctly identified what Mahler thought of as the reminiscence of Brahms. Compare mm. 11ff. of the first movement of Brahms's First Symphony with mm. 147–48 of the first movement of Mahler's Fourth. She may also be correct that Mahler's assertion that Brahms got it from Weber refers to the Act II Trio from *Der Freischutz*, mm. 10ff and especially mm. 94ff., both for Aennchen.

26 Henry-Louis de La Grange, *Mahler*, 1 (New York: Doubleday, 1973), 550. The same story is repeated in the revised French edition (*Gustav Mahler: chronique d'une vie*, I [Paris: Fayard, 1979], 841, where the crucial phrase is "remplie de réminiscences de tous genres."

27 *Zitattechniken in der Symphonik des 19. Jahrhunderts* (Sinzig: Studio, 1998), 140. Richard Specht, *Gustav Mahler* (Berlin: Schuster u. Loeffler, 1925²), 25.

28 "Als Komponist war [Bruckner] selbstbewusst genug, um diese Aehnlichkeiten als Abhängigkeiten und damit als Schwächen zu erkennen." Egon Voss, "Wagner-Zitate in Bruckners Dritter Sinfonie? Ein Beitrag zum Begriffr des Zitats in der Musik," *Die Musikforschung*, 49 (1996), 403–06, 406.

29 Kenneth Hull, "Brahms the Allusive: Extra-Compositional Reference in the Instrumental Music of Johannes Brahms," PhD dissertation, Princeton University, 1989.

30 See the article on *Allusion* in the *New Princeton Encyclopedia of Poetry and Poetics*, ed. Alex Preminger and T. V. F. Brogan (Princeton, NJ: Princeton University Press, 1993), which begins, "A poet's deliberate incorporation of identifiable elements from other sources...."

31 The supposed letter to [Felix] Otto Dessoff is quoted in Kalbeck, op. cit. 1, 152. Kenneth Hull (see "Brahms the Allusive," 27, n. 14) does not find the letter in Brahms' published correspondence because Kalbeck (or his printer) has miscited the date. The (undated) letter is clearly from mid-June 1878, not July 1888, as Kalbeck says. It can be found in the Brahms *Briefwechsel*, 16, ed. Carl Krebs (Deutsche Brahms Gesellschaft, 1920), 191–92. The exchange between Brahms and Dessoff covers five letters and is interesting enough in this connection to be quoted in some detail. See the Appendix to this essay.

32 One could flesh out this point further with other instances of Brahms rejecting claims about allusion, for example in his Scherzo op. 4 and in the C-minor Piano Quartet, or with his care to acknowledge the Scarlatti quotation in Opus 72 (1876).

33 Hull, "Brahms the Allusive," 24. Linda Hutcheon, *A Theory of Parody* (New York: Methuen, 1985), 43, quoted in Hull, 39.

34 "Auf die Form wie auf den Geist der ersten Periode [Brahmsens] hat ohne Zweifel der letzte Beethoven einer grossen Einfluss gehabt. Um den Genius dieses Meisters scheint Denken und Sinnen des jungen Brahms wie um eine Sonne gekreist zu haben. In einem Werke, dem in vielfacher Beziehung hochinteressanten Trio Op. 8, findet dieser Kultus einer geradezu rührenden Ausdruck. Das zweite Thema in seinem letzten Satze, vom Cello so schön eingeführt, ist eine offenbare Umspielung vom Hauptgesang aus Beethoven's 'Liederkreis an die ferne Geliebte'—dieselbe Melodie, die am Ende des Werkes die Worte der Widmung trägt: 'Nimm sie hin denn, diese Lieder.' Man begegnet dieser Art symbolischer Verwendung bedeutender Melodien in den Kompositionen von Brahms bis in die neueste Zeit herein."

35 Quoted from Hermann Kretzschmar, *Gesammelte Aufsätze über Musik* (Leipzig: Studio, 1910), 1, "Johannes Brahms," 151–207, 158. I would also note that Brahms removed what some have heard as a quotation of Schubert's setting of *Am Meer* from the slow movement of Opus 8. I have not yet traced the history of the assertion of this quotation previous to the first volume of Kalbeck's biography of Brahms (1908).

36 Walter Frisch, "Brahms and Schubring: Musical Criticism and Politics at Mid-Century." See note 2 above.

37 Johannes Brahms, *Briefwechsel*, 8, ed. Max Kalbeck (Berlin: Deutschen Brahms-Gesellschaft, 1915), 215–16: "politischen Anspielungen in meinem Requiem . . . 'Gott erhalte': fängt's gleich an—im Jahre 1866." This is doubtless a reference to the Prussian-Austrian war of early 1866, and the musical reference is to the cello part in m. 3 of the first movement. In his postscript of the next morning, Brahms apologizes for his somewhat ill-humored joke at Schubring's expense.

38 Hanslick's brief review, reported in Selmar Bagge's article "Johannes Brahms" in the *Allgemeine musikalische Zeitung, Neue Folge* (I [1863] cols. 464–65) says "die Unselbstständigkeit dieses zweiten Scherzo würde uns bedenklich genug dünken, um den Satz lieber ganz zu streichen." (Kretzschmar, in the first edition of his *Führer durch den Konzertsaal* of 1887, says the same thing.) It has, he says, "mehr als die nöthige Aehnlichkeit mit dem Scherzo aus Beethoven's zweiter Symphonie." He goes on, "Wir gehören nicht zu jene entsetzlichen Reminiscenzen-Jägern, die bei jedem D moll-Akkord ausrufen: Ha, 'Don Juan'!" and he says that he was not going to chide Brahms for the "Anklänge an Beethoven's 'Scene am Bache'" in the Adagio of the Serenade. But this was too close and too prominent. In a similar vein, he faults the first movement of the A-major Violin Sonata, op. 100, for its "etwas zu merklich an das Preislied in den 'Meistersingern' anklingenden Thema." "Brahms' neuesten Instrumental-Kompositionen" (1889) quoted from Eduard Hanslick, *Aus dem Tagebuch eines Rezensenten*, ed. Peter Wapnewski (Kassel: Bärenreiter, 1989), 40.

39 ". . . er ein solches Werk drucken oder aufführen lässt, ohne die auffallendsten Reminiszensen zu entfernen." Both van Noorden and Bagge are quoted in Norbert Meurs, *Neue Bahnen? Aspekte der Brahms-Rezeption 1853–68* (Köln: Studio, 1996), 139.

40 ". . . weil er an keinem der vorhergegangenen Meister nachweisbar anlehnt oder gar einem noch epigonenhafteren und doch so zeitgemässen Eklektizismus fröhnt, weil er auch nicht selbstgenügsam eine einzelne, ursprünglich zwar originelle Stimmungs- und Ausdruckweise zur Manier verknöchern lässt, sondern weil eine echt künstlerische Inspiration ihm eigenthümliche musikalische Gedanken zuführt."

41 "Störend sind uns vorübergehende Anklänge auf Seite 61 an den ersten Satz der Pastoralsymphonie gewesen. Derartige Reminiscenzen, wie unwillkührlich sie auch auftauchen mögen, müssen und können von jedem Componisten vermieden werden." From a review in the *Deutsche Musikzeitung*, 3 (1862), 179–82,

quoted in Norbert Meurs, *Neue Bahnen*, op. cit., 148 and 155. Meurs's book is full of evidence of the negative attitude of critics of all stripes during the 1850s and 1860s toward alleged thematic resemblances.

42 Anthony Newcomb, "Once More Between Absolute and Program Music: Schumann's Second Symphony," *19th-Century Music*, 7 (3 April 1984, Essays for Joseph Kerman), 233–50, 245 n. 26.

43 "Es ist sehr bemerkenswerth, wie ein und dasselbe Motiv von verschiedenen Meistern benutzt ist, ohne das dabei von einem Plagiat die Rede sein kann."

44 Wilhelm Joseph v. Wasielewski, *Robert Schumann, Dritte, wesentlich vermehrte Auflage* (Bonn: Emil Strauss, 1880), 210, n. 1. The Haydn Trio is given variously to Joseph Haydn, Michael Haydn, and Ignaz Pleyel. Cf. Hoboken XV/3, the Haydn *Gesamtausgabe*, Ser. XVII, II, Anhang 2, where the passage quoted by Wasielewski is on 272.

45 "Auch das Nachschlagen im Scherzo [here Joachim inserts a bit of musical nota-tion: an eighth-note rest followed by an eighth note, three times], das sich bei der Ausführung unpraktisch erweisen dürfte. Schon im ersten Satz des Schu-mannschen A dur-Quartetts, das doch viel langsamer geht, klingt es unruhig. Aber wie rund und aus dem Ganzen ist sonst das Scherzo geraten. Es gemahnt manchmal an letzten Beethoven, so konzentriert ist der Bau, und eigentümlich die Wendung der Melodie."

46 See David Brodbeck, "Medium and meaning: new aspects of the chamber mu-sic," *The Cambridge Companion to Brahms*, ed. Michael Musgrave (Cambridge: Cambridge University Press, 1999), 98–132, 109. The letter of Clara Schumann is in *Clara Schumann, Johannes Brahms: Briefe aus den Jahren 1853–1896*, ed. Ber-thold Litzmann. 2 volumes (Leipzig: Breitkopf & Härtel, 1927), I, 371. The letter of Joseph Joachim is from Johannes Brahms, *Briefwechsel*, 5 (Berlin: Deutschen Brahms-Gesellschaft, 1908), ed. Andreas Moser, 307–08. Incidentally, it appears that Brahms changed the accompaniment on Joachim's advice before sending the piece to the printer, since no such syncopated accompaniment appears in the printed version of the theme.

47 ". . . am Schlusse . . . hat Schumann hier wiederum Beethovens 'ferne Geliebte' heraufbeschworen, die schon im 14. Takt erschienen war." I quote here from the fourth edition of 1920: Hermann Abert, *Robert Schumann* (Berlin: Schlesische Verlagsanstalt, 1920, 69. It is curious that he has just quoted as a "sehnsuchtige Seufzer" for Clara, the very phrase that Schumann wrote out in his letter to Clara of 9 June 1839, quoted just below, which has only the vaguest resemblance to the Beethoven phrase.

48 Clara und Robert Schumann, *Briefwechsel. Kritische Gesamtausgabe*, ed. Eva Weissweiler (Basel and Frankfurt: Stroemfeld/Roter Stern, 1987), II, 562. The entire passage is as follows: "Schreibe mir, was Du bei dem **ersten** Satz der Phan-tasie Du Dir denkst? Regt er auch viele Bilder in Dir an? Die Melodie [here a manuscript insertion in musical notation] gefällt mir am meisten darin. Der "Ton" im Motto bist **Du** wohl? Beinahe glaub ich's."

49 I like Robert Alter's trenchant statement of the distinction. "Whereas allusion implies a writer's active, purposeful use of antecedent texts, intertextuality is something that can be talked about when two or more texts are set side by side, and in recent critical practice such juxtaposition has often been the willful or whimsical act of the critic, without regard to authorial intention." *The Pleasures of Reading* (New York: Simon & Schuster, 1990), Ch. 4, "Allusion," 112.

50 See Charles Rosen, "Influence: Plagiarism and Inspiration," in *On Criticizing Music: Five Philosophical Perspectives*, ed. Kingsley Price (Baltimore: Johns Hopkins University Press, 1981), 16–37, a slightly revised veresion of the same article in *19th-Century Music* 4 (1980/81), 87–100.

51 Max Kalbeck, *Johannes Brahms*, III/1 (Berlin: Deutsche Brahms-Gesellschaft, 1910), 109 n. 1. To the comment of "einer Exzellenz, die sich viel auf ihre musikalische Bildung zu gute tat," that "Es ist merkwürdig, wie das C-Dur-Thema in Ihrem Finale dem Freudenthema der "Neunten" ähnelt," Brahms is reported to have replied "Jawohl, und noch merkwürdiger ist, dass das jeder Esel gleich hört." The version of the anecdote given without source by Richard Specht in his 1928 biography of Brahms is slightly different. He attributes the remark to "a musical wiseacre of [Brahms's] acquaintance" who "expressed his enthusiasm over the C-minor Symphony and added that it was only regrettable that the theme of the finale was so like the one in the Ninth Symphony." I am quoting from the English translation by Eric Blom: Richard Specht, *Johannes Brahms* (London: J.M. Dent, 1930), 98.

52 Reinhold Brinkmann, *Johannes Brahms, die Zweite Symphonie: späte Idylle* (Munich: Edition Text & Kritik, 1990). Musik-Konzepte, 70, esp. 19–26. English translation in Reinhold Brinkmann, *Late Idyll: The Second Symphony of Johannes Brahms* (Cambridge, MA: Harvard University Press, 1995), trans. Peter Palmer, esp. 33–53.

53 See the reflection of Brahms's continuing impatience with reminiscence hunting in the letter to (Felix) Otto Dessoff of 1888 [recte 1878] reported by Kalbeck (*Johannes Brahms*, op. cit. Vol I, 152 n. 1 and quoted in the appendix to this essay.

54 ". . . der durch ein Zurückrufen der Stimmung des 1. Satzes Deiner 2. Sinf. entstanden ist, am Ende gar directe Reminiscenzen enthält, und so will ich warten bie die Sinf. erscheint (was übrigens schon lange genug dauert) um wenigstens darüber beruhigt zu sein," 175.

55 "Aber Anklänge an meine 2te sind gewiss nicht in Deinem Quartett, das wäre mir doch aufgefallen," 176.

56 "Das berühmte anspruchslose 4tett will ich nun doch drucken lassen, da Du mich über die Reminiszenzlosigkeit beruhigt hast und ich aus Deinen Zeilen herauszulesen glaube, das Du, wenn Du auch keinen Rath giebst, es für anständig genug hältst. Hast Du etwas dagegen, wenn ich es Dir widme? *Du darfst es sehr ungenirt sagen!*", 180.

57 "Von der Reminiszenzlosigkeit wollte ich Dich überzeugen, aber S[imrock] hat noch keine Partituren weiter abziehen lassen," 182.

58 "Nein, dass Dir das nicht aufgefallen ist gehört zum Unglaublichen! Oder ist mein Gewissen so zart, dass es richtet, wenn der Beschädigte selbst nicht nur nicht klagt, sondern wie es scheint nicht einmal weiss, dass ihm etwas entwendet wurde? Sieh Dir einmal den beiliegenden Zettel an und dann sage, ob ich nicht Recht habe," 187.

59 "Dass ich nun eine Variante im Schlusssatz Deines 1. Theiles im Gedächtnis behalten haben sollte ist schier unmöglich, denn selbst Deine populärsten Stellen behalten sich nicht gleich auswendig, wie viel weniger aus dem Zusammenhang gerissene Phrasen; und doch, da steht's. Nun habe ich Dein Stück 3mal gelesen und es ist mir nicht aufgefallen und heute früh 6 Uhr sitze ich beim Café und lese wieder und wie ich an die Stelle komme, denk' ich, mich rührt der Schlag, denn ich wollte heute das 4tett an Gurckhaus schicken. Nun bitte, sage mir umgehend, ob jetzt auch noch eine Ähnlichkeit da ist," 188.

60 "Du wirst über meine Reminiszenzen-Jagd wahrscheinlich lachen; aber nachdem ich das Unglück erlebt habe, dass das erste der 4 Lieder (Mein Falk hat sich verflogen) genau so anfängt wie ein Lied von Jensen, das ich in meinem Leben nicht gehört und gesehen habe, und zwar in der nämlichen Tonart und Bewegung durch 2 ganze Takte, so wäre es mir furchtbar peinlich, wenn mir, noch dazu bewusst, wieder etwas dgl. passierte. . . . Zudem klammert sich Publikum und Kritik mit wahrem Entzücken an eine Ähnlichkeit, sei sie noch so äusserlich und das verdirbt einem dann das bischen Spass vollends," 189.

61 "Ich bitte Dich, mache keine Dummheiten. Eines der dummsten Capitel der dummen Leute ist das von den Reminiszenzen. Die betreff. kleine Stelle bei mir ist, so vortrefflich auch alles Übrige sein mag, wirklich ganz und gar nichts. Bei Dir aber ist gerade die Stelle von einer allerliebsten warmen, schönen und natürlichen Empfindung. Verdirb nichts, rühr nicht daran, Du kannst gar nicht oft so schön sprechen—doch, Du fängst ja erst an zu plaudern! Eigentlich hätte ich nichts sagen und hernach mir das herrenlose Gut nehmen sollen. Keine Note darfst Du daran ändern. Schliesslich weisst Du natürlich, dass ich bei der Gelegenheit auch und viel schlimmer gestohlen habe. Die Volkmannsche Rem[iniszenz] is gar nicht der Rede werth. Die Floskel war lange vor Volkmanns Geburt da, das hat aber nicht im geringsten gehindert, dass er eben wieder ein sehr hübsches Stück daraus gemacht hat," 191–192. This last bit probably refers to a passage in Dessoff's letter in which he says "My conscience is burdened also with yet another worry, which I shall also copy out, and on which I would appreciate your opinion" ("Mein Gewissen ist auch noch mit einer anderen Sorge belastet, die ich ebenfalls aufschreibe und über die Du mir gefälligst Deine Meinung sagen willst"), 189.

Some Theoretical Thoughts about Aspects
of Harmony in Mahler's Symphonies

DAVID LEWIN

I. Double-Interval Cycles and the Finale of the First Symphony

A DOUBLE-INTERVAL CYCLE is a series of pitch classes whose successive intervals are i, j, i, j, and so forth indefinitely. Example 1 shows such a cycle in the diatonic context of E major. Here interval i is a diatonic third down (modulo the octave), and interval j is a diatonic fourth up (again modulo the octave).

Example 1

A double-interval cycle, diatonic in E major.
Intervals i, j, i, j, etc.; i=diatonic 3rd down (mod 8v); j=diatonic 4th up (mod 8v).

D♯ B E C♯ F♯ D♯ G♯ E A F♯ B G♯ C♯ A D♯ B E

The upper arrow on Example 1 indicates that the cycle links into itself here, where the series of pitch classes is starting to repeat. The D♯ at the left of the example is thereby linked with the D♯ toward the extreme right. But we need not wait for the cycle to close and repeat, before noticing other possible common-tone links. The lower arrow on the example shows such a link: the opening D♯ is the same pitch-class as the D♯ in the sixth order-position of the example. Even though the cycle is not yet repeating *in toto*, the pitch-class link is available for constructive musical purposes. Example 2 shows a scheme that will be relevant for analysis of a musical passage we shall soon consider.

Example 2

The cycle of Example 1: some links and segments

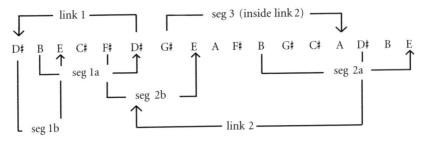

Let us start at the B in order-position 2 of the example. The arrow labeled "seg 1a" follows the cycle along, from the B to the D♯ in order-position 6. The arrow labeled "link 1" connects this D♯ to the D♯ at the far left of the cycle, in order position 1. From that D♯, the arrow labeled "seg 1b" takes us to order-position 3, thus overlapping the beginning of segment 1(a) and closing a visual loop on the example.

The arrow labeled "seg 2a" takes us along the cycle, from the penultimate B on the page to the note just after the rightmost B, thus suggesting kinetically a link involving those B's. The end of segment 2(a) cyclically overlaps segment 1(b). Following the arrow labeled "link 2," we can move along the cycle from the D♯ of segment 2(a) to the other D♯, and then proceed in the environs of that D♯, resolving F♯-and-D♯ to G♯-and-E in segment 2(b). And the arrow labeled "seg 3" takes us along the cycle so as to fill out the interior of link 2.

Example 3 shows pertinent features from the opening of Beethoven's Piano Sonata op. 14, no. 1. The brackets on Example 3 correlate with brackets from Example 2. Of special interest in the top staff of Example 3 is the way in which various registers articulate various cycle-segments. At the linking D♯ in the melody, the end of segment 1(a), in one register, is distinguished from the beginning of segment 1(b), in another register. And from the end of segment 1(a) in the melody, the later segment 3 continues in the same register, a phenomenon that projects musically the continuation of segment 3 from segment 1(a) along the abstract cycle of Example 2.

Example 4 gives a segment from another double-interval cycle, this one

Example 3

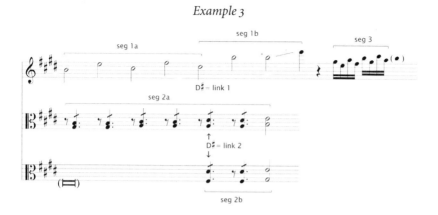

Example 4

A segment from a double-interval cycle in twelve-tone equal temperament.
Intervals i, j, i, j, etc.; i = 6 pc-semitones; j = 5 pc-semitones

Eb A D G# C# G C F# B F Bb E A Eb

definitely measured with semitones, rather than diatonic or just intervals. While the cycle is not complete on Example 4, the given segment has interesting properties in itself. It is bounded by the linking pitch classes A and Eb; there are no other pitch-class links between; and the ten notes between the linking A's fill out the total chromatic. In an earlier article, I tried to show that the segment of Example 4 is basic to large pitch structure in the second movement of Webern's Piano Variations, Op. 27.[1] Example 5 lays out the given segment in registers, indicating alternating intervals of 6 and 5; those familiar with the piece will find the layout suggestive.

My approach here was heavily influenced by the work of Catherine Nolan, who proposed studying this double cycle.[2] Example 5 suggests how various characteristic three-note chords of Webern's movement project in reg-

Example 5

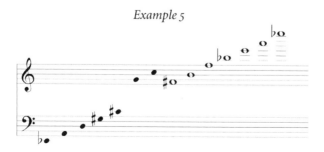

ister three-note segments of the cycle as a whole. The three-note chords are thereby synecdochic for the cycle as a whole. This feature, observed by Nolan, enables me to interrelate large-scale pitch structure with large-scale rhythmic structure. Example 6 shows how.

The pairs of loud three-note chords in the movement mark exactly the written bar lines that begin mm. 4, 9, 4bis, 9bis, 15, 20, 15bis, and 20bis. (In each case, the lower chord of the pair takes the metric accent of the barline.) The resulting pattern projects alternating numbers of five and six things—namely, written measures—in the rhythmic domain of the piece. That permits me, in the cited article, to explore the function of the written $\frac{2}{4}$ time signature for the piece, which enables the measurements of Example 6. While we do hear strong three-eighths patterning in the rhythmic foreground at the opening of the movement, that happens only *before* the beginning of Example 6. The example also leads me to explore certain salient isorhythmic patterns in the music.

Example 6

Segment from a rhythmic double-interval cycle in Webern's op. 27, II.
Durations of five and six measures alternate, where the "measures" are Webern's written $\frac{2}{4}$.
Pairs of loud (056)-trichords are indicated.

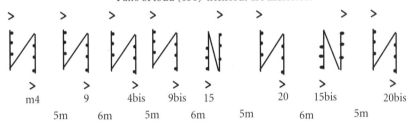

Example 7 shows a segment from another double-interval cycle. Subsegments 2 and 3 fill in the retrograde of segment 1, minus the linked G's.

Example 7

A segment from a double-interval cycle.
Intervals i, j, i, j, etc.; i = M2 or diatonic 2nd or 2 semitones; j = m3 or diatonic 3rd or 3 semitones. Some segments are indicated.

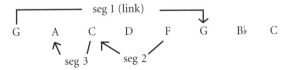

The open noteheads of Example 8 show how Wagner projects those segments in harmonizing the Grail Motif from *Parsifal*—here transposed to C major.

Example 8

Example 9 reproduces the series of Example 6, showing two new subsegments. Segments 4 and 5 engage the G-links, so projecting the entire retrograde of segment 1, including those links.

Example 9

The cycle-segment of Example 7; some further segments.

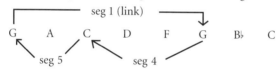

Example 10 sketches Mahler's variation on Wagner's Grail Motif, at the first appearance of the Paradiso Theme in the last movement of the First Symphony (rehearsal 26). Mahler's segments 5 and 4 respectively extend Wagner's segments 3 and 2, so as explicitly to include the G-links. The $^6_4$ harmony, over the repeated linking G's, is nicely inventive. Heard at the end of segment 5, the $^6_4$ is *wesentlich*, tying the end of segment 5 to its beginning, on the C harmony. Heard as the beginning of segment 4, the $^6_4$ is *zufällig*, passing on in the bass to

Example 10

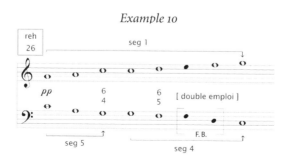

the subsequent harmony over F. The $^6_5$ harmony over that F is also inventive, as a species of *double emploi*: we hear the chord first as an F harmony and then as a D-minor harmony, enabling segment 4 of the cycle to be projected cognitively into the bass line, as indicated by the bracketed noteheads on Example 10. The fundamental bass structure thus projects first the step G-F and then the step D-C, enabling the stepwise intervals of the underlying cycle to function in the bass. Rameau's *double emploi* is exactly the opposite: he would hear first a D-minor harmony and then an F-major one, so that the fundamental bass could explicitly *avoid* the stepwise progressions, moving instead as G-D-F-C.

Example 11

The cycle-segment of Examples 7 and 9, put into minor.
Intervals i, j, i, j, etc.; i=m2 or diatonic 2nd or 1 semitone; j=M3 or diatonic 3rd or 4 semitones. Some new segments shown.

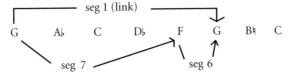

Example 11 gives a minor version of Example 7, with a new segmentation. This structure can be heard in the first phrase of Mahler's Inferno Theme, as shown in Example 12.

Example 12

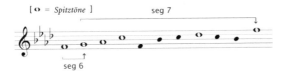

The open noteheads of the example show how the segmental structure of Example 11 is projected by the local high points (*Spitztöne*) of the melody. In this scheme, structural weight goes onto the melodic D♭, rather than the melodic B♭, and we find Mahler's performance notation enforcing exactly that point, as shown by Example 13.

Example 14(a) gives again the cycle of Example 11, bracketing new segments 8 and 9. Example 14(b) gives Example 11 with the linking G's omitted.

Example 14(b) then comprises a German-sixth chord in F-minor, plus the resolving (octave) C's. These matters are projected strongly at the opening of the movement, as shown in Example 15.

Example 13

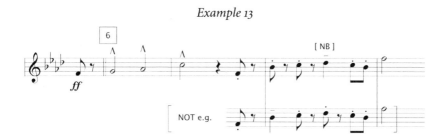

Example 14

(a) The minor segment of Example 11; some further arrangements.

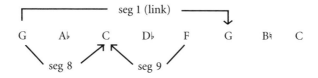

(b) Harmonic interpretation of the minor segment, omitting Gs.

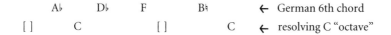

Example 15

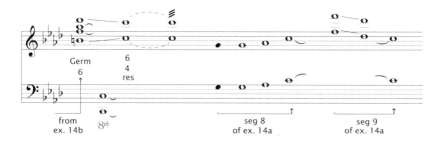

Example 16

Example 16 sketches the "breakthrough" version of Mahler's Paradiso theme. The parenthesized F in the bass along with the indication "quasi $^6_4$?" will be discussed later. There is certainly much happening here that cannot be directly referred to the double-interval cycle we have been exploring. For instance, the eleven-nine-seven harmony over the second G in the bass, and the following Bb-major harmony, interrelate with the Inferno theme transformed into major, as suggested by Example 17. The "quasi $^6_4$" here is suggested by the heavy accents on F in the bass ('celli, bass and three bassoons) under the C of the Inferno melody and again under its high F.

Example 17

Beyond that, in the breakthrough theme of Example 16 one can analyze several indirect references to our double-interval cycle. Example 18, for instance, sketches on the left the bass line for Wagner's Grail theme and then, on the right, the melody for Mahler's breakthrough theme.

Example 18

We have already heard (in Ex. 8) how Wagner's bass line can be related to our cycle, as suggested by the linkage-and-segment-arrows on Example 18. We can now hear how the melody of Mahler's breakthrough theme, after its opening G, retrogrades Wagner's bass line, explicitly projecting the C-link by repeating the melodic C.

Example 19

(a) The cycle-segment of Examples 7 and 9; the right-hand G does not turn back
to F, but breaks out of the G-link (=seg 1), pressing on to B♭ via Mahler's
"breakthrough" segment at "break!"

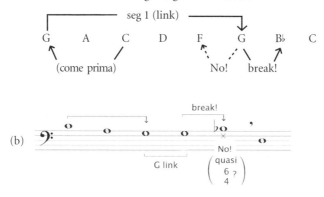

Example 19(a) shows how an extension of our cycle-segment beyond the G-link can give rise to a B♭. The B♭ "breaks through" the linking G, as indicated by the rightmost arrow. The dotted arrow marked "No!" emphasizes that the structure does *not* turn back from the rightmost G to fill in the segment between the two G's. Example 19(b) shows how this idea pertains to the bass of Mahler's breakthrough theme. The F that does not appear in Mahler's bass line is marked by an X on the staff; the B♭, as it were, substitutes for the F. The harmony is, in that reading, marked "quasi $^6_4$?" As such, it resonates with the "quasi $^6_4$" event on Example 17. Were the F in the bass of Example 19(b), the bass-line would project our cycle perfectly, using the G-link.

II. An Ikonic Sonority in the Adagietto of the Fifth Symphony

The term "ikonic," as I am going to define and use it here, raises semiotic questions and problems. But I find the word suggestive nonetheless, possibly influenced by the ways I have heard Ralph Shapey talk about "graven images" in his music. By an ikonic sonority, then, I shall here mean specifically a musical *Ding an sich*, referential as a point of departure and arrival, not necessarily dependent on other sonorities for whatever meaning we sense in it.

In traditional theories of common-practice tonality, such ikonic characteristics are possessed by the tonic triad as an abstraction, or as projected in register and timbre by particular instruments within a composition. But in those theories the tonic has other characteristics as well, beyond the ikonic. In Schenkerian theory, for instance, diminution of the tonic triad projects a special sort of structure, an *Ursatz* that works as a background for both large- and small-scale melodic and harmonic activity within a piece. In fundamental-bass theories, or in Riemannian function-theory, the tonic triad spawns other harmonic triads in its image, giving rise to progressions of triads through a musical passage or piece. In all traditional theories, the behavior of the tonic triad is intimately connected with what we perceive as the establishment and effect of a key.

A musical sonority that works as ikonic, however, need *not* necessarily possess any such tonic-triadic properties. The sonority need only be something particularly marked as referential for our attention, whether by temporal priority or by some other accentual means. Almost certainly the first such ikonic sonority of substantial influence on the European canon is Wagner's Tristan Chord, shown in Example 20(a).

Example 20

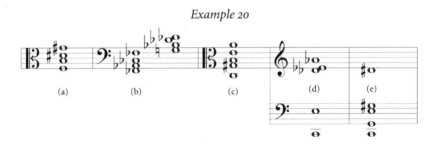

The sonority is marked as ikonic by its frequent recurrence as a point of departure or arrival in a large variety of contexts. Significant too is its temporal priority: it is the first harmony we hear in the music-drama. Examples 20(b) through (e) show other ikonic sonorities in the post-Wagnerian canon. 20(b) symbolizes the opening sonority of the *Augures printaniers* from Stravinsky's *Sacre*. 20(c) symbolizes the opening of Schoenberg's orchestral piece, op. 16, no. 3. 20(d) symbolizes the opening sonority of Act 1, Scene 2 from Berg's *Wozzeck*, and 20(e) the opening sonority of his clarinet piece, op.

5, no. 4. In each case, the ikonic sonority enjoys temporal priority, as the first verticality of its piece or passage.

That is significant, for we have a certain psychological propensity to mark any event that seems to initiate a new chain of events in time as something at least potentially referential. I used to ask my composition students to imagine attending a new play in a traditional fourth-wall proscenium theater, at which the curtain rises upon a chicken in mid-stage, who peers out this way and that at the audience and then struts off stage right. In what ways, I would ask the students, would their sense of what is to come, later in the play, be constrained by the opening? The exercise seemed particularly useful to me because the technical education of musicians in the United States was so heavily biased, at mid-century, by a focus upon cadences and closures—predisposing students to think of the temporal arts as *abbetont*, in Riemann's terminology, at the expense of their *anbetont* aspects.

The sonorities of Example 20 all have a certain atonal character, despite aspects of tertian harmony that our ears today might hear within them. Their atonal character for early-twentieth-century ears is, I think, somewhat in the spirit of my chicken on the proscenium stage: atonality, in the historical context of the early-twentieth century, helps each sonority project an ikonic character as *Ding an sich*. But there is no abstract necessity for an ikonic sonority, as such, to be intrinsically atonal. Indeed I shall assert as ikonic for Mahler's Adagietto a highly consonant sonority which is perfectly consistent with diatonicism and/or traditional tonality. Example 21 symbolizes that sonority.

Example 21

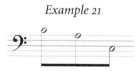

I have written it as a beamed arpeggio, rather than an abstract simultaneity, partly because of the way Mahler presents it at the opening of the piece, and partly because its constituent pitch classes C and A often exercise their influence staggered in time and register, as the piece continues. I shall now examine how the ikon of Example 21 does in fact work its influence over the *Stollen, Stollen, Abgesang* of the Bar form that constitutes the first large section of the movement, mm. 1–38 (rehearsal 2). I shall show that an ikonic mode of hearing, while perfectly consistent with functional tonality and modal diatonicism here, can nevertheless subsist independently of those categories, and in a dialectic relation with them, just as the Tristan Chord can in Wagner's drama.

Example 22

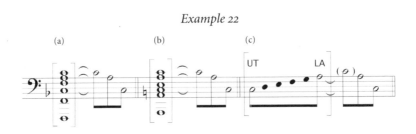

From this point of view, it would be non-ikonic hearing to call the ikonic sonority "5̂ and 3̂ in F major," as if some Platonic F major chord or key had necessarily *preceded* the ikon in Mahler's musical discourse—a phenomenon suggested by the bracketed sonority to the left of Example 22(a). This hearing is non-ikonic, though to be sure plenty of F-major structures will *follow* the ikon, as Mahler's piece progress. In like fashion, it would be non-ikonic hearing to call the ikonic sonority "3̂ and 1̂ in A minor," as if some Platonic A minor chord or key had necessarily *preceded* the ikon in Mahler's discourse—a phenomenon suggested by the bracketed sonority to the left of Example 22(b). This hearing is non-ikonic, though to be sure there will later on be a heavy A minor cadence embedding the ikonic A and C at the end of the second *Stollen* (m. 19, rehearsal 1), long *after* the ikonic opening.

And as regards modal diatonicism, it would be non-ikonic hearing to say that the ikonic sonority "embeds Ut and La of a natural hexachord," as if some Platonic hexachord had necessarily preceded the ikon in Mahler's discourse— a phenomenon suggested by the bracketed sonority to the left of Example 22(c). This hearing is non-ikonic, though to be sure there will shortly follow just such a hexachord, that shapes the opening of the principal theme *after* the ikon has been heard.

Example 23

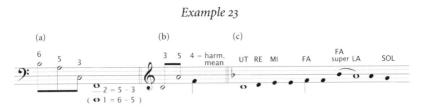

In contrast, the hearings of Example 23 *are* ikonic, since they respect the possibility of hearing the ikon as a *Ding an sich*, not dependent on some categorically *preceding* phenomenon. Example 23(a) hears the note F in the bass of m. 3, and the parenthesized F an octave below that, an implicit ground-bass for the tonality of the piece, as *terzi suoni* in the sense of Tartini, difference-tones acoustically or at least conceptually generated by the ikonic pitches themselves. And Example 23(b) hears the treble-clef F in the melodic register of m. 3 to be generated by an ikonic C and A in the spirit of Zarlino, who analyzes an abstract major sixth as a composite of a perfect fourth below and a major third above, so that tones in proportion 5:3 (like the ikonic upper A and lower C) may admit a harmonic mean that is 4 (like this F).[3] Example 23(c) then shows how the harmonic structure of Example 23(b) can get filled in, in the spirit of Zarlino's Part 3, to produce a natural hexachord for the beginning of the theme in Mahler's piece.

I do not mean to claim that the ikonic hearings of Example 23 are somehow "better" than the non-ikonic hearings of Example 22, or that we somehow "ought" to listen only ikonically to this music. In a similar spirit, I would not myself argue (though I know others who would) that hearing the Tristan Chord as an ikonic *Ding an sich* generating other chords and melodies is somehow "better" than having intuitions of functional tonality as we listen to the opening of the music-drama. But it is significant, for me, that we *can* listen ikonically as well as in other ways, so that a dialectic among modes of hearing becomes operative in our perceptions—in the Mahler piece as in Wagner's drama.

Example 24

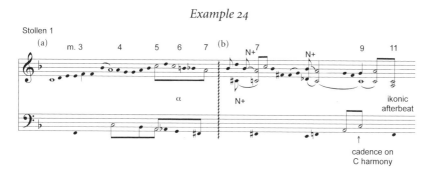

Example 24(a) shows further aspects of the first *Stollen* influenced by the ikon. Events up to m. 4 have already been discussed in that regard. From m. 4 to m. 5, the melody rises to an ikonic high C, while the bass descends ikonically from C to A, so that at m. 5 an ikonic C-over-A sounds in the outer voices. Then the melodic C, inflected by its upper neighbor, descends chromatically through a minor 3rd to ikonic A at m. 7, while the bass A of m. 5 descends in syncopated parallel minor 17^{ths} below, to F♯ at m. 7. The gesture is labeled "alpha" for future reference.

Example 24(b) picks up the narration from there, and carries it to the end of the first *Stollen*. Approaching m. 7, the ikonic C-A verticality is inflected by preceding half-step upper neighbors, labeled "N+" on the example. This event receives poignant acoustic prominence because of the chromatic cross-relation and enharmonic ambiguity involving the C♯.[4] Halfway through m. 8 the double upper neighbors are heard again; the C♯ now works as D♭. Approaching the cadence of the *Stollen* at m. 9, the bass moves ikonically from A up to C. The melody rests on G in m. 9, supporting the cadential moment with a C harmony.

After the cadence of m. 9 the melody of the second *Stollen* begins in the 'celli—not visible on Example 24(b)—over which the violins produce a long ikonic afterbeat for the first *Stollen*, as shown on the example.

Example 25

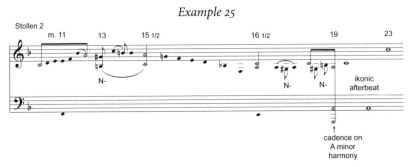

Example 25 shows ikonic aspects of the second *Stollen*. Here the ikon is consistently inflected by its half-step *lower* neighbors, labeled "N-" on the example. This inflection ultimately leads to a full cadence in A minor at m. 19. The second *Stollen* thus cadences on A-minor harmony where the first *Stollen* cadenced on C-major harmony; the large-scale C-A relation, first one, than the other, is arguably ikonic, especially since each cadence is followed by a long ikonic afterbeat.

Example 26

Example 26 focuses on ikonic material in the *Abgesang* of the theme. Measure 26 introduces again the half-step upper-neighbor pair N+; the upper neighbor to C is again spelled as C♯, and in the immediate continuation it works melodically as C♯. Over mm. 27 and 28 we hear the retrograde of the alpha gesture from Example 24(a). Returning our attention to Example 26, halfway through m. 29 we hear the music land heavily on the upper-neighbor dyad; there is now strong support for the prolonged B♭-minor harmony, though it takes a while even now before the strings abandon written C♯ for D♭. The half-step neighbors N+ then resolve, with voice crossing, to the climactic $^6_4$ chord halfway through m. 30—a climactic ikonic dyad.

I should stress once again that I am not offering my ikonic analysis as a *substitute* for a fundamental-bass analysis, or a Schenkerian analysis. The ikonic hearing complements other modes of hearing, in a dialectical manner.[5]

Example 27

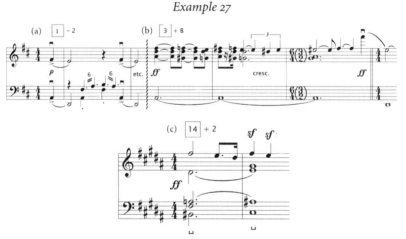

Another example of Mahler's ikonic technique will be instructive, and useful for our later work. Example 27(a) gives the beginning of the theme in the first movement of the Ninth Symphony. The F♯-E gesture works as an ikon here, an ikon which includes the entrance of the F♯ on a *weak* quarter of its measure, but *with a certain accent appropriate to an entrance*—here the downbow marked for the violins, which play here for the first time in the piece.

Example 27(b) shows the ikonic F♯-E filled in with a chromatic passing tone; the F♮ was prepared when we heard the theme in minor some eighteen measures before. Accent on the weak-beat F♯ that opens the example is provided by the first entrance in the symphony of the three trumpets as a choir. The music builds to a big climax at the end of the example, where the theme returns with the downbow high F♯.

Example 27(c) shows the ikonic F♯-E reharmonized in the middle of the movement. There is a cymbal crash, fortissimo, at the barline. The example sets into motion a very extended chromatic turbulence that crests fifteen

measures later, where the music of the example comes back even more force-
fully, with octave and fifteenth doublings above in flute and piccolo, and with
trombone and tuba choir swelling the harmony. The cymbal crash is now
fortississimo, and the bass drum beats fortississimo along with the cymbal
crash. Mahler marks this moment as the climax for the entire movement with
his parenthesized message for the conductor, "(*Höchste Kraft*)."

III. Diatonically Essential Modal Mixture as a Thematic Principle in the Adagio of the Ninth Symphony

For diatonic tonal music, a certain species of chromaticism resides in the use
of secondary leading tones and secondary fourth degrees, the latter generally
harmonized as secondary dominant sevenths or secondary subdominants. I
like to think of this chromaticism as having a melodic ancestry in mutational
Mis and Fas of hexachordal diatonicism. Example 28 shows what I mean.

Example 28

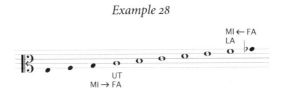

A further species of chromaticism involves modal mixture. Within the
context of a diatonic major or minor mode, this practice introduces chromatic scale degrees that are diatonic within the parallel minor or major mode.

Modal mixture, so defined, can involve a straightforward alternation of
parallel major and minor tonic triads, as at the opening of Schubert's G-ma-
jor Quartet, or Strauss's *Zarathustra*. Without a broader context, one tends
to hear the overall mode as major in this case, for both cultural and acoustic
reasons.[6] I will not call such major/minor alternations of tonic triads "*diatonically essential* modal mixture," because no *melodic* modes are necessarily
involved.

I will also not attach the term, "*diatonically essential* modal mixture," to a
context where a certain phrase in major or minor is followed by an echoing
phrase in the parallel minor or major. The two modes here are not *essentially mixed*; they are rather compared or contrasted, so that the metaphor
of "mixture" is not appropriate. This consideration would apply as well to
echo phrases with some variation, as at the beginning of the last movement
in Schubert's quartet. I shall reserve the term, "diatonically essential modal

mixture," for musical contexts in which the two parallel diatonic modes essentially interpenetrate, the one the other.

In this connection the role of contexts is crucial. To illustrate the point, let us study various contexts within Example 29, which gives pitches and rhythms for the opening of the Adagio in the Ninth Symphony.

Example 29

In the context of mm. 1 and 2 there is no modal mixture whatsoever. The entire context, except for the secondary leading tone at G♮, is diatonic within D♭ minor. If we look at the key signature we may be fooled into thinking that B♭ and C flat are mixture tones in a D♭-major context. But that involves conceptualizing a sonorous context *larger* than mm. 1 and 2 in themselves, where we are listening securely in D♭ minor.

Let us now consider the context of the chords in m. 3 of Example 29, including our response to the entrance of the full string choir here. In this context, there is definitely essential modal mixture. We are likely to hear the major mode governing the three-chord progression, partly because the melodic $\hat{3}$-$\hat{2}$-$\hat{1}$ is in major, partly because the first vertical harmony of the piece, where the complete string choir enters as such, is a major triad, partly because if we hear the B♭ harmony as a mixture event on the sixth degree, we can easily rationalize the chord as signifying a deceptive cadence.

But when we broaden our context to include Example 29 as a whole, things are not so straightforward. The broader context is not arbitrary: it demarcates the descent of the opening melodic gesture in mm. 1 and 2, as far as a melodic cadence on the tonic scale-degree D♭ at the end of Example 29. In this connection, Mahler instructs that the violins are to play on the fourth string throughout mm. 1–3 and following. Now the B♭ harmony at the end of the example is not so chromatic; the harmony is rather quite consistent with the D♭-minor ambience of mm. 1 and 2 in themselves. Listening within the context of Example 29 as a whole, we will find it quite possible to hear the example in D♭ minor throughout, with the G♮ as before, and with only one chromatic mixture tone—namely the F♮ which begins the theme at m. 3, the F♮ where the entire string choir begins to sound.

The mixture sensation is remarkable because the *Gestus* of the F♮ so clearly suggests what later eventuates—that this note is the Schenkerian *Kopfton* for an eventual theme in D♭ major. The character of the *Kopfton* is radically colored by its sounding the unique chromatic mixture tone in the special context of Example 29 as a whole. Major and minor modes are indeed interpenetrating, within yet larger contexts.

Example 30

Example 30 gives pitches and rhythms for the first phrase of the theme proper. The interpenetration of major and minor continues in the second half of m. 3, where the tenor voice of the chorale, with its minor-mode 3̂-2̂-1̂, imitates the soprano from the first half of the measure, with its major-mode 3̂-2̂-1̂. The F♭ of the first cellos thereby evokes the F♭ that "should" have been played by the violins, at the beginning of m. 3, in the minor-mode context of Example 29. As such, the first cellos' F♭ refuses to yield to the F♮ of the second cellos and basses; this gives rise to a pungent harmony that epitomizes the essential interpenetration of minor and major modes. The F♭ over F is not *simply* an appoggiatura to E♭; it is an essential harmony in itself.

At the beginning of m. 4 all harmonies and voices return to the major mode and remain there through the cadence on the last quarter of m. 4. I say "return," having in mind the specific context of mm. 3 and 4, in which the F♮ that begins the theme at the entrance of the string choir has a powerful initiating force, making us feel that the theme, in *this* particular context, begins in the major mode, rather than with mixture in the minor mode.[7]

The final weak-beat harmony of Example 30 prolongs the cadential tonic. The other weak-beat harmonies of the example all inflect the strong-beat harmonies that follow them. The first and last strong-beat harmonies are initiating cadential major tonics. The other strong-beat harmonies on the example are specially annotated. These are the harmonies that carry the interpenetration of modes in the context. B♭ major instead of B♭ minor signifies the pull of D♭ minor, giving us the sixth-degree harmony in that mode. G♭ major instead of G♭ minor signifies a return to D♭ major, giving us the fourth-degree harmony in that mode.[8]

I shall call the B♮ and G♭ harmonies of Example 30 *emblematic*, because they represent thematically the forces of the respective D♭-minor and D♭-major modes here.

Example 31

Example 31 illustrates a hypothetical continuation from the middle of m. 3 to the beginning of m. 4, remaining in D♭ minor throughout. The bass F♮ is now a secondary leading tone, though when F♮ sounds together with F♭ we are reminded that F♮ is not *simply* a leading tone, just as F♭, in the actual music, is not *simply* an appoggiatura. The tenor voice of Example 31 is diatonic within the G♭ minor that is being tonicized, and the soprano voice is diatonic in D♭ minor.

The preceding remark brings sharply to our ears an awareness that the soprano voice of actual mm. 3–4, in Example 30, is diatonic throughout in the D♭-major mode. That highlights even more the emblematic B♮ harmony halfway through m. 3. The mixture harmony carries the *entire* force of the D♭-minor mode in the context of mm. 3 and 4. "In the context" again; in the context of mm. 1–4, the B♮ harmony resonates cognitively with the diatonic minor mode heard in mm. 1 and 2, as discussed earlier in connection with Example 29.

Example 32 sketches the next phrase of the theme. From the D♭ cadence of m. 4, the bass moves down chromatically to B♭. The bass line of the example as a whole thus arpeggiates B♭-minor harmony, harmony on the sixth degree of D♭ major, harmony earlier denied by the emblematic B♮-major of the opening phrase. B♭-minor harmony also appears over the first half of m. 6. The G♭ harmony halfway through m. 5 is the other emblematic harmony of the opening phrase, supporting the D♭-major mode. The note C♭ in the bass of Example 32 is a secondary dominant 7th for the emblematic first-inversion G♭ harmony that follows. Over mm. 5–6, then, the D♭-major mode is asserting itself very

Example 32

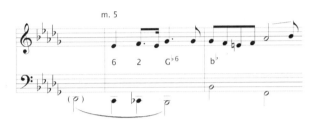

strongly. F♭, the once-powerful minor-mode sixth degree, is here transformed enharmonically into the secondary leading tone E♮ in the turn figure about F♮, all to the greater glory of that 3rd degree in the major mode.

Example 33 sketches in simplified texture the third and fourth phrases of the theme. The sketch articulates three transformational levels for the mixture structure of this music; the levels are labeled (a), (b), and (c). Level (a), reconstructed from the actual music, is a hypothetical Ur-version of the passage in D♭ major throughout, diatonic except for some secondary leading tones. Emblematic harmonies are indicated on the sixth and fourth degrees of the D♭-major mode: B♭-minor on the sixth degree, G♭-major on the fourth.

Level (b) of the example begins, as the diagonal arrow suggests, with the familiar emblematic substitution of B♭♭-major harmony for B♭-minor harmony, thereby representing the sixth degree of the D♭-minor mode. The enharmonic

Example 33

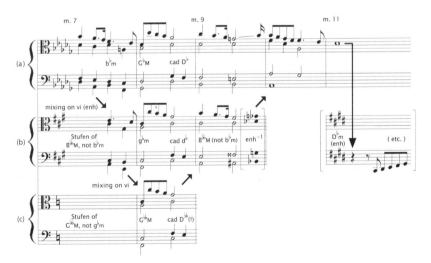

notation, A major and so forth, is for convenience only. Level (b), properly speaking, is diatonic in Db minor, but its signature asserts Bb major as the governing local mode. The reason for this will shortly become clear. Some salient harmonic features are annotated on level (b). At the beginning of m. 8, the Gb-major harmony of level (a), emblematic for the Db-major mode, is denied on level (b) by the Gb-minor harmony there. Halfway through m. 8, the plagal cadence is now in Db minor, rather than Db major. At the beginning of m. 9, the harmony of level (b) clings to Bb major, not Bb minor, re-emphasizing the emblematic mixture harmony.

At the beginning of m. 10, the music of level (b) returns to level (a), rejoining the major-mode Ur-version. Example 33(b) analyzes the pivot harmony for the return, in the last half of m. 9, as the emblematic return-harmony of Gb major, inflected by a G♮ that is derived from the overlying melody of level (a) at that moment. The pivot involves an implicit diminished-seventh chord that appears explicitly on Ur-level (a), where it tonicizes Ab major; on level (b) the diminished-seventh sound, abetted by the tenor voice's motion from Fb to G♮, is heard at first as a tonicization of Cb minor, the second-degree harmony in the context of Bb major. The tonicization of Cb minor is all to the greater glory of the Gb-major root, the emblematic harmonic root that returns us to level (a).

Level (c) is entered from level (b) by mixture on the sixth degree of the mixed sixth degree itself. The harmony of escape from level (b) to level (c) is thus G♮ major, an ironic ficta comment on the overlying Gb major of level (a). Gb major would be the emblematic harmony of *return from level (b)* to level (a); instead, the actual music provides G♮ major as a harmony of *escape from level (b)* to level (c). The plagal cadence at m. 10 of level (c), coming to rest on D♮ major as local tonic, provides an equally bizarre ficta inflection of the Ur-tonic Db major, which overlies it on level (a).

Level (c) returns to level (b) at the beginning of m. 9. A further irony here is that the Bb-major harmony of level (b), familiar as an earlier emblem of *escape to level (b)* from level (a), now is heard as a harmony of *return to level (b)* from level (c).

After the unharmonized cadence tone at the beginning of m. 11, the A section of the ABA' theme is finished. As shown by the downward arrow on Example 33, the bassoon begins a small interlude in Db minor before the B section of the theme.

One should compare the melody of mm. 9–11 in the music with the melody of mm. 2–3, displayed in Example 29. The melody of mm. 2–3 is a model

for the minor-mode approach to a major-mode 3̂-2̂-1̂ and the gesture is repeated in the melody of mm. 9–11.

Our study of Example 33 has sensitized us to the constructive force of
Bᵇ-major harmony, substituting for Bᵇ-minor, as an emblem of entry into the
Dᵇ-minor mode, and also to the force of Gᵇ-major harmony as an emblem of
return to the Dᵇ-major mode. Example 34 reinforces these impressions very
compactly.

Example 34

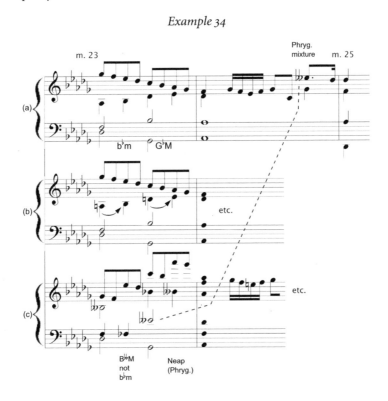

The example sketches the approach to the cadence for the entire ABA'
theme, at the end of the A' section. Level (a) reconstructs an Ur-cadence, diatonic in Dᵇ major through the $^6_4$ chord of m. 24. Bᵇ minor, not Bᵇ major, occurs
on the second quarter; the second half of m. 23 does the first half over again
"in IV," IV being an emblematic harmony here.

Level (b), with its secondary leading tones in m. 23, takes weight away
from the emblematic subdominant harmony and adds weight to the unmixed
sixth-degree harmony. Those secondary leading tones are enharmonically revised at level (c), so as to become mixture tones. The Bᵇ is now a mixture sixth

degree, pointing towards full emblematic B♭-major mixture harmony on the following beat. This harmony emblematically substitutes for the tonicized B♭ minor of level (b). The second half of m. 23 on level (c) does the first half of the measure over again "in IV" (the emblematic *Stufe* of the return); within that *Stufe*, the E♭♭ harmony, "mixture♭VI/IV," gives an emblematic-escape within the emblematic-return of the IV *Stufe*.

The return to major mode finally discharges upon the cadential $^6_4$ harmony of m. 24. The ♭VI-of-IV harmony pivots, becoming a Neapolitan harmony of D♭ major in this connection.

The long dotted line on Example 34 shows that the E♭♭ pitch and harmony in m. 23 prepare and color the E♭♭ in the melodic cadence figure of m. 24. To that extent, we can still hear the E♭♭ of m. 24 as ♭-VI-of-IV, an emblematic-escape within an emblematic-return. To be sure, the note can (also) be analyzed as a "Neapolitan" or "Phrygian" $\hat{2}$-of-D♭. The point is that its appearance in the *local* context of mm. 23–25 is set up by the ♭-$\hat{6}$-of-IV event of m. 23. The association of m. 24 with thematic events of the Scherzo is another matter, not involved in the *local* context under discussion.

On Example 34, the melodic figuration during m. 23 of level (c), as in the actual music, was possibly suggested by Wagner's "War es so schmählich?" theme, from the last scene of *Die Walküre*. More to the point, the rapid climb of the violins here, over all strings from fourth to first, is an effective way to suggest an ultimate ascension to a more ecstatic higher altitude, rising from the prayerful but heavily earth-bound sounds of the fourth strings that characterized melodic activity at the opening of the movement. At the end of the movement—and of the symphony—the violins will be hovering ethereally on the high A♭ and F heard at m. 24 of level (c). Example 35 shows the violin parts for the last eight measures of the symphony.

Example 35

The example makes other associations as well. The rhythm of the second violins as they execute the chromatic turn figure suggests a melodic turn figure that occurred at a different pitch level in the B section of the ABA' theme,

m. 14 of the movement. The pitches and pitch-classes of the chromatic turn around F suggest other occurrences of the figure at that pitch-class level. One instance can be recalled from Example 32, where the E♮ was the first non-diatonic note within the D♭-major melody of the theme proper. Another instance can be recalled from Example 30, where one can follow the pitch classes for a chromatic turn that starts on the melodic F that opens the theme. The pitch-class turn continues with the imitating F♭ halfway through m. 3 in the tenor voice of the chorale, and then goes on to the F♮ in the bass at the end of m. 3, moving from there to the bass G♭ at the beginning of m. 4.

The ambience of Example 35 is especially propitious for associative reflection because all harmonic activity has stopped, and we are left only with evanescent wisps of melody, divested as it were from their harmonic underpinnings. In that connection I can entertain an even more remote pitch-class association, namely with Example 27(b), where the trumpet motif from the first movement turns enharmonically around the same pitch-classes. Thereby I can associate the emblematic notes G♭ and F♭ of the last movement with the ikonic F♯-E of the first movement, despite the radical difference in tonality. Indeed, one might say that in this hearing, the end of the symphony dissolves not only metric pulse and harmonic progression, but also the binding forces of tonality, so that we are left only with the *Sachlichkeit* of the pitches in themselves.

IV. Modernism and the Preceding

What has this study of Mahler to do with modernism? I am not sure, but I think the following review is to the point.

In the finale of the First Symphony, I am struck by the way Mahler, without completely abandoning common-practice harmony, invents new syntactic uses for common-practice vocabulary, adapting it to the formalism at hand, the formalism of the double-interval cycle. Striking in that connection are Mahler's new uses of $^6_4$ chords, of the *double-emploi*, and of the B♭ $^5_3$ breakthrough chord, a $^5_3$ that is used as if it were a derived inversion of the $^6_4$ whose bass-note F belongs in the non-breakthrough pattern of bass intervals.

In the Adagietto of the Fifth Symphony, Mahler's ikonic thinking links his practice with more overtly modernist post-Wagnerian composers, but his ikon is in some respects all the more radical because of its extreme acoustic consonance. For me, this suggests a link as well between Mahler and various post-modernist composers who work ikonically, if less subtly. I think particularly of the early American minimalists—Reich, Riley, Glass, and others. Mahler points the way to a practice where impressions of tonality can grow out of consonant ikonic listening, rather than entering into dialectic tension against ikons more dissonant in themselves.

In the Ninth Symphony Adagio, I am struck by the relentless thematic allegories of Mahler's emblem harmonies, supersaturating the harmonic texture with tokens of escape and return. The saturation can be focused in single chords, like the one at the end of m. 3 that superimposes F♭ in the tenor over F♮ in the bass, or the one at the end of m. 9 that embeds a G♯ inside a first-inversion G♭ harmony: the single chords have definite meanings here, as allegorical vertical structures within the mixture narratives. Those narratives also endow the melodic *Kopfton* F♮ of Mahler's theme with a pungent character as a unique chromatic mixture-tone in one pertinent D♭-minor context. And Mahler's allegories make logical an otherwise well-nigh nonsensical modulation, from a locally cadential D♭-major tonic just before m. 9, to a cadential D♭-major $^6_4$ chord at the beginning of m. 10, only three chords later. Without the allegorical context, imagine giving a student the schema of Example 36 as an exercise in harmonization! And imagine telling the student in that connection that only one chord could be used, for each half of m. 9! The preposterous fantasy shows how far we are here from talking about simple harmonic technique, in following through the logic of allegories for departure and return in Mahler's broad compositional thinking, allegories that motivate the emblematic B♭♭-major harmony at the first question mark of the example, and the emblematic G♭-major harmony, in first inversion with embedded G♯, at the second question mark.

Example 36

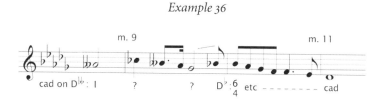

The unremittingly allegorical techniques of diatonically essential mixture hereabouts also enable a highly serialized total chromaticism in the melody of mm. 7–11. Example 37(a) shows the serial aspect of the passage, bracketing the four whole-tone trichords that together project the total chromatic in Webernian fashion.

Example 37

Example 37(b) segments the entire melodic line of the two phrases into beamed spans that project five consecutive ordered forms of the trichords. Segment 4 subsumes segment 1 as a subsegment. Segment 4 is an ordered retrograde-inversion of segment 3, and segment 5 is an ordered pitch-class retrograde-inversion of segment 2. The repeated F of segment 5 cadences the A section of the theme with the same succession of pitches, F-F-Eb-Db, that began the theme in m. 3.

If we find it difficult to make the harmonic practice of Mahler square with the rubric of modernism, I think that is because of the profoundly diatonic basis that underlies so many of his most sophisticated musical conceptions, as indeed all of those studied in this essay. We are accustomed to thinking of diatonicism as a conservative—if not indeed reactionary—trait in an early-twentieth-century Viennese composer's style. Perhaps in our present historical position, we can think of the matter with more sophistication, focusing not so much on stylistic materials in the abstract as on the ways in which they are used to build and project far-reaching compositional trains of thought—as Schoenberg would put it, not Style but Idea.

Notes

1 David Lewin, "A Metrical Problem in Webern's Op. 27," *Music Analysis* 12, no. 3 (1993), 343–354.

2 Catherine Nolan, "Hierarchic Linear Structures in Webern's Twelve-Tone Music," PhD dissertation, Yale University, 1989. Not only does Nolan analyze Webern's piece using the double cycle, she also investigates all abstract interval cycles (mod 12) as such, and all double-interval cycles, which she calls "trichordal cycles."

3 Gioseffo Zarlino, *Le istitutioni harmoniche* (Venice, 1558), 165. Facsimile edition by Broude Brothers (New York, 1965). Part 3, Chapter 20: ". . . dico che lo Essachordo maggiore ha la sua forma dalla proportione . . . tra questi termini radicali 5 & 3 . . . gli estremi della sua proportione possono esser tramezati dal numero Quaternario, in cotal maniera 3.4.5; & lo potremo dire composto della forma della Diatesseron, & della forma del Ditono."

4 The C♯, as spelled, betokens a secondary leading tone inflecting the dominant-of-G-minor, the harmony of A-over-F♯ in m. 7.

5 In a somewhat similar spirit, I do not mean to deny the relevance of other considerations, such as the inter-opus recollection, when the Adagietto begins, of the Lindenbaum episode from the end of the Wayfarer songs. Even if some listeners might be unaware of that recollection, Alma would certainly not have missed it, and very likely Mahler was addressing the reference to her ears. The Lindenbaum episode, however, is preceded by a very extended dominant preparation, unlike the opening of the Adagietto in the symphony. Thereby one hears the beginning of the Lindenbaum a good deal more in the sense of Example 22(a).

   The opening of the Adagietto also recalls in technical ways the opening of Beethoven's first Rasumovsky quartet (op. 59, no. 1), which also begins with a C-A-C verticality, withholding the note F until a melodic *Haupstimme* has entered with C-D-E-F. The emotional or psychological transformation, from the Beethoven piece to the Mahler, seems considerably more obscure.

6 The acoustic reasons are stronger the closer we are to hearing sustained sounds in just intonation, rather than keyboard sounds in equal temperment. This is the case for both the Schubert and the Strauss passages.

7 The way in which locutions such as "return" here depend on the articulations and interrelations of various contexts is a subject of theoretical investigation in my article "Music Theory, Phenomenology, and Modes of Perception," *Music Perception* 3/4 (1986), 327–393.

8 My reference to "sixth-degree" and "fourth-degree" harmonies will indicate that a *Stufen*-theory, rather than a Riemannian function-theory, is pertinent when discussing forthcoming matters. While function-theory can label both G♭-major and G♭-minor harmonies as "subdominants" (rather than "fourth-degree harmonies") in the respective modes of D♭ major and D♭ minor, function-theory will assign the label of *Parallelklang* ("relative harmony") to the B♭-minor harmony

in the key of Db-major, while assigning the different label of *Leittonwechselklang* to the Bbb-major harmony in the key of Db minor. The Riemann labels do not indicate why the one harmony might substitute for the other. Calling both harmonies "sixth-degree harmonies" in keys with the same tonic note does so indicate.

Hermann Erpf's sensitive analysis of this passage on pages 135–136 of *Studien zur Harmonie- und Klangtechnik der neueren Musik* (Wiesbaden: Breitkopf and Härtel, 1969, reprint of 1927/1955), which uses an extended Riemannian function theory, suffers from this problem. The persistence of *Stufen*-theories in Vienna past the time of Riemann is aptly discussed by Robert Wason in *Viennese Harmonic Theory from Albrechtsberger to Schenker and Schoenberg* (Ann Arbor: UMI Research Press, 1985).

Beyond the Bourgeoisie:
Social Democracy and Musical Modernism
in Interwar Austria and Germany[1]

KAREN PAINTER

HISTORIANS OF IDEAS and culture have by now thoroughly documented the impassioned attempts to create a new art incorporating interwar political ambitions in the United States and Europe, above all in the Soviet Union and the Weimar Republic.[2] The decades of Socialist Realism and proletarian culture, particularly in Germany and Austria, with the famously political struggles of the Kroll Opera, have tended to make the history of music in this period appear a struggle between modernist aesthetics and socialist aspirations.[3] The adherents of these respective programs—composers and cultural commentators alike—allegedly contended to fill the vacuum left by what they perceived as the disintegration of bourgeois musical culture. Yet a re-examination of musical life and output, especially one that takes into consideration works lying beyond the modernist canon as it has survived into the present, suggests a far closer relationship between modernism and a Social Democratic agenda than traditionally presented. Such a revised history, moreover, challenges the current, popular battle-cry that new music has abandoned the public.

The debates over socialism and modernism—with Hindemith, Weill, and Eisler on the one side, and the Second Viennese School on the other—were freighted with individual artistic agendas and slogans like "*Gebrauchsmusik*" or "art for art's sake." Such manifestos could not accurately portray compositional aims and listening experiences.[4] To be sure, the Left's political agendas for art in the Austrian and German Republics often differed from the ambitions of composers. But both socialist and modernist proponents started from the belief that bourgeois musical culture had self-destructed and must be replaced by a more expansive and encompassing cooperation between artist and public. This shared conviction entailed many parallel approaches for the production, performance, and reception of music. For what is needed, I will argue, is a broader conception of modernism. We understand the creation of interwar musical culture better if we conceive of modernism less a formalist aesthetics than as a new context of performance. Interwar modernism was not a hermetic commitment and it was intrinsically political not because ideological dogmas were supposed to guide composition, but because it proposed that music (but not "the musical work" with its atavistic connotation of an artist separable from his public) was to be heard in a new context of performance by a reconceived audience. The question remained, however, whether such an engagement could be viable given the pressures of populist dogma on the far Left and far Right. The space for accessible innovation was always threatened, and already by the 1930s was closing.

In the Social Democratic milieus of Vienna and Weimar Germany, modernism entailed a commitment to engaging a proletarian audience. What this listening experience entailed has been all but ignored by music historians, who instead have focused on innovations in genre (Zeitoper, for example), new movements such as the Neue Sachlichkeit, or projects of the kind exemplified by Brecht and his collaborators: all topics that can be easily absorbed into a canonical music history.[5] In fact, there is an abundance of writings, in newspapers and specialized journals, which records the expectations and aspirations that were both attributed to and encouraged from workers. This essay explores how socialism opened up listeners and composers alike to the language of modernism. The majority of composers and performers of new music were at some point involved with the *Arbeitermusikbewegung*—certainly more than traditional history surveys have acknowledged.[6] Socialist ministers or cabinet ministers in Germany and Austria supported a wealth of proletarian choral and musical groups which offered opportunities to young and ambitious musicians. Even established artists had an incentive to work in socialist venues, not least because the reactions of audience and press tended to be positive. Preferring reportage to criticism, populist and workers' newspapers usually sought to capture the mood at an event in enthusiastic terms; the discourses of critique and analysis belonged to a bourgeois intellectual tradition. The battles against modern art were mainly a bourgeois phenomenon.

The very idea of proletarian music depended on a Marxian, universalist aesthetic and, at the same time, a specific responsibility to the class-based communities in which it was produced (or at least performed). Art music subsisted in a class-stratified society but promised a cultural unity, a contradiction that testified both to its achievement and to its limits. Certain genres cut across class lines with little difficulty. The success of music in film—itself an art form which had supposedly originated in the working class[7]—proved the viability and accessibility of contemporary music, even music that was undeniably "modernist" in idiom. Silent film was an excellent venue for contemporary music, insofar as a large audience could experience a novel musical language in a context in which its meaning and coherence were guaranteed; thus, even a score as innovative and challenging as Gottfried Huppertz's for Fritz Lang's *Metropolis* (1926) could achieve popularity. Often, memorable segments of film music were arranged for piano, such as the "machine music" from *Im Anfang war das Wort,* scored by Claus Clauberg, a composer of socialist cabaret and film music. Composers working in cinema also contributed to socialist causes in the concert hall. Edmund Meisel wrote his celebrated score for Sergei Eisenstein's *The Battleship Potemkin* in 1925, the same year his "Red Symphony" was premiered in Neukölln (a proletarian district in Berlin). Upon his premature death, Meisel was eulogized for the "unforgettable, revolutionary music" he had composed for film.[8]

Most of the leading composers and conductors associated with "modern" music became involved, to greater and lesser degrees, with musical institutions that sought an audience and perhaps even a means of music production that extended beyond the bourgeoisie and bourgeois expectations. Musicians born into a working class without traditional music training achieved notable success; the self-taught musician and conductor Hermann Scherchen is a good example. After the Great War, Scherchen adapted Russian revolutionary songs, learned as a prisoner of war, for German workers' choruses, two of which he directed (the Berlin Schubert Chorus and the Mixed Chorus of Greater Berlin). At the same time, Scherchen remained committed to new music. His conducting career began with the Berlin premiere of *Pierrot lunaire,* thereafter presented in a German tour. Scherchen's involvement with the International Society for Contemporary Music, which he helped found, extended to his conducting at many of its festivals, including the premiere of the Three Fragments from *Wozzeck* in Frankfurt in 1924. But the wide range of activities undertaken by Rudolf Réti is perhaps the best instance of the interlocking spheres of socialism and modernism. From the early 1920s through 1934, Réti was a music critic for the *Arbeiter Zeitung* and director of the music department at the Volkshochschule. A composer as well, his works frequently deployed folk materials, some of which were explicitly political. Yet, like Scherchen, he was also a champion of new music, serving as the secretary of Schoenberg's Society for Private Musical Performances (1918–21), co-editor (with Alban Berg and Paul Stefan) of the *Musikblätter des Anbruchs* (1920–28), and founding member and secretary of the Austrian section of the International Society for Contemporary Music.

There were, admittedly, formidable challenges to developing a music that was both artistically advanced and suitable for the working class. One complication arose from the opposed associations that concert music had for the middle classes and the proletariat. For the bourgeoisie, concert music was supposed to elevate and unite individual listeners by means of its universal language; outside the concert hall, amateur music-making counted merely as cultivated entertainment. But for the proletariat, it was concert music that provided entertainment while music-making instead served to elevate individuals and unite them into a single community. The difference was an important one. The process of elevating the community through music thus took place in the concert hall for the bourgeoisie, but wherever amateurs could make music together in the case of the proletariat.

I. Musical Politics

The Crisis of the Bourgeois Musical Public

Forty years ago, Jürgen Habermas singled out the bourgeois reading public as the formative force creating modern civil society.[9] In Central Europe, during the nineteenth century, the musical public played a similar role in establishing a public sphere. By 1918, however, this public no longer possessed the cohesiveness to exert a political as well as aesthetic influence. It seemed quaint to recall, in the pages of the Social Democratic organ *Kunst und Volk*, that Goethe had once sighed in exasperation, "Ah, the public!" In Vienna, the journal continued, the Viennese had long since forgotten that the word "public" was once used in the singular, not the plural. "Every city, every theater, even various seat categories in the same city, have their own, distinctively profiled public"; the artist as well had his own public which "correspond[ed] with his goals and follow[ed] his efforts."[10]

The end of the war, and above all the revolutions in Central Europe, compelled artists to ask what political implications their work had for reconstructing society. Composers and writers on music alike had to come to terms with the sociopolitical transformation in one way or another. Theorists of every stripe felt it necessary to abandon, or at least revise, older notions of an aesthetic sphere that remained above and apart from the constitution of a political community. Even before World War I, any confidence in the bourgeois public as a community of independent "individuals" had flagged. For reasons emanating from both the Left and Right—either by way of a wave of working-class socialism or through the specter of imperialism and nationalism—the idea of "a public" was no longer secure. The public was in danger of appearing—or was, in fact, depending on the perspective—more of a mass subject to its own collective emotions than an aggregation of cultivated individuals. This reconceptualization of the public came on the heels of the transition from the "Liberal" ascendancy in politics in the 1860s and early 1870s to the rise of mass democratic parties, on the one side, and nationalist populist rivalries, on the other—not only in Vienna, but throughout European society. The evolution of "a public," into fragmented, potentially volatile urban populations was a basic premise of social theorists. Right-wing ideologues such as Gustave Le Bon and Vilfredo Pareto offered scathing critiques of mass emotionalism, but Marxists as well depended on and stressed collective organization in advancing the working-class cause. And academic sociologists such as the Liberal Ferdinand Tönnies believed that *Gesellschaft*—a fragmented society versus a cohesive community—was replacing *Gemeinschaft*.[11]

Before World War I, forays beyond absolute music—from Mahler's Eighth Symphony to Strauss's *Sinfonia domestica*—can be seen as a desperate effort to breathe new life into bourgeois genres. But after the War, composers and critics had to recognize that the bourgeois public was no longer a politically relevant audience. German commentators on the Left and the Right reassessed bourgeois cultural premises—about canonical forms, for example, as well as about the belief that music elevated audiences through a dialectic of work and pleasure. The result was either a reaffirmation of bourgeois values in an insistently conservative vein (for example Hans Pfitzner's String Quartet in C♯ minor, op. 36, subsequently recomposed into his Symphony in C♯ minor, op. 36a) or an attempt to forge a new, broader audience conceived as a single community rather than as a group of individuals with similar training and shared moral values.

With music critics, the spectrum of ideologies about musical audience ran from Karl Blessinger's right-wing political sympathies, which would lead him to contribute the first book on music and National Socialism, to the pro-republican Paul Bekker, who became the *bête noire* of conservative nationalists. Both adopted a rhetorical commitment to socialism but remained committed to bourgeois musical traditions. Blessinger's "Musical problems today and their solutions," published in 1919, the first year of the Weimar Republic, appropriates notions similar to Oswald Spengler's proto-fascist ideas of "Prussian socialism," proposed the very same year. Blessinger calls for a "thorough-going renewal" of musical life. "It is high time to turn to our work, and I welcome every co-worker in this project . . . Work—work and construction—is necessary, if thought should become deed." Musical listening, he would have his readers believe, entailed none of the contemplation and reverence experienced by past generations. Rather, it entailed great emotional intensity that shattered the staid atmosphere of the concert hall. Blessinger regretted the "tasteless" architecture of many halls, which interfered with the emotions evoked by the performance; the "uniform, identical rows of seats," for example, had a "most sobering effect" on audiences.[12]

Blessinger's critique of bourgeois values and the call for labor in a nationalist context held no sympathy for the democratic revolutions in Central Europe. He believed that earlier Social Democratic initiatives in art music had failed. Admirable as it was to draw all levels of society together, there was no demonstrable need for art music in the lower classes: "The many attempts to elevate workers spiritually and culturally did not actually find a positive response, which is indeed to be expected." The problem, he continued, extended beyond any particular class: "As is the case among the bourgeoisie, so only a certain percentage among the working classes nurture aspirations for higher cultural meaning. Others are indifferent, or even antagonistic, towards these inclinations." Blessinger was, moreover, concerned that developing an aesthetic sensibility in the masses could risk dangerous consequences by heightening their drive for pleasure. In support, he cited the philosopher Moritz Geiger (1880–1937): "One should ask whether it is phenomenologically defensible to use all means to try to awaken aesthetic pleasure in people and then complain about the growing drive for pleasure among the Volk."[13]

Blessinger also leveled a radical critique at the century of the bourgeoisie and its musical products. The hallmark of musical logic, "so-called 'motivic work,'" had no value of its own. He criticized music of the New German School for the fact that motivic work occurred outside the development section, and he cited an alleged "poverty" of absolute music in Brahms and his generation.[14] The main solution to the "problems" of contemporary musical life was to revive the art and discipline of listening. Blessinger called upon Germans to strive for a more productive experience of music. His central chapter concludes with Goethe's words: "One cannot experience or enjoy, without at the same time becoming productive. This is the innermost trait of human nature."[15] Rejecting the bourgeois notion of *Bildung*, Blessinger condemned a technical understanding of music as useless detail—"the frog's perspective"—and espoused a broader notion of action in lieu of analysis and reflection (an approach resonant with National Socialist ideology).[16]

Paul Bekker was equally critical of initiatives to revive musical culture. He felt that the current socialist aesthetic agenda was a spurious solution to the problem of the audience. The proclamation ("Aufruf von Künstlern und Dichtern") signed by Richard Strauss, the playwright Gerhart Hauptmann, the painter Max Liebermann, and others did not go far enough toward establishing governmental and social roles for music. Bekker was also troubled by the facile adoption of socialist rhetoric, with its assumption that all culture must reflect class division. "The *Volk* needs its poet and artist; it needs all of its workers, including the 'white-collar.'"[17] While advocating a new role for music that would not be mere "luxury," Bekker defended Schoenberg for composing music that was purely "intellectual." We listen to music "in order to perceive a new intellectual web within ourselves," he commented after hearing Schoenberg's Second Quartet. He admired Schoenberg as a composer who "possesses the courage and determination to scorn . . . demands for a merely materialist understanding and to follow solely the idealist impulse to shape the manifestation of music's spiritual fundamentals." Schoenberg's creativity was revealed in his ability to avoid convention and yet "shape the music so strongly" that even skeptical listeners can recognize "the deep, inwardly glowing intensity as well as the coherence and logic of its structure." Music, Bekker continued, should be "an intellectual event of the most extreme tenderness" not "a play of sonorities which babbles according to our ear's conventional laws of beauty."[18] Like Blessinger, Bekker was suspicious of bourgeois musical culture; at the same time, he strongly resisted any class divisions. He hoped for a music that could appeal to bourgeoisie and proletariat alike, although the community he longed for would have to be constituted through art, not politics. Bekker and Blessinger had opposing political commitments, Left and Right, but they shared the common conviction of the postwar moment that art had to speak to and for a new political community, and that the aesthetics of the nineteenth-century liberal bourgeoisie—still privileging pleasure over labor—were inadequate for the harsh demands of the twentieth century.

Socialism and New Music

Around the turn of the century, initiatives to extend art music beyond the bourgeoisie were intended to integrate or control the working class rather than to help them define a separate identity. Concert series and performing groups offered the same repertoire to workers, but at lower prices. A "Volks-squartet für classische Musik" was founded in Vienna in 1890 and hailed as entirely consistent "with the democratic tendencies of our time."[19] The underlying goal of its founder, August Duesberg, however, was to divert "the discontented and the revolutionary-minded from dark thoughts" into a musical culture that would provide "a safeguard from their own soul."[20] The Viennese Workers Symphony Concerts, founded in 1905, boasted access to "the largest and most beautiful concert hall of Vienna" (the large hall of the Musikverein), a venue which, while offering workers an opportunity to hear a symphony in its entirety (rather than in isolated movements), largely replicated the musical offerings of other series.[21]

After the War, writers and organizers not only saw the value of bringing serious music to the proletariat, they suggested that the revolutionary working class must have a special vocation for modern works. Artistic planning became more ambitious, and the Workers Symphony Concerts not only continued, but aspired to nurture a socialist culture for the new Republic. Paradoxically, the new enhanced agenda followed in part because of the very limits of Socialist power. As early as 1919 the Social Democratic Party of Austria found itself stalemated in a great coalition with the conservative Christian Socialists on the national level, but they still controlled the city and Land of Vienna. Within the metropolis they shifted their attention from such issues as socializing heavy industry to making Vienna into an incubator for working-class culture. The great housing projects of the period were the most noted and famous institutional expression of this aspiration, but in general working-class culture became the chosen terrain for projects of transformation. The working class was designated as both subject and object of this program: the collective actor that could bring about a Social Democratic culture, and the population that would be transformed through new, clean, collective apartments communally arranged or through new music meant both for enjoyment and for edification. The very project of workers' music had become more earnest than, for example, the idea of a proletarian production of *La Traviata*—a proposal of the aesthetics professor and music critic Richard Wallaschek, who would later be scoffed at by a colleague dismissing him as "dry, and amusingly learned."[22]

To be sure, the Social Democratic party had organized cultural initiatives before the First World War. The tireless David Josef Bach had devoted continuing effort to the Social Democratic Center for the Arts (*Kunststelle*) and remained convinced that the working class was a responsive audience for serious modern music. Bach boasted of the workers' enthusiasm for *Verklärte*

Nacht (but at a time, 1922, when the music was no longer representative of the composer's modernist idiom). "The unthinkable has happened. We have performed Arnold Schoenberg, none other than the hated Arnold Schoenberg, and his *Verklärte Nacht* has enjoyed a greater success than the work has had practically anywhere else. . . . We want to remain true to ourselves, and true to the revolutionary duty."[23] In fact, the workers' appetite for modern music *was* limited, the lack of interest, when acknowledged, was blamed on social conditions. Paul A. Pisk, Schoenberg's student and the secretary of his Society for Private Musical Performances as well as a composer whose music and writings reflect a deep commitment to a socialist aesthetic, lamented that as a result of increased class conflict, new music could no longer unify the people to the extent that Mahler's had. Music in everyday life—in the cinema, dance halls, taverns, and other sites of entertainment—did not allow workers to develop the creativity necessary to grasp "another level" in music. Pisk still hoped, writing in 1925, that in the future there would be attempts to create "a new music that can truly express the feelings of the proletariat."[24]

The idea that embracing musical modernism might bring about social change initially came from politicians and art historians. In 1921, the Social Democrat Oskar Pollak proposed that revolution in art was the harbinger of political revolution: art, more than anything else, "senses the future."[25] But it would remain for Hans Tietze, in a 1926 article on "Socialism and Modern Art," to emphasize that political revolution had always coincided with artistic revolution. Tietze did not, however, see any role for art criticism in the production and reception of a modernist aesthetics: judging quality should occur only later. All that mattered for the moment was that the critic communicate the "general vitality" of music and its "revolutionary meaning."[26] Such an unreflective approval of modernism as a source of political as well as aesthetic vitality came close to the anti-intellectualism that would inform Goebbels' rationale for prohibiting arts criticism after 1936.

Musicians, in turn, argued that modern music was necessary for political progress. In an article titled "Can the Worker Have a Relationship to Contemporary Music?" Pisk explained that the lack of musical education among workers had the advantage that "modern" music was no less accessible to them than classical music was. Establishing an awareness of contemporary music was essential to forming a new *Weltanschauung*, Pisk argued.[27] David Josef Bach often addressed the practical difficulties of performing new music, implying that such difficulties were the main hindrance to establishing an appreciative audience. He urged the programming of new and lesser-known works, despite the need for extra rehearsal time—not to mention the time "to create a public." Bach went so far as to suggest that programming Beethoven had a financial exigency. "With few rehearsals or even without rehearsals, it is certainly cheap, financially, to play Beethoven. . . But it is also morally cheap to perform Beethoven." Anticipating the attention Beethoven would receive in the composer's 1927 centennial celebrations, Bach insisted that the proletariat has "the possibility and the right to be addressed by new art."[28] Similar slogans calling for new music were occasioned in 1930 by the annual commemoration of the March 1848 revolution in the Viennese Workers Symphony Concerts, since the program included less new music than in the previous season. Bach did not concede, or even believe, that "modern" music was less suitable to a proletarian audience; he explained that it merely required more study. The example he gave, Hanns Eisler's new choral music, was telling, for Eisler had recently quarreled with Schoenberg over the need for accessibility in modern music.[29]

Forging a tie between new music and the working class took on fresh urgency in the period of the world economic crisis. In 1929, the *Sozialistische Kulturbund*, a Social Democratic umbrella organization, established a prize to encourage the composition of orchestral music suitable for workers' concerts. The jury consisted of leading musical figures—Hindemith, Scherchen, and the musicologists Alfred Einstein and Georg Schünemann.[30] Novel compositional techniques and media were enthusiastically reported in the pages of the Social Democratic *Kunst und Volk*. Frank Warschauer's writing on electronic music is a good example of this innovative journalism.[31]

The most ambitious linking of contemporary music and socialist reform was proposed by Pisk in an article on "new" music for the "new" generation. It was not coincidental, he argued, that "important modern composers" were Social Democrats who, in turn, were more receptive to new music and in fact claimed to share a "will" towards a "new musical culture." This culture, I would suggest, encompassed listening habits as well as modes of composition. At the century's start, Pisk recalled, youth had become disenchanted with Wagner and Brahms, whose *Weltanschauung* was outdated. Now, however, the composer became allied with the artist and worker in an attempt at liberation from the past (their shared "revolutionary will") and in an orientation to the future. Audiences, Pisk presumed, were open to those artists whose work seemed relevant, however modern its language: "The *Volk* will gladly welcome in its ranks anyone who has something to say to it and above all artists, who speak to its soul." Intellectual constraints did not matter, because "music is an art of emotions and of the soul." Pisk reported that already there were workers who "love" modern music and who believe it speaks to them; whether as performers or listeners, they were "involved" with modern music. His purpose was not to document a new phenomenon (no evidence or individuals were cited) but to encourage a receptivity, in spirit if not in deed. The working class should retain "a lively hope in artists." He therefore warned composers that modern music was at a crossroads: it could become either an "occult science" or "pathbreaking in the new artistic feeling" that would arise in connection with the *Volk*. He proclaimed, "The red flags of socialism wave for musicians as well. If we follow them, the path to a new musical culture will not have as many thorns. We want to follow!"[32]

Establishing a proletarian audience served the art form as well, even beyond any particular political benefits. Bach explained that art is dangerous when it merely "satisfies" the listener through a "dream"—it is cheap to laugh or cry, to be noble or brave. Instead, the artist must be the mouthpiece of society, expressing what "society thinks and feels at the deepest level." Repeated listening, as well as a degree of reflection (*Betrachtung*), would allow the listener to understand how an artist and his milieu belong together.[33]

The Viennese Workers Symphony Concerts, in their novel programming, gradually acclimatized proletarian audiences to the demands of contemporary music. Initially, new music was heard only when conductors programmed their own works, and presumably the personal connection helped make the music more accessible.[34] Moreover, the selection was suitable to a musically untrained audience. The first new music performed, in January 1918, was a program of excerpts from Julius Bittner's operetta *Du lieber Augustine: Szenen aus dem Leben eines wienerischen Talents*, premiered at the Volksoper the preceding summer; the program was conducted by the composer and had Emilie Bittner as soloist. Julius Bittner would have had additional appeal to proletarian audiences. As an examplar of amateur music-making, largely self-trained, he composed in his spare time, working as a lawyer and judge until his mid-forties (1922), when he gave up the legal profession for music.[35]

The second inclusion of new music, again a concert conducted by the composer, was carefully programmed with an eye toward accessibility. Karl Prohaska's Serenade, op. 20, for small orchestra, was grouped with canonic and appealing works employing much larger forces (Beethoven's first *Leonore* overture, Mendelssohn's Violin Concerto, and Schumann's Overture, Scherzo and Finale). Prohaska was a beloved teacher, well-known to the audiences of the Workers Symphony Concerts through several appearances as keyboard soloist.

The third instance of programming a composer as conductor was Oskar Fried, renowned for his interpretation of contemporary music. He programmed his *Erntelied* (Harvest Song) with Mahler's Second Symphony (although Mahler had urged him not to pair anything with the symphony). Fried, as a self-made professional musician, was a good model for the working classes; his training had been "on the job" rather than at conservatory. After years of the Workers Symphony Concerts programming isolated examples of contemporary music, in 1920, Bach, founder and impresario of the series, made public a plan that each concert should include one new or little known work.[36] It would take some time to realize his ambition.

In four of its five last seasons, 1929–34, the Viennese Workers Symphony Concerts each featured at least one contemporary work. Even works-in-progress were presented; for example, a program of excerpts from Prohaska's opera project on the French Revolution, *Madeleine Guimard,* with a libretto by the celebrated Socialist Lily Braun.[37] There had been a gradual but clear increase in the programming of new music. By 1923–25, a significant number of programs included contemporary music, and by 1925–28, half of the programs each year did so. During his two seasons as principal conductor of the concert series, Webern resisted the usual practice of programming new music that was political in nature. The only exceptions were for the annual March 1848 commemoration. In 1925, the concert featured Beethoven, Brahms, Weber, and Mendelssohn, but concluded with Webern's own orchestration of Liszt's "Workers' Chorus." The fact that Webern was a "bold" composer of "modern music" mattered to a proletarian audience—or so the *Arbeiter Zeitung* believed should be the case, in reporting that one of the most joyous evenings of the 1925–26 season was to experience "devotion and profound emotion" at Webern conducting. It is not hard to see the political significance in the critic's pleasure at how Webern exposed the many hidden inner "little voices in the music."[38]

By the end of the 1920s, the programming of political music and new music was a tradition at the Viennese Workers Symphony Concerts. In 1930, Webern opened the program with a political work by the Berlin composer and critic Heinz Tiessen, *Vorspiel zu einem Revolutionsdrama* (1926); the concert continued with a series of canonic works, songs by Schubert and Wolf (with Paul Pisk accompanying), Reger's Requiem and Beethoven's "Eroica." By contrast, at the 1929 March celebration held at the railroad workers' union in Simmering, Maria Gutmann conducted an entire program devoted to political works (including Russian folk songs, a choice that would have been interpreted as ideological, given the connection to the Soviet Union and communism). The following season, Webern declined to conduct a political work by Rudolf Réti, *Aufruf an die Armee der Künstler*, arguing that the music was difficult for his chorus and that they would not agree to sing it.[39] It was a flimsy excuse, however, as the work had been sung by two workers' choruses the previous year, in the same concert series. Moreover, the program included the Viennese premiere of both Webern's own orchestration of Schubert's *Deutsche Tänze* (D. 820) and Milhaud's Violin Concerto—both fairly demanding works.

Did Webern focus on the standard repertoire out of practical exigency, as a young conductor who could not yet secure international appearances or high-profile European performances? Conducting the Viennese Workers Symphony Concerts allowed Webern to develop his repertory as well as build a reputation through the ample press coverage the series received. He did, however, conduct new music in other venues. The conservatism in the Viennese Workers Symphony Concerts, notwithstanding their programming of recent music, perhaps stemmed from an underlying ambivalence about political music. Was Webern perhaps unable to share the optimism of the Social Democratic music theorists that the working class had a particular vocation for radical experimentation in music? These concerts—and the new politicized constituency for modernism in general—favored music of bolder gestures and regularized musical vocabulary rather than the taut, exquisite craftsmanship and intensity of timbre which Webern (who had, most likely, been parodied as the intellectual and melancholic composer Max in Krenek's *Jonny spielt auf*) was exploring in his own compositions. Webern's hesitation about the repertory of the Workers Symphony suggested that the claims of proletarian aptitude for modernism might be premature. They also foreshadowed the precariousness of the Viennese experiment in cultural politics as a whole. In 1934, the Social Democrats would stage an insurrection against the authoritarian encroachments of a rightwing-dominated Republic; they would go down in defeat as their housing blocks were shelled and captured. Cultural politics had not been a strong enough fulcrum on which to base social or political revolution. The search for a modernist artistic mission had reflected that weakness indirectly, but sought to compensate for it. The working-class revolution had been stalemated since 1919–20, all the more reason to claim the working class's revolution for art must remain triumphant. But here, too, as Webern perhaps understood, there were reasons to doubt. For a decade and a half, modernism was linked to the ideal of a democratized and aesthetically-sensitive public: revolutionary as a class and encouraging the most experimental art. Then that public was suppressed. The question remains whether it would ever have sustained the most rigorous experimentation of the era. But given the unremitting hostility of the reactionary forces that prevailed, perhaps the question is moot.

II. Modernism in Theory and Practice

THE LIBERATION OF PITCH AND THE AESTHETICS OF RHYTHM

What implications for musical composition and performance might follow from a re-conceived and democratic public? Musicians, critics, and theorists on both the Left and the Right agreed that emphasizing rhythm was the most promising way to build a unified musical community—and the repertoire that developed in the interwar years proved them correct. In his book on "work and rhythm," first published in 1896, the social historian Karl Bücher lamented that rhythm had become irrelevant in German culture and society. He maintained that its power to "excite pleasurable feelings" would both alleviate the stultification of labor and produce art universally accessible to audiences. A culture steeped in art forms that emphasized rhythm would, Bücher believed, reconcile physicality with intellectual and spiritual life. Bücher's tract continued to appear in expanded editions over the next decades, with sections added on the work songs of various nationalities, cultures, and employment (pilot songs, trucker songs, etc.). A 1930/31 volume on socialism and music reprinted its discussion of rhythm as an "economic principle of development."[40]

In the interwar years, rhythm and motion became critical to practitioners and theoreticians of disparate aesthetic and ideological orientation. The young academic Gustav Becking drew on the research of his teacher, Hugo Riemann, in developing a practical approach to musical analysis and listening. Becking believed that a composer's distinctive musical style could be determined through his rhythmic writing. His *Habilitation*, later published as *Der musikalische Rhythmus als Erkenntnisquelle*, proposed that music is best experienced by beating one's head or arm in the air.[41] During these same years, the composer Carl Orff and dance instructor Dorthée Gunther founded a school and pedagogical method based on percussion-based music and movement, later marketed to the Hitler youth; their method remains in use to this day. At the other end of the ideological spectrum, Ernst Kurth developed a philosophical and analytical system which conceived of music as motion (*Welle*, or wave, was the governing concept), under the rubric of a book on Bruckner's symphonies. Whether populist or philosophical, a conceptualization of music as rhythm served to intensify the listening experience, with the goal that the art form was not mere entertainment or a status symbol but instead was a profound transformative act.

Rhythm became a metaphor for the vitality and energy of art, life, and human consciousness. The rhythm of typing could be coordinated with re-cordings of popular dances, as Helga Weigel proposed, to enhance the work-er's energy and dispel any nervousness.[42] Various contributions to *Kunst und Volk* show a fascination with rhythm, even in the atemporal arts. An article devoted to "rhythm in the visual arts" relied on developments in science (the new quantum theory of wave mechanics advanced in the mid-1920s) and philosophical principles (mostly specious) in order to advance the conception of matter as substance "built of vibrating centers of energy." Now that time was a fourth dimension, "all of the world's activity [was] rhythm." Music was the art form closest to nature, because its vitality derived from rhythm. This amounted to a radical revision of classical aesthetics based on *mimesis*, that "art holds up the mirror to nature." (The notion of matter "built of vibrating centers of energy" no longer seems so far-fetched, in view of the develop-ment of string theory in subatomic physics.) The connection between sound and image came naturally to the author, Richard Harlfinger, an illustrator of music books. Harlfinger insisted that rhythm is both time and space, citing the example of ocean waves, which are perceived by the eyes as if the ears heard the "rhythmic beating" of the surf. This generalized sense of rhythm was to open up his readers to new developments in the visual arts; modern painting, it was claimed, could no longer adhere to realism ("cold and pho-tographic") but should be "infused by the warm heartbeat of the artist." An artist uses "free, creative energy" to perfect the imperfections in the world.[43] Experiencing rhythm was seen as crucial to productivity and satisfaction in the workplace.

The same aesthetic was applied to other performance arts, in particular film, such as Hans Richter's avant-garde film *Rhythmus* (1921), which in turn influenced Mies van der Rohe's glass houses. The film and theater critic Fritz Rosenfeld argued that rhythm is "the secret of every work of art, and the core of theater." For Rosenfeld, not only did every play have its own rhythm, but every performance as well. He defines music as that which "connects the events through rhythm."[44] The writer Erich Kästner took occasion to criti-cize such philosophizing in the very same journal, *Kunst und Volk*. The lines "Everything is rhythm / Rhythm is everything / Soul is a feeling for rhythm / Intellect is rhythm in feeling," by the poet and novelist Hermann R. Bartel, struck Kästner as an example of a prevalent "diarrhea of feeling."[45]

The supreme example of this emerging practice of aestheticization through rhythm was a new genre, *Sprachchor* ("speaking chorus"), in which rhythm transformed the sound of the masses into music.[46] Two hundred peo-ple might, in one instance, read aloud the same poem simultaneously. Groups dedicated to this genre were founded in Germany, Belgium, and Austria. Maria Gutmann, who was a writer as well as a conductor of such choruses, offered the following allegory for the invention of *Sprachchor*:

> The masses crowd on the streets. They demand. Individual voices
> are loud, but the space encompasses them. First there are a hundred,
> then a thousand, then it is *all*. The masses cry out: unconstrained
> by rules, without order, incomprehensible. *One* will—but then one
> word hits another, splits the masses into individual calls. Suddenly
> a rhythm connects all voices into one chorus; suddenly the disor-
> der of individuals calls becomes an organized, vocal expression. The
> *will* of the masses has won.

Gutmann heralded *Sprachchor* as the epitome of socialist art. "Nowhere is there a clearer organic development of a hot vitalism (*Lebensgefühls*) into a coherent form of expression, into an art work." Modern youth, Gutmann claimed, were "not satisfied with being a public," for they wished to express their feelings: in essence, to represent themselves. "People who want to struggle together, play together, and to shape their lives together, have a deep need to give back this communal living in an art work." The mass chorus did not exist merely to recite but actually to "embody" the art work. Music became motion. "Today it is not only the human voice but also the entire body that is a means for artistic expression. It would be wrong to have the organism of the living body imitate the rhythmic exactitude of a machine. The danger of such a mechanization of the mass choruses is that it becomes rigid and is no longer able to shape and make live and new *every* poem."[47]

The importance of rhythm in new music, according to the young musicologist Hans Engel, writing in 1930, derived from the inspiration of the machine. In an article on the "rhythm of time," he scorned as "primitive" the idea of seeking jazz and popular dance rhythms in "new music" (a term he placed in quotations)—he compared it to looking for waltz rhythms in Schumann and Wagner. But he welcomed the use of machine rhythms in new music, citing an inner connection between man and machine. Engel saw the machine as inspiration in Hindemith and Stravinsky, along with the explicit representations of machines in Honegger's *Pacific 231*, Weill's *Der Lindbergflug*, and Max Brand's *Machinist Hopkins*.[48]

Rhythm, more than any other parameter of music, symbolized political action. Tiessen's *Vorspiel zu einem Revolutionsdrama* opens with a solo bass drum; the high point of the battle is again represented in the percussion alone, and the final climax recalls the rhythm from the opening. The aesthetic consequence of such prominence in rhythm was to undermine the hegemony of a pitch-based musical system. So too in Orff's choral settings of Brecht from 1930–31, which deployed a percussion ensemble and three pianos; in one setting, 700 intellectuals worship an oil tank. Although these are stylistically very similar to *Carmina burana*, composed five years later during the Third Reich, Orff would deny any connection to his earlier political and artistic ties to communism and the Left.

SCHOENBERG AND THE SECOND VIENNESE SCHOOL

Although the Second Viennese School was not to produce a music for the masses, the realization that the bourgeois concert audience had given way to new publics prodded innovation in revealing ways. It is worthwhile asking more insistent questions about the music itself and not just the musical public in this period. Did the commitment to a radically democratized public and context for music not lead to any consequences for the composers most associated with interwar modernism, Schoenberg, Berg, and Webern? Was rhythm to remain the only parameter that could be reworked for the sake of the new audience?

The emphasis on rhythm before 1945 tended to bring a simplification and a regularization of pulse and any further divisions—unlike the emancipation of timbre, which entailed a highly complex configuration of "orchestral polyphony" (to use Strauss's term and Mahler's concept). Certainly a simplicity of meter and palpable sense of momentum were unattractive to Schoenberg, Webern, and, to some degree, Berg in the interwar years. Rather they pressed ahead with their challenges to pitch-dominated structures. Remarkably, given the demands on audiences unfamiliar with their musical language, they believed that experimentation might help to link the most uncompromising innovation and the expectations of a working-class audience. Indirectly at least, the awareness of socialist aspirations and the atmosphere of sociopolitical change could encourage artistic experimentation—just as the Russian revolution prodded painters and architects to develop such abstract modes as constructivism.

The fact that the political ideals of Webern and of Schoenberg, in particular, were far from those of the Left should not deflect attempts to assess their compositions in a sociopolitical context. In the case of Schoenberg, the composer's own conservative impulses were often contrary to Social Democratic ideals. Any Austrian patriotism also remained secondary to hopes for eventual unification with Germany; throughout the 1920s many on the Austrian Social

Democratic Left also retained hope for the union of the two new republics. But what was important for a composer's trajectory during this period was less any agreement or dissent from particular political measures; it was the continuing sense that Vienna and Austria were laboratories for modernity and that he was participating in an ongoing drama of cultural innovation.

Reinhold Brinkmann has observed that Schoenberg's break from tonality involved a conscious experimentation in scoring types and genres of increasing complexity, from Lied to solo piano (Three Piano Pieces, op. 11), to orchestra (Five Orchestra Pieces, op. 16), and finally to opera (*Erwartung*).[49] Schoenberg followed a similar path, I will suggest, in his attempts to build a broader audience base beginning in 1925—perhaps an unconscious reaction to the opportunities provided by the apparent stability of Social Democracy in Vienna. First, as if rejecting the possibility that he himself was compromising the rigor of his compositional aesthetic, Schoenberg poked fun at neo-classical composers in his Three Satires, opus 28, late in 1925. In December, Schoenberg was taken by surprise at the public acclaim of *Wozzeck*, with its proletarian themes brilliantly executed through a full array of traditional forms, translated into a modernist idiom that was both lush and brash. The very next month, Schoenberg, probably both envious of and inspired by his student's success, began to cycle through the various performing forces associated with an elite public, in each case making his compositional language more accessible and eliminating complexity in counterpoint and sonority. The different genres included chamber music (the Suite for Piano, Three Winds, and Three Strings, op. 29), orchestral music (Orchestra Variations, op. 31), opera (*Von heute auf morgen*, op. 32), and solo piano (Piano Piece, op. 33a).

It is often said that while correcting proofs for *Von heute auf morgen*, Schoenberg began work on the Piano Piece, op. 33a. However, it is also true, and perhaps more significant, that he took up this curious piano work in the midst of setting old German folk tunes. Scholars have wondered why Schoenberg would publish a piano composition as the first part of an opus long before composing the remaining component. (There is no proof, in surviving sketches, that Schoenberg had even planned the second piano piece by 1929, when he published the first.) In fact, he turned to Opus 33a three days after completing two of the three settings for chorus (the third, "Es gingen zwei Gespielen gut," which demanded extensive sketches, would only be completed sometime over the next three months). While relatively simple, these settings nevertheless involved four-part writing. It was only after beginning work on the Piano Piece that Schoenberg achieved his most extreme simplicity, in arranging the four German folk songs for voice and piano. The final arrangement of "Es gingen zwei Gespielen gut"—Schoenberg's pride and joy, which would always be presented first when the various groupings of folk songs were published—was being finished in the same month Schoenberg composed the first of the Six Pieces for men's chorus, op. 35. His acute interest in self-presentation, I would suggest, led him to ensure that Universal would publish his Opus 33a, with its abstract, elite vocabulary, the very same year, 1929, that the folk songs were to be premiered in a workers' concert. The piano work would then be seen as not an individual piece but part of a larger opus, and therefore more central to the composer's activities.

Given Schoenberg's antagonism towards socialism, it is not surprising that he wished to deflect attention away from his own contribution to the movement. The ten-month interruption in his compositions for men's chorus—in itself unusual for Schoenberg—saw another deliberate act of self-promotion. This time, Schoenberg did not set elite and popular genres in opposition, but made a radical statement against the musical form with the greatest possible audience: film music. He audaciously composed a work for an imaginary film and thereby asserted his complete independence from and maybe even subtle contempt for an audience in this growing industry of musical composition. The same month he completed the *Begleitungsmusik zu einer Lichtspielszene*, he completed the remaining four choral pieces commissioned for performance by workers. Schoenberg's concern with his public image extended beyond compositional practices. In one letter to Pisk (from the very same year his Bach arrangement and folk songs were presented on a Workers Symphony Concert) Schoenberg resisted being seen as a supporter of Social Democracy.[50]

Schoenberg received the commission for the folk song arrangements in April 1928, and while he does not seem to have completed any before December of that year, as early as May he wrote Karl Lütge (who had arranged for the commission and sent him the folk songs) to complain about the songs assigned to him. Two had "no noteworthy melodic traits," and one was "downright trivial." The one song he had found interesting, "Es gingen zwei Gespielen gut," would not yield a suitable setting, "since it is so hard, like Bach."[51] The reference to Bach is not surprising; that same month, Schoenberg began work on his orchestration of Bach's Prelude and Fugue in E♭ major, BWV 552. Schoenberg emphasized a connection to Bach through programming, including his Bach arrangements in a special Viennese Workers Symphony Concert on November 10, 1929. Bach, the quintessential German composer, was a peculiar choice to celebrate the founding of the Austrian republic, but also a revealing one in view of Schoenberg's wish for a grossdeutsch unification that would combine Austrian as well as German territories in a single state. More specifically, it suggests an emphatic elitism, designed to offset the effect of his German folk songs heard, on the same program, following Brahms's "Beherzigung." "Es gingen zwei Gespielen gut" was probably the final song completed in both of the groups—that for voice and piano, and that for unaccompanied mixed chorus. But Schoenberg probably also had begun work on the song first; he took pains with the canons in the chorus, devoting the most sketches to its fourth strophe, which contains two reverse canons.

Schoenberg had good reason to be concerned about how his works would fare in the workers' musical movement. The composer himself, and biographers in his wake, have minimized his early connection to socialism and his conducting of workers' choral societies, but there is growing evidence to suggest a strong involvement.[52] David Josef Bach continued to cite Schoenberg's sympathy and involvement. In 1905, a time when the integration of workers into bourgeois musical tradition was prized, Bach reported in the *Arbeiter Zeitung* about Schoenberg: "what made him proud was that he could teach a small workers' chorus—if I remember correctly, that of the metal workers in Stockerau—some Brahms choruses." (In this same article, which followed a performance of *Verklärte Nacht*, Bach portrayed Schoenberg as a "self-made man in all regards" and whose works were so complex that the composer himself could not play them on the piano. Schoenberg must not have been pleased to read, in the same article, that he "had learned nothing at all from books" or that a "self-righteous music teacher" did not believe Schoenberg "could have composed his quartet himself.")[53] The article did nothing to foster the reputation of the young Schoenberg who, since returning to Vienna in the summer of 1903, still had no regular employment and had seen few performances of his music, and certainly none by any elite musical institutions. Moreover, the society Schoenberg and Zemlinsky founded in Vienna, the Vereinigung schaffender Tonkünstler, had been dissolved a few months before Bach's review in the worker's press, despite its ambitious programming of large works. A quarter-century later, when Schoenberg held one of the highest musical posts in the German academic community, he would have been troubled to see the proletarian press still claiming that he not only "has a lively interest in our movement" but that this interest extended back to his youth, when he reputedly conducted five Viennese workers' choral organizations.[54]

Schoenberg's case demonstrates that proponents of modernism could participate in the working-class musical milieu even without personally supporting its political agenda. Aesthetic and political aspirations need not be aligned. Schoenberg's ambivalence between populist accessibility and the demands of modernism is most acute in his arrangement of "Es gingen zwei Gespielen gut." The character of political, proletarian choral music is avoided in all regards. There is no strong rhythmic pulse, nor any segmentation into clear phrasing—in fact, the phrasing of the original folk melody is blurred over. The bass is as active a line as the other three voices, offering little grounding in harmony or rhythm. Variation form is itself unusual for a choral setting, and Schoenberg's execution particularly so. Already the statement of the theme (stanza 1) has a complex texture in the three voices, which complicates the idea of its merely "accompanying" the folk melody in the soprano. The second stanza (the first variation) has more profile than the first: the folk melody, now in the tenor, is stretched into a syncopated structure. The strong profile is set off against the momentum of the other lines, which ascend in scalar eight-note patterns (initially canonically). This contrapuntal clarity, however, soon dissolves. The beginning of the third stanza is completely absorbed into the ongoing musical process, rather than marking a structural break. The melodic line, back in the soprano, is ornamented and commands less attention. It is preceded by three staggered entrances, each different, the third of which is an inversion of the melody. After the initial sketch, Schoenberg gave the soprano a dramatic climax at m. 24; the inner voices move in parallel sixths. The final cadence is prepared in the alto and bass, which is the first point where the eighth-note pulse ceases. The remaining stanzas, particularly the fourth, are rigidly structured and required more sketches than the rest of the setting. The final stanza brings closure through a slower tempo and a supreme sense of order: a single canon throughout. This was the only one of the folk songs that Schoenberg set three times, yet it remained impractical and ill-suited to its task. As the story goes, there was insufficient rehearsal time for it to be included in the premiere of the three folk songs in the Viennese Workers Symphony Concerts. But Webern left the song out of the subsequent performance a month later and again when he recorded the songs, a year and a half later.[55]

Schoenberg's ambivalence with respect to his Social Democracy and a wide audience in the years 1928–30 is nowhere found in Webern. In 1923, Webern became chorus master of the Singverein of the Kunststelle and, in 1927 and 1928, of the Viennese Workers Symphony Concerts, affiliations which he retained until the two organizations were dissolved. Despite his involvement with socialist music-making, Webern's output, at least in terms of genre and compositional aesthetics, was more distanced from proletarian music than Berg's and Schoenberg's. Schoenberg would newly compose his workers' choruses (and use his own texts), while Webern's, again, were but an orchestration of Liszt. Webern's only other foray into a populist genre was orchestrating

Schubert dances, D. 820, premiered in a Viennese Workers Symphony Concert in November 1931. Nonetheless, for all the trappings of tradition in genre and scoring, Webern's modernist idiom does resonate with socialist aesthetics. The radical brevity of expression has often been interpreted as a reaction to the expansiveness of Romantic music, but socialist musical culture, in its programming as well as its compositional styles, may have been a more direct source. (In this context, Schoenberg's famous observation that Webern's Bagatelles, op. 9, offer "a novel in a single gesture," published in the preface to the score,[56] may read in another sense, as more than a purely aesthetic judgment, with its allusion to the most bourgeois of literary genres imparting an elite stature to his student.) Webern's turn away from thematic development can also be seen as a rejection of bourgeois criteria for musical logic and edification. His compositional principles of symmetry and canon suggest a fascination with constructing an object in exquisite dimensions, an extreme craftsmanship with attention to detail and a relationship between form and function—the very same values promulgated during the two preceding decades by such artistic reform circles as the German Werkbund or the Austrian Sezession.[57] The idea of design theory for a mass culture, typified by the Werkbund, offers a useful model for serialism in general, because while expertise in music theory was valued and deemed necessary for the construction of the work, it was not essential for the listener's appreciation.

It was not lost on the proletarian press that modernism provided new ways of listening, free from convention and training. In his review of Webern's String Trio, op. 20, for the *Arbeiter Zeitung*, Paul Pisk mentioned only in passing that the work is twelve-tone. What mattered was that the music "releases for the listener a very remarkable row of timbral stimulation." For Pisk, it was easier to grasp the "character" of a composition than to follow a "melodic line." The listener could obviously enjoy the performance—the flageolet, pizzicato, playing on the bridge of the instrument are qualities he singled out—even when it was not possible to hear the wide intervals as a coherent melody. Pisk even avoided stating that musical training enhanced the listening experience, and conceded only that careful study of the score was necessary for "a clear impression of the form and art work." Pisk did regret that this "individualizing music" failed to resonate with a large public, but he attributed its lack of popularity to the fact that chamber music, by its very nature, could not address a large audience. If written for a large ensemble, however, even the most radical twelve-tone music could move the working class. Social Democracy was prepared to appropriate the most demanding aesthetic innovations, and there was no reason for the avant-garde to turn its back on the mass audience.

Socialist Aspirations and Modernist Aesthetics

"The revolution in listening, unleashed by Beethoven, has found its culmination in Arnold Schoenberg," the young conductor Jascha Horenstein pronounced in a German proletarian singers' magazine.[58] It was not surprising to see Beethoven cited as a precursor to artistic and political developments, especially in reviews which, like Horenstein's, appeared in the aftermath of the centennial in March 1927, when the composer was appropriated by a range of political parties.[59] Horenstein did not explain how Schoenberg revolutionized musical listening in his discussion of the choral music, or why this was relevant to the working class, but his terms are provocative. Did Schoenberg, like Beethoven, compel the listener to perceive a new form as shaped by the thematic material, rather than recognize an existing, conventional form?

In reconstructing the relationship of modernist aesthetics to socialism, it makes sense to speak in terms of the goals of listeners and composers, rather than a codified set of aesthetic principles, such as thematic invention, formal clarity, or the unity of form and content. In an article on proletarian musical culture, Julius Bittner made the plea that training someone to listen was more important than training him or her to play an instrument.[60] The gamut of styles and genres presented to proletarian audiences or composed for them, from Eisler's mass songs to Schoenberg's choral music, was too large to support generalizations about collective aesthetic identity.

It is difficult to establish direct influence for socialist ideology on compositional practice, despite exceptions like Hanns Eisler, who aspired to a universal musical style that drew on proletarian genres and presumed styles. In view of the overlapping spheres of activity of so many musicians and social activists, it is reasonable to ask what parallels exist between socialist music and modernist music. Given the intensity of the activity and idealism, we should expect that the socialist embrace of music and its ensuing presence in cultural politics had a profound effect on how music was heard and what impact it had outside the concert hall.

Theodor Adorno, to cite the most notable theorist of music's social responsibility, all but ignores reception on the part of the audience or public.[61] One of the most notable innovations emerging from the alleged confrontation between modernism and socialism was an attention by critics to the historic moment in which working-class members of society might be released from their need to be only laborers and instead become interpreters of, and thereby participants in, musical exchange. Despite the rhetoric of denigrating the musical public, to which composers and writers from Schoenberg to Adorno and beyond have repeatedly fallen prey, a definition of modernism

should have included, at least as one defining condition, the idea of an audience that was decisively reconstituted from more than a bourgeois collection
of individuals. Socialism and modernism could and did meet briefly in a new
evaluation of the audience and of listening. The dream of socialist art, which
since 1989 admittedly seems hopelessly utopian (if not a dangerous prelude
to Stalinist conformity), was, in fact, not a vision about the socialist artist. It
was a belief about the role of art for an idealized public, one that might be
sufficiently liberated from material scarcity and sufficiently grounded in the
traditions of culture that it could play an active role in encouraging even the
·most radical amendments to that tradition. The ideal audience would mediate between the traditions of art that it had thoroughly assimilated and those
gifted individuals who might decisively renew them, even to the point of rupture. In that way the ideal public, conceived by Viennese Social Democracy,
was itself to be the very oxygen for modernism and not its adversary. We need
not judge here whether such a hope was irremediably naive, but in an era
when it seems to have become so totally remote we should at least recover its
inherent premises and promise.[62]

Understanding differences in concert preparation is one way of evaluat-
ing the new audience of modernism; musical training was essential for the
bourgeoisie, while public participation was valued by the proletariat. While
studying the score or playing an arrangement at home encouraged reflection
and analytic listening, political music-making promoted a common, public
experience of intensity and momentum. The songs and music for socialist
rallies emphasized effect (*Wirkung*) over lyricism, unity, and other abstract
criteria. In such a culture, aesthetic traditions of the nineteenth century and
earlier were irrelevant. Concerns over the relationship between form and
content and demands for balance and symmetry were deemed useless abstractions. Clarity and vitality became paramount. The proletarian composer
would be praised for directness and clarity in melodic writing and simplicity
in harmonic language—in short, music evaluated according to an aesthetic
of effect. The father of Austrian socialist music, Josef Scheu, saw the purpose
of workers' songs as expressing the "thoughts, feelings, and elevated ideas,
for which we live and die." Well before the artistic and intellectual current
of vitalism influenced musical aesthetics in general, Scheu emphasized that
"effect" and "energy" made for truthful expression in "liberation songs" and
"work songs."[63] The Hungarian composer and political activist Béla Reinitz
won admiration because, according to Scheu, his music "goes for the direct
effect, and suffuses the listener, without allowing him to relax. It intentionally produces a mass effect and turns decisively to the emotions and to the

ears, without any consideration for ears accustomed to musically delectable bites."[64] In Réti's *Aufruf an die Armee der Künstler*, for example, artists are "soldiers of the revolution marching to the barricades of the spirit." The review in the *Arbeiter Zeitung* spoke of the music's powerful effect on the workers audience. Noting the allusions to Mahler, the reviewer admired the "striking march rhythms and melodies."[65]

For all the obvious differences between socialist and modernist music, such as an emphasis on accessibility rather than on rigor and construction, the parallels and cross-influences are more revealing. Despite the difference in the value placed on immediacy, high modernism, like socialism, was based on a functionalist aesthetic. Ideas were stated or alluded to, but rarely developed with any sense of ornamentation or elaboration. The avoidance of repetition and harmonic rhythm meant that immediate perception was more important than synthesis and goal-oriented listening. Function was prioritized over any presentational quality, in which material did not in itself signify anything, but merely served as preparation (closure, or other structural boundaries). The brevity characteristic of much serial music seemed to imply a value on action, not reflection. Despite the common polemics against modern music as "abstract," the idea of "absolute music," which apotheosized abstraction, was a legacy of bourgeois musical culture but not, in theory or in practice, a burden felt by the musical avant-garde. In socialist music, as in modernist compositions, the hermeneutic process itself was usually surprisingly simple, complicated though the language of modernism was. A relationship to genre was often attenuated in modern music and did not exist in most socialist music. In the latter venue, a composition was either wholly transparent in what it communicated (that is, through a text or programmatic title), or it was presented as pure music, yet free of any intimations of the absolute.

In socialist art music, as with modernism in general, there was a suspicion of genre as a means of communication. Workers' programs were constituted overwhelmingly of vocal works and program music—works in which a text or hermeneutic paradigm prevails over any features inherited from genre and convention. The only traditional genre for new music in workers programs was the concerto, which for the very same reason—its historical freedom from tradition—remained important for modernist composers throughout the century. The sense of music-making as a craft and skill was most evident in the soloist, whose virtuosity promised excitement and "effect." In some venues, genre was rejected altogether as a means of communication. The program for a workers' concert might list "Solo for violin" and the performer's name, without any reference to a composer. In one instance—meetings of the German Communist party and German Communist Youths in 1924—the program opened with an entry "Music," and again after the intermission, listing only the performer, a violin virtuoso.[66] Genre was problematic because it interfered with the direct engagement of the listener, so important to socialist writers. As David Josef Bach put it, music should be *experienced*, not *contemplated*. Reading about music would not give the worker access to the art form.[67] This did not, however, mean abandoning the intellectual appreciation of music altogether. The composer Paul Josef Frankl contributed an article on "musical comprehension" to *Kunst und Volk*, in which he argued that an audience's enthusiasm in the concert hall merely confirms the superficiality of the "capitalist concert business." A true musical understanding requires "the unification of emotion with reason."[68] And the journal itself perpetuated the idea of music as edification by publishing program notes for the Workers Symphony Orchestra Concerts prior to the event itself.

In the bourgeois aesthetic of subjectivity, moral progress required intentionality. To be moved or transported was a self-conscious aspiration. Socialist music, on the other hand, was in itself an expression of solidarity and liberation; in structure or content, it required no similar process of self-transformation, redemption, or purification. Emancipation from bourgeois culture meant dissolving the link between pleasure and moral inspiration. By contrast, socialist music, like much modernist music, did not require—or permit—emotional identification from the listener. A composition could be tender, irate, or passionate, but the musical unfolding did not therefore entail self-identification with the emotional state. Protagonists like Pierrot or Wozzeck could be profoundly moving, but the art work did not encourage self-projection because the characterization and circumstances were so very specific. Identification with the composition's emotional or narrative current meant, at some level, a self-validation through art, an act for which there was no place in socialist culture. Instead, music would provide a feeling of solidarity based on a group association. In this sense the musical agenda of the 1920s paralleled the efforts of Brecht and Erwin Piscator in contemporary Berlin to create an "epic theater" that rejected what they felt was a spurious emotional identification of audience and characters.

By the end of the 1920s Social Democratic cultural attitudes moved even further from inherited bourgeois aesthetic conventions and toward musical values that permitted more of a rapprochement with modernist endeavors. There was a turn against program music, in part because it allowed for a passive, comfortable experience of art, in which an audience might become absorbed in a topic that had no overt political significance. The jury for a composition prize established by the *Sozialistische Kulturbund* to encourage orchestral music for the workers spoke out against "mere program music."[69] David Josef Bach in turn warned about the dangers of an escapist art, where a particular social class finds it "more comfortable to be in the theater than outside the theater." Operetta epitomized music that satisfied a dream-wish rather than served the political function of "serious art."[70] In the Social Democratic press, there were also attempts to justify abstraction in art[71]—the correlative in music being atonality.

The most compelling parallel between socialist experiments and modernist aesthetics was a focus on a single parameter, whether pitch or timbre, rhythm or register, without claims of integration into a single economy. The *Sprachchor* served as more than a political symbol representing the people on stage. The designated role of a speaker in much socialist music put speech in the forefront of the performance. It was therefore unlike, for example, the spoken dialogue in a Singspiel, which replicated dialogue or human interaction, presumably in realistic manner. In Tiessen's *Aufmarsch* (1931), the performing forces included mixed chorus and speaker, with an accompanying wind band. Works for spoken choruses allegedly opened up the listener to experiencing music as rhythm and sound, not melody. As with atonal music, the listener had fewer points of reference and so focused more on the nonmelodic facets of music—rhythm, counterpoint, thematic ideas, timbre. By contrast, to name one example, early reviewers of Mahler's Sixth show horror at the prominence of percussion in the finale, as if the pitch-dominated economy of music had collapsed into disorderly noise.

There remained, of course, a danger in a musical language that abandoned balance and integration, but instead appealed through its immediacy. Such art risked political exploitation, or at least losing its idealistic ambitions; one example is Edmund Nick. His emphatically modern *Leben in dieser Zeit*, with a text by Erich Kästner and a jazz orchestra accompanying soloists and chorus, was performed in a Viennese Workers Symphony Concert in 1931. Whereas Kästner would find himself condemned as a degenerate author, Nick became a popular composer of songs and musicals in the Third Reich.

The speaking chorus often had a political role, proclaiming a text with a particular message. Some such instances are Ottmar Gerster's *Das Lied vom Arbeitsmann* (1929) and *Wir!* (1932), composed to a text by Hendrik de Man (a cousin of Paul de Man), a socialist whose emphasis on the psychological irrationality of the working classes would carry him toward fascism by the mid-1930s and eventually to collaboration with Belgium's German occupiers. Nor was film music immune to this transformation from socialist aspirations to Nazi ambitions. Walter Ruttmann, who wrote so enthusiastically in the *Kunst und Volk* in 1929 about the potential for a wide audience through sound film—responding to a commission to make a film entitled *Symphony of the Earth*, which would explore the visual "rhythm" of the world—would join forces only four years later with Leni Riefenstal on the screenplay for *Triumph of the Will*, which Hitler commissioned to record the 1934 Nazi party convention in Nuremberg.

These developments in musical expression revealed a fundamental dilemma of the German and the Austrian socialists. As Thomas Mann recognized in 1930—when in the pages of *Kunst und Volk* he called on the progressive bourgeoisie to support the Social Democrats—their policies protected the German "intellectual legacy," including its precious musical heritage.[72] Yet as their Communist rivals pointed out, this old commitment to bourgeois culture also seemed to condemn the party to stagnation between Left and Right. Could, however, artistic as well as political innovations open up to a more dynamic style—including the stress on rhythm and massed speaking voices—without accepting the collectivist attitudes, communist or fascist, that threatened its own destruction?

One means of protecting against collectivist policies that sought to suppress the individual, rather than elevate him or empower him by assimilation into a larger community, was the artistic celebration of diversity and independence. Many new political forms of artistic expression—speaking choruses, movement choruses, *Agitproptruppen*—privileged the moment through a collection of segments. Montage came to have more authenticity than claims of total unity. The working-class experience contributed decisively to what became the modernist legacy: music of the moment, divorced from ahistoricist claims; an audience from whom participation, not contemplation, was demanded; a value on rhythm rather than tonality; the breakdown of the hermetically-sealed musical experience and an opening up to theater, drama, and mass politics. This politics proved more unpredictable than its early Viennese proponents, such as Bach, had ever envisaged. Conceived as a project for emancipation and cultural enrichment, working-class music helped to expose the whole spectrum of a political art no longer securely contained in familiar bourgeois concepts. But if such music could foster these enlightened ends, it was also capable of mobilizing the crudest kind of collectivism. In its own modest but decisive way, Viennese working-class musical experience after World War I helped to foreclose any simple relapse of music into tradition or unambiguous rationality.

POSTSCRIPT: SOCIALISM, FASCISM, AND THE AMBIGUITIES OF
MODERNISM

It is well known that the receptivity to modernism was greatest in urban
centers, where bourgeois liberalism was allegedly so vulnerable. The Social
Democratic experiment in Vienna, increasingly beleaguered after the rise of
Austrian fascism, ended with the armed clashes of February 12, 1934, much as
Social Democracy—and, to a large extent, artistic modernism as well—had
met defeat in Germany a year earlier. Many of the protagonists of the socialist and the modernist agenda fled into exile immediately, or within a brief
period. The premise of their shared program—faith in an enlightened audience, which, even without the bourgeois legacy of artistic training, might become critical participants in an aesthetic awakening—was largely disavowed.
But with the rise of a new political order, the particular elements of socialist
and avant-garde aesthetics—whether in architecture, drama, or music—had
the potential to be exploited for very different ends. Fascism, paradoxically,
claimed the mantle of modernism alongside its more archaic yearnings. Some
ideological commentators—and writers on music—were prepared to make
the transition. Erstwhile socialists, like Hendrik de Man, proved willing to ac-
commodate the new politics of fascism and came to see the masses as moved
by dark and irrational psychological impulses, to be controlled rather than
empowered.[73] The idea of speech as music, so crucial to the spoken chorus,
was transferred to the massive Nazi rallies, where speech after speech provided the sonic program to which lights, flags, and military maneuvers were
choreographed. The stage was set for the politicization of rhythm.

The fascist appropriation of stylistic elements that had earlier served a
Social Democratic agenda is not, however, sufficient reason to reject such
experimentation outright. The individual components remain ideologically
ambiguous, just as the elements of a political or economic program—public
works, provision of leisure-time activity, organization of labor unions—might
serve fascist, democratic, or Social Democratic programs. Ultimately, I would
suggest, it is the political message of an aesthetic statement or development,
not its particular formal resources, that determines its political meaning.

Of course, there were dangers in identifying an aesthetic program with
any collectivist ideological program—socialist, democratic, communist or
fascist. The history of the 1930s and indeed of the next half-century amply
illustrates the political appropriation that might follow. There were aesthetic perils as well: banality and kitsch might easily derail any effort to inspire
a mass audience, as the cruder products of Eisler, Copland, or Orff testify.

Nonetheless, even repressive regimes could permit some significant art, precarious though the effort might remain. And for better or worse, few artists choose to create without any reference to wider social or political conditions (witness the many artistic, and pseudo-artistic, responses to 9/11). Ultimately, the history of aesthetic developments is a history not just of successive innovations in artistic production, but also of the evolving image of the intended public. Who will be reading, viewing, or listening? Who will be inhabiting the planned housing community or city?[74] And not only what individual, but what community will be reading, viewing, residing, or listening? The artist's posing of that question has served as an impulse to modernism and innovation as much as his explorations of medium and technique; and those artists at work in the Central European metropolises of the early-twentieth century, before and after the First World War, allowed no evasion of the question.

Notes

1   I am grateful to Joseph H. Auner, Robert Koelzer, and Charles S. Maier for their comments on this essay.

2   See, for example, Carol J. Oja, *Making Music Modern: New York in the 1920s* (New York: Oxford University Press, 2000); Neil Edmunds, *The Soviet Proletarian Music Movement* (Oxford and New York: Peter Lang, 2000); and Bryan Gilliam, ed. *Music and Performance During the Weimar Republic* (Cambridge: Cambridge University Press, 1994).

3   On the politics of the Kroll Opera, see John Rockwell, "Idealism and Innocence: The Failure of Opera Reform in the Late Weimar Republic," in a forthcoming volume edited by Thomas Crow and Karen Painter, for the Issues & Debates series at the Getty Research Institute.

4   See in particular the charges made in Joseph H. Auner, "Schoenberg and His Public in 1930: The Six Pieces for Male Chorus, Op. 35," *Schoenberg and His World,* ed. Walter Frisch (Princeton: Princeton University Press, 1999), 85–125. Schoenberg's fascination with the idea of a broader public, around 1930, should be understood as part of a larger rapprochement of socialism and modernism.

5   Ironically, the wealth of scholarship on the workers' musical movement has adopted the methodology of a bourgeois collector, gathering sources without subjecting them to scrutiny or according them any aesthetic status. The most useful among these collections are Werner Fuhr, *Proletarische Musik in Deutschland 1928–1933* (Göppingen: Alfred Kümmerle, 1977); Reinhard Kannonier, *Zwischen Beethoven und Eisler. Zur Arbeitermusikbewegung in Österreich* (Vienna: Europa, 1981); Inge Lammel, *Arbeitermusikkultur in Deutschland, 1844–1945* (Leipzig: VEB Deutscher Verlag für Musik, 1984).

6   See, for example, the treatment of the interwar period in Robert P. Morgan, *Twentieth-Century Music. A History of Musical Style in Modern Europe and America* (New York and London: W. W. Norton, 1991), 151–324, which discusses only Hindemith's *Gebrauchsmusik* (220–29).

7   Grete Ushely argued that movie houses were thronged by proletarian audiences long before the intelligensia became interested in the medium. See her "Film als Volkskunst," *Kunst und Volk: Mitteilungen des Vereines Sozialdemokratische Kunststelle* 3, no. 6 (February 1929), 173.

8   *Arbeiter illustrierte Zeitung 48*, 1930; reproduced in Lammel, *Arbeitermusik-kultur*, 195.

9   Jürgen Habermas, *Strukturwandel der Öffentlichkeit: Untersuchungen zu einer Kategorie der bürgerlichen Gesellschaft* (Neuwied am Rhein: H. Luchterhand, 1962).

10 Theodor Haas, "Julius Bittner," *Kunst und Volk: Mitteilungen des Vereines Sozialdemokratische Kunststelle* 4, no. 5 (January 1930), 138–39. The Goethe quotation can be found in *Conversations of Goethe with Johann Peter Eckermann*, trans. John Oxenford, ed. J.K. Moorhead; intro. Havelock Ellis. (New York: Da Capo Press, 1998), 21, entry of 10 Nov. 1823.

11 Ferdinand Tönnies, *Gemeinschaft und Gesellschaft: Abhandlung des Communismus und des Socialismus als empirischer Culturformen* (Leipzig: Fues, 1887, trans. José Harris and Margaret Hollis as *Community and Civil Society*, ed. José Harris (Cambridge and New York: Cambridge University Press, 2001).

12 Karl Blessinger, *Die musikalischen Probleme der Gegenwart und ihre Lösung* (Stuttgart: Benno Filser, 1919), iv, 55–56.

13 Blessinger, *Probleme der Gegenwart*, iv, 96; quoting from Moritz Geiger. "Beiträge zur Phänomenologie des ästhetischen Genusses," *Jahrbuch für Philosophie und phänomenologische Forschung* 1, no. 2 (1913), 567–84.

14 Blessinger, *Probleme der Gegenwart*, 36.

15 The quotation is from Goethe's "Über den sogenannten Dilettantismus. Oder die practische Liebhaberey in den Künsten," *Propyläen* 1, no. 1–2; 2 no. 1 (1799). Published as part of Paralipomena. Vorarbeiten und Bruchstücke, in *Goethes Werke. Weimarer Ausgabe* I, 47 (Weimar: H. Böhlau, 1887–).

16 Blessinger, *Probleme der Gegenwart*, 82.

17 Paul Bekker, "Der Geistige Arbeiter" (1918), *Kritische Zeitbilder,* Gesammelten Schriften, 1 (Stuttgart and Berlin: Deutsche Verlags-Anstalt, 1921), 211.

18 Paul Bekker, "Neue Kammermusik. Deutsche Erstaufführung von Schönbergs fis-moll-Quartett in Frankfurt," *Frankfurter Zeitung*, 30 December 1918; from the Arnold Schönberg Center, Vienna.

19 From Theodor Helm's concert report from Vienna, *Musikalisches Wochenblatt* 22 (1891), 121; quoted from Margaret Notley, "*Volksconcerte* in Vienna and Late Nineteenth-Century Ideology," *Journal of the American Musicological Society* 50, no. 2–3 (1997), 443.

20 August Duesberg, *Ueber Hebung der Volksmusik in Hinsicht auf das "Erste Wiener Volksquartett für classische Musik"* (Vienna: Lesk und Schwidernoch, 1892), 23; quoted from Notley, "*Volksconcerte* in Vienna," 444.

21 *Arbeiter Zeitung*, Vienna, 12 December 1905; quoted from Johann Wilhelm Seidl, *Musik und Austromarxismus: zur Musikrezeption der österreichischen Arbeiterbewegung im späten Kaiserreich und in der Ersten Republik* (Vienna, Cologne, and Graz: H. Böhlau, 1989), 121. David Josef Bach, "Fünfunzwanzig Jahre Arbeiter-Sinfonier-Konzert," *Kunst und Volk: Mitteilungen des Vereines Sozialdemokratische Kunststelle* 4, no.2 (October 1929), 41.

22 Richard Specht, "Mahlers Feinde," *Musikblätter des Anbruch* 2, no. 7–8 (April 1920): 284.

23 David Josef Bach, *Arbeiter Zeitung*, 14 November 1922; quoted in Seidl, *Musik und Austromarxismus*, 151.

24 Paul A. Pisk, "Zur Soziologie der Musik," *Der Kampf. Sozialdemokratische Monatsschrift* 18, no. 5 (May 1925), 186–87.

25 Oskar Pollak, "Sturm und Drang von heute," *Der Kampf* 14, no.2/3 (February 1921), 88.

26 Hans Tietze, "Sozialismus und moderne Kunst," *Der Kampf* 19, no.12 (December 1926), 548.

27 Paul A. Pisk, "Kann der Arbeiter ein inneres Verhältnis zur zeitgenössischen Musik finden?" *Kunst und Volk: Mitteilungen des Vereines Sozialdemokratische Kunststelle* 2, no. 2 (February 1927), 5.

28 David Josef Bach, "Wie feiern wir Beethoven," *Kunst und Volk: Mitteilungen des Vereines Sozialdemokratische Kunststelle* 1, no. 7 (August 1926), 6–7.

29 David Josef Bach, "Märzfeiern," *Kunst und Volk: Mitteilungen des Vereines Sozialdemokratische Kunststelle* 4, no. 7 (March 1930), 228.

30 Werner Fuhr, *Proletarische Musik in Deutschland, 1928–1933* (Göppingen: Alfred Kümmerle, 1977), 115.

31 Frank Warschauer, "Klangzaubereien elektrischer Musikerzeugung," *Kunst und Volk: Mitteilungen des Vereines Sozialdemokratische Kunststelle* 4, no. 4 (December 1929), 115–19.

32 Paul A. Pisk, "Neue Musik dem neuen Menschen," *Kunst und Volk: Mitteilungen des Vereines Sozialdemokratische Kunststelle* 4, no. 1 (September 1929), 8.

33 David Josef Bach, "Sozialismus und Kunst," *Kunst und Volk: Mitteilungen des Vereines Sozialdemokratische Kunststelle* 5, no. 5 (July 1931), 92.

34 David Josef Bach, "Rechenschaftsbericht für 1928," *Kunst und Volk: Mitteilungen des Vereines Sozialdemokratische Kunststelle* 3, no. 10 (June 1929), 283.

35 Bittner also published in *Kunst und Volk*, making a plea for support of the school of the Verein für volkstümliche Musikpflege.

36 David Josef Bach, *Arbeiter Zeitung*, 10 November 1920; quoted in Seidl, *Musik und Austromarxismus*, 145.

37 Lily Braun, *Die Liebesbriefe der Marquise Madeleine Guimard. Eine lyrische Oper in drei Akten* (Berlin, Grunewald: H. Klemm, 1923).

38 *Arbeiter Zeitung*, 21 April 1926; quoted from Seidl, *Musik und Austromarxismus*, 159.

39 Kathryn Bailey, *The Life of Webern* (Cambridge: Cambridge University Press, 1998), 139–40.

40 Karl Bücher, "Der Rhythmus als ökonomisches Entwicklungsprinzip," *Arbeit und Rhythmus* (Leipzig: Teubner, 1896), excerpted in *Musik und Gesellschaft. Arbeitsblätter für soziale Musikpflege und Musikpolitik*, ed. Fritz Jöde and Hans Boettcher (1930/31), rpt. ed. Dorothea Kolland (West Berlin: Das europäische Buch, 1978), 44–46.

41 Gustav Becking, *Der musikalische Rhythmus als Erkenntnisquelle* (Habilitationschrift, University of Erlangen, 1922; Augsburg: B. Filser, 1928).

42 Helga Weigel, "Musikalisher Rhythmus als Mittel der Leistungssteigerung bei der Schreibmaschinenarbeit," *Musik und Gesellschaft*, 60–61.

43 Richard Harlfinger, "Der Rhythmus in der bildende Kunst," *Kunst und Volk: Mitteilungen des Vereines Sozialdemokratische Kunststelle* 1, no. 3 (April 1926), 8. Harlfinger illustrated *Unsere Lieder: Singbuch für Österreichs Wandervögel*, which appeared in editions in 1912, 1918, and 1923, as well as an edition of farmer's music for two violins or mandolin and guitar (1925). He also illustrated a book of Austrian fairytales in 1936.

44 Fritz Rosenfeld, "Das Theater Tairoffs," *Kunst und Volk: Mitteilungen des Vereines Sozialdemokratische Kunststelle* 4, no. 8 (April 1930), 247.

45 "Alles ist Rhythmus / Rhythmus ist alles/ Seele, ist Gefühl für Rhythmus / Geist, ist Rhythmus im Gefühl." Quoted in Erich Kästner, "Diarrhoe des Gefühls," *Kunst und Volk: Mitteilungen des Vereines Sozialdemokratische Kunststelle* 5, no. 3 (January 1931), 62, 64–65. Hermann R. Bartel published a collection of poetry in 1907 and two novels, *Der Mumien-Magier* (1928) and *Der weisse Elefant* (1937).

46 There was considerable attention to the Sprechchor in the *Kunst und Volk: Mitteilungen des Vereines Sozialdemokratische Kunststelle*. In addition to the article discussed below, the preceding years saw writings by Adolf Müller, "Der Sprechchor," 1, no. 8 (September 1926), 9–10; Emil Müller, "Der Sprechchor im Wahlkampf," 2, no. 4 (April 1927), 1; Wolfgang Schumann, "Die Sprechchorbewegung," 2, no. 6 (September 1927), 9–10; and Elisa Karau, "Zur Sprechchorbewegung," 2, no. 9 (December 1927), 2–3.

47 Maria Gutmann, "Sprechchöre," *Kunst und Volk: Mitteilungen des Vereines Sozialdemokratische Kunststelle* 3, no. 1 (September 1928), 14–15. Gutmann collaborated with the writer Helene von Weilen in adapting the popular fairytale by Wilhelm Hauff, *Zwerg-Nase*, into a radio drama, the script of which was published by the populist Viennese press. In the Third Reich, she also published the diary of a cancer victim, introduced in a remarkable tale of her discovery of the diary and its signification. See her forward to *Aus dem Tagebuch einer*

Unbekannten, in the series *Deutsche Illustrierte Romane* (Berlin: Dr. Selle-Eysler, 1936).

48 Pamela Potter points out that during the Third Reich, Engel dabbled in race theory (*Most German of the Arts: Musicology and Society from the Weimar Republic to the End of Hitler's Reich* [New Haven: Yale University Press, 1998], 188). But already in this article he linked national and racial types to the various structures of rhythm. Hans Engel, "Rhythmus der Zeit," *Musik und Gesellschaft,* 54–56. See also Frank Mehring, "*Welcome to the Machine!* The Representation of Technology in *Zeitopern,*" *Cambridge Opera Journal* 11, no. 2 (1999), 159–77.

49 Reinhold Brinkmann, "Schoenberg, Op. 16," *Komponisten des 20. Jahrhunderts in der Paul Sacher Stiftung,* ed. Hans Jörg Jans (Basel: Paul Sacher Stiftung, 1986), 63–70.

50 See Schoenberg's letter to Paul A. Pisk, 22 October 1929; from Hans Moldenhauer, "Paul Amadeus Pisk and the Viennese Triumvirate," *Paul Pisk. Essays in His Honor,* ed. John Glowacki ([Austin] College of Fine Arts, University of Texas, 1966), 209.

51 Arnold Schoenberg, Letter to Karl Lütge, 30 May 1928; quoted in from Schoenberg, *Sämtliche Werke* (Mainz: B. Schott's Söhne; Vienna: Universal Edition, 1966–), 18, 1, xxx.

52 Joseph H. Auner, 98–99; R. John Specht, "Schoenberg Among the Workers: Choral Conducting in Pre-1900 Vienna," *Journal of the Arnold Schoenberg Institute* 10 (1987), 28–37; and Albrecht Dümling, "'Im Zeichen der Erkenntnis der socialen Verhältnisse': Der junge Schönberg und die Arbeitersängerbewegung," *Zeitschrift für Musiktheorie* 6 (1975), 11–21, which reproduces an unknown letter from Schoenberg to David Josef Bach from July 1895.

53 David Josef Bach, "Feuilleton. Arnold Schönberg," *Arbeiter-Zeitung,* 17 December 1905, rpt. as Plate 88, Arnold Schoenberg, *Lebensgeschichte in Begegnungen,* ed. Nuria Nono-Schoenberg (Klagenfurt: Ritter, 1992), 47. The work under discussion was the D-major Quartet. The occasion for the article was a performance of *Verklärte Nacht.*

54 Walter Hänel, *Deutsche Arbeiter Sänger-Zeitung* 30, no. 11 (1929), 234, review of the premiere of "Glück," Op. 35, no. 4, in a broadcast by the Erwin Lendvai Quartet; reprinted in Arnold Schoenberg, *Sämtliche Werke,* 18, 2, XLV–XLVI.

55 Schoenberg, *Sämtliche Werke,* 18, 1, xxx.

56 In the passage, Schoenberg goes on to speak of the "joy in a breath." This sensuous yet non-sensual metaphor was common in the early-nineteenth century. Arnold Schoenberg, preface to Anton Webern, *Sechs Bagatellen: für Streichquartett, op. 9* (Vienna and New York: Universal-Edition, 1924).

57 See Frederic J. Schwartz, *The Werkbund: Design Theory and Mass Culture before the First World War* (New Haven: Yale University Press, 1996).

58 Jascha Horenstein, "Arnold Schönbergs Chorwerke," *Deutsche Arbeiter-Sänger-*

Zeitung 28, no. 7 (1927), 125; reproduced in *Schoenberg: Sämtliche Werke*, 18, 2, xlii.

59 See David Dennis, *Beethoven in German Politics, 1870–1989* (New Haven and London: Yale University Press, 1996).

60 Julius Bittner, "Proletarische Musikkultur," *Kunst und Volk. Mitteilungen des Vereines Sozialdemokratische Kunststelle* 1, no. 5 (June 1926), 5–6.

61 See Adorno's *Aesthetic Theory*, trans. Hullot-Kentor (Minneapolis: University of Minnesota Press, 1997).

62 For a similar argument in the visual arts, see T. J. Clark, *Farewell to an Idea: Episodes from a History of Modernism* (New Haven: Yale University Press, 1999).

63 Josef Scheu, "Die Arbeiter-Gesangvereine und ihre Bedeutung für die Sozialdemokratische Partei," quoted without citation in Albrecht Dümling, "'Im Zeichnen der Erkenntnis der Socialen Verhältnisse': Der junge Schönberg und die Arbeitersängerbewegung," *Zeitschrift für Musiktheorie* 6 (1975), 16–17.

64 Andreas Németh, "Béla Reinitz, ein Musiker des Proletariats," *Kunst und Volk: Mitteilungen des Vereines Sozialdemokratische Kunststelle* 1, no. 2 (June 1926), 7.

65 *Arbeiter Zeitung*, Vienna, 28 November 1930; from Kannonier, *Arbeitermusikbewegung in Österreich*, 104.

66 Both programs are reproduced in Lammel, *Arbeitermusikkultur*, 123, 163.

67 Although the author of the letter is unidentified, it appears to be David Josef Bach, and it is quoted in his article "Fünfundzwanzig Jahre Arbeiter-Sinfonie-Konzert," 41.

68 Paul Josef Frankl, "Vom Verständnis des musikalischen Kunstwerkes," *Kunst und Volk* 2, no. 8 (November 1927), 13. Frankl was the composer of the Lustspiel Overture, which was performed on the 1927 Christmas Day program of the Viennese Workers Symphony Concerts. He is absent from the standard lexika of the period.

69 Georg Schünemann, "Die Arbeiter-Sinfonie," *Deutsche Arbeiter Sänger Zeitung* 30, no. 9 (1929); quoted from Fuhr, *Proletarische Musik*, 174.

70 David Josef Bach, "Sozialismus und Kunst," 91.

71 See Leo Herland, "Der Ausdruck in der neuen Kunst," *Kunst und Volk: Mitteilungen des Vereines Sozialdemokratische Kunststelle* 3, no. 8 (April 1929), 217, 222. Ironically, this same author would publish a book on physiognomy in the Third Reich, to be revised in 1956 and in subsequent editions over the ensuing three decades.

72 Thomas Mann, quotation from *Kunst und Volk: Mitteilungen des Vereines Sozialdemokratische Kunststelle* 5, no. 2 (November 1930), 34.

73 Hendrik de Man, *The Psychology of Marxian Socialism* (1926), trans. Eden and Cedar Paul; intro. Peter J. Steinberger (New Brunswick, NJ: Transaction Books, 1985).

74 On the politics of urban planning see Eve Blau, *The Archictecture of Red Vi-enna, 1919–1934* (Cambridge: MIT Press, 1999); also Helmut Gruber, *Red Vienna: Experiment in Working Class Culture, 1919–1934* (New York: Oxford University Press, 1991) and Anson Rabinbach, *The Austrian Socialist Experiment: Social De-mocracy and Austromarxism, 1918–1934* (Boulder: Westview Press, 1985).

Schoenberg's Byron:
The "Ode to Napoleon Buonaparte," the Antinomies of Modernism, and the Problem of German Imperialism

JUDITH RYAN

WE KNOW, OF course, of Chapman's Homer, but who or what exactly was Schoenberg's Byron? On the simplest level, it was a German edition of Byron's works that Schoenberg brought with him when he came to America: the four-volume Meyers Klassiker edition assembled and annotated in 1911 by Friedrich Brie.[1] Schoenberg would have been familiar with the German tradition in which Byron embodied a particular kind of heroic ideal,[2] and he certainly would have known that Byron died while fighting to help free the Greeks from the Turks. If he had read Byron's works attentively, he would have noticed that the English poet was both a Philhellenist and a proto-Zionist: Byron frequently linked the Greeks and the Jews as oppressed peoples with whom he identified.[3] One of Byron's most successful volumes of poetry was his *Hebrew Melodies* (1815), a project designed to hark back to primitive Jewish traditions; the poems were put to music by Isaac Nathan, whose settings consisted of arrangements of Jewish religious and folk melodies. These poems mourn the lost land of the Jews, basing their depictions of Jewish culture on scenes from the Old Testament. They are also full of aggressive warriors like Sennacherib and cruel tyrants like Herod and Belshazzar. These most accessible of Byron's poems clearly delineate themes that would have spoken to Schoenberg at the time of his exile. I do not know how many of his possessions he was able to bring with him to America, but the fact that his four-volume Byron was among these objects is clearly significant.

Schoenberg's decision to use Byron's "Ode to Napoleon Buonaparte" as the text he set to fulfill a commission given him in 1941 by the American League of Composers may thus seem an unremarkable choice. But it raises many more questions than at first meet the eye—or the ear. Schoenberg's unfinished essay, "How I came to write the *Ode to Napoleon*" (1943), gives a number of answers, but still leaves much unexplained.[4] Perhaps the most intriguing question is one Schoenberg did not anticipate in 1941 when he first began to write op. 41 or even in 1943 when he embarked on his explanatory essay: how the composer himself understood the text when he set about fulfilling a subsequent request, the 1944 proposal of the U.S. Office of War Information that he prepare a German version for broadcast as part of the American propaganda against Nazism. The task of putting Byron into German while taking into account the exigencies of an already existent melodic line forced Schoenberg to pay close attention to every single word of the text: he could hardly allow himself to be swept along by vague underlying sentiments. Each detail of the poem had to make sense, not only musically, but also semantically, in this new context. Could Byron's ode be expected to work equally well when addressed to listeners who were the actual enemy of the audience for which Schoenberg's music had first been composed? How, just to give one very obvious example, might a German audience be expected to respond to the poem's concluding stanza in praise of George Washington, whose name did not bear the same emotional associations for them as it did for the original American audience? Imagining the German response to these lines of the poem is not easy.

Before tackling the puzzle of the two different audiences for the "Ode to Napoleon," we need to step back and size up in a more panoramic way the aesthetic issues Byron's poem posed for Schoenberg, especially with respect to the problems of modernism. Opus 41 is modernist in a different sense from Schoenberg's compositions of the first decades of the twentieth century, but, in its own way, it is still very much a modernist piece.

Significantly, Schoenberg's first choice for a text on which to base the composition commissioned by the American League of Composers was Maeterlinck's *The Life of the Bee* (1901). While it is not surprising that Schoenberg might look back to the aestheticist movement, which had been one of his primary sources of textual material for his first atonal pieces, it is odd that he should have thought in the first instance of a prose text of over 400 pages. What interested Schoenberg in *The Life of the Bee* was its study of the relation between the drones and the queen: he believed this description might go some way toward explaining the attitude of individual Germans to the Führer. In "How I came to write the *Ode to Napoleon*," Schoenberg claims that it was precisely Maeterlinck's aestheticism that ultimately made him decide not to use *The Life of the Bee*: "Maeterlinck's poetic philosophy gilded everything that was not already gold." An additional problem that Schoenberg does not mention in this essay, however, was Maeterlinck's fascination with bees and their social organization. For the Belgian writer, the hive is a "strange little republic" that abounds in "faith and mystery and hope."⁵ In his admiration for the social forms of bee colonies, Maeterlinck is hardly alone, of course. The prospective audience for Schoenberg's composition would have had to overturn a long cultural tradition that had imbued the social arrangements of the hive with positive associations. Even careful cutting and splicing of passages from *The Life of the Bee* would be unlikely to yield a text that fit neatly with the argument Schoenberg had hoped to present. The problem with Maeterlinck was not just with his aestheticist style; it was also with his ideas.

When Schoenberg turned from Maeterlinck to Byron, he still did not depart radically, in the first instance, from the kind of text to which he had so often recurred in the past. His initial conception was to set the famous poem "The Isles of Greece" from Canto III of *Don Juan*. In contrast to the ironic tone of Byron's epic satire, "The Isles of Greece" is a sixteen-stanza inset lyric presented as an example of the "sort of hymn" Juan may have sung when traveling in Greece. Though highly rhetorical, the poem is also eminently lyrical: it is an elegy for the loss of the nation's former culture in the current barbaric age of the early-nineteenth century. "The Isles of Greece" includes numerous shifts in mood that would have provided grist to Schoenberg's compositional mill. In contrast to the difficult "Ode to Napoleon," "The Isles of Greece" would have allowed Schoenberg to inveigh against tyranny in a firm and decisive manner—in the penultimate line, for example, the speaker declares: "A land of slaves shall ne'er be mine." For generations of readers, "The Isles of Greece" has proved eloquent and moving; it is not only poetically more accomplished, but also easier to understand than the "Ode to Napoleon." Why did Schoenberg reject his initial impulse to use the famous hymn from *Don Juan* to express the call to freedom that he deemed essential in 1941?

To resolve this question, we need to explore the problem of audience address that Schoenberg confronted in composing his piece for the American League of Composers. The speaker of "The Isles of Greece" is figured as a Greek who laments the decline of his country's culture since its high point in classical antiquity. From Schoenberg's perspective, a parallel can be drawn between the decline of classical Greece and the decline of the German cultural tradition—all the more so given the long tradition in which German writers had themselves developed this analogy. With appropriate changes of proper names, geographic and personal, Byron's "Isles of Greece" might seem to pour forth directly from the mouth of a German opponent to the cultural and political ideology of the Nazis. The difficulty was that a lament for the decline of German culture ran the risk of being seriously misunderstood by the American audience. What Schoenberg needed was not a text that would express his own views, but something that could help to focus more sharply the ideas of his American listeners.

The attack on Pearl Harbor in December 1941 motivated Schoenberg to reflect on his indebtedness to the United States, and the poem he finally settled on, Byron's "Ode to Napoleon," did just this in its concluding stanza, with its rather clumsy allusion to "the Cincinnatus of the West," George Washington. Furthermore, the ode itself developed the contrast between tyranny and freedom that Schoenberg wished to address in this piece. As commentators have not tired of pointing out, however, Schoenberg's selection of this text is an awkward and unconvincing one. The ode seems particularly inappropriate for the early forties because of the potential parallel between Napoleon and Hitler. Reinhold Brinkmann argues that the "Ode to Napoleon" only works within the context of World War II if it is given a "selective" reading that highlights its "impassioned appeal against tyranny" and its hope for "a liberated human race."[6]

Yet if the text was so problematic, why did the U.S. Office of War Information wish to broadcast the composition into Germany as part of its counter-propaganda program? In order to understand this, we need to recall the point of view from which Byron's text is written: that of an admirer of Napoleon disappointed by the emperor's defeat at Waterloo. The opening stanza of the ode questions Napoleon's heroism, suggesting that the nobler course of action after his defeat would have been to commit suicide:

> 'Tis done—but yesterday a King!
> And arm'd with Kings to strive—
> And now thou art a nameless thing
> So abject—yet alive!
> Is this the man of thousand thrones,
> Who strew'd our Earth with hostile bones,
> And can he thus survive?

These lines hammer home the idea that Napoleon's survival after his defeat at Waterloo is as much a matter of shame as the fact of his military failure. This suggests a quite specific "selective reading" for the German audience. In the fall of 1944, Hitler was increasingly under pressure from the Allies, losing ground on both the eastern and the western fronts, but he had not yet capitulated. He had recently survived the attack on his person by German military officers under the leadership of Claus von Stauffenberg on July 20, 1944. "Is this the man of thousand thrones, / Who strew'd our Earth with hostile bones, / And can he thus survive?" Indeed, viewed from the perspective of this second audience, German citizens in Germany who might be wooed away from Hitler, Byron's text is remarkably apposite. Byron's poem, with its forceful expression of a bewildering gamut of emotions including admiration, disappointment, scorn, disgust, and many others, might well speak to a segment of the German population who were struggling to sort out complicated and often conflicting feelings about Hitler. The text successfully upholds lofty ideals of honor and freedom while showing how the previously admired leader has fallen drastically short by these measures. It models a more complex and sophisticated response than propaganda texts, with their simplistic contrasts between good and evil.

Seen from this angle of vision, the ode even anticipates the problem subsequently addressed by the Mitscherlichs in their influential study, *The Inability to Mourn.*[7] A text like Byron's "Ode to Napoleon" that articulated the struggle to wean oneself away from a misguided emotional attachment could have provided a therapeutic instrument for postwar Germany as it tried to disengage from its wartime loyalty to Hitler. The third stanza of the poem states that future times might learn from Napoleon's fall:

> Thanks for that lesson—it will teach
> To after-warriors more
> Than high Philosophy can preach,
> And vainly preached before.
> That spell upon the minds of men
> Breaks never to unite again,
> That led them to adore
> Those Pagod things of sabre-sway,
> With fronts of brass, and feet of clay.

No wonder Schoenberg thought, in 1944, that "many people will relate it to Hitler and Mussolini,"[8] or that he gave the speaker's part to the music publisher Schirmer in the hope that the work would be performed in postwar

Germany. The stanza claims that people will never again fall under the spell of a charismatic leader who promulgates evil ideas. Subsequent stanzas argue, by appealing to an entire sequence of examples from world history, that the truly heroic leader is one who recognizes when his rule has turned into tyranny and who chooses to abdicate his office. Of Lucius Sulla, the Roman dictator who resigned in 79 B.C., the text maintains: "His only glory was that hour / Of self-upheld abandon'd power."

The question "who is speaking?" in the text of Schoenberg's Opus 41 thus has a complicated answer. We have been taught to distinguish between author and speaker; but in the case of Byron's "Ode to Napoleon Buonaparte" we might just as well admit that there is little difference between the two. In essence, it is Byron's own ambivalent relationship to Napoleon that finds expression in the poem. Schoenberg, however, does not occupy the same position as Byron toward the text. For this reason, it would be better to regard the text of Opus 41 as a dramatic monologue, spoken by someone who is as much an imagined persona as the speaker of Schoenberg's later piece, *A Survivor from Warsaw*, op. 46 (1947). The speaker of Opus 41 is, in effect, at one and the same time the Byron who voices his disappointment over Napoleon's fall from greatness and the German who sees his admiration for Hitler coming undone.

Though cogent for the 1944 German version of the text, designed for broadcast into wartime Germany, this argument does not hold up with respect to the original American audience for whom the work was composed in 1941/2. How could Schoenberg have conceived that this text might "speak" to that audience? In order to understand the text's function from this perspective, we need to bear in mind Schoenberg's long-held belief, as formulated in his *Four-Point Program for Jewry* (1933), that the Jewish struggle against anti-Semitism tended to alienate potential supporters who were not Jewish.[9] For this reason, Schoenberg did not want to take the position of a Jewish victim in this important wartime composition (*A Survivor from Warsaw* is a postwar work based on a radically changed set of assumptions). There is good reason to believe, furthermore, that in 1941 few Americans knew that Hitler was already proceeding toward the "final solution." As Max Frankel has shown, American newspapers tended to bury articles about the fate of Jews in Germany and German-occupied lands in the inside pages rather than displaying them as front-page stories. In the period 1939–1945, the *New York Times* rarely mentions Hitler's actions against the Jews on the front page, and only once (in December 1942) was this topic treated in a lead editorial.[10] Despite the more active work of *The Post*, *The Nation*, and *The New Republic*,[11] the larger American public simply lacked full information about the horrors to which European Jews were being subjected. Schoenberg thus needed to find an argument against Hitler that might appeal to the American majority. The fear of invasion by the Japanese that had been unleashed by the attack on Pearl Harbor in December 1941 had brought home to Americans just how important the idea of independence was to them. For Schoenberg to present Hitler as a "new Napoleon" aiming to conquer as much foreign territory as he could was a way of aligning his composition with the American fear of being invaded. Against the backdrop of Pearl Harbor, the implicit message that Hitler was a new Napoleon would raise in the minds of American listeners the specter of being invaded from across the Atlantic as well as from across the Pacific. The "selective reading" of Byron's ode for this group of listeners thus focused on the problem of imperialism,[12] and the speaker of this version is to be visualized as someone who is concerned about contemporary threats to American independence.

Schoenberg's personal views about the threat posed by Hitler were, to be sure, more closely linked to his racial policies; from Schoenberg's perspective, Hitler's imperialist ambitions were dangerous primarily because they would entail a vast spread of these policies throughout the lands he conquered. On the related issue of colonialism, furthermore, Schoenberg's ideas were by no means simple. In view of the fact that many countries were now limiting the number of Jewish emigrés from the Nazi Reich, he urged that a territory be found where they could settle without posing a burden on other nations. In contrast to those who advocated a return to Palestine, Schoenberg urged that money be raised by subscription to purchase land in Uganda. In taking up this idea, Schoenberg recurred to proposals that originated during the German colonial period, when the focus of overseas settlement was in Africa.[13] Ironically, Schoenberg's views about a new homeland for the Jews share the colonialist notion that Africa was essentially an empty space.

On the topic of empire, Byron's "Ode to Napoleon" lists a series of tyrants, despots, and emperors from classical antiquity to the sixteenth century. Byron's ode presents Napoleon as the most recent in this line, an emperor who should learn the lessons of his predecessors. Superimposing upon this configuration Schoenberg's implication that Hitler is yet another member of this sequence, we can see Schoenberg using the poem as a way of appealing to American anti-imperialist sentiment. The poem's tribute to George Washington in the final stanza clinches what, from this perspective, must be read as an attempt to remind the American audience of its roots in the struggle against empire.

For Byron, the Washington stanza was far from crucial to the ode. In fact, he only composed it, and the two stanzas that precede it, in response to his publisher's request to make the poem longer so that he could avoid paying stamp tax, which was levied on texts of less than one sheet. Byron later removed them from the ode again, and the 1981 authoritative edition of his works reproduces these twenty-seven verses under the heading "Additional Stanzas." [14] The German edition of Byron that Schoenberg had brought with him to the United States does not include these three stanzas: he would not have discovered them until he purchased an English edition at the beginning of 1942. This meant that when Schoenberg produced the German version for the 1944 broadcast, he had to translate these stanzas from scratch, in contrast to the rest of the poem, where he worked energetically to rewrite the Meyers Klassiker version so that it would better accord with the vocal line of his composition. Schoenberg's translation of the ode's final lines give them a dignity they do not possess in the original English. Byron writes:

> Yes—one—the first—the last—the best—
> The Cincinnatus of the West,
> Whom envy dared not hate,
> Bequeath'd the name of Washington,
> To make man blush there was but one!

Schoenberg's rendering does not entirely manage to avoid banal rhymes, but at least he avoids the awkward rhyming of "Washington" with "one" and eliminates entirely the unfortunate blushing motif. Most importantly, he introduces the concept of freedom in an emphatic position, the last line of the poem:

> Ein Cincinnatus der Neuen Welt,
> ihr größter, hehrster, reinster Held
> hat diesen Wunsch erfüllt,
> den Namen Washington vermacht
> der Menschheit, der er Freiheit bracht'.

Schoenberg's ending implicitly links Washington, who "brought freedom to humankind," with Prometheus, the bringer of fire, who had been the subject of the final stanza in the shorter version of Byron's poem. In Schoenberg's German text, Washington's gift of freedom functions as a positive counterpoint to Prometheus's theft of fire. Washington is at once part of the historical and the mythological networks that inform the poem.

Reinhold Brinkmann has shown how carefully Schoenberg went through the Meyers Klassiker translation, painstakingly adjusting the German to accord with Byron's diction.[15] Such adaptations were not always possible, however, and in several instances Schoenberg actually changed his original composition to accord with the new German wording: Brinkmann illustrates this procedure by examining the opening lines of the seventh stanza, where Schoenberg made musical changes to take account of a difference in word order—and hence in stress patterns—in the second line.[16] While Schoenberg's alterations in the musical line between the 1941 and the 1944 version can be explained by such exigencies of the German, his reworking of the Meyers Klassiker translation cannot always, or certainly not always entirely, be accounted for by an appeal to the needs of the original music. Beginning with stanza five, Schoenberg undertakes revisions of the German that go well beyond minor shifts in speech intonation or meaning. These changes stem, I believe, from two different considerations: first, many of Schoenberg's revisions to the German of the edition he had brought with him into exile clarify some of the historical and mythological allusions in the poem; second, some of his reworkings bring themes to the foreground that were important for the topical reference of the poem to his 1944 German audience. Taken together, these two types of alteration would have made the larger themes of the poem clearer than they were in Byron's English, which assumes a thorough grounding in history and the classics. Perhaps Schoenberg was trying to correct the baffling impression Opus 41 had made on its original American audience, which scarcely knew how to react at the first performance.[17] It is hard to know whether Schoenberg had been unaware of the difficulties the ode's many allusions would cause twentieth-century American readers—to say nothing of listeners who would have less time to puzzle over the poem's wording—after all, he himself had originally become familiar with the text in a German edition that included helpful footnotes. Here and there, Schoenberg revises the Meyers edition so that it will render Byron's original more accurately;[18] but more often, his changes reveal a desire to clarify and explicate.

The first of these major changes is definitely of the explicative type—not a retranslation so much as an unwritten footnote pulled up into the text itself. This is the passage:

> Is it some yet imperial hope
> That with such change can calmly hope? (ll. 41–2)

The Meyers Klassiker edition stays fairly close to the original:

> Läßt ihn ein kaiserliches Hoffen
> Kalt sehn den Schlag, der ihn getroffen? (52)

To be sure, this version fails to represent the crucial word "yet"; but Schoenberg goes well beyond the small adjustment it would have required to incorporate this idea. Instead, he renders the lines:

> Nimmt ruhig seinen Sturz er hin
> Weil er noch Hilf' erhofft von Wien?[19]

These lines, with their distinctively Austrian rhyme, suggest that Napoleon was hoping that relatives of his wife, Marie Luise of Austria, might persuade Vienna to come to his assistance after the defeat at Waterloo. While this notion helped flesh out the historical context of the ode in a very concrete way, it limited the parallel that Schoenberg wishes to draw between Napoleon and Hitler (Austria was already part of Hitler's Reich), and diminishes the identification Byron implies between his own lingering "imperial hope" and that of his former idol, Napoleon.[20]

Less awkwardly explanatory is Schoenberg's inclusion of Milo's name in stanza 6, where the English alludes to him only by recounting the story of Milo's death when the oak to which he was tied rebounded when he tried to break his bonds by splitting the tree ("He who of old would rend the oak / Dreamed not of the rebound," ll. 46–47). Toward the end of the same stanza, Schoenberg again paraphrases Byron's image of the "forest prowlers' prey" (l. 53) by stating more straightforwardly that Milo's suffering was ended when he was eaten by a wolf ("Ein Wolf rasch endet Milos Leid—," Sch., 99). To be sure, Schoenberg does not include Sulla's name in stanza 7 or Charles V's in stanza 8. But in these instances, there is good reason to regard the contrasting references to "the Roman" and "the Spaniard" as predominantly an attempt to indicate that different emperors in different historical periods nonetheless had the good sense to abdicate at the appropriate time, thus setting an example that Napoleon has failed to follow. It could well be argued that the allusions to the Roman and the Spanish Empires takes precedence in these stanzas over precise identification of the specific emperors involved.

In one instance, Schoenberg even identifies a transferred epithet and shifts it back to its logical referent in his translation. When Byron writes, in stanza 14, "Then haste thee to thy sullen isle / And gaze upon the sea" (ll. 118–119), the adjective "sullen" is clearly a poetic transference from Napoleon himself to the island where he will be exiled. The translator of the Meyers Klassiker edition retains Byron's arrangement of noun and epithet, but he uses an adjective that could more logically be applied to an island than "sullen," thus virtually eliminating the rhetorical figure Byron employs: "Zur düstern Insel nun entrückt, / Starr in des Meeres Branden!" (54). Schoenberg's rendering of these lines as "Auf deiner Insel laß dich nieder, / Das Meer starr haßvoll an" (Sch., 100), however plain it may be by comparison to the original, nonetheless reveals a translator well schooled by working with Greek and Latin texts in the German high school tradition where decoding transferred epithets would have been everyday fare.

More interesting than these indications of a particular approach to translation are those passages where Schoenberg chooses to intensify major themes he wished to highlight in the 1944 translation. His predecessor in the Meyers Klassiker edition had already decided to render Byron's phrase, "ill-minded man" (l. 10) as "Tyrann" (51), thus anticipating the word "tyrant" midway through the poem (l. 89), as well as the references to the tyrannical rulers Nebuchadnezzar in stanza 3 and Timour (Tamburlaine) in stanza 15. Schoenberg foregrounds this idea throughout his translation beginning with a seemingly minor change in the opening stanza from "Mann" to "Herr" (l. 5). The Meyers translator's decision to render "a man of thousand thrones" as "ein Mann von tausend Reichen" (51) may have been one of the things that first motivated Schoenberg to imagine that the text might invoke Hitler, with his "Tausendjähriges Reich," to listeners in the 1940s. A striking change that accentuates the present relevance of the ode for the German audience of 1944 is Schoenberg's reworking of Byron's lines about the Roman Sulla:

> His only glory was that hour
> Of self-upheld abandon'd power. (ll. 62–63).

Schoenberg sacrifices the sustained breath of this brilliant formulation for a more mundane paraphrase that spells out in clear, if rather wooden, terms the point he is trying to convey to listeners in Hitler's Germany:

> Moralisch doch sei er geschätzt,
> Der zwangfrei Macht durch Recht ersetzt. (Sch., 99)[21]

What really happened after Lucius Sulla's retirement from his cruel dictatorship in 79 B.C. is less important for Schoenberg's purposes here than the suggestion that abdication by Hitler—or his removal—would return a state of law to Germany. The emphatic positioning of the contrasting terms "Macht" and "Recht" in the final line of this stanza would carry the idea much more persuasively than Byron's more poetic phrase, "self-upheld abandon'd power," which needs quite elaborate parsing before it can be fully understood.

The three last stanzas of the ode, those that Byron had added only to reduce the stamp taxes for his publisher, had not been included by the Meyers Klassiker translator. For these "additional stanzas," Schoenberg was on his own. There are moments here where he does very well, as in his version of the lines:

> Where is that faded garment? Where
> The gewgaws thou wert fond to wear,
> The star—the string—the crest? [22]

Schoenberg's translation is a masterpiece of fluid rearrangement:

> Der Tand von längst verblichner Tracht,
> Mit Stern und Schwur und Fransenpracht—
> Wer wird danach noch fragen? (Sch., 101)

And, as we have already seen, Schoenberg devises a conclusion to the poem that considerably strengthens Byron's awkward lines about George Washington. Yet in these last three stanzas, Schoenberg also takes care to use wording that is equally applicable to Napoleon and Hitler. For example, he paraphrases Byron's convoluted lines "When that immeasurable power / Unsated to resign / Had been an act of purer fame / Than gathers round Marengo's name"[23] as "bliebst du Konsul, statt Cäsar, / hättst edlern Ruhmes Tat vollbracht, als zuschreibt dir Marengos Schlacht" (Sch., 101). On a simpler level, he renders Byron's word "king" [24] as "Kaiser." More pointedly, Schoenberg replaces Byron's reference to "remembrance"[25] with an explicit reference to pangs of conscience ("Gewissens Plagen," Sch., 101), a phrase that might have evoked moral twinges in the Germans who were listening to the U.S. War Office's broadcast of this piece. Clearly, Schoenberg was thinking carefully about his potential audience when he worked on the language for the 1944 German version.

These considerations of the text and its relation to its two very different intended audiences may help us understand, at least intellectually, what Schoenberg may have seen as the potential appeal of the ode. Why do audiences not find the piece more attractive, then? The composition is vigorous and forceful, but it does not touch us in the quite same way as Schoenberg's later piece, *A Survivor from Warsaw*. We feel that the "Ode to Napoleon" is deliberately holding back from what is conventionally thought of as the "aesthetic"—even from the kind of modernist aesthetic represented by some of Schoenberg's most radically atonal compositions.

The transition from the instrumental introduction to the voice part may help us approach this problem. Perhaps this moment in the piece (mm. 24–28) can best be understood as a shift from interior to exterior monologue. With its agitated, scurrying effects, the introduction suggests conflict in several senses: military, political, intellectual, and emotional. The rest in m. 25 is intriguing, because it suggests that these conflicted moments have come to an end: at the same time, however, two groups of instruments—the second violins and the cellos—do not join in this rest, but begin to play harmonics instead. When the voice declares, in the following measure, that "'tis done," a further ambiguity emerges, since this is not the announcement of an ending, but the start of a complexly articulated meditation on the undoing of Napoleon. The first violins and violas now join the other strings with harmonic chords that give the statement "'tis done" a somewhat surreal quality. The unearthly harmonics hint at a contrary understanding of the apparently decisive action announced by the voice. And, as if this were not enough, the voice and the instrumental parts consider several different ways of "reading" the opening syllables of the poem: while the piano accompaniment and the Sprechstimme experiment with nuanced versions of a reading of "'tis done" as an iambic foot (mm. 26 and 27),[26] the violins propose reading it as a spondee (m. 27)—although to be sure, these pizzicato chords, with their light metallic sound, countermand the usual heavy tread of this foot (an effect heightened by the dissonance introduced by the D in the second violin part). The result is something far less decisive than Mephisto's "es ist vollbracht" in Goethe's *Faust*. Schoenberg plays deconstructively with Byron's opening words, suggesting that what has been "done" at the battle of Waterloo is not an ending but the beginning of a difficult intellectual struggle about the meaning of Napoleon's defeat. For the 1940s listener, the questions this raises refer not only to Napoleon, but also to the history of seductive leadership that Byron had hoped would end with the French emperor.

Why did Schoenberg create, in the *Ode to Napoleon Buonaparte*, a piece of music that arouses serious resistance to the expectations even of informed listeners? On one level, Schoenberg may have been responding to Byron's particular use of irony, which itself aimed to "confound readerly expectations."[27] On another level, however, he was concerned not just to sway his listeners emotionally, but also to get them thinking. What Schoenberg heard as "170 different shades of irony, contempt, sarcasm, parody, hate, and outrage" (one for almost every line of the 171-line poem) modeled a nuanced movement of thought and feeling that posed a challenge to both his American and his German audiences.[28] In addition, his tendency in the "Ode to Napoleon" to follow speech intonations—admittedly rather bombastic ones—as closely as possible severely minimizes the latent tension between song and speech, keeping the listener in a more active mental state. Despite the difficulty of the text, which requires a range of historical and cultural knowledge to be understood completely,[29] the setting throws the emphasis on the progression of ideas.

This emphasis can be likened to Brecht's estrangement effect, though it is of course accomplished by very different means. The *Ode to Napoleon Buonaparte* is designed to have a compelling impact on its listeners, but at the same time to prevent them from being emotionally carried away. Were this otherwise, the stanza about breaking the charismatic sway of tyrants would in effect be countermanded. This stanza actually contains an allusion to the description of Nebuchadnezzar's dream in the Book of Daniel. Daniel interprets Nebuchadnezzar's dream of a "great image" "fearsome to behold": its head "was of fine gold, its chest and arms of silver, its belly and thighs of bronze, its legs of iron, its feet part iron and part clay."[30] The various body parts, regardless of their substance, shatter, whereupon the image grows into a huge mountain filling the whole earth. Daniel interprets the dream as an allegory of a sequence of mighty kingdoms, each of which is destroyed in turn, to be supplanted finally by the coming of the kingdom of heaven. Byron's ode anticipates that the spell Napoleon and his predecessors cast over the minds of men will ultimately be broken, like the great image in Nebuchadnezzar's dream. From Schoenberg's perspective of the 1940s, however, Napoleon was not the last of the line: Hitler is another figure who harbors what Byron calls in the ode "some yet imperial hope" (l. 41). But charismatic influence must come to an end, and so Schoenberg's music itself resists the temptation to continue that charisma. The resistance the composition offers to our desire for the aesthetic is an essential aspect of its attempt to create a new modernist aesthetic that urges complex reflection and intellectual struggle at the expense of the siren call of emotion.

Notes

1 *Byrons Werke*, trans. A. Böttger et al., ed. Friedrich Brie (Leipzig: Bibliographisches Institut). The edition I was able to procure from Widener Library is undated, but Brie dates his introduction December 1911. The Widener copy, designated on the title page as a "kritisch durchgesehene und erläuterte Ausgabe," has a pencil note on the copyright page indicating that it was donated to Harvard in 1930.

2 In addition to Brie's almost hundred-page introduction on Byron's life and works, Schoenberg may also have read Helene Richter's large biography, *Lord Byron: Persönlichkeit und Werk* (Halle and Saale: Max Niemeyer Verlag, 1929), which includes an entire chapter on Byron as a "Napoleon of Poetry" (183–211).

3 For a more detailed and sophisticated account of this aspect of Byron's thought, see Caroline Franklin, "'Some samples of the finest Orientalism': Byronic Philhellenism and proto-Zionism at the time of the Congress of Vienna," in *Romanticism and Colonialism: Writing and Empire, 1780–1830*, ed. Tim Fulford and Peter J. Kitson (Cambridge: Cambridge University Press, 1998), 221–242.

4 Arnold Schoenberg, "How I Came to Compose the *Ode to Napoleon*," *Journal of the Arnold Schoenberg Institute* 2, no. 1 (1977), 55–7.

5 Maurice Maeterlinck, *The Life of the Bee*, trans. Alfred Sutro (New York: Dodd, Mead and Company, 1901), 67–8.

6 "Arnold Schönberg's 'Ode to Napoleon Buonaparte,' op. 41," notes accompanying Edition Abseits compact disc, EDA 008–2, 39.

7 Alexander und Margarete Mitscherlich, *Die Unfähigkeit zu Trauern* (Munich: R. Piper & Co. Verlag, 1967).

8 Cit. Brinkmann (see n. 6), 39.

9 See Alexander L. Ringer, *Arnold Schoenberg: The Composer as Jew* (Oxford: Clarendon Press, 1990), esp. chapter 7, 116–149.

10 Max Frankel, "Turning Away From the Holocaust," *The New York Times*, 150th anniversary issue, November 14, 2001, H10.

11 Ibid.

12 In fact, Byron's views on empire, like his views on Napoleon, were complex. Saree Makdisi comments: "That Byron did not share the kind of imperial attitudes expressed by Disraeli and Burton does not […] necessarily mean that he opposed imperialism altogether" (*Romantic Imperialism: Universal Empire and the Culture of Modernity* (Cambridge: Cambridge University Press, 1998), 134.

13 This was a suggestion originally made by the English, who did not want to see the Jews establish themselves in Palestine. Among the Zionists, the Uganda Project was promulgated by Theodore Herzl, but it was rejected after his death in 1904 by the Zionist Congress. See *A Four-Point Program for Jewry* in Alexander Ringer, *Arnold Schoenberg: The Composer as Jew*, 234–243.

14 Lord Byron, *The Complete Poetical Works*, ed. Jerome J. McGann (Oxford: Clarendon Press, 1981), 3, 265–6.

15 Brinkmann, (see n. 6), 40.

16 Ibid., 41.

17 See Arnold Schoenberg, *Complete Edition*, 24, part 2.

18 Another example of a revision that aims for greater accuracy is Schoenberg's rendering of lines 100–101, where Byron's formulation "Weighed in the balance, hero dust / Is vile as vulgar clay," seriously mistranslated in the Meyers edition as "Nicht schwerer wirst der Helden Staub als anderer du finden," becomes the more acceptable "Der Helden Staub zeigt in der Waage / Mit Lehm denselben Preis" (Sch., 100).

19 Ibid., 99. Subsequent references to Schoenberg's German version of the poem refer to this edition.

20 Byron's views on this point are well presented by Michael Williams in "Byron's 'Napoleon' Poems: 'Some yet imperial hope,'" *Unisa English Studies*, XXIX, no. 1 (1991), 13–23.

21 The Meyers version runs: "Sein einz'ger Ruhm, daß er entsagt, / Frei, da noch seine Macht geragt" (53).

22 "Additional Stanzas," ll. 14–16, Byron, *Complete Poetical Works*, 3, 265.

23 Ibid., ll. 3–5.

24 Ibid., l. 10.

25 Ibid., l. 13.

26 Actually, they read "'tis done" as a trisyllable, preserving a trace of the elided pronoun "it."

27 Caroline Franklin, "Some samples of the finest orientalism," 223.

28 Letter to Orson Welles of 13 September, 1943, cit. Reinhold Brinkmann (see n. 6), 39.

29 The Meyers Klassiker edition contains explanatory notes, translating the epigraph about Hannibal and giving the names of figures like Milo, Sulla, Charles V, Maria Luise of Austria, and Dionysus the Younger, all of whom remain unnamed in the poem. Schoenberg may thus have underestimated the problems the multiple allusions in the poem would present to an audience unaided by such annotations.

30 Daniel 2:31–33.

Ideologies of Serialism:
Stravinsky's *Threni* and the
Congress for Cultural Freedom*

ANNE C. SHREFFLER

Music and Politics: Methodological Considerations

THAT THE DEVELOPMENT of serial music after 1945 was affected by the Cold War is probably not a controversial statement anymore. Why shouldn't music have also responded to the same forces that steered post-war painting and literature into an increasingly material-based abstraction? In Western Europe, the effects of politics on cultural life after the war were drastic and immediate because of the need to reject both Fascist aesthetics and the restrictive artistic policies implemented in the Soviet block in 1948. Many of the innovations in European New Music after 1945 can be read as responses to these two pressures: on the one hand, composers embraced musical idioms and techniques that had been forbidden by Nazi cultural policies; on the other, they systematically and ostentatiously exercised the freedom that was denied their Eastern counterparts.[1] In the U.S., lacking a past that needed to be exorcised, the political dimension was less explicit in discourse about music in the immediate post-war years. Implicitly, however, the compositional avant-garde was politicized by endorsing two cornerstone Cold War values: belief in the supremacy of the methodologies of hard science and in the value of personal and political freedom.[2] Modernist art, in particular abstract expressionism, was believed to articulate these values sufficiently clearly that it could be instrumentalized by the U.S. government in its campaign to spread American cultural values after the war.[3] Recent studies have revealed the "cultural cold war" to have been much broader in scope and better financed than was previously thought.[4] The propagation of modernist music, while secondary to the much more visible and profitable world of the visual arts, was also part of this larger program.[5]

While the musical avant-gardes in both North America and Europe can be linked in some general ways with Cold War politics, the impact on specific composers or pieces is difficult to prove. One problem is that the two spheres are conceptually incommensurate; while "politics" on the one hand refers to a wide range of activities, ideas, and social structures, the term "artworks" on the other denotes a class of objects which may be in themselves quite complex but are at least individually identifiable. Relating political phenomena to specific artworks is like trying to identify the effect of global weather patterns on the begonia in your garden. The literal incomparability of the political and aesthetic spheres and the difficulty of describing exact relationships between them has led to a tendency to treat them as if they were completely unrelated. This tendency is exacerbated by notions of the autonomy of art, which became so central to Western culture after 1800 and flourished until the end of the twentieth century.[6] Talking about politics and music creates anxieties about besmirching music's transcendent purity with such mundane and unappetizing things as policy, laws, and struggle.[7]

While Western aesthetics claim the artwork's autonomy from the political sphere, Marxist-inspired approaches recognize the relationship with the outer world as an essential feature of art. Discussion of the relationships between music and politics is here facilitated by the fact that the actors themselves acknowledge their political motivations. Yet if we can only speak of "political" or "ideological" music when it is overtly intended as such, then the entire sphere of Western autonomous music is placed out of reach. In practice, the category "political music" has been used almost exclusively in connection with the Left; the Western avant-garde's claim for political neutrality through aesthetic autonomy has been taken at face value by mainstream critics. Ideological critique of the avant-garde carried out by the Left—by such figures as Cornelius Cardew or Konrad Boehmer—does not seriously question this neutrality, because the debate is framed entirely in terms of leftist assumptions about the relationship between music and politics. (A book like Cardew's *Stockhausen Serves Imperialism* only perpetuates the East-West dichotomy and paralyzes real discussion.[8]) It seems impossible to discuss the political implications of art that is not consciously politically conceived.

If the aesthetic sphere is separate from the political, as is implicit in the

Western position, how can there be an ideology of serialism? Even if we allow that the polarized political situation after World War II affected the development of serialism in a general way, how can this impact be seen on the level of institutions and individuals, and ultimately in musical works? Can we recognize "ideology," not just in the general sense of "a manner or the content of thinking characteristic of an individual, group, or culture," but in the more specific and political sense of "the integrated assertions, theories, and aims that constitute a sociopolitical program"?[9] And finally, assuming we can, what do we gain by politicizing the unpolitical?

First, one must broaden the definition of "politics" beyond the specific actions of governments and the impact of these actions on individuals and institutions to include the reverse: how individuals influence each other and, by extension, institutions and governments. Shifting the focus from the macrosocial level (from concepts such as the state, market, or class) to the individual level allows us to paint a more nuanced picture: not just to see who was Right and who was Left, but rather to observe how people functioned within the networks of prestige, prizes, and jobs.[10] These individual actions can be fitted again into a larger political context because the value judgments that influence artistic decisions are never completely personal ones, but are articulated using existing language and framed within (or against) accepted value systems.[11] Second, it is useful when dealing with works of art to shift the focus from the works themselves to their reception and use. The question is not, therefore, what does the work itself express (as a statement of its immutable essence), but rather how has the work been understood? Answers to the latter question are changeable, depending on the historical situation. Even in an ostensibly apolitical context, certain styles and techniques are marked in specific ways according to various hierarchies of prestige, value, and taste.[12] The pointedly apolitical stance of much Western postwar avant-garde music should not dissuade us from trying to identify such markings; indeed much writing about avant-garde music, in focusing exclusively on compositional techniques, seems designed to mask the real pressures upon it from the outside. In a statement that can be applied to the arts as well, Edward Said writes, "Culture works very effectively to make invisible and even 'impossible' the actual affiliations that exist between the world of ideas and scholarship … and the world of brute politics, corporate and state power, and military force."[13]

Another means of linking music and politics is through the analysis of concepts common to both. It can be useful to look at how political rhetoric seeps down into the nooks and crannies of individual consciousness, even of people who considered themselves to be apolitical. A good example of this is the key concept "freedom," which after the war acquired a set of highly specific yet vastly different associations in American, West European, and Soviet political discourse. In America, the word became a cipher for Western democracy. Freedom also became an important concept in discourse about the arts in the West, most notably as the guiding principle of Abstract Expressionism.[14] The Communist system, on the other hand, also claimed freedom as a central concept: freedom from capitalist oppression and from exploitation by the ruling class. In writings about New Music, freedom is also a basic notion, providing as it did justification for the limitless expansion of musical language through pioneer-like exploration of its materials.

The different, even opposite meanings attributed to the term freedom do not reveal an inherent conceptual ambiguity—since for each individual speaker the concept's meaning is clear—but rather the power of political ideology to endow a concept with a specific, socially binding meaning that becomes valid for certain groups of people. An individual may consciously resist this meaning, but in doing so he or she still recognizes its authority. Analysis of concepts and how they were used by different groups provides a useful conceptual link between governmental and individual politics, and even between politics in the general sense described above and works of art. I believe we should do this analysis, because our knowledge and even our perception of works of music are shaped by the words we use to think about them. In analyzing a serial piece, we cannot avoid using words like freedom and control if we want to talk about its materials and how they are used. These musical concepts, though not identical to their political usages, are analogous to these, and unthinkable without them: as the composer Mathias Spahlinger put it, "The thought structures and ways of feeling that are thematicized in music are analogous to those with which political structures are formed, or, they are the same."[15]

In the following I would like to explore further the concept of freedom in both political and musical discourse within the post-war context. This focus allows us to move among the different levels—between the Gulf Stream and the begonia, so to speak—by looking at a specific case in which the U.S. government used advanced music as cultural propaganda for Western liberal ideals: the Congress for Cultural Freedom and its sponsorship of Stravinsky's *Threni* at the 1958 Biennale in Venice. Several threads of the problem are visible in this case study: the specific aims and means of the Congress for Cultural Freedom, the East-West political divide that caused it to be formed in the first place, the individual motives of people like Nabokov, Stravinsky, and others in allowing themselves to be instrumentalized by the organization, the perception of Stravinsky's serial works as representing the specific brand of freedom propagated by the U.S. governing elite, and the structure of *Threni*, which articulates an aesthetic of freedom and control on its own terms.

The Concept of Freedom in Artistic Discourse

Freedom is the oxygen of modernist art and at the same time a source of one of its greatest anxieties. On the one hand, modernist art demands and obtains freedom from tradition and from conventional expression: this is expressed in the freedom to develop "secret languages."[16] On the other hand, if this freedom is exercised too relentlessly, the human subject is annihilated or becomes invisible, and without the subject, freedom becomes irrelevant. (This anxiety mirrors the constant and massive tensions in post-industrial society between individual freedoms and collective responsibility.)

In the two decades after 1945, composers whose work was quite different in many other respects shared a material-based conception of music that called for a fundamental rethinking of the nature of sound and its organization. If there is a common denominator in the diverse techniques and approaches called "serialism," then it is the notion of granting autonomy to the different qualities of musical material. In the absence of an *a priori* harmonic system, pitch and rhythm were no longer privileged as the defining features of musical content; their qualities of differentiation (and notatability) could be extended to "the other characteristics of sound: dynamics, mode of attack, timbre," as Boulez put it in "Éventuellement...," an important early serial manifesto.[17] Using a vivid contemporary metaphor, Milton Babbitt describes this expansion of musical possibilities in terms of splitting the musical atom: "Along with this increase of meaningful pitch materials, the number of functions associated with each component of the music event also has been multiplied.... Each such 'atomic' event is located in a five-dimensional musical space determined by pitch-class, register, dynamic, duration, and timbre."[18]

In this atmosphere of experiment, freedom to explore also involved freedom from outmoded convention; one of the perceived advantages of the new techniques was that they allowed the systematic elimination of extra-musical associations and traditional gestures. This can only be done, according to Boulez, by extending the existing twelve-tone technique, "which, up to now, has been largely an instrument of destruction and hence bound up with what it wanted to destroy [the conventions of tonal music], but to which our first object should be to give [it] its autonomy." Similarly, George Rochberg wrote in 1963: "Today, the sound material of music enjoys an autonomy never before accorded it. This is due largely ... to its liberation from what Sessions calls 'the musical train of thought,' the process of establishing logical connections between melodic phrase shapes and the harmonic progression which support them."[19]

Paradoxically, much of the music that was produced under the aegis of the new freedom was in fact anything but free in its construction. As Babbitt put it (continuing the previous quotation), "these five components [pitch-class, register, dynamic, duration, and timbre] not only together define the single event, but, in the course of a work, the successive values of each component create an individually coherent structure, frequently in parallel with the corresponding structures created by each of the other components." According to Boulez, the contradiction between freedom and control was necessary, and indeed inherent to the situation, since the higher-level freedom, that is, freedom from convention, could only be achieved through a renewed focus on discipline and control of the materials. Along with the liberation of sound came its voluntary reimprisonment, as the musical materials, after having declared their independence, were organized into what Boulez called an "integrated rhetoric." "It is amusing," Boulez writes, "to find the avant-garde exalting the freedom of an accepted discipline, while conservatives side with the freedom of anarchy."[20]

What interests me here is not the particular compositional technique being described (Boulez's serialism was not Babbitt's, nor was it Rochberg's), but rather how all these composers insist on a rhetoric of freedom. As in science, artistic freedom is here understood as needing to be exercised by following strict rules. This understanding of freedom was particularly widespread in the early Cold War period and was accompanied by a large-scale rationalization of society—of industry, higher education, corporations, and the military—as well as by the development of the specifically American academic version of music theory.

Musical discourse, always metaphorical, here draws upon political discourse for its vocabulary and syntax. The concept of autonomy used in the writings above (and the examples could be multiplied) is evoked as an unambiguously positive feature. The image of the newly-gained autonomy of the different parameters of music, which in turn allows an expansion of resources, is a familiar one from the political sphere. The concept of freedom was apparently so indispensable to writings about serial music that even the system's constraints had to be described in its terms: "liberation from the musical train of thought," "freedom of an accepted discipline." The language used to describe serial music therefore depends upon and articulates the specific understanding of freedom in the West during the 1950s, encompassing its political and scientific dimensions, and including the overwhelmingly positive value judgment attached to it.

The Concept of Freedom in Political Discourse

The notion of freedom in discourse about music in the early Cold War cannot be separated from the polarized political situation. The texts just cited echo political discourse by seeking to gain for musical material the same independence that the individual artist has claimed since the eighteenth century. Western notions of freedom through the autonomy of the individual, prevalent since the American and French Revolutions, acquired a new sharpness in the early Cold War as Western societies sought to define their definition of freedom against a different one: freedom from capitalist oppression and from exploitation by the ruling class. "J'ai choisi la liberté! ...," wrote the composer Hanns Eisler in 1948, shortly after his politically-motivated deportation from the United States.[21] Eisler's words intentionally echo the title of a book by a recent Russian defector to the U.S., Victor Kravchenko's *I Chose Freedom*, and reverse its meaning.[22]

At stake are two fundamentally different notions of freedom, collective and individual: music's freedom in Socialist Realism was assumed to follow automatically from society's freedom,[23] whereas in the West, New Music disconnected itself intentionally from society as individuals exercised their freedom in what they perceived to be a context of apolitical neutrality. It is because of this underlying tension that freedom becomes such a crucial concept in writings about New Music and in the New Music itself; the Western notion of freedom provided justification for the limitless expansion of musical language, but just as importantly, it staked out a position opposite to the Socialist-Realist aesthetic.

The political polarity set up a force field which individuals and institutions could not escape or ignore. The implementation of the Zhdanovian artistic reforms in the Soviet Union in 1948, and the specific criticism of Western modernism that they contained, forced a confrontation with the West. The musical reforms, disseminated through the publication of a manifesto drafted by Eisler and issued at the International Congress of Composers and Music Critics in Prague in May 1948, denounced "formalism"—clearly implied were all modernist styles including twelve-tone music—and called for music that was more accessible to the masses.[24]

One of the most influential of the numerous Western responses was Theodor W. Adorno's article "Die gegängelte Musik" ("Music Led By the Nose").[25] Questioning whether art can be steered at all by external forces, Adorno rejected the manifesto's basic presupposition: that art can ignore the historical imperatives of its development and simply be shaped anew in a utopian social order:

> [The manifesto] assumes that the collapse of individualistic society
> has to point to organization as the higher form—even with respect
> to those things whose very existence means freedom and the resis-
> tance of the living against organization. It has always been the task
> of art, ever since there has been a developed barter society (Tausch-
> gesellschaft), to oppose the ever increasing institutional grasp on life
> and to hold up against this an image of man as a free subject. Unfree
> art however can only present an image of freedom in its negation
> of bondage. (64)

Here Adorno articulates the central paradox of artistic freedom; if art is led ("gegängelt") by externally-imposed requirements, then it cannot serve its primary function of revealing the lack of freedom and brutal subjugation of the individual that takes place in any society. In a society that compels the artist to follow Eisler's manifesto, "Kunst darf nicht frei sein, weil sie als frei ausspräche, daß die Menschen es nicht sind" ("Art is not allowed to be free because it would then be able to pronounce that people are not," 52). The ideal relationship between the artwork and society should be a dialectical one: the status of the artwork as art depends on an autonomy that allows it to stand outside society in order to criticize it but which must at the same time be close enough to register its every tremor.

Adorno's position that art, by definition, "means" freedom and resistance of the living individual against the organizational (above all economic) restraints imposed by society, encapsulates the Western viewpoint; in the early years of the Cold War, the belief that freedom was a necessary condition for art was taken to be so self-evident that it became a kind of mantra. The Cold War context gave the notion of artistic freedom as one of the principal features of modern democratic society a defensive twist. Because of the knowledge that this freedom, whether for notes or for people, was denied elsewhere, it was not enough to conceive of it as mere autonomy; it had to be flaunted by those that possessed it. The moral superiority claimed by the Western position was such that one can almost speak of a compulsory artistic freedom, which moreover had certain limits; artists were free to be "cubists, surrealists, dodecaphonists and existentialists," but not to be landscape painters or tonal symphonists.[26] Serge Guilbaut writes about the visual arts, "Avant-garde art succeeded because the work and the ideology that supported it ... coincided fairly closely with the ideology that came to dominate American political life after the 1948 presidential elections. This was the 'new liberalism' ... [which] not only made room for avant-garde dissidence but accorded to such dissidence a position of paramount importance."[27] Musical discourse, therefore, not only drew upon political discourse by borrowing its words; musical practice and musical language were also drawn into the political force field. It was not possible to disengage oneself from the maelstrom, because the institutions involved in music's commissioning and performance were buffeted along by its winds; moreover, each work would be interpreted in light of the associations given to it by its political context.

The Congress for Cultural Freedom

In the aftermath of the war, the political categories Left and Right (the former still in the thrall of Stalinism, the latter exemplified by a failed criminal regime) were believed by many American political thinkers to be no longer applicable to the complexities of the current situation. The difficulty of finding a position from which to attack Communism that was not situated on the Right was acute. In his influential book of 1949, Arthur Schlesinger postulated a "Vital Center" defined by "The Politics of Freedom," as articulated in the book's title. Its central thesis: "The conception of the free society—a society committed to the protection of the liberties of conscience, expression and political opposition—is the crowning glory of western history."[28] In this view the notion of individual freedom, particularly freedom of thought and of artistic expression, formed the essential core of Western democracy and at the same time defined its primary difference from both Fascism and Communism.

Exactly this conception of freedom lay behind the creation of the Congress for Cultural Freedom (CCF)—whose very name made a political statement in this context—an American-backed, CIA-funded organization set up as part of the ambitious program to rebuild European cultural life after the war.[29] The CCF was organized as part of a larger effort by of the U.S. government to provide a counterweight to the Communist Information Bureau (Cominform), founded in 1947. The CCF's main goal was to respond to Soviet cultural propaganda by actively disseminating Western liberal ideals through cultural exchange. This pro-Western propaganda was not to be addressed to the Soviet Union itself, but rather to parts of the world deemed susceptible to Soviet influence: Asia, Africa, Eastern Europe, and most crucially, Western Europe. Here the involvement with Communism in intellectual circles, particularly in France and Italy, was viewed with suspicion; because Paris was felt to be especially precarious, the CCF set up its main office there (under the name Congrès pour la Liberté de la Culture).[30] The CCF supported books, art exhibits, symposia, music festivals, and journals, including *Encounter* in London, *Preuves* in Paris, and *Der Monat* in Berlin, which, not coincidentally, first published Adorno's essay quoted above. The CCF leadership was made up of American and European intellectuals, politicians, and artists, many of them former Communists, who were drawn from a group known as the non-Communist Left. Figures with a wide range of political sympathies received support from the CCF, although artists who were currently too closely associated with Communism were excluded. Though anti-Communist by definition, the CCF leadership took pains to distance itself from right-wing politics and rejected McCarthyism, nationalism, and religious movements.

The CCF's aims were set out in a brochure issued at the organization's founding in June 1950 in Berlin: *Freedom Takes the Offensive*, which contained a "manifesto adopted by leading intellectuals of the free world."[31] (See Fig. 1)

Figure 1

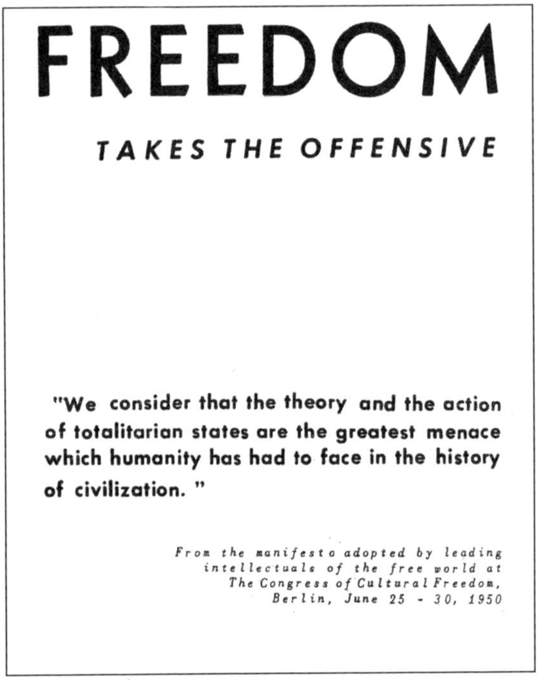

FREEDOM

TAKES THE OFFENSIVE

"We consider that the theory and the action of totalitarian states are the greatest menace which humanity has had to face in the history of civilization. "

From the manifesto adopted by leading intellectuals of the free world at The Congress of Cultural Freedom, Berlin, June 25 - 30, 1950

The authors included Arthur Koestler, Sidney Hook, and Nicolas Nabokov. As the title of the brochure makes clear, the CCF transformed freedom from a concept inscribed onto a banner, as it were, into something active and even aggressive. The euphoria of the moment comes across in many of the texts, as freedom was brandished as the new weapon in the "battles of our time."[32]

These battles, as it turned out, were fought on the comfortable terrain of concert halls, exhibition galleries, and five-star hotels. Major festivals were launched in Paris (1952), Rome (1954), Venice (1958), and Tokyo (1961). Because the American composer and Russian émigré Nicolas Nabokov was in charge of running the CCF's operations (his title was Secretary General), music was at the center the organization's activities, which also included art shows and presentations by literary figures.

The Paris festival, "Masterpieces of the Twentieth Century," while more ambitious than the other festivals, was typical in its desire to make a splash; staging a high-profile "event" evidently took priority over any kind of thematic or even political coherence (although the disproportionately American emphasis and the exclusion of avowed Communists were obvious).[33] The month-long festival (April 30 through June 1) featured mainstream organizations including the Boston Symphony Orchestra, the New York City Ballet, and the Vienna Philharmonic; it also launched the career of the young and then-unknown soprano Leontyne Price. Avant-garde music was also performed under the aegis of the festival (albeit in a marginal role), including most notably the world premiere of "Music for Two Pianos" by Pierre Boulez, later known as *Structures 1a*.[34]

But the best-known contemporary composer at the festival was Igor Stravinsky, represented with nine pieces,[35] including new stagings of *Le sacre du printemps* and *Orpheus* with choreographies by George Balanchine. Nabokov had also tried very hard to include a staged performance of Stravinsky's recent opera, *The Rake's Progress*, in what would have been its French premiere, but this did not come about. Stravinsky himself attached much importance to the fact that his appearance at the festival marked his re-entry into Parisian musical life after an absence of fourteen years. So, even though the music of many other living composers, including Virgil Thomson, Aaron Copland, and Samuel Barber was also played, it was still Stravinsky's festival. Colin Mason reported: "But the triumph of Schoenberg, Bartók, Milhaud and Britten was nothing compared to Strawinsky's. It was clearly the intention of the festival that this should be so. ... For he is the sole survivor of a generation of giants, the greatest living master of music, and this is the year of his seventieth birthday."[36] Stravinsky's much-heralded post-war "debut" in the French capital did not feature his newest music; festival audiences experienced the old composer presiding over performances of his most well-known earlier works. He was presented more as a legendary historical figure than as a living composer. (This impression might have been different if *The Rake's Progress* had been performed; but even so, Stravinsky would have still been represented by the neoclassical style characteristic of his works since the 1920s.) The festival's programming, emphasizing well-known masterpieces and established ensembles, reflected all in all a distinctly conservative perspective on twentieth-century music at the half-century mark.

The political purpose of the festival was well known to Stravinsky and was in fact widely recognized at the time.[37] The goal, literally to put artistic freedom on display, was articulated at every opportunity by Nabokov, in interviews and in articles such as the one that opens the special issue of the *Revue musicale* of April 1952.[38] The *New York Herald Tribune* reported in December 1951: "One of the principal motives of the Congress in sponsoring the Spring festival, it was said, is to combat the current Communist party line in Europe which has been insulting Western art and culture as 'decadent.'"[39] To drive the point home that the right to free artistic expression is not to be taken for granted, the program book reprinted polemical condemnations from the Nazi or Soviet press of many of the pieces on the program (these had been collected at Nabokov's request by his friend H.H. Stuckenschmidt, whom Nabokov characterized as "an old friend of the Congress").[40] The message was twofold; not only was the Western composer free to follow his impulses, but also the music itself represented freedom by breaking through the boundaries of convention. Nabokov's broad mainstream programming and relative neglect of the avant-garde indicates that he believed that this message could be conveyed with almost any twentieth-century music composed outside the Soviet block.[41] In other words, the style of the music seems to have been less important than the circumstances under which it was composed. Partly because the political purpose of the festival was so obvious (and moreover destined to fall on deaf ears in the predominantly left-leaning intellectual circles of Paris), it was not a success, although due to its sheer size and scale it did create the intended stir.[42]

I have described the Paris festival in order to establish, first, Stravinsky's prominent role in an event whose political nature was evident, and second, that he was well informed about the CCF and its goals, which he evidently shared, given his own anti-Soviet stance.[43]

Stravinsky's association with Nabokov and with the CCF lasted for many years after the Paris festival. *Canticum Sacrum, Movements* for piano and orchestra, *Threni*, and *Abraham and Isaac* were among the works with whose commissioning Nabokov was closely involved. In addition to the generous commissions (usually at least $5000), Stravinsky received substantial fees for conducting his works at these performances (from $1500 to $2500 per appearance), and very generous travel expense subsidies (upwards of $2000 for each trip), all of which was financed by the Congress for Cultural Freedom.[44] For the Paris festival alone Stravinsky received $6500.[45] He would have received an additional $5000 for conducting *The Rake's Progress*. (For the sake of comparison, the average annual family income in 1952 in the U.S. was $3900.)[46] Although a detailed study of Stravinsky's finances in these years would be necessary to get a complete picture, it appears as if Nabokov's commissions and engagements provided a substantial percentage of Stravinsky's income after 1950; it seems clear, moreover, that the CCF provided much, if not most, of the direct support for Stravinsky's late work.

Threni

Let us look more closely at one example, *Threni: Id est Lamentationes Jermemiae Prophetae* for vocal soloists, chorus, and orchestra (1957–58), whose commission and first performances took place under the auspices of the CCF; subsequent performances were organized with Nabokov's support (see Fig. 2). The letter from Nabokov to Stravinsky shows how such commissions were initiated and presumably financed by the CCF while appearing to come from a third party, here the Norddeutscher Rundfunk (North German Radio) in Hamburg. After initially declining, Stravinsky fulfilled this commission (for which Nabokov offered $5000 plus a $2500 conducting fee) with the composition of *Threni*, which was premiered September 23, 1958 at the Biennale in Venice, with the composer conducting.[47] Immediately following the Biennale, Stravinsky conducted four further performances of *Threni* in Switzerland. These performances were also organized by Nabokov.[48]

The new piece, then, was commissioned and performed under the most generous possible terms. Artistically the circumstances were also ideal, as the chorus and orchestra of the North German Radio were of excellent quality. Why does it matter—or does it matter—that all this was made possible by the CIA, who supported this and other projects for its own political motives? Stravinsky, although well-informed about the CCF, did not know who his patron really was; Nabokov had always identified Julius Fleischmann and his foundation as the source of the support.[49] The traditional view has been moreover that the composer preserves his artistic autonomy regardless of the

Figure 2. Letter from Nicolas Nabokov to Igor Stravinsky,
Paul Sacher Foundation, Stravinsky Collection.
Used with kind permission of the Paul Sacher Foundation.

CONGRÈS POUR LA LIBERTÉ DE LA CULTURE

104, BOULEVARD HAUSSMANN, PARIS VIIIᵉ · EUROPE 55-15

LE SECRÉTAIRE GÉNÉRAL

CONFIDENTIAL.   17th June, 1957.

Mr. Igor Stravinsky,
1260 North Wetherley Drive,
Hollywood,
California.

Dear Igor Fëdorovitch,

Once more, many warmest greetings and good wishes
for your health and happiness. Oh how I should have liked
to have been in Los Angeles and heard the first performance
of "Agon". I hope it went well and look forward to having
a chance of seeing the score. Could I get a copy from the
Booseys and the Hawkses? At any rate, I am planning to be
in Dartington in August and am immensely looking forward to
seeing you there.

Here is the gist of the proposal which I indicated in
my cable: Rolf Liebermann, Director of the Radio in Zuerich,
who is, as you know, a very good friend of mine, has now been
appointed Director of the Hamburg Radio which has become one
of the most important radio stations of Europe. I saw him
last Friday and discussed my Tokyo plans with him. Prospects
for the Tokyo project look very promising, by the way, but I
shall not know the definite decision for approximately another
month. Rolf Liebermann made the following proposal which, combined with the Tokyo possibilities could I believe, be of interest to you: Would you accept a commission from the Hamburg
Radio to write a work of your choosing of approximately 20-minutes'
playing time or longer, for a first performance by the Hamburg
Radio in September 1958 under your direction?

This work would be performed within the framework of two or
three special public concerts, organised by Liebermann and myself
under the title "Les Concerts Européens" on the occasion of a
European Cultural Conference which will be sponsored by the
University of Hamburg and the European Institute, with my collaboration, and to which we intend to invite between 25 and 30 of
the most important European philosophers, writers, poets and
scientists. The other two concerts of "Les Concerts Européens"
would include the first concert performance of "L'Atlantide" by
Manuel de Falla and works by Schoenberg, Webern and Bartok.

/...

circumstances of a piece's origin. This may be true from the perspective of
the composer, who does not feel pressure to compose in a particular way (and
there is no evidence that commissions from the CCF came with any strings
attached). And for a work-centered historiography the source of the commission indeed would not much matter.

But it matters a great deal to cultural analysts and historians who wish to understand the dynamics of a given political and cultural moment. And *Threni*, read as a text in a dialogue about cultural freedom, confirms at one level everything the CCF stood for, while at another level it reveals the fragility and utter precariousness of that freedom. This complex and even contradictory message is the appropriate one for an artwork; if the piece had merely reiterated the political message, it would just be propaganda. *Threni* is therefore not a piece of "political music," but in articulating a dialectic of freedom and control, it addresses some of the central issues of its time, which were also directly analogous to those at the core of the CCF's philosophy.

In the following (partial and incomplete) analysis, I hypothesize that the piece's articulation of restriction, boundedness, inexorability, and, ultimately, profound hopelessness makes it on the one hand an unsuitable choice for the optimistic and rather simplistic message of the CCF, but that on the other hand *Threni* served the CCF as an ideal example of the kind of music that could only be produced in the West. It is necessary to focus on the work's "internal" features—its serial musical language, its use of chorus, its text-setting, and its religious, almost liturgical tone—as well as its context and reception, because all these elements are connected. A political interpretation cannot come straight from the "primary musical facts themselves," as Reinhold Brinkmann points out, but rather is developed out of the associations given to the music by its receivers. While the use of categories that pieces seem to share with political ideas (such as freedom, or in Brinkmann's example, "the violation of norms") "because of the increasing abstraction necessarily entails a coarsening of the categories," these categories can and must be specified by examining how they work in that particular piece of music: "in the musical text as the only possible location of individuation and of social concreteness."[50]

Threni, a setting in Latin of the Lamentations of Jeremiah, is based on a single twelve-tone row, which is varied by rotation and permutation as well as by the traditional operations of transposition, inversion, retrograde, and retrograde inversion (see Ex. 1a). A passage from the first elegy, given in

Example 1a. Row of Igor Stravinsky's Threni

Example 1b, illustrates the work's severity as well as the strictness of its row technique. The flugelhorn and tenor soloist, paired in a duet, are accompanied by the syllabic declamation of the women's chorus and by upper strings (Vn. I and II, Vla.). The entire passage sounds in the narrow registral space of slightly more than two octaves (d to f♯²); this is in sharp contrast to the low bass of the immediately preceding passage (mm. 37–41).

The tenor voice and flugelhorn (a tenor bugle) are more than a timbral pair; they are pitch counterparts as well. Each unfolds the retrograde form of the row (the flugelhorn does this continuously with few repeated notes, while the tenor presents two incomplete rows before finally completing one in m. 53). The pitch imitation between the two voices in addition to the fixed registers create the impression of a canon, but the varied rhythms and the tenor's fragmentary rows break up whatever canons are temporarily formed. The dialogue character of these two voices—or, perhaps more accurately, their double monologue character—is emphasized after m. 57 when the other instruments and voices drop out, leaving the flugelhorn and tenor alone to continue reiterating their row form, ending on the same pitch an octave apart, as they began.[51]

The women's chorus unfolds, with interruptions, two statements of the row's retrograde inversion form. The final note of this (and of the other) row form is E♭/D♯, which the chorus marks by repetition; in m. 56, the voices in the three upper staves converge on this pitch. The three serial voices—the flugelhorn, tenor, and chorus—seem to be locked in their repetitive row statements and circle around within a narrow registral space like tigers pacing around a cage.

The accompanying strings are even more drastically reduced. They have only three pitches, C, D, and F (all in register 4), and no rhythmic independence. Even though the choice of the three notes can be explained as a serial derivation of the chorus's row,[52] the strings' reiteration of its three pitches negates the row's E♭/D♯ centricity.

Threni was Stravinsky's first thoroughly serial piece. It was also his response to "total serialism"; according to David Smyth, Stravinsky copied out the row for Boulez's *Structures 1a* in his sketches for the piece.[53] Boulez's row seems to have had no real impact on Stravinsky's composition; in any case Stravinsky's serial technique is worlds away from Boulez's. The twelve-tone row in the passage just discussed is used neither as material to generate mathematically-related variants, as in Boulez, nor as a basis for motivic development, as in the Viennese School, but rather as itself. In the passage from *Threni* discussed above the row *is* the material: much of the piece is indeed a

Example 1b. Igor Stravinsky, Threni:
Lamentationes Jeremiae Prophetae *(1957–58): De Elegia Prima, mm. 37–61.*
Translation: How doth the city sit solitary, that was full of people! How is she
become as a widow! she that was great among the nations, and princess
among the provinces, how is she become tributary!

Example 1b. (continued)

series of "sounding rows" (here Adorno's famous criticism would have been more apt than it was with Webern). The row canons are not disguised in order to serve some other musical end, but simply assert and reassert in readily audible fashion their own bounded materiality. The piece does not employ serial structures as a kind of subcutaneous control, but enacts control itself. This control is reflected in the work's form as well, which displays a large scale tripartite symmetry reproduced in small on more local levels.

It seems clear that *Threni* has something to say about freedom, but what? Does the piece deny the possibility of freedom by putting obsessive order on display? Or does it confirm the value of freedom by representing its opposite? Or does it dissolve the perspective of the human subject (a necessary condition for freedom) by subsuming it into the collective and confining it within endlessly-circling canonic structures? Or do these apparent strictures signify a higher freedom (as in Bach's strict contrapuntal music), sought through the grace of a divine power?

The latter two interpretative hypotheses are far richer than the first two, since they do not try to eliminate the tension between freedom and control that is a defining feature of this music. The piece does not deliver a message as one-sided as the CCF's, in which freedom is always connoted positively, restriction negatively. Neither does it present a simple mirror image of this value structure. Instead, by constantly rupturing the seemingly controlled surface, the piece's serial language enacts the fundamental tension inherent in the notion of order. This tension can be heard even in the passage discussed earlier, where there are breaks in the seemingly controlled surface. I have already mentioned the interruptions in the tenor's presentation of its row and the rhythmic differences between the two melodic voices that disrupt the canon. The strings also seem to contradict the serial surface: their repeated seconds and minor thirds sound modal, even "Russian." Moreover, the drastically reduced pitch and registral dimensions in this passage are compensated by the rich timbral variety achieved by the use of different instrumental families and textures (solo brass vs. solo voice; solo male voice vs. choral female voices; choral voices vs. choral strings, melodic linear textures vs. tremolo ostinato-type textures). What *Threni* presents to us is not the order of a well-oiled machine, but rather the fragile, even precarious order of modern urban society.

Threni is ultimately a piece of religious music, not only because of its Biblical text (whose excerpts were selected by Stravinsky), but because of how the text is treated.[54] The Lamentions of Jeremiah are set not as a piece of concert music, but as if for liturgical use. This can be heard in the speaking choruses in the first and fifth elegies, which sound like the congregation at prayer, and in the prominent solo role of the second bass, who—most notably at the beginning of the third elegy—with his unaccompanied solo alternating with choral entrances represents the role of the priest leading the congregation at prayer. The text's message proceeds from a third-person description of the destruction of Jerusalem and the slaughtering of its population to a more personal level as the narrator describes the torments inflicted upon him. He pleas for God's mercy, which he believes has been withheld from him. After begging for divine retribution of his enemies, he prays for God to remember his ordeal and to confer His grace again upon the people.[55]

Although the text would lend itself to a subjective, pseudo-dramatic setting (a monologue in the voice of Jeremiah, for example), in *Threni*, the personal level has been expunged in favor of the collective voice of the people. The solo voices are anonymous; they rarely sing alone, but are instead deployed in duets, trios, or quartets, which are usually strictly canonic and always bound by serial structures (only the second bass has a prominent solo role; he represents the priest, as mentioned above, who as mediator between the congregation and God does not speak for himself). The chorus is omnipresent, not least because it intones the Hebrew letters that begin each verse; these in turn do not belong to the text proper, but are objective markers of its structure. This "impersonal" approach to the text prevents it from becoming an expression of an individual's pain. The piece's serial language further augments the distance between the music and the searing content of the text. The story is recounted (and the words are usually understandable), but the listener is not drawn in to share the experience of pathos.[56] At the end of the piece ("Converte nos," mm. 405–end) an increased tonal centricity is heard, ending in the A-minor-sounding chord A-C (which however occurs *within* the serial structures); the progress from "sounding rows" to tonal allusion could support a reading of the piece as a religious narrative, in which the human subject progresses from pain in slavery to freedom through God's mercy.

A thirty-five-minute serial cantata, *Threni* is a stringent, ascetic, and decidedly unspectacular work. In the context of the Venice Biennale and the Swiss concerts that followed, *Threni* was dissonant on several levels. Not only was it the only post-war serial piece on any of the programs, it was also much less inviting than the other twentieth-century pieces programmed (which included Bartók's Concerto for Orchestra, Berg's Violin Concerto, and Hindemith's Konzertmusik for string orchestra and brass),[57] and certainly less appealing to the average festival audience member than the music by G. Gabrieli,

Pachelbel, and J.S. Bach also heard at the Biennale (not to mention "a jazz jam session of the latest polyphonic jazz bands of the United States").[58] On the Swiss tour that followed the Biennale, *Threni* was paired with Beethoven's Ninth Symphony, whose fourth movement presents an exaggerated optimism which was more consistent with the CCF's message than *Threni*'s. But *Threni*, as Stravinsky's first newly-commissioned work for a CCF festival, would have also been conspicuous within the context of Stravinsky's own works: the new piece must have come as a shock to those expecting music like the *Sacre du printemps*, *Symphonies of Wind Instruments*, and *Oedipus Rex*, all of which had been featured in earlier festivals and were also played in Venice. Even Stuckenschmidt, who was closely associated with the CCF and an admirer of Stravinsky's music, was not taken with the new piece: "Threni is the strictest, most dissonant twelve-tone piece that the over seventy-year-old master has written after his conversion to the musical language of Schoenberg and Webern; the piece sounded strange and out-of-place in the context of Venice," he wrote about the premiere.[59]

Even though *Threni*, an anti-festival piece par excellence, was not really at home in the Venice Biennale, it was still perfectly suitable for the CCF's purposes. As Adorno's essay "Die gegängelte Musik" (and the CCF manifesto in far less subtle fashion) made clear, exposing ruptures and contradictions is exactly the proper role of art in a free society. As political propaganda *Threni* was ideal because it could only have been a product of a Western society. Nabokov must have been satisfied, even though he personally preferred Stravinsky's neoclassical music, because *Threni* went against practically every single dictum in the Eisler manifesto. *Threni* therefore, in spite of the ambivalent relationship to freedom that it articulates, had excellent propaganda value.

Finally, in addition to serving the CCF's purposes admirably, *Threni* at the same time staked Stravinsky's claim to be a living composer who was involved with the most recent avant-garde trends, and not just "the sole survivor of a generation of giants."[60] Stravinsky's choice of serial technique carried a double association. First, it was unambiguously associated with the cutting edge of advanced music in Europe and the U.S.[61] Second, at least as far as the CCF was concerned, it was equally unambiguously associated with an anti-Communist, or more precisely an anti-Soviet aesthetic, in that it broke practically all the rules that had been set for Soviet music after 1948. (That there was a type of politically progressive European music that was marked by the use of advanced idioms complicates the situation, but does not alter the CCF's view of things.) The political and artistic "meanings" of serial technique in this particular context existed regardless of whether or not Stravinsky meant to create these associations or even thought about them.[62]

I would like to end with three observations,

1. The example of the CCF shows how advanced music was instrumentalized for political purposes in the West, that is, as liberal democratic propaganda promoted as an alternative to Communist artistic policies (even if the CCF's efforts were not ultimately successful). This points up one significant difference between the European and the American cultural environments after the war: in Europe, advanced styles continued to be conceived as oppositional to Fascism (i.e., on the Left), whereas in the U.S., they were part and parcel of an anti-Communist, high-technology, scientific Cold War ideology. (The U.S. could not have produced a Nono.)

2. The aesthetic modernism of post-war Europe and the U.S. cannot be viewed as apolitical because its main concepts developed in the context of, and specifically in opposition to, the diametrically different notion of freedom advocated by Communist governments. The oft-proclaimed aesthetic autonomy grew out of an intentionally oppositional stance, even in cases where the art was unrelated to the CCF or any specific program.

3. But post-war modernism was not just reactive; it also partook of and contributed to a political discourse about the central ideas of the time: freedom and control, the role of individual and the role of society, the relationship to tradition and the desire to create a blank slate, local and international culture, and many more. Artworks engaged with these ideas and were in turn received in the context of the larger ideologies that these ideas represented. Ideology is therefore not just something found on the Left; it was also intrinsic to "unpolitical" music in the West. In the case of serial music, its very hermeticism—performed in acts of autonomy, of erasure, and of scientific order—reveals its stake in Cold War tensions.

Notes

*   I would like to thank Reinhold Brinkmann, Lydia Goehr, Felix Meyer, and Simon Obert for their comments and suggestions on an earlier draft of the paper. I also benefited from the discussion of the draft by graduate students and colleagues at the Graduiertenkurs in Blonay, Switzerland, in July 2002.

1 Inge Kovács points out how the Western avant-garde developed, not coincidentally, as a mirror image of the Communist cultural program: "Vor diesem Hintergrund fällt auf, daß die westeuropäische Avantgarde zunehmend genau das propagierte und darstellte, was von stalinistischer Seite Verfolgungen ausgesetzt war. Insofern ist ihre Entwicklung um 1950 vor der Folie des Kalten Krieges zu verstehen, ohne daß damit andere Erklärungsansätze ausgeschlossen werden sollen, vor allem der Kontext der jüngst überstandenen NS-Diktatur und des Zweiten Weltkrieges," in Gianmario Borio and Hermann Danuser, eds., *Im Zenit der Moderne: Die Internationalen Ferienkurse für Neue Musik Darmstadt, 1946–1966*, 1 (Freiburg im Br.: Rombach, 1997), 129.

2 See Martin Brody, "'Music for the Masses': Milton Babbitt's Cold War Music Theory," *Musical Quarterly* 77 (1993), 161–192; also William Brooks, "The Americas, 1945–70," in Robert P. Morgan, ed., *Modern Times: From World War I to the Present* (London [etc.]: Macmillan, 1993), 309–48.

3 This has been amply documented; see Serge Guilbaut, *How New York Stole the Idea of Modern Art: Abstract Expressionism, Freedom, and the Cold War*, trans. Arthur Goldhammer (Chicago and London: University of Chicago Press, 1983).

4 See Peter Coleman, *The Liberal Conspiracy: The Congress for Cultural Freedom and the Struggle for the Mind of Postwar Europe* (New York: The Free Press, and London: Collier Macmillan, 1989), Frances Stonor Saunders, *Who Paid the Piper? The CIA and the Cultural Cold War* (London: Granta Books, 1999), and Volker R. Berghahn, *America and the Intellectual Cold Wars in Europe: Shepard Stone Between Philanthropy, Academy, and Diplomacy* (Princeton and Oxford: Princeton University Press, 2001).

5 For studies of music's role in the American government's attempts to fight Communist propaganda see Ian Wellens, *Music on the Frontline: Nicolas Nabokov's Struggle against Communism and Middlebrow Culture* (Hants, U.K. and Burlington, Vermont: Ashgate, 2002) and Mark Carroll, *Music and Ideology in Cold War Europe* (Cambridge: Cambridge University Press, 2003).

6 See Lydia Goehr, "'Music Has No Meaning to Speak of': On the Politics of Musical Interpretation," in Michael Krausz, ed., *The Interpretation of Music: Philosophical Essays* (Oxford: Clarendon Press, 1993), 177–190; and Jürg Stenzl, "'Reinlichkeitsgefühl in Kunstdingen': 'Politische Musik'—Skizze einer Begriffsgeschichte," *MusikTexte* no. 39 (1991), 48–55. Both Goehr and Stenzl identify the separation of music and politics as a consequence of the development of an aesthetic of autonomy in the late-eighteenth century and warn against mistaking this historical situation for a universal one.

7 Stenzl writes, "Religion, Hygiene und Virginitätswert durchkreuzen sich..." in implicit assumptions about music's protected space; he identifies the origins of this anxiety as historically specific to German culture, see "Reinlichkeitsgefühl," 53.

8 Cornelius Cardew, *Stockhausen Serves Imperialism and Other Articles* (London: Latimer New Dimensions Ltd., 1974); Konrad Boehmer, "Karlheinz Stockhau-

sen oder: Der Imperialismus als höchstes Stadium des kapitalistischen Avant-gardismus," *Musik und Gesellschaft* 22 (1972), 137–50.

9 These are two of the definitions in Webster's *New Collegiate Dictionary*. For a discussion of the various meanings of ideology, see Terry Eagleton, *Ideology: An Introduction* (London and New York: Verso, 1991).

10 As Georg Iggers writes, "[In the 'New Cultural History'], the sources of exploitation and domination were not to be found primarily in institutionalized structures, in politics or in the e[c]onomy, but more importantly in the many interpersonal relations in which human beings exert power over others.... Foucault in an important sense replaced Marx as the analyst of power and of its relation to knowledge," *Historiography in the Twentieth Century: From Scientific Objectivity to the Postmodern Challenge* (Hanover, NH and London: Wesleyan University Press, 1997), 99.

11 Mathias Spahlinger writes, "vielleicht fragt kunst nur danach, was schön oder häßlich ist; was aber einer gesellschaft für das eine oder andere gilt, ist politisch nicht gleichgültig" ("Perhaps art asks only what is beautiful or ugly, but what a society holds to be one or the other is politically not irrelevant"), see "wirklichkeit des bewußtseins und wirklichkeit für das bewußtsein: politische aspekte der musik," *MusikTexte* No. 39 (1991), 40.

12 See my "The Myth of Empirical Historiography: A Response to Joseph N. Straus," *The Musical Quarterly* 84 (2000), 30–39. Jennifer DeLapp has shown how serial techniques were associated with anti-Communism in the charged political climate of the 1950s in the U.S.; see her "Copland in the Fifties: Music and Ideology in the McCarthy Era" (PhD Dissertation, University of Michigan, 1997). Amy Beal examines the U.S. government's interest in promoting avant-garde music by initiating and supporting the Internationale Ferienkurse für Neue Musik in Darmstadt in its early years, see "Negotiating Cultural Allies: American Music in Darmstadt, 1946–1956," *Journal of the American Musicological Society*, 53 (2000), 105–139.

13 Quoted in Lydia Goehr, "The Politics of Musical Interpretation," 180.

14 See Guilbaut, *How New York Stole the Idea of Modern Art*, especially 187–89.

15 "Die in musik thematisierten denkformen und fühlweisen sind denen, mit denen staat gemacht wird, analog oder sie sind diese selbst." Spahlinger, "wirklichkeit des bewußtseins," 41.

16 I refer here to Robert P. Morgan, "Secret Languages: The Roots of Musical Modernism," in Monique Chefdor, Albert Wachtel, and Ricardo Quiñones, eds., *Modernism: Challenges and Perspectives* (Urbana, IL: University of Illinois, 1986), 33–53.

17 "Possibly ... ," in *Stocktakings from an Apprenticeship*, trans. Stephen Walsh, 115. The original essay was published in *Revue musicale* 212, April 1952; it was later included in Pierre Boulez, *Relevés d'apprenti*, collected and edited by Paule Thévenin, (Paris: Éditions du Seuil, 1966), 147–82. Dominique Jameux dates the

essay 1950: see his *Pierre Boulez*, trans. by Susan Bradshaw (Cambridge, MA: Harvard University Press, 1990), 44. This essay contains the infamous sentence, "... any musician who has not experienced ... the necessity of dodecaphonic language is USELESS" (*Stocktakings*, 113) which Boulez re-used in his essay, "Schoenberg is Dead."

18 Milton Babbitt, "Who Cares if You Listen," in Elliott Schwartz and Barney Childs, eds., *Contemporary Composers on Contemporary Music* (New York: Da Capo, 1978), 245.

19 Rochberg, "The New Image of Music," *Perspectives of New Music* 2 (1963–64), 4.

20 Boulez, "Possibly ...," 112.

21 Hanns Eisler, "J'ai choisi la liberté! ...," *Les Lettres françaises*, 29 April 1948, 1, in Hanns Eisler, *Musik und Politik: Schriften 1948–1962*, ed. Günter Mayer (Leipzig: VEB Deutscher Verlag für Musik, 1982), 10–13.

22 Victor Kravchenko, *I Chose Freedom: The Personal and Political Life of a Soviet Official* (Garden City, NY: Garden City Publishing, 1946). Published simultaneously in French, the controversial book was widely discussed—and roundly rejected—in Parisian left-wing intellectual circles, for whom it represented a heresy. See Tony Judt, *Past Imperfect: French Intellectuals, 1944–1956* (Berkeley [etc.]: University of California Press, 1992), 112–13.

23 This is articulated in Eisler's essay "Gesellschaftliche Grundfragen der modernen Musik" (1948): "Nach all diesen Exzessen und Experimenten scheinen die Aufgaben der Musiker in unserer Zeit vielleicht darin zu liegen, die Musik in einer zuerst vielleicht bescheideneren Weise in eine höhere Form der Gesellschaft zurückzuführen, vom Privaten zum Allgemeinen. Und diese höhere Form ist eine Gesellschaft von freien Menschen, in der die Ausbeutung des Menschen durch den Menschen aufgehoben ist," *Musik und Politik*, 22.

24 Two versions of the manifesto can be found in *Musik und Politik*, 26–31. The manifesto was published in Russian in *Sowjetskaya Musyka* 5 (1948), 7–8, in German in the *Österreichisches Tagebuch* 3 (1948), 32, in Czech in *Hudebni rozhledy* 1 (1948), 40. The Czech congress closely followed the Soviet congress of February 1948, at which Shostakovich, Prokofiev, Khachaturian, and other Soviet composers were reprimanded for succumbing to the "formalist movement." The "Decree on Music" formulated on this occasion by Zhdanov was a model for the later Czech manifesto. See William W. Austin, *Music in the 20th Century, From Debussy through Stravinsky* (New York and London: Norton, 1966), 434, 458–59. A summary of these events was published in English: see Alexander Werth, *Musical Uproar in Moscow* (London: Turnstile Press, 1949).

25 "Zugrunde liegt [dem Dokument] die Vorstellung, daß der Zerfall der individualistischen Gesellschaft ohne weiteres auf Organisation als die höhere Form weise—auch dort, wo die Sache ihrem eigenen Sinn nach Freiheit und den Widerstand des Lebendigen gegen Organisation meint. Denn es war Aufgabe der Kunst, seit es überhaupt eine entwickelte Tauschgesellschaft gibt, der immer weiter fortschreitenden institutionellen Umklammerung des Lebens zu

opponieren und ihr ein Bild des Menschen als eines freien Subjekts entgegen-
zuhalten. Im unfreien Zustand aber ist Kunst des Bildes der Freiheit mächtig
nur in der Negation der Unfreiheit"; Adorno, "Die gegängelte Musik," in his
Dissonanzen. Einleitung in die Musiksoziologie, ed. Rolf Tiedemann (Frankfurt
a.M.: Suhrkamp, 1973), 51–66 (Gesammelte Schriften, 14). Originally published
in *Der Monat,* May 1953, but written before the spring of 1949. See letter from
Adorno to René Leibowitz, 15 April 1949, Paul Sacher Stiftung, Basel (hereafter
cited as PSS), Leibowitz Collection.

26 Colin Mason, "The Paris Festival," *Tempo* 24 (1952), 19. Martin Brody also notes
that one rationale for offering a privileged position to avant-garde art was to
ensure the "cultural diversity" characteristic of a liberal, pluralistic society, that
is, not to abandon the field to popular culture, see "Milton Babbitt's Cold War
Music Theory," 182.

27 Guilbaut, *How New York Stole the Idea of Modern Art,* 3.

28 Arthur Schlesinger, *The Vital Center: The Politics of Freedom* (Boston: Houghton
Mifflin, and Cambridge, MA: The Riverside Press, 1949). Other thinkers also
contributed to the post-war American conception of freedom: see Arthur Koestler, *The God that Failed: Six Studies in Communism* (London: Hamish Hamil-
ton, 1950); Sidney Hook, ed., *John Dewey: Philosopher of Science and Freedom*
(New York: The Dial Press, 1950). Countless school textbooks and works of popular history from this time echo this particular understanding of freedom: for
example Gertrude Hartmann's *America: Land of Freedom* (Boston: D.C. Heath
& Co., 1946).

29 Although related in spirit to the Marshall Plan (which did provide some of the
funding), the CCF operated on a much more modest scale. (The burgeoning
literature on the CCF is summarized in notes 4 and 5.)

30 Sidney Hook wrote in 1949: "The informational re-education of the French
public seems to me to be the most fundamental as well as the most pressing task
of American democratic policy in France, towards which almost nothing along
effective lines has been done." Quoted in Saunders, *The Cultural Cold War,* 70.

31 *Freedom Takes the Offensive: From the manifesto adopted by leading intellectuals
of the free world at the Congress of [sic] Cultural Freedom, Berlin, June 25–30, 1950*
[Berlin, 1950]. Typescript. I consulted an original held in the Schweizerische
Osteuropabibliothek in Bern.

32 *Freedom Takes the Offensive,* 1. The war metaphors culminate in the heading
"U.S. Atom Bombs—Defenders of Liberty" in James Burnham's article "Rhetoric and Peace," 28. Although bellicose language is used throughout the brochure,
none of the other authors advocates actual violence.

33 For the staging of *Le sacre du printemps* for the festival, the choreographer Balanchine had requested Picasso as set designer, but, Nabokov wrote to Stravinsky on June 27, 1951, "naturellement, après les dernières cabrioles du camarade
Picasso, surtout son impardonnable toile sur les massacres de Corée, il est hors
de question que nous ayons recours à lui. Picasso est devenu un triste sire qui

se met au service de la propagande soviétique et malheureusement il n'y aura rien à faire dans cette direction." Stravinsky responded on July 3: "Evidemment Picasso eut été le plus desirable s'il n'etait juge 'indesirable'." Original orthography. PSS, Stravinsky Collection. Translated excerpts from the Stravinsky-Nabokov correspondence have been published in Stravinsky, *Selected Correspondence*, II, ed. and with commentaries by Robert Craft (London and Boston: Faber & Faber, 1984), 381–82.

34 Boulez must have been at that time associated in some way with the CCF; in addition to the premiere of *Structures*, the article cited above, "Éventuellement...," was first published in a special number of *La Revue musicale* devoted to the festival; see No. 212 (April 1952), Numéro Spécial: "L'Oeuvre du XXe Siècle: Exposition Internationale des Arts sous les auspices du Congrès pour la Liberté de la Culture."

35 *The Firebird, Orpheus, Le sacre du printemps, Concerto in D, Scènes de ballet, Oedipus Rex, Symphony in C, Capriccio* for piano, and *Symphony in Three Movements*. See Wellens, *Music on the Frontline*, 139.

36 Mason, "The Paris festival," 15.

37 The Stravinsky Nachlass contains articles from the *New York Herald Tribune*, the *Los Angeles Daily News*, and other newspapers about the festival and its political goals. See Saunders, *Who Paid the Piper?* (120–24) for a summary of responses to the festival in the French press. The reviews I have collected, from *The Score, Tempo, Österreichische Musikzeitschrift,* and *Melos,* also show ample awareness of the organization's political goals.

38 Nicolas Nabokov, "Introduction a L'oeuvre du XXe Siècle," *La Revue musicale* 212 (April 1952), 5–8; see especially the article's close (8).

39 Paul V. Beckley, "Boston Symphony, City Ballet Going to Paris Festival in May," *New York Herald Tribune*, December 28, 1951 (PSS, Stravinsky Collection).

40 Letter from Nabokov to Stuckenschmidt, February 26, 1952, Stuckenschmidt-Sammlung, Akademie der Künste, Berlin. I have not been able to locate a copy of this program book. It would be interesting to investigate whether Nicolas Slonimsky's *Lexicon of Musical Invective*, which appeared one year later, had any connection to Nabokov or to the political context.

41 Nabokov disliked the music of Shostakovich and Prokofiev intensely, in (large?) part for political reasons. See his article, "The Case of Dmitri Shostakovich," *Harper's Magazine* (March 1942), 422ff, in which he describes Shostakovich's political career in great detail and ascribes to him "one hundred per cent Stalinist-Communist" loyalties (426).

42 On the overwhelmingly left-wing sympathies of French intellectuals at that time, see Tony Judt, *Past Imperfect*. Ian Wellens quotes a contemporary review of the festival that called it "a very popular fiasco," see *Music on the Frontline*, 45.

43 Nabokov kept Stravinsky informed about all his political activities; in a letter

of December 23, 1950, Nabokov described to his friend how he had been involved in the founding of the CCF, "une seconde resistance anti-communiste." He promised to send Stravinsky the CCF manifesto. The letter, in the PSS, Stravinsky Collection, is in Russian (except for a few French phrases like the one quoted above). I am very grateful to Elena Dubinets for translating it for me. Stravinsky's own anti-Soviet opinions hardly need expounding upon, as the Bolshevik revolution had forced him into permanent exile and robbed his family of their estate and their wealth. On Stravinsky's right-wing leanings, see Stephen Walsh, *Stravinsky: A Creative Spring. Russia and France, 1882–1934* (New York: Knopf, 1999), 520–22.

44 It is not entirely clear whether Nabokov knew that the CIA was behind the CCF at this time; Stonor Saunders believes that he must have known, but Nabokov writes to Stravinsky on May 5, 1967 of his horror upon discovering this (see Stravinsky, *Selected Correspondence*, 2, 419). The question remains open.

45 See contract between Stravinsky and the Congress of the Cultural Freedom, dated October 12, 1951. PSS, Stravinsky Collection (Nabokov correspondence).

46 "Family Income in the United States: 1952," published by the Bureau of the Census, U.S. Department of Commerce (viewed at www2.census.gov/prod2/popscan/P60–15.pdf on September 15, 2002).

47 Letter from Nabokov to Stravinsky, June 17, 1957, PSS, Stravinsky Collection.

48 "Vorläufige Programmzusammenstellung für Venedig und Schweiz, September 1958," PSS, Stravinsky Collection (Nabokov correspondence).

49 Nabokov mentions Fleischmann in letters to Stravinsky of November 13, 1951 and November 25, 1952 (PSS, Stravinsky Collection).

50 "Bringt notwendig aufgrund der wachsenden Abstraktion eine Vergröberung der Kategorien mit sich," "am Notentext als dem einzigen möglichen Ort von Individuation wie gesellschaftlicher Konkretheit." Reinhold Brinkmann, "Ästhetische und politische Kriterien der Kompositionskritik," in Ernst Thomas, ed., *Darmstädter Beiträge zur Neuen Musik 13* (Mainz: Schott, 1973), 39.

51 This texture anticipates the (vocal) tenor duets in the Diphona I and II sections.

52 Derived from chorus's row by selecting order numbers 3, 4, and 5 notes apart: 1 2 3 4 5 6 7 8 9 10 11 12 (1).

53 Unpublished study, cited in Joseph N. Straus, *Stravinsky's Late Music* (Cambridge, New York [etc.]: Cambridge University Press, 2001), 33. This information is not contained in Smyth's article, "Stravinsky as Serialist: The Sketches for Threni," *Music Theory Spectrum* 22 (2000), 205–224, which, in describing the origins of Stravinsky's row in detail without reference to Boulez, implicitly indicates that the *Structures* row had no real influence on the composition. Stravinsky, we recall, would have had the opportunity to hear the premiere of Boulez's piece at the CCF's Paris festival in 1952.

54 The text's subject, the destruction of a city, combined with the dedicatee (the North German Radio in Hamburg), would have recalled for contemporary lis-

teners and especially for the original performers the fire-bombing of Hamburg in 1943.

55 The text setting has been discussed by Hansjörg Pauli, see "On Stravinsky's 'Threni,'" *Tempo* 49 (1958), 16–33.

56 Luigi Nono's *Il canto sospeso* does something even more extreme, in that the texts—letters from prisoners of war who did not survive—are imbedded in multi-parameter serial structures and are rendered inaudible. But in both cases, emotional distance and the avoidance of a cheap pathos that would be inappropriate to the gravity of the situation are achieved.

57 See "Vorläufige Programmzusammenstellung für Venedig und Schweiz, Sept. 1958," PSS, Stravinsky Collection.

58 See letter from Nabokov to H.H. Stuckenschmidt, February 13, 1958, Stuckenschmidt-Sammlung, Akademie der Künste, Berlin.

59 "Die 'Threni' sind das strengste, dissonanteste Zwölftonstück, das der über siebzigjährige Meister nach nach seiner Bekehrung zu Schönbergs und Weberns Tonsprache geschaffen hat; sie klangen in diesem venezianischen Rahmen befremdlich," H.H. Stuckenschmidt, *Zum Hören geboren: Ein Leben mit der Musik unserer Zeit* (München und Zürich: R. Piper & Co., 1979), 268. Nabokov did not mention the piece a single time, either negatively or positively, in his subsequent letters to Stravinsky. In his memoirs, he related that although he had never been comfortable with Stravinsky's shift to twelve-tone idioms, they remained friends; see his *Bagázh: Memoirs of a Russian Cosmopolitan* (New York, 1975), 179.

60 Mason, "The Paris Festival," 15.

61 Boulez's programming of *Threni* in the fall of 1958 in his concert series Domaine Musical, in which only the most important New Music was featured, can be seen as evidence of the piece's avant-garde pedigree. (He had programmed the European premiere of *Agon* in the Domaine series in October 1957.) The fact that the Paris performance of *Threni* was from all reports a disaster does not alter this fact. Boulez tried to make it up to Stravinsky by programming and conducting the piece in other venues, for example in Munich in March of the following year. It does seem, however, that Stravinsky's close association with Nabokov and the CCF (as well as with political reactionaries such as Nadia Boulanger) negatively affected the reception of his music in Paris after 1952. To confirm this and to explain *how* the reception was affected would require another study.

62 That is, it would be simplistic and wrong to ascribe to Stravinsky, in his decision to adopt the twelve-tone technique, motives such as the desire to "keep up with Boulez." (I agree with Joseph Straus on this point; see his *Stravinsky's Late Music*, 35.)

The Essence and Persistence of Modernity

KLAUS KROPFINGER

THE QUESTION I would like to consider here is: Has modernity run its course, or is it in actuality still at the top of our agenda? I pose the question not just with respect to aesthetic theory, but above all to artworks that represent, now as ever, the idea of modernity, no matter what label one may eventually decide to pin on them.

Modernity and Avant-Garde Consciousness

When I speak of the modern in music, of the modern in thought about art, and of the modern in the specific art that represents this thought, I am interested in a quite specific distinguishing quality, or more precisely, in a specification. I will speak of the modern above all, if not exclusively, as an art of the avant-garde. However, it is precisely the concept of the avant-garde that has been swept into a critical maelstrom. In an essay entitled "Die Aporien der Avantgarde," Hans Magnus Enzensberger has insisted that "the 'avant' in avant-garde contains its own self-contradiction, for it can only be described as such *a posteriori.*"[1] For Enzensberger, the problem is that composers (or artists of whatever stripe) who deem themselves avant-garde or are declared as such by contemporaries can only make good on the claim historically, that is, after the fact, in order to be recognized as such. However, is this historical justification really the deciding factor? Reflecting on Enzensberger's reservations, Carl Dahlhaus has emphasized that "to claim that one is anticipating the future" is irrelevant to composers for whom the term avant-garde is coined. As an example, he names Karlheinz Stockhausen, who declared that he composes for the present; he leaves the future to later generations.[2] Even aside from the question of who should count historically as avant-garde, one could object that Stockhausen is by no means a composer who creates with his eyes turned backward, and that he never thought of himself in such terms. For Stockhausen, as for other artists with the new in mind, the deciding factor is, as always, the intention to progress creatively, to create the new in an emphatic sense, regardless of any later evaluation.[3] Consider the essay entitled "Erfindung und Entdeckung. Ein Beitrag zur Form-Genese," where Stockhausen speaks of a "new land for musical discoveries once again" opening up.[4] In an article on "Elektronische und instrumentale Musik," he emphasizes that

> In the first half of the century, the compositions "Ionisation" by Edgar Varèse and "Construction in Metal" by John Cage already laid the road for a fully new development, completely independent of pitched music. The beginnings of *musique concrète* were also stimulated by Varèse and Cage.[5]

In the introduction to "No. 6: Gruppen für 3 Orchester (1955–1957)," he stresses that

> With "Gruppen," a new development of "instrumental music in space" began. The new form of multi-layered time compositions of instrument to instrument is also made clear in the outer form.[6]

From such statements, it is completely clear that Stockhausen, wide awake, situated himself in the historical current of new compositional tendencies and developments. He knew how to continue these developments with the musical capacities proper to him and with the creative sixth sense tailored to auspicious means of the new. His creative consciousness was *avant-goût*. Although he worked with such intensity and direction toward the future, he was in essence indifferent as to his future worthiness of the term avant-garde. He himself said (quoted by Dahlhaus with good purpose[7]): "If we of today expect that much more contemporary music will be performed. . . then we must also expect of coming generations that they make their own music and not fill up their time again predominantly with old music, and that they will be more vital and more in tune with the present than most people today."[8] Thus, the slogan of "fury of disappearing" does not apply to his music, as it does not apply to that of Schoenberg, Boulez, Cage, Varèse, and many others, regardless of the ridiculous appeal to performance statistics—one of the fetishes of superficial criticism. Rather, one must turn to what Baudelaire says in the *Journaux intimes*:

> All ideas are, in themselves, gifted with an immortal life, like a person.
>
> All created forms, even those by man, are immortal. For the form is independent of the material and it is not the molecules that constitute the form.[9]

In order to show once and for all that the issue is not the decoration of an avant-garde façade, but rather the creative state of mind that aims at the definitively new, I turn to Luigi Nono. An essential trait of Nono's creative personality is his sensitivity to the aspects of the past that point toward the future and that demand actualization. He opens himself in order to discover and to create the new. Among others, Walter Benjamin acquired a quite fundamental significance for him.

> Benjamin in my view is a thinker who really aided me to free myself further from several schemata, from a prejudice, from a model. And I believe that the most important thing is to separate oneself ever further from such schemata. To achieve this, one must free oneself from specialization. As a composer, one can never be only a composer. In an age in which interdisciplinary work is possible, this is important for us in the same degree as in earlier times, when one studied astronomy, physics, logic, rhetoric, and music. Today, I believe, there can be no question that a musician must know what is afoot in philosophy, in physics, in painting and architecture, and in life in general.[10]

For Nono, the new is absolutely central. It is attainable only if one opens one's horizons—an opening of horizons understood as a function of an unconditional orientation forward!

And what, after all, did Boulez refer to when he said "Schoenberg is dead" if not to the act of surpassing in the sense of compositional progress? The goal: to trump and to leave behind the classical hero of the avant-garde. Was not this statement explicitly linked to a critique of Schoenberg's method of composition? As Boulez saw it, this method was inadequate, for it did not really use the possibilities that lay within the compositional principle of twelve-tone music. Was not the idea of serial composition also propelled by avant-garde consciousness? Once again, he cared little whether this impulse would actually claim a leading position. Does not this constellation of historical developments in the area of musical technique show that the compositional consciousness is the decisive matter, not its consciously bold declaration? If something can be branded after the fact as definitively ahead, this is ultimately secondary, or even insignificant for the state of consciousness and its realization at the time of creation.

When I emphasize the aspect of avant-garde, I am of course also well aware of what Adorno says in the *Aesthetic Theory*: "Further, the concept of the avant-garde, reserved for many decades for whatever movement declared itself the most advanced, now has some of the comic quality of aged youth."[11] To reply to such *moquerie*, one can use Adorno's own statement later in the book: "Only the most advanced art of any period has any chance against the decay wrought by time."[12] Adorno's jab aimed not least at the flashy exhibition of a word that deserves to be used only in its essential sense. And it's exactly this that I demand.

A Term of Surface Without Foundation: Post-Modernism

The focus on avant-garde seems more than ever unavoidable when one looks at the importunate, fashionable concept post-modernism.[13] It stands for an attack on basic principles, for an indiscriminate lash against modern art and against the modern in general. One hears cries not just that the high modern, once sovereign, has aged and burned out, but above all that the whole age of modernity is over.

But what should one think of a concept that the composer Wolfgang Rihm has disqualified as a "journalistic slogan that has achieved the status of a general mood"?[14] He has ironically described the concept as belonging "to the modern climbing gear for sportive tourists in the artistic Alps"[15] and has dismissed it as jingoistic swagger.[16] In a quite similar tone, Helmut Lachenmann has spoken of post-modernism as a style of "smart-alecky dressing up" [*post-modern gestylte Schlaumeierei*][17] and as a type of mimicry of progress. Despite his "objections to this term as early as 1980," in which he spoke of a "'post-modernity' of kitsch and arbitrariness," of a "pluralism" that had degenerated to "promiscuity,"[18] Heinrich Klotz, an art historian equally talented in word and in analysis, later used the word "without hesitating as a pure designation that is universally recognized."[19] However, the word lacks precision, for Klotz needed "imposed diagnoses,"[20] however critically tinged, to make it work.

In the face of all dialectics of modernity and post-modernity, there is one higher point of view, that of a sustained modernity. The points of departure, orientation, and support for this are above all as follows:

First, Habermas's idea of an "incomplete modernity"[21] can be read from the following single sentence: "I think that we should learn from the aberrations that have accompanied the project of modernism, from the errors of the extravagant programs of abrogation, rather than give up on modernity and its project altogether."[22]

Second, Wellmer's critique on ambiguity is implicit within post-modernism. On the one hand, movements understood as post-modern are directed at the "defense of conditions without which modernity would bury the potential for humanity of which it alone is capable." On the other, they claim "the turn away from technocratic modernity as a withdrawal from modernity itself."[23] Wellmer emphatically rejects this regressive aspect of post-modernism:

> It can hardly be doubted that [Charles] Jencks is among those champions of a post-modern architecture and city planning that are radically modern according to the definition discussed here.[24] The clearest indicator of this is his emphasis on the relationship between an urban life style and democracy. To a certain extent, Jencks construes his 'post-modern' critique of modern architecture from the perspective of a democratically conceived city planning. Despite his intention, his critique of modern architecture is in so far, no critique of the Enlightenment, but rather part of a 'critique of instrumental reason.'[25]

Third, as mentioned above, Heinrich Klotz formulated a critique of the concept of post-modernism in 1980,[26] a critique invoked again in his *Kunst im 20. Jahrhundert*, as can be seen in the subtitle of his book: *Moderne—Postmoderne—Zweite Moderne*.[27] For what else would this imply but the restitution of modernity, that is, a modernity that is retained and sustained. This idea resonates with the words of Wolfgang Welsch. With respect to Werner Hofmann, he writes "that post-modern art takes up and develops the structures of modern art,"[28] and, echoing Lyotard's destination, intended for post-modernism,[29] that it "continues the work of the avant-garde movement."[30] But at this point, one must ask if Klotz's dictum regarding the "end of the avant-garde"[31] is correct with respect to the specific sense of the term sketched above. Does not this consciousness, directed as it is toward the transcendence of boundaries, aim beyond itself at precisely the point at which it, under the rubric of post-modern, turns against a "technocratically perverted modernity"?[32] Even here, the critical attitude of an avant-garde is maintained as an artistic, principled stance, not as a historicization characteristic of a limited historical period. Only when judged according to this criterion can the consciousness claim a genuine artistic self-evidence—just in the sense of Wolfgang Rihm's statement: "What the avant-garde once was—a sign of an especially intense art—existed before the concept of the avant-garde. And it exists today."[33]

One must also reflect on an issue of cultural politics often pointed out by Habermas, one that touches on and even affects day-to-day politics. In the wake of Hans Sedlmayer's demonization of the explosive contents of aesthetic modernity, a neo-conservatism has fought "to take programmatic leave" of modernity through an "appeal to 'post-modernity.'"[34]

"Great works wait"

Even Adorno himself expressly and illuminatingly emphasized the issue of a sustained modernity in order to enter into the discussion of modernity and post-modernity. Adorno's dictum that "Great works wait"[35] has stood await-ing its own realization; the phrase means that "Great works persist," that they gain in stature as they hold out.

With respect to the modern, Adorno's reflections sharpen the designation "great works" in a specific way:

> Only the most advanced art of any period has any chance against the decay wrought by time. In the afterlife of works, however, qual-itative differences become apparent that in no way coincide with the level of modernity achieved in their own periods. In the secret *bellum omnium contra omnes* that fills the history of art, the older modern may be victorious over the newer modern.[36]

This aspect of an art that persists through the passage of time because of its quality was and continues to be what brings forth an actual avant-garde that is immune to decay, for it is the motivating creative impulse behind an ad-vanced art of particular quality. According to Jürgen Habermas, to this phe-nomenon corresponds a "radicalized" consciousness of modernity:

> Modern is valid now as that which helps a spontaneously-itself-re-newing actuality of the Zeitgeist to become objective expression. The signature of such works is the new, which is overcome and de-

valorized by the novelties of the next style. But while the merely
fashionable passes into the past and becomes old-fashioned, the
modern maintains a secret connection to the classic. As always, the
classic is that which survives the ages.[37]

In this understanding of modernity, progress gains an intensity that hides a
dialectic. The avant-garde strives for progress, but for a progress that—including a specific artistic quality—lasts beyond whatever is currently modern.
Habermas continues:

> As always, the classic is that which survives the ages. Of course, this
> power takes the sign of modernity no longer from the authority of
> a past epoch, but rather alone from the authenticity of a past actu-
> ality. This conversion of today's actuality into that of yesterday is
> consuming and productive simultaneously. As Jauss has observed, it
> is the modernity itself that creates its classicality. We now speak of
> classical modernity as if it were self-evident.[38]

Progress surmounts itself, step by step, but precisely in this way it stores an
enormous artistic potential.

There are famous examples of this dialectic in the arts. In music, Arnold
Schoenberg represents it in a consummate manner. In the essay "Der dialektische Komponist" of 1934, Adorno emphasized this characteristic trait of
Schoenberg's perpetually progressing procedures of composition. Beyond the
issues of reception that Schoenberg brings up, Adorno focuses on the new
quality of artistic consciousness that arises from the tension between compositional intention and compositional material, citing Stefan George that "The
highest strictness is simultaneously the highest freedom." This quality lends
Schoenberg's works a considerable historical endurance:

> The resistance to Schoenberg has its most evident reason in the fact
> that every work from his hand, and certainly every phase in the his-
> tory of his music, confronted us with new enigmas that could not be
> mastered with knowledge of what went before, or even of his own
> most recent production. . . . Although each work by Schoenberg fol-
> lows the previous one in a compulsory way, they by no means grow
> out of each other. . . . After Schoenberg, the history of music will
> no longer be fate, but will be subject to human consciousness. . . .
> This consciousness struggled free of the abyss of the subconscious,

of dream and desire, fed itself on its material like a flame, until the light of a true day transformed all the contours of music. This is its greatest success between the extremes, no longer play, but truth itself. This success places the name of Schoenberg, the greatest living musician, in the landscape of the one who first found the conscious sound for the dream of freedom: Beethoven.[39]

Problems of the Material

If this new creative consciousness defined, as it always had, the dialectic of Schoenberg's historical position—the dialectic of actuality and persistence, it is nonetheless precisely the mental stance of the "dialectical composer" that characterizes his connection to tradition. It would be a mistake to assume that Schoenberg's grappling with the musical material meant a break with all connections to the past. The opposite is the case! But the compositional consciousness would now integrate the past according to his method of critical assimilation. What once was formed and sounded as formed material would now be perceived as the mere material of sound, structure, and configuration. It could be accessed in the service of creative freedom. Freedom in the treatment of past material would be taken as a duty in the sense of a new compositional strictness. To take one example, Pierre Boulez finds an important point of orientation in the chorale variations and arrangements of Johann Sebastian Bach. In general, as he himself has stressed, German music has had the strongest influence on him, "from afar, so to speak," in particular with respect to form.[40]

The extent to which Schoenberg's creative spirit presents an experimental laboratory for musical material of the past is documented by the enormous volume of his writings, not to speak of his music. The writings show an astonishing horizon of historical orientation, an orientation that always stands on or departs from a critically illuminating analysis. For Schoenberg, the Gordian knot was an infinitely fascinating puzzle that had to be untangled and unraveled. The Janus-faced character of Schoenberg's compositions that combine prospective and retrospective features participate in this dialectic, for they follow classical formal qualities or patterns such as sonata form even while they are twelve-tone. Pierre Boulez clearly and famously took account of this in his critical statement that "Schoenberg is dead." Boulez presented this text in 1951 as a lecture at Darmstadt. At the occasion, among other things he said that

Since the pre-classical and classical forms which predominate are historically unconnected with dodecaphony, a yawning chasm opens up between the infrastructures of tonality and a language whose organizational principles are as yet but dimly perceived. . . . the architecture annuls any possibility of organization that the new language may possess. The two worlds are incompatible: and yet one has tried to justify the one by the other.[41]

However, Boulez does not content himself with such sweeping statements. While he esteems Schoenberg's compositions written between ca. 1910 and 1920/23 (Opus 24), in the end he aims his critique at specific works within Schoenberg's twelve-tone oeuvre, among them such as the Quintet for Flute, Oboe, Clarinet, Horn, and Bassoon (Wind Quintet), op. 26 (1923/24) and the Variations for Orchestra, op. 31 (1926–28). According to Boulez, compositions such as these have a grave flaw. "In a word, Schoenberg never concerned himself with the logical connection between serial forms as such and derived structure."[42] Nonetheless, no matter how great Boulez's critical distance with respect to Schoenberg's artistic orientation and his compositions after Opus 24 may be, there is one perspective under which the two composers approach each other decidedly. It is this perspective that encapsulates the dialectical composer: it is the relation of the composer to the material. Despite all differences in creative habitus, Schoenberg and Boulez are joined by the "change. . . in the way the composer behaves toward his material,"[43] noted by Adorno, also characterized as "a contradiction not inside the artist, but between the power in him and what he found before him."[44]

Thus, Boulez himself characterized his compositional procedure as "the proliferation of materials."[45] He conceives this tendency to proliferate as "dangerous. . . , as it can lead to a density which is always the same, to a greatest density, to a highest tension or a most extreme variation in every instant." So he saw himself forced in many cases "to reduce, to cut down the possibilities or to bring them in a sequence such that they developed in time and did not overlap, which would have been too compact."[46] It is not coincidental that the book that contains his interviews with Célestin Deliège and Hans Mayer is entitled *Wille und Zufall* [Will and Chance].

It would be an important and interesting task to engage for once not just with individual theoretical writings, but fundamentally with the enormous increase in the quantity of theoretical writings by modern composers, published or not. At this point, I can only allude to this task.

Variants of Avant-garde Consciousness

It is no surprise that precisely Boulez—equally perceptive and discriminating in analysis as eloquent and open to future compositional horizons—accompanies his creative products in this way. Here it is illuminating to note that even, or one should say precisely, Boulez is skeptical of an infinite musical progress by means of new technology. He expresses this quite clearly in the article "At the Edge of Fertile Land," the title of which refers to the famous picture by Paul Klee.[47] Within this fertile land, Boulez was open to new sounds, even and especially those beyond the tempered scale. He described John Cage's prepared piano as a solution and as a pointer in the right direction. However, he keeps his distance from the type of experimental music advocated by Cage. Cage argues for "centers of experimental music. . . . In these centers, the new materials, oscillators, turntables, generators, means for amplifying small sounds, film phonographs, etc. [should be] available for use."[48]

There is no doubt that Cage advocates the infinite fertile land. But even, or precisely, he cannot escape from the dialectic of freedom and necessity or strictness. Cage goes far beyond the mere preparation of instruments. By means of chance operations, the musical material is kept open for a wide range of possibilities, a range that includes not only the composer and the performer(s), but also the listener(s) or recipient(s).[49] In this way the composer becomes in the end his own recipient, as can be visualized in the case of the score of *Variations V*. It is a score that consists of notes: "Notes . . . on that which has just happened, and . . . these notes moreover take into consideration that somebody else, too, could make the piece."[50] Here, Cage gives his own definition, i.e., a new definition of score.[51] In this openness that prepares for the future, one can recognize last but not least the spirit of Charles Ives and Edgar Varèse. Cage, however, goes much further. Aside from the fact that he persistently and without pause creates new things, he extends music into life. Music becomes and is declared as life itself, like all activities of daily life. And, one could say, Cage develops himself finally to an experimental object of himself.

Cage's dialectical combination of freedom and strictness is to discover and develop the sensibility of the material with respect to the necessity of its organization as freedom of choice. Cage's artistic path is paved with examples of this stance and the procedures that arise from it. The result of his studies with Schoenberg is characteristic enough. As he himself wrote:

Five years later, when Schoenberg asked me whether I would devote my life to music, I said, "Of course." After I had been studying with him for two years, Schoenberg said, "In order to write music, you must have a feeling for harmony." I explained to him that I had no feeling for harmony. He then said that I would always encounter an obstacle, that it would be as though I came to a wall through which I could not pass. I said, "In that case I will devote my life to beating my head against that wall."[52]

Cage's lifelong confrontation with the wall was extremely productive. In acting thus, he owed not only Schoenberg, but he also felt himself equally in debt to predecessors, especially to Satie and Varèse, but also Henry David Thoreau and Charles Ives.[53] Cage's consciousness of the past was creatively stimulated. He transformed received "material" into the mental potential of a strictly forward-looking personality that Dieter Schnebel pointedly described in 1971. "John Cage is perhaps the most important innovator in the most recent music,"[54] an "Avant-gardist—ahead of the Avant-garde."[55]

Schnebel himself is one of the German composers who partake of Cage's fertile land without false shame. To take but one example, a composition such as *ki-no*, in which slide projections and films combine with sounds to echo through the room, cannot be conceived without Cage as a predecessor pointing the way.[56]

Schnebel is an example of the enormous influence that Cage had well beyond the United States, even beyond those artists who were part of his artistic community, such as David Tudor, Earl Brown, Morton Feldman, and Christian Wolff. Among them, Feldman counts rightly as a composer of extraordinary stature. While he experimented with different types of musical notation, his main interest lies "in different densities and combinations of timbres, usually played very softly."[57] His *Piece for Four Pianos* (1957) is one example.

As has been noted, this piece leaves a final impression that reminds one much of Webern:[58] the four pianists play nothing more than a single part "to produce 'a series of reverberations from an identical sound source.'"[59] Of course, it is neither the gentleness nor the subtleties that define alone the impression made by this music. Beyond that it is the sparseness of the sound, a sparseness that corresponds to a hesitating, step-by-step musical process. It is as if the composer dedicated himself to experiencing the touchstone of time.

A close friend of Cage,[60] Henry Cowell emphasized that such pieces, despite their many patent stylistic differences, are linked by a common point of view with compositions by Christian Wolff, Pierre Boulez, and John Cage. They are linked through the "concentration on unusual connections between space and time, and less through new melodies and chords; and the same through the conviction that, no matter whether they are arrived at by chance or on purpose, all musical connections are of potential interest and are worthy of investigation."[61]

Aside from Feldman, Stockhausen has dealt with the relation between space and time, and has in addition investigated musical relationships such as how different tempi produce shifting musical layers with sliding temporal relations. While Feldman injects freedom into his scores by means of improvisatory elements of performance, freedom is a structural consideration in a composition such as Stockhausen's *Gruppen*. As Stockhausen writes:

> Several independent orchestras surround the listener—in "Gruppen" there are three. The orchestras play, each under its own conductor, in part independently and in different tempi. From time to time they meet in a common sonic rhythm. They call to and answer each other. One echoes the other. At various times, one hears music from the left, from the front, or from the right. The sound migrates from one orchestra to the next, and so forth."[62]

Stockhausen's *Carré* offers an additional way to modulate musical sounds in space and time. The vibrations back and forth of the sounds take on an important structural function. All of these layers, directions, and specifically artistic crystalizations of the avant-garde themselves form a fertile land without borders, an enormous range of compositional summits of invention and material, ready to be used artistically and spanning both generations and historical trends.

In a letter written to me in 1991, Wolfgang Rihm explained his connection to Arnold Schoenberg, whom he perceives as the great sower of this fruitland:

> In my view, Schoenberg as a total, unabridged figure stands *unretuschiert* [in his original stature] as a most contradictory spirit and a generative human being of incredible energy. He furthermore is for me the *battery*, the source from which recharge is offered. (I experience Webern and Berg—with all love—as quite dependent on this recharge.) Schoenberg remains the primary source.[63]

In this contemporary example, one can see the power to survive and power of inspiration of a genuine classical modernism—a power to which

Adorno testified. There is no trace of somnolence or desiccation in the individual, creative avant-garde consciousness, which acts as an inspiration with undiminished viability. And if one were to need only one more additional example, then the compositional activity and creatively oriented reflection of Helmut Lachenmann would suffice to prove the power of survival of a completely avant-garde consciousness of material. It is a consciousness of material that demonstrates the sensing and molding of instrumental qualities, layers, and structures of sound, as well as its mental contouring and structuration.[64]

Persistence of the Avant-Garde

Rihm is also a striking example that this impulse which radiates from individual artists and instills an avant-garde consciousness is limited neither to one individual nor to one event. He describes his first aural impression of Varèse's *Arcana* as a formative experience, as an initiation.[65] Next to Schoenberg, Varèse became a highly important composer and a further point of orientation for him.

In general, Rihm himself best describes the comprehensive horizon of his orientation. "One can only build on fascinating works, not on 'techniques.' As there are many fascinating works in serial music, I see no reason why something there should be passé."[66] Rihm's experience of Varèse is illuminating: it is the fusion of artistic-humanist stance and compositional quality that continues to have an effect. When he writes that Varèse compositionally worked off the shock of his "initiation to *Sacre*" throughout his life,[67] Rihm intimates an aspect of artistic experience which he sees as possibly constitutive of artistic creativity altogether and upon which he has reflected at length: "creation as crisis."[68] In this consciousness of crisis, one can see a hidden connection to the broken structure of contemporary avant-garde composition, and in addition to its critical consciousness of context. With respect to the workshop, crisis means not least the composer's step-by-step decisions that, despite all ruptures, lead to a sonic configuration defined by a "density (not just on paper!), richness (not just in the sonic *cloth!*), strangeness (not just as zest!), clarity (precisely in darkness!), fantasy (which can be spun forth and which is not at an end at the end of the piece!), unforced quality (precisely at the most forceful moment!), unresolved quality (which seethes on!)."[69] From this perspective, the structural realization of these qualities—always seen as Rihm's expressivity—gains a dimension that reaches much deeper. It is an existential music in which an avant-garde comprehensively realizes its stance. To cite only one example among many, *fremde szenen I-III / versuche für klaviertrio / erste folge* [*foreign scenes I-III / essays for piano trio / first sequence*].

Rihm's wide horizon contains an additional perspective, insofar as Luigi Nono is for him a very special, permanent battery. And not just for him. Helmut Lachenmann underlines that

> Only Nono and Cage seem to be messengers of hope. . . . Only they seem to point up horizons and abysses that can still be explored. In them that creative agitation that is the only peace allowed to us is protected: secure insecurity rather than insecure security."[70]

When Lachenmann—who lived, studied, thought, and composed together with Nono for two years (1958–1960)—designates Cage and Nono in a single breath as pillars of hope, he speaks, at least with respect to Cage, in full knowledge of the late Nono. Earlier (1959), Nono held his American colleagues among composers in contempt, thinking specifically of the imitators of Cage.

Lachenmann values Cage as "a great provocative spirit and exemplary practician of radical freedom who awakes creative awe."[71] But in spite of his high respect for both Nono and Cage, Nono still ranks higher.

> Nono always conceived composition as an act in which the responsibility of the artist had to orient itself with respect to history and the societal situation. From a technical point of view, at least at that time, this meant the conscious control of connotations with which the musical material is indelibly permeated, because of the role of the material in society through tradition and convention. The composer reacts to these connotations in his decisions in one way or another.[72]

This stance reminds us of the great, almost forgotten composer and pianist Stefan Wolpe, who was forced into exile by the Nazis. *Form IV, Broken Sequences*, written in 1969, three years before his death, seems to be composed of both dispersed and malformed material. Its gestures take possession of the tattered curtain of history.

Memory, desperation, and the will to resistance simultaneously carry and characterize the structural image of this and many other compositions by Wolpe. It is not too much to say that it is not only in compositions such as this[73] that one hears the musical reflection of what has quite rightly been characterized as Wolpe's "permanent sense of displacement that the exile experiences, regardless of where he is."[74] In this connection, we are also conscious of the fact that Wolpe had been a politically engaged composer since his youth. Until 1933 he was dedicated to the idea of a radical socialism.[75]

In this all-inclusive perspective Wolpe stands next to Nono and Lachenmann, despite all differences in style and technique. His proximity is not least one that touches on the beginning of Adorno's *Dialektik der Aufklärung*:

> In the most general sense of progressive thought, the Enlightenment has always aimed at liberating men from fear... Yet the fully enlightened earth radiates disaster triumphant.[76]

Lachenmann artistically crystallized the fundamental problem of destroyed hope. According to his own commentary, his opera *Das Mädchen mit den Schwefelhölzern* [*The Matchgirl*]

> is full of messages, both clear and veiled: critique of society, existential loneliness, "regressive" protest—the capital of the little girl, the matches, which she lights to warm herself, to get an image of luck—while she freezes to death. In my youth I have known Gudrun Ensslin, who came like me from a family of pastors, full of ideals, Protestant in the radical sense; she joined the Red Army Fraction, and at the beginning of her dubious career in the movement of political protest she ignited a huge department store; she perished in 1977, by suicide or murder, in any case as a victim of an indifferent society, a society feigning blindness and deafness.[77]

Lachenmann's specific profile as an avant-garde composer is immediately recognizable in all its contours when he closes the statement with the words: "*Messages, hommages*: As a composer, only the narrative and its structure is important to me. All must come from there."[78]

In truth, Lachenmann's music, like that of Nono, presents a quite specific dialectic. Represented by a never-ending quest for new sounds by means of specially prepared instrumental sounds and structures within the horizon of concrete utopian goals, its progressive traits are inseparably connected with an abyss of desperation.

Lachenmann's work for string quartet, entitled *Gran Torso*, is an example of this exceptional, advanced world of sounds.

Nono's composition *Risonanze erranti* is an especially striking example of the "dialectic of enlightenment" that overshadows all hope. It compositionally reflects in sonic material a poem by Ingeborg Bachmann—"Keine Delikates-sen"—and various poems by Herman Melville.[79]

A particular characteristic of all these compositions, including that of Stefan Wolpe, is the broken structure, a broken quality that does not spare the individual sound. In connection with this, the compositional structure of Nono's *Risonanze erranti* is permeated by what Walter Benjamin called the "tiger's leap into the past": he inserts short but highly expressive speaking fragments of works by Johannes Ockeghem (1425–1496), Josquin Des Prez (ca. 1450) and Guillaume de Machaut (ca. 1300). Thus, the words and syllables of Bachmann's poem correspond with the echoes of the past, with words like "Malheur me bat," "Pleure," and "Malheur." From this confrontation between past and present, the future yawns before us.

Nono was a member of the Italian communist party, but his political convictions were unmistakably characterized by humanistic ideals closely linked with an anti-fascist position. This is the basis for his composition *Musica manifesto no. 1*, which blends present fight with peaceful future together. It is highly characteristic of Nono's sense of a dialectic of material that he recommended that I superimpose both parts of *Musica manifesto no. 1—Non consumiamo Marx* (composed with sound material from the Paris uprisings of 1968) on *Un volto del mare* (the sonic image of an ocean idyll)—to play them simultaneously.[80] As a contemporary event in every case, the score grows from the reciprocal interaction of sound and active, even creative reception. Cage would have applauded!

Lachenmann writes in his text *Affekt und Aspekt*:

> Moreover, aesthetic programs whose perspectives direct themselves into the future are legitimate, and they will come up again and again, and exactly there, where music understands itself as something which is especially binding and not as—to quote Manfred Trojahn—"a playground for privatizing invention of Musical Composition."[81]

In a conversation, Luigi Nono expressly applauded the motto that Ferruccio Busoni inscribed at the head of his *Entwurf einer neuen Ästhetik der Tonkunst* (*Sketch of a New Aesthetic of Music*), first published in 1907, a text that Busoni sent to Arnold Schoenberg and that Schoenberg commented on, in part through the addition of musical examples.[82] Nono held Busoni's *Sketch* in his hand as he visited Schoenberg's house together with Nuria in 1964.[83] I should add that Busoni and Schoenberg regarded each other with real respect. In 1912, Schoenberg wrote to Kandinsky:

Dear Mr. Kandinsky,
   Wouldn't you like to ask for a contribution from Busoni? He is very closely connected with us. Read the 1 February issue of *Pan* or his *New Aesthetics of Music*.[84]

The motto to Busoni's *Entwurf einer neuen Ästhetik der Tonkunst* reads as follows:

> "What seek you? Say! And what do you expect?"
> "I know not what; the Unknown I would have!
> What's known to me, is endless. I would go
> Beyond the end: The last word still is wanting."[85]

These are words in the spirit of the avant-garde. They reverberate in Lachenmann's words: "For me, Nono was the example of a radical seeker. . ."[86] It is this spirit that makes all objections to the so-called aporias of the avant-garde collapse in disarray.
   It is this spirit alone that counts.

Translated by Keith Chapin

Notes

1   Hans Magnus Enzensberger, *Einzelheiten* (Frankfurt am Main: Suhrkamp, 1962), 299ff. Translation in Carl Dahlhaus, "Progress and the avant garde," in *Schoenberg and the New Music*, trans. Derrick Puffett and Alfred Clayton (Cambridge: Cambridge University Press, 1987), 15. I wish to thank Helga von Kügelgen for editing the German version of the manuscript.

2   Carl Dahlhaus, "Progress and the avant garde" (cf. n. 1), 15. Pierre Boulez would prefer to substitute the term "contemporary music" for "avant-garde music." But when he writes: "We would, then, prefer not to speak any more of 'Avant-garde,' but of contemporary composition in an actual and bellicose sense," he changes nothing but the word—the concept remains unchanged. Actual music can, as a "bellicose" one, be nothing but pioneering, consequently oriented forward, towards future. (cf. Pierre Boulez: "Wie arbeitet die musikalische Avantgarde," in Boulez, Werkstatt-Texte, trans. Josef Häusler, Frankfurt am Main/Berlin 1972, 179)

3   Peter Bürger has problematized the concept of the "new." By historicizing the "modern," he distinguishes the change in artistic means of presentation (which is always at hand) from a change of the system of presentation. See Peter Bürger,

Theorie der Avantgarde (Frankfurt am Main: Suhrkamp, 1974), 85 and 113, n. 14. What he passes over is the fact that a change in the system of presentation (such as the departure from a central perspective or, in the musical arena, the departure from tonality) does not occur instantaneously, but rather owes its genesis to a stepwise change in the means of presentation. As opposed to a historically defined "avant-garde movement," this sequence of gradual steps is grounded in an artistic consciousness that is indebted to an artistic self-criticism anchored in a personal artistic consciousness that in turn strives to go beyond what has been achieved and is opposed to all anonymity of an artistic movement.

4   Karlheinz Stockhausen, *Texte zur elektronischen und instrumentalen Musik*, Texte Band 1: Aufsätze 1952–1962 zur Theorie des Komponierens (Cologne: M. DuMont Schauberg, 1963), 225.

5   Ibid., 145.

6   Karlheinz Stockhausen, *Texte zu eigenen Werken und zur Kunst Anderer: Aktuelles*, Texte Band 2: Aufsätze 1952–1962 zur musikalischen Praxis (Cologne: M. DuMont Schauberg, 1964), 71.

7   Carl Dahlhaus, "Progress and the avant garde" (cf. n. 1), 15.

8   Stockhausen, *Texte zur elektronischen und instrumentalen Musik*, 188.

9   Charles Baudelaire, *Oeuvres Complètes*, ed. Y.G. Le Dantec, Bibliothèque de la Pléiade (Paris: Gallimard, 1954), 1230.

10 Klaus Kropfinger, ". . . kein Anfang—kein Ende. . . Aus Gesprächen mit Luigi Nono," in *Musica* 42 (1988), 168.

11 Theodor W. Adorno, *Aesthetic Theory*, ed. Gretel Adorno and Rolf Tiedemann, trans. Robert Hullot-Kentor, Theory and History of Literature, 88 (Minneapolis: University of Minnesota Press, 1997), 24–25.

12 Adorno, *Aesthetic Theory* (cf. n. 11), 41.

13 The brief discussion of the modernism/post-modernism problem may seem arbitrary if one considers the different material conditions of music as opposed to architecture, painting, sculpture, and literature. Wolfgang Rihm has discussed this in "Musik ist immer abstrakt" (cf. Wolfgang Rihm: "Wieviel Modernen braucht die Musik?" in Heinrich Klotz, ed. *Die Zweite Moderne*, München: C.H. Beck, 1996, 141. As, however, "post-modern" music nevertheless is discussed, music can't be kept away from the problematic quality of that term (cf. Otto Kolleritsch, ed.: *Wiederaneignung und Neubestimmung. Der Fall "Postmodern" in der Musik*, Wien/Graz, 1993).

14 Wolfgang Rihm, *ausgesprochen: Schriften und Gespräche*, 1, ed. Ulrich Mosch, Veröffentlichungen der Paul Sacher Stiftung, 6, no. 1 (Winterthur: Amadeus, 1997), 391. One must ask to what extent, or even if, Rihm's compositions should be thought of as post-modern; cf. Hermann Danuser, *Die Musik des 20. Jahrhunderts* (Laaber: Laaber, 1984), 400, 402. On the other hand, it is doubtless at least questionable to declare the concept of the avant-garde as outmoded or as left behind historically. Even here Wolfgang Rihm advances an interpreta-

tion of the avant-garde that is based on the principle behind the concept, *not* on one of its historically conditioned forms. He writes, "What the avant-garde once was—a sign of an especially intense art—existed before the concept of the avant-garde. And it exists today. One can even perceive a decisive intensification of the situation. Today, even the insipid art trade can no longer make the pretense that it is avant-garde" (1, 390).

15 Ibid., 396.

16 Ibid., 396; "Just the use of the word post-modern guarantees presence in the zones of contemporary thought. Unfortunately, the word also guarantees its level: flat."

17 Helmut Lachenmann, *Musik als existentielle Erfahrung: Schriften 1966–1995*, ed. Josef Häusler (Wiesbaden: Breitkopf and Härtel, 1996), 143.

18 Heinrich Klotz, "Post-Moderne?" in *Jahrbuch für Architektur* (1980/81): 7.

19 Heinrich Klotz, *Kunst im 20. Jahrhundert. Moderne—Postmoderne—Zweite Moderne*, 2d ed. (Munich: C. H. Beck, 1999), 148.

20 Ibid., 148.

21 Jürgen Habermas, "Die Moderne—ein unvollendetes Projekt," in *Die Moderne— ein unvollendetes Projekt*, third ed. (Leipzig: Reclam, 1994), 32–54, esp. 49ff.

22 Ibid., 49.

23 Albrecht Wellmer, "Kunst und industrielle Produktion: Zur Dialektik von Moderne und Postmoderne," in *Zur Dialektik von Moderne und Postmoderne: Vernunftkritik nach Adorno* (Frankfurt am Main: Suhrkamp, 1985), 127ff.

24 Charles Jencks, *The Language of Post-Modern Architecture* (New York: Rizzoli, 1977).

25 Wellmer, "Kunst und industrielle Produktion" (cf. n. 23), 128.

26 Klotz, "Post-Moderne?" (cf. n. 18), 7–9.

27 Klotz, *Kunst im 20. Jahrhundert* (cf. n. 19).

28 Cf. Wolfgang Welsch, *Unsere postmoderne Moderne* (Weinheim: VCH, 1987), 192.

29 Jean-François Lyotard, et al., *Immaterialität und Postmoderne* (Berlin: Merve, 1985), 30.

30 Welsch, *Unsere postmoderne Moderne* (cf. n. 28), 194.

31 Klotz, *Kunst im 20. Jahrhundert* (cf. n. 19), 153.

32 Wellmer, "Kunst und industrielle Produktion" (cf. n. 23), 127.

33 Wolfgang Rihm, *ausgesprochen: Schriften und Gespräche*, 1 (cf. n. 14), 390.

34 Jürgen Habermas, "Die Kulturkritik der Neokonservativen in den USA und in der Bundesrepublik," in *Die Moderne—ein unvollendetes Projekt*, 97.

35 Adorno, *Aesthetic Theory* (cf. n. 11), 40.

36 Adorno (cf. n. 11), 41.

37   Habermas (cf. n. 21), 34.

38   Habermas (cf. n. 21), 34.

39   Theodor W. Adorno, "Der dialektische Komponist," in *Gesammelte Schriften*,
     17 (Frankfurt am Main: Suhrkamp, 1982), 198–203 passim. Translated by Susan
     H. Gillespie as "The Dialectical Composer," in Theodor W. Adorno, *Essays on
     Music*, selected with introduction, commentary, and notes by Richard Leppert
     (Berkeley: University of California Press, 2002), 203–7 passim.

40   Pierre Boulez, *Wille und Zufall. Gespräche mit Célestin Deliège und Hans Mayer*
     (Stuttgart/Zurich: Belser, 1977), 16ff.

41   Pierre Boulez, "Schoenberg is dead," in *Stocktakings from an Apprenticeship*, col-
     lected and presented by Paule Thévenin, translated by Stephen Walsh, and with
     an Introduction by Robert Piencikowski (Oxford: Clarendon, 1991), 209–214,
     here 212.

42   Boulez, "Schoenberg is dead" (cf. n. 41), 212.

43   Adorno, "The Dialectical Composer" (cf. n. 39), 205. The problematic implica-
     tions of Adorno's concept of material—discussed by Albrecht Wellmer among
     others with respect to the critique of Peter Bürger (cf. Wellmer, *Zur Dialektik
     von Moderne und Postmoderne*, 58ff.)—has been thematized by Carl Dahlhaus
     under the rubric of dialectic conceptuality. He writes that "the concept of mu-
     sical material is a compositional-technical and at the same time an aesthetic,
     historical-philosophical, and a sociological category," and that "Not only is the
     material with which Schoenberg, Webern, and Cage operate different, but the
     concept of material itself: the category of material in its relation to other con-
     cepts such as technique, language, and structure. . . . The terminological investi-
     gation of the concept of material turns accordingly into a historical one: defini-
     tion dissolves itself into the writing of history." Carl Dahlhaus, "Adornos Begriff
     des musikalischen Materials," in *Schönberg und andere*, 339, 341. The problem-
     atic involved in Adorno's concept of material, along with its complexity, only
     goes to show its relevance to the far-flung and complex network of associations
     and orientations of a genuinely creative compositional consciousness.

44   Adorno, "The Dialectical Composer" (cf. n. 39), 205.

45   Boulez (cf. n. 40), 15.

46   Boulez (cf. n. 40), 15.

47   Pierre Boulez, "'At the Edge of Fertile Land' (Paul Klee)," in *Stocktakings* (cf. n.
     41), 158–172. The climax, if one will, of this text is in the last paragraph. It begins
     as follows. "I thus refuse to believe in the idea of 'progress' from instrumental to
     electronic music; there is only a shift in the field of action" (172).

48   John Cage, *Silence* (Middletown: Wesleyan University Press, 1967), 6.

49   Cf. Dieter Schnebel, "Abwege: Konsequenzen der jüngsten Musik," in *Denkbare
     Musik: Schriften 1952–1972* (Cologne: M. DuMont Schauberg, 1972), 267.

50   Richard Kostelanetz, *John Cage* (Cologne: M. DuMont Schauberg, 1973), 48 .

51 Kostalanetz (cf. n. 50), 47ff.

52 Cage, *Silence* (cf. n. 48), 261.

53 "His [Thoreau's] point was that he could not support a government that en-
dorsed slavery and waged an imperialist war against Mexico. His imprisonment
set Concord tongues wagging, and so he concluded that justifying his action
would make an instructive lecture for the Concord Lyceum. He gave it twice,
ultimately titling it 'Civil Disobedience,' and then his bluestocking friend Elizabeth Peabody printed it, in May 1849, in a volume she edited called *Aesthetic
Papers.* Understandably it was ignored. But by the end of the 19th century, it
had begun to make itself felt, and, by the middle of the 20th, it had an eager
audience. To many, its message still sounds timely: there is a higher law than the
civil one, and the higher law must be followed even if penalty ensues. So does
its consequence: 'Under a government which imprisons any unjustly, the true
place for a just man is also a prison.'" *The New Encyclopedia Britannica,* 11, 15th
ed. (Chicago: The University of Chicago Press, 1985), 726 (2nd col.).

54 Schnebel, *Denkbare Musik* (cf. n. 49), 373.

55 Dieter Schnebel, "Avantgardist—der Avantgarde voraus," in Kostelanetz, *John
Cage* (cf. n. 50), 9–18.

56 Schnebel, *Denkbare Musik* (cf. n. 49), 345 ff.

57 William Bland, "Morton Feldman," in *The New Grove Dictionary of Music and
Musicians,* 6 (London: Macmillan, 1980), 455.

58 Alfred Frankenstein, in *High Fidelity,* 10, no. 1, January 1960, 68.

59 Bland, "Morton Feldman" (cf. n. 57), 455.

60 Kostelanetz, *John Cage* (cf. n. 50), 125. According to Cowell, Schoenberg realized
quite well that Cage was more interested in his philosophy than in learning
technical procedures.

61 Kostelanetz, John Cage (cf. n. 50), 128ff.

62 Stockhausen, *Texte* (cf. n. 6), 71.

63 Rihm (cf. n. 14), 275.

64 To read Lachenmann's writings is to realize very quickly that terms like "material," "structure" and not least "avant-garde" play a quite decisive role. For example, Lachenmann states that "new functional relationships and new types of
the dialectic between" new sounds and new forms can be created through the
"mutation of the concept of material" by means of a disruption of the "false
magic" of material. Lachenmann (cf. n. 17), 148ff., 197.

65 Rihm (cf. n. 14), 94ff. "Next to Schoenberg, Edgard Varèse is a quite important
composer for me. . . . And there lay this record: *Arcana* by Edgard Varèse. I had
already heard it said that there was something to it. I had never heard it and
asked the man behind the desk to put the piece on. I stood there for the whole
twenty-five minutes that it lasts, and it was for me the initiation."

66 Rihm (cf. n. 14), 391.

67 Rihm (cf. n. 14), 95.

68 Rihm (cf. n. 14), 99–107.

69 Rihm (cf. n. 14), 392.

70 Lachenmann (cf. n. 17), 207.

71 Lachenmann (cf. n. 17), 306.

72 Lachenmann (cf. n. 17), 206.

73 The title *Displaced Spaces*, composed in 1946, sounds like an echo of the designation "displaced persons."

74 Cf. Anne Shreffler, "Wolpe and the Black Mountain College," in *Driven into Paradise: The Musical Migration from Nazi Germany to the United States*, ed. Reinhold Brinkmann and Christoph Wolff (Berkeley: University of California Press, 1999), 294.

75 Austin Clarkson, "Stefan Wolpe," in *The New Grove Dictionary of Music and Musicians*, 20, 512. In a short surviving biographical sketch, Wolpe wrote only "I was in the socialist movement and was also a religious pacifist." Cf. Thomas Phleps, *Stefan Wolpe—Eine Einführung* in: *Stefan Wolpe: Lieder mit Klavierbegleitung 1929–1933*, ed. Thomas Phleps (Hamburg: Peer Musikversand GmbH, 1993), 3.

76 Max Horkheimer and Theodor W. Adorno, *Dialectic of Enlightenment*, trans. John Cumming (New York: Herder and Herder, 1972), 3. See however Habermas's critique in *Der philosophische Diskurs der Moderne*, 2nd ed. (Frankfurt am Main: Suhrkamp, 1989), 130–157.

77 Lachenmann (cf. n. 17), 210.

78 Lachenmann (cf. n. 17), 210.

79 "Misgivings" (1860), "Apathy and Enthusiasm" (1860/61), "Dupont's Round Fight" (1861), "The Lake," "An Uninscribed Moment," "The Conflict of Convictions" (1860/61), "To the Masters of the 'Meteor'" (1888).

80 The simultaneous superimposition represents a statement by Jürgen Habermas in support of an "adamant Enlightenment": "Who declares the project of Modernity as to coincide with the consciousness and the public-speculative actions of individual terrorists, comports no less short-circuiting than someone who would declare the uncomparably more continuous and more extensive terror, which is executed in the dark, in the cellars of the military—and Secret—Police, in the camps and psychiatric institutions, as to be the raison d'être of modern state (and its positivisticly excavated legal government), only because this terror makes use of the means of the public compulsory apparatus of state." (See Habermas [n. 21], 48–59.)

81 Lachenmann (cf. n. 17), 70.

82 See the edition with an afterword by H. H. Stuckenschmidt (Frankfurt am Main: Suhrkamp, 1974), 62–75.

83 Cf. Enzo Restagno, *Nono* (Turin: Edizioni di Torino, 1987), 21.

84 Schoenberg wrote this on an undated piece of paper, probably at the beginning of February 1912. Cf. *Arnold Schoenberg, Wassily Kandinsky: Letters, Pictures and Documents*, ed. Jelene Hahl-Koch, trans. John C. Crawford (London and Boston: faber and faber, 1984), 45.

85 Ferruccio Busoni, *Sketch of a New Esthetic of Music*, trans. Thomas Baker (New York: Schirmer, 1911); reprinted in *Three Classics in the Aesthetics of Music* (New York: Dover, 1962), 75.

86 Lachenmann (cf. n. 17), 207.

"Vom Pfeiffen und von alten Dampfmaschinen," Virgil Thomson, a Reply to Milan Kundera, Kurt Schwitters, and My Galoshes: Perspectives on "Modern" and "Modernism"

LEO TREITLER

WHO WROTE THESE words, and when?

> We are witnessing a Herculanum and
> Pompeii for Music. Music is no more.

It was Heinrich Schenker, in 1910.[1] But it could have been countless others, right down through the annals of Western music as far back as we can read them. Observing that, Charles Rosen commented a few years ago that "... the death of classical music is perhaps its oldest continuing tradition."

All such Jeremiads look back, to a classic tradition or golden age whose stability and endurance are threatened with subversion by the new.

Jacques de Liège wrote in 1330, "Music was originally discreet, simple, masculine, and of good morals; have not the moderns rendered it lascivious?"[2]

Giovanni Maria Artusi famously attacked Claudio Monteverdi's music in his "Artusi, or Of the Imperfection of Modern Music" of 1600. (These pejorative references to "modern" and "the moderns," incidentally, mark a change from the earliest uses of the duality "ancient/modern" recorded in the ninth century when it was neutrally a chronological differentiation.)

On the other hand, chances for the survival of serious music are worried over from the side of the modernists as well. Milton Babbitt, in his famous essay "Who Cares if you Listen," wrote "If such music is not supported, the concert-going activity of the conspicuous consumer of musical culture will be little disturbed. But music will cease to evolve, and, in that important sense, will cease to live."[3] This, too, can be found in multiple versions and in discourse about all the arts. The view is forward, to the future. Either way it is music in motion that is under assessment, and music's movement through history that is the ground of its evaluation. What is always striking in such assessments is the exclusion of the present—any present—as anything other than the past's future or the future's past, in a vision of history in which past and future push ineluctably against one another.

An allegorical text by Franz Kafka evokes this vision:

> He has two antagonists: the first presses him from behind, from the origin. The second blocks the road ahead. He gives battle to both. Actually, the first supports him in his fight with the second, for he wants to press him forward, and in the same way the second supports him in his fight with the first, since he drives him back. But this is only theoretical. For there are not just two opponents but also he himself, and who really knows his intentions? In any case his dream is that some time in an unguarded moment—and this would require a night darker than any night has ever been yet—he jumps out of the fighting line and is promoted, on account of his experience in fighting—to the position of umpire over his antagonists in their fight with each other.[4]

"Looking Forward" is the title of Virgil Thomson's 1945 essay about what he calls the "modernistic" period which, he wrote then, is "now drawing to a close."[5] "The first thing the intellectual world of music will have to do once the shooting [of WWII] is over is to get on with the business of closing off the modernistic epoch, which has been at once our inheritance from the nineteenth century and the means of our liberation from it." The language of struggle goes on: "But the war cries of modernism will have to have died down still farther before the children of peace can really start to enjoy the benefits of all the forays and all the campaigns that we now middle-aged have engaged in to establish the twentieth century's right *to be itself.*" I take Thomson's "right to be itself" to refer to a (mostly neglected) kind of historical representation in which the past is represented as having an ontological present, that is, as the present experience of its contemporaries rather than as its future's past or its past's future.

"The war cries of modernism" had not died down when I was living in West Berlin as a student during the late 1950s. They blended with Cold War cries sometimes, as in the disruption of Hermann Scherchen's performance of *Moses und Aron* by hecklers from East Berlin, to cite one extreme episode. But I heard softer expressions as well.

Berlin winters were wet, as I had been warned. Half-melted gray slush lay on the streets much of the time, and I was glad to have brought with me a pair of galoshes suited to keep my feet dry and protect my shoes and trouser bottoms from that mess (Fig. 1). As I rode back and forth on the U-Bahn, fel-

Figure 1.
Illustration by
Mary Frank

low passengers fixed their eyes on them with intense stares, as though they would have vaporized them. I had my own thoughts ("what are *they* staring at?"), about how *their* unprotected feet must have felt, especially the feet of young women in their high-heeled pumps and minimal sandals. One day I asked the opinion of my landlady—she was the hermeneut for all my Berlin experiences—about what might be so fascinating and even threatening about my galoshes. She shot back "sie sind nicht modern," that is, not chic or stylish, not *comme il faut*. The stares told me that it isn't correct to sacrifice chic to comfort. Altogether the experience taught me something about the dictatorial character of modernism, despite its avowed freedoms. It is the imperatives that accompany ideas of modernism of whatever cast that come through.

Milan Kundera is a novelist and literary essayist with music in his blood. He grew up as the son of a concert pianist and director of the Conservatory of Music in Brno. Until he settled in Paris at the age of forty-six he lived under a totalitarian, Soviet-influenced Marxist regime in Czechoslovakia. His writings about music history and aesthetics bristle with signs of his having had his fill of socialist realism and materialist historiography.

In the essay "Improvisation in Homage to Stravinsky," an apt title for a rambling chapter in Kundera's *Testaments Betrayed*,[6] modernism fails again to find its own ontological present, thriving instead as a parasite on the rehabilitation of an aesthetic that, writes Kundera, had prevailed from the beginning of Western music in the Middle Ages up to J.S. Bach, more specifically, *Die Kunst der Fuge*. This is a more peaceful vision of the relation of modernism to romanticism than Virgil Thomson's; the modern simply passes back over romanticism without a struggle in heeding what Kundera dubs "The Call of the Past." What drives this backward *jeté* are the imperatives of the art of music itself, which Kundera sets free, without any notion of the imperatives of a future-oriented, progressive modernity. Here the reaction against Marxist doctrine shows.

Either Kundera's strong gravitation to the music and career of Stravinsky has led him to this historical view of modernism, or he has come to it first and seized on Stravinsky as its paragon. He presents it in this second way, writing that in the mid-twentieth century, music's thousand-year history became totally present, totally available, nowhere more than in the Stravinsky *oeuvre*. One feels a clash with Adorno coming on.

To bring that rehabilitated aesthetic to the surface Kundera rekindles the controversy stirred up by the famous passage in Stravinsky's *Chronicle of My Life* (1935): Music is "powerless to express anything at all—a feeling, an attitude, a psychological state. Music's *raison d'être* does not reside in its capacity to express feelings." Why, in 1993, did Kundera rouse this sleeping dog which most people by then had been content to let lie? Because "an aesthetic of feeling" was given priority and had become self-evident in the eighteenth and nineteenth centuries, and modernism, recall, is founded on the rehabilitation of an aesthetic that had prevailed before that time, an aesthetic free of human subjectivity. To retrieve it entailed either detour around or struggle against romanticism.[7]

Again, for Kundera the principles of socialist realism haunt this story. Rousseau had assigned priority to melody as the vehicle for the aesthetic of feeling, and Zhdanov had condemned formalist composers because their music could not be whistled. Under socialist realism the principles of the eighteenth and nineteenth century were transformed into dogmas that blocked modernism. Although Kundera insists that the dynamics of the history of art are internal to the arts themselves and do not lie in political or social forces, his theory is nonetheless a projection of Cold War ideologies onto the domain of music history.

So he launches a big polemic against the critics of Stravinsky's questionable proclamation (I say questionable not only because of the question about authorship but because I believe the duality that it poses is dubious, and in any case it is contradicted by Stravinsky's music). And after Zhdanov and Co., the biggest target is Adorno and his criticism of Stravinsky in *The Philosophy of Modern Music*, of his "antipsychological furor," his "indifference toward the world," "his desire to objectivize music" in "a kind of tacit accord with the capitalist society that crushes human subjectivity." This last Kundera labels as the sort of "short circuit" with which he characterizes Adorno, a style with which, indeed, some of the brightest members of a younger generation of music scholars has been infected and which has been criticized by others beside Kundera.[8]

Kundera, like many other interpreters of Adorno, pro and con, shows no awareness of a different side of Adorno's hermeneutic which might have tempered his outburst "Will we ever be done with this imbecile sentimental Inquisition, the heart's Reign of Terror?"

Adorno began a little-noticed, very short essay published 1930 in the journal *Anbruch* under the title "Motive V: Hermeneutik" this way (with ellipses):

> Hermeneutics has been banned. With good reason: because it shrank the content of music to the domain…of the multiplicity of subjective experience and of individual soul-stirrings,…because it distorts while it reports, and can never be made to correspond unambiguously to the musically objective. Nevertheless in the criticism of hermeneutics as of "subjectivity" altogether people have gone too far and lost true objectivity. For music has been torn loose—as empty play—from all of its values or contents…
>
> Nevertheless it is not yet the case that there is no chance for hermeneutics today. The affects offer themselves to it as interpretable material…The energy of yore becomes visible as empty spaces in works that have decomposed, which their mere sounds in the present no longer fill. It is to this empty space that hermeneutic interpretation must direct itself.

This opening is followed and exemplified by eight hermeneutic sketches of no more than a paragraph each. Here is a characteristic one:

> The closing group of the finale of Mozart's A major piano concerto: above an organ-point with mechanically inflected accompanying figure between tonic and dominant with a melody that really just drives within one step of a second after another with the movement of the preceding, in order suddenly, without giving way, to split up into the smallest little motivic parts: that closing group, whose dense work closes off all the development and dynamic of the remainder of the movement, as if its enclosure wanted to reel in the time that before had been flowing freely: how like it is to the clock, as which the philosophers of the 17th century once thought their world; which at first a godly builder had set in motion and now left to itself, trusting to its mechanism. It is a magic mechanism, an unknown onlooker outside shows it the time while it itself controls the time in which it is enclosed. Inside everything remains the same the world is a dream of its sleeping builder. But when the clock of Mozart's closing group in the coda begins for the third time, when its metallic sound begins softly to drip in the cool subdominant, then it is as if the half-forgotten work has occurred to the master, as if he had taken hold, removed his spell from it: time empowers itself with the power of the clock and, reconciled, it plays for itself its epilogue before falling silent.

Reinhold Brinkmann, in an essay whose title I have incorporated into mine,[9] has rather tellingly portrayed this way that Adorno had of revivifying the music of the past while circumventing the false dichotomy posed by Stravinsky (*pfeiffen* and *alte Dampfmaschinen* are images in Adorno's interpretations of Hindemith's Viola Concerto, op. 36, and the opening of Mahler's First Symphony, respectively) . The interpretive procedure, writes Brinkmann, is a response to "gesture" and "tone" (Alban Berg's concept) as components of a "musical physiognomy" (a reference to the subtitle of Adorno's book, *Mahler: A Musical Physiognomy*).[10]

Such a physiognomy does not lend itself to proof or certainty or to a strict intellectual order. Rather it gives itself up to a chancy dependence on experience in order to arrive at something essential. It is a gamble, dependent on a widening field of association. The premises of Adorno's interpretation of art, relying thus on insight and intuition, are themselves artistic, hardly scientific. His "physiognomics" presents itself as a gesture of humanity; in an inhuman world it seeks a human face in its objects.

No modernist artist provides a clearer counterexample to Kundera's dogma that the movements of art are driven exclusively by their own internal dynamics than Kurt Schwitters. Under the banner of Dada, Schwitters joined with other artists and writers to express, through exhibitions, performances, and publications, their disaffection with the bourgeois world that had made World War I. The year after its conclusion, 1919, was a year of the most explosive creativity for him.[11] He began making collages—MERZ-pictures, he called them (taking the second syllable of *Kommerz* in a letterhead for a *Kommerz und Privatbank*)—incorporating found scraps and materials from modern life. He had his first exhibition in the gallery *Der Sturm* in Berlin along with Klee and Molzahn. In the same year, he published the poem *An Anna Blume,* which was largely responsible for establishing his reputation.

In his own words, "During the war, the unrest was terrible. I couldn't use what I had learned in the Academy and the new possibilities were not yet fully developed. And suddenly the glorious revolution arrived…Now the excitement really began…After the revolution I felt myself free and had to cry out my jubilation to the world. Since we were an impoverished country, I had to do this economically, using what I could find. One can also shout with waste from the dustbin, and that's what I did. I nailed and glued it together. I called it MERZ, but it was my prayer of thanks for the victorious conclusion of the war…Everything was destroyed anyway and it was necessary to build something new from the pieces."[12]

This combination of necessity and freedom produced a multifaceted aesthetic of subtlety and depth. The waste materials used in the collages are apprehended in the light of their original contexts and continue to offer a wide range of allusive possibilities, as, for example, the texts of newspaper scraps which could evoke strong feelings—this in contrast to the collages of the cubists that began to be made eight years earlier. An example (Fig. 2): MERZ-bild 25A from 1920 shows word fragments that can be recognized: upper left *Reichsk[anzler]* and *blutigen,* lower left in very small print *Generalleutnant* (next to 732), further down on the left *Hungersn[ot] Erhöhung* and "*Gegen der Stillegung,*" upper right "*Offener Brief, Mathias, Die Korrupt[ion].*"[13] Think of such fragments from our reading of the daily press jostling each other in our anxious minds today. At the same time these waste materials are treated and perceived as independent aesthetic objects released from their mundane functions. (Schwitters spoke of their *entformung* and *entgiftung.*) And when

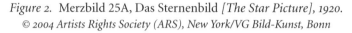

Figure 2. Merzbild 25A, Das Sternenbild *[The Star Picture], 1920.*
© *2004 Artists Rights Society (ARS), New York/VG Bild-Kunst, Bonn*

they are so regarded the juxtaposition of their colors, forms, and textures
make for abstract compositions with their own beauty (he spoke of them
as *konsequent*). (See Figs. 3, *Kleine Seemansheim* and 4, *Konstruktion für edle
Frauen.*) In their multiple communications these works transcend the duality
of form and feeling.

Figure 3. XIX Bild, Kleines Seemannsheim *[Small Sailors' Home]*, 1926.
© 2004 Artists Rights Society (ARS), New York/VG Bild-Kunst, Bonn

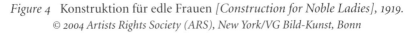

Figure 4   Konstruktion für edle Frauen *[Construction for Noble Ladies], 1919.*
© *2004 Artists Rights Society (ARS), New York/VG Bild-Kunst, Bonn*

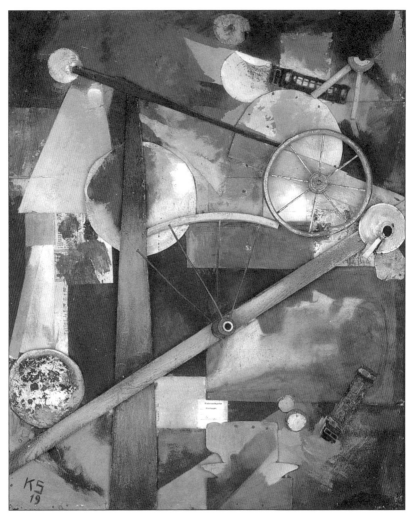

I conclude this collage of mine with a reading of *An Anna Blume,* which
is a kind of counterpart of the visual collages, calling attention to the playfulness and irony that has virtually every aspect of language and poetry as its
object, but also to the play of convention and to the aspect of allusion.

AN ANNA BLUME

O du, Geliebte meiner siebenundzwanzig Sinne, ich
liebe dir!—Du deiner dich dir, ich dir, du mir.
—Wir?
Das gehört (beiläufig) nicht hierher.
Wer bist du, ungezähltes Frauenzimmer? Du bist
—bist du? Die Leute sagen—du wärest—laß
sie sagen, sie wissen nicht, wie der Kirchturm steht.
Du trägst den Hut auf deinen Füßen und wanderst
auf die Hände, auf den Händen wanderst du.
Hallo, deine roten Kleider, in Weiße Falten zersägt.
Rot liebe ich Anna Blume, rot liebe ich dir!—Du
deiner dich dir, ich dir, du mir.—Wir?
Das gehört (beiläufig) in die kalte Glut.
Rote Blume, rote Anna Blume, wie sagen die Leute?
Preisfrage: 1.) Anna Blume hat ein Vogel.
            2.) Anna Blume ist rot.
            3.) Welche Farbe hat der Vogel?
Blau ist die Farbe deines gelben Haares.
Rot ist das Girren deines grünen Vogels.
Du schlichtes Mädchen im Alltagskleid, du liebes
grünes Tier, ich liebe dir!—Du deiner dich dir, ich
dir, du mir,—wir?
Das gehört (beiläufig) in die Glutenkiste.
Anna Blume! Anna, a-n-n-a, ich träufle deinen
Namen. Dein Name tropft wie weiches Rindertalg.
Weißt du es, Anna, weißt du es schon?
Man kann dich auch von hinten lesen, und du, du
Herrlichste von allen, du bist von hinten wie von
vorne: "a-n-n-a."
Rindertalg träufelt streicheln über meinen Rücken.
Anna Blume, du tropfes Tier, ich liebe dir.[14]

O thou, beloved of my twenty-seven senses,
I love thine!
Thou thee thee thine, I thine, thou mine, we?
That (by the way) is beside the point!
Who art thou, uncounted woman,
Thou art, art thou?

People say, thou werst,
Let them say, they don't know what they are talking about.
Thou wearest thine hat on thy feet, and wanderest on thine hands,
On thine hands thou wanderest.
Hallo, thy red dress, sawn into white folds,
Red I love Eve Blossom, red I love thine!
Thou thee thee thine, I thine, thou mine, we?
That (by the way) belongs to the cold glow!
Eve Blossom, red Eve Blossom, what do people say.
    PRIZE   1. Eve Blossom is red.
QUESTION: 2. Eve Blossom has wheels.
                    3. what colour are the wheels?
Blue is the colour of your yellow hair,
Red is the whirl of your green wheels,
Thou simple maiden in everyday dress,
Thou small green animal,
I love thine!
Thou thee thee thine, I thine, thou mine, we?
That (by the way) belongs to the glowing brazier!
Eve Blossom,
Eve,
E-V-E,
E easy, V victory, E easy,
I trickle your name.
Your name drops like soft tallow.
Do you know it, Eve,
Do you already know it?
One can also read you from the back.
And you, you most glorious of all,
You are from the back as from the front,
E-V-E.
Easy victory.
Tallow trickles to strike over my back!
Eve Blossom,
Thou drippy animal,
I
Love
Thine!
I love you!!![15]

In an afterword Schwitters wrote

> My poetry is abstract. Like MERZ painting it makes use of given ele-
> ments such as sentences cut out of newspapers or taken down from
> conversations, drawn from catalogues, posters etc. with and without
> alteration. (this is terrible) Such elements need not suit the meaning,
> for there is no meaning any more. (This is terrible too.) Nor is there
> any elephant now, there are only parts of the poem. (This is fright-
> ful) And you? (Buy war bonds!) Decide for yourself where the poem
> stops and the frame begins.[16]

Schwitters initially joined the Dada movement, but separated his work
from it. "I compared Dadaism at its most exalted form with MERZ and came
to this conclusion: whereas Dadism merely poses antitheses, MERZ recon-
ciles antitheses by assigning relative values to every element in the work of
art. Pure MERZ is pure art. Pure Dadaism is pure non-art; in both cases deliberately so."[17]

With this differentiation Schwitters made a claim for a modernism distinguished by what it is and is for, rather than by what it is not and is against.
Or, to put it in terms that I engaged earlier, a modernism whose being is in its
own presentness, not in its relation to a past of which it is the future, or to a
future of which it is the past.

Notes

1   *Neue musikalische Theorien und Phantasien*, 2, *Kontrapunkt* (Stuttgart and Ber-
    lin, 1910), vii.

2   *Strunk's Source Readings in Music History*, ed. Leo Treitler (New York: Norton,
    1998), 277.

3   Ibid., 1311.

4   "ER: Aufzeichnungen aus dem Jahre 1920. Beschreibungen eines Kampfes," *No-
    vellen, Skizzen, Aphorismen aus dem Nachlass* (Prague: Velag Heinrich Mercy
    Sohn, 1936) 287.

5   *The Musical Quarterly* 31 (1945),

6   Milan Kundera, *Testaments Betrayed: An Essay in Nine Parts*, trans. Linda Asher
    (New York: Harper Collins, 1995).

7   I just mention in passing that this revival belongs with a whole network of dis-

torted historical representations of music, even the earliest music we know—e.g., the wide-spread dogma that medieval music was but the expression of numerical proportions, that its composers had no interest in the meanings or feelings of the words they intoned in their music.

8 Charles Rosen writes about "Adorno's attempt to unite art and society with a facile metaphor," and cites Carl Dahlhaus's comment about Adorno's attempts to unite musical analysis and sociology, "The verbal analogies perform the function of hiding a gap which the argument could not close." See "Should we Adore Adorno?" *New York Review of Books* (October 24, 2002), 63.

9 See Reinhold Brinkmann, "Vom Pfeifen und von alten Dampfmaschinen: Zwei Hinweise auf Texte Theodor W. Adornos," in *Beiträge zur musikalischen Hermeneutik*, ed. Carl Dahlhaus (Regensburg: G. Bosse, 1975), 113–20.

10 See Theodor W. Adorno, *Mahler: A Musical Physiognomy*, trans. Edmund Jephcott (Chicago: The University of Chicago Press, 1992).

11 Regarding Schwitters' relationship to the Dada phenomenon, as manifested especially in his collages, see Dorothea Dietrich, *The Collages of Kurt Schwitters: Tradition and Innovation* (Cambridge: Cambridge University Press, 1993).

12 From Schwitters' autobiographical statement in *Gefesselter Blick*, a book on the new advertising art by Hans and Bodo Rasch, 1930. Cited by Monica J. Strauss in her catalogue essay for *Kurt Schwitters: Collages and Other Works on Paper* (Beverly Hills, CA: Lewis Newman Galleries, 1988).

13 I follow here the discussion of this work in Dietrich's book, 112–114.

14 Kurt Schwitters, *Anna Blume Dichtungen* (Hannover: Paul Steegemann, 1922), 7–8.

15 This is Schwitters's own (hardly literal) translation of the poem. Reprinted in Werner Schmalenbach, *Kurt Schwitters* (London: Thames and Hudson, 1970), 204.

16 See note 12. Translation by Werner Schmalenbach, in *Kurt Schwitters* (London and New York: Abrams, 1967).

17 See note 11.

Of Aprons, Buses, and Bridges:
Kafka's Judgment

PETER J. BURGARD

In "Das Urteil" the reader is forced to judgment. This judgment, grounded in the logic and shifting perspective of the narrative, is that the father is correct in *his* judgment and that the son is right to commit suicide.

The curious thing about Kafka's texts is that they are exceptionally welcoming to whatever degree of complexity one wishes to bring to bear on and then derive from them, even though they are in many ways actually very simple—in their language, in the extreme spareness of their plots, in their stark literality (metaphors are few and far between in "Das Urteil," for example, which might be one justification for a very literal reading). Indeed, it is probably that very simplicity that invites such extraordinary critical complexity, that allows us to supply—in the Goethean sense of "suppliren," the supplement—such symbolism and metaphoricity to them. Kafka himself seems to have contributed to this by remarking on how full of "abstractions" the story is. Here I want to devote my energy to teasing some of that simplicity back out of the highly articulated complexity that has come to inform readings of "Das Urteil"—in part also in order to circumvent the scholarly constraint of accounting for all previous research, a constraint that, particularly with writers like Kafka, easily chokes off any less "scientific" approach to his work or approaches by anyone who isn't a Kafka scholar.[1] Put another way, through Kafka's simplicity I hope to reclaim some measure of freedom in responding to his work.

"Das Urteil" is a short story about a young businessman named Georg

Bendemann, who on a sunny spring Sunday morning writes a letter to a friend in Russia. After he has finished writing the letter, he takes it across the hall to show it to his father, apparently so that the father will know that he has written it. Whereupon the father launches a surprising, even shocking attack on his son, first questioning whether and then denying that Georg has this friend in Russia. Georg is unable to counter the attack, and when his father—remarking on what a good child Georg had been, only to have become a devilish human being—sentences him to death by drowning, Georg carries out that sentence, running outside and throwing himself off a bridge. A funny story, in other words. Funny, of course, not so much because of what happens to Georg—one might say this is fairly serious stuff—but as always in comedy, because of discrepancy. In this case it is the dramatic discrepancy between the reader's expectations (formed by a story that sees events primarily from Georg's perspective) and what actually happens in the text. Kafka himself apparently couldn't keep from laughing when reading his work aloud to friends. This discrepancy that lends a delicious black humor to the story does not, I will argue, reflect any rupture in the logic of the narrative, but results instead from its structure.

The structure of the story is fundamentally bipartite and articulated spatially. The first part takes place in Georg's room, where he is thinking about the letter he has written; there is a brief transition when he goes from his room into his father's, and then the second part, save Georg's one-paragraph race out the door to jump off the bridge at the end, takes place in the father's room. This structure reflects the one major shift in perspective that occurs in the story—the shift from a *monologic* to a *dialogic* situation. One can, however, detect more minute shifts in narrative perspective throughout the text, starting with an omniscient narrative that gradually turns inward but then turns outward once again at the end. The stations would be: 1) the first paragraph, which starts authorially with "Es war an einem Sonntagvormittag im schönsten Frühjahr";[2] 2) the second paragraph, which begins by telling us "Er dachte"[†] and thus revealing that the narration has already begun to enter Georg's perspective; 3) the third paragraph, where we already find ourselves fully in free indirect discourse with the beginning question, "Was wollte man einem solchen Manne schreiben,"[‡] a question Georg is asking himself, but not in quotation marks; 4) the conclusion of the first part of the story with

---

[*] "It was a Sunday morning at the very height of spring" (49)

[†] "He was thinking"(49)

[‡] "What could one write to such a man" (50)

direct discourse, the quotation from Georg's letter to his friend; 5) the transitional movement across the hallway, described by an omniscient narrator;
6) the direct discourse of the dialogue between Georg and his father; 7) the
return to Georg's perspective, if not free indirect style, when we learn that
he "fühlte sich aus dem Zimmer gejagt" (38)[*]; and 8) the return, at the very
end, to omniscient narration: "In diesem Augenblick ging über die Brücke ein
geradezu unendlicher Verkehr" (38).[†] One might also describe the narratorial
viewpoint as beginning with omniscient third-person narration in that first
paragraph of the text, moving to limited omniscient narration when we enter
Georg's perspective in the second, then to free indirect discourse, then to the
direct discourse of the quoted letter, then back to limited omniscient narration during the transition from Georg's room to his father's, then to a mixture
of direct discourse and limited omniscient narration in the dialogue between
them, where most everything is direct discourse, but where numerous revelations of what Georg is thinking are nevertheless interspersed, then to limited
omniscient narration alone as Georg races out of the house to the bridge and
his own demise, and finally, in the last line, back to omniscient third person
narration, thus coming full circle and instantiating a surprising closure in the
narrative structure of the story that belies the non-closure that that "endless"
traffic on the bridge seems to suggest.

But what of that one major shift in perspective I mentioned, the one that
helps to articulate the bipartite structure I have claimed the story has? Again,
in examining the complexities of the shifting narrative perspective throughout the text, one can lose track of the simpler, more basic shift from an essentially monologic situation to a dialogic one. Those many shifts in perspective
just outlined—and one could go into greater detail and ascertain many more
minute shifts—may well be one of the main reasons why it seems so difficult
to get a handle on this story: namely, because the text is literally and (thus)
figuratively *shifty*. This difficulty and the shifts that ground it may in turn
explain the inordinate number of different readings of the story. My point
is that these many perspectival shifts function as red herrings, so to speak,
as distractions from the greater, overarching narrative simplicity of the story,
blinding readers to that *one* major shift, from monologue to dialogue, that
means the most, that defines the structure and with it the theme of the story.

The two parts of the story swing on a single perspectival hinge, much as

---

[*] "felt like he was being chased out of the room" (63)

[†] "At this moment an unending stream of traffic was just going over the bridge"
(63)

they swing, spatially, on the hinges of the doors whose thresholds Georg must cross to enter his father's room—from the perspective of an isolated individual to an intersubjective realm where there is more than just that individual's point of view and where the latter is thus relativized and put to the test. Kafka even has Georg's father emphasize this shift when he says "'Du bist wegen dieser Sache zu mir gekommen, um dich mit mir zu beraten'" (32).[*] Obviously, this consultation does not turn out very favorably for Georg; obviously, Georg's perspective does not pass the test of the intersubjective realm.

The second part of the text provides the *context* by which the first part can be judged, and that single, isolated point of view in the first part veritably invites judgment. But it is not the father who is doing this particular judging, since he wasn't privy to Georg's thoughts while he wrote the letter. In addition to the father's judgment, there is the judgment that we, the readers, whom the text, through this structure and this perspectival shift, has placed into the position of Georg's judges, must make. Herein lies the performative aspect of "Das Urteil," "The Judgment," as well as, we shall see, in the way the text proves the father right and the son wrong, performing its own judgment and execution of Georg.

The sense of Georg's perspective being put to the test and our being put in the position of judge along with, but not analogously to, Georg's father, is heightened by a narrative peculiarity in the dialogue between father and son, in their verbal duel. It is not simply direct discourse, or rather, with two very brief exceptions, it *is* the direct discourse of Georg's father without narratorial embellishment, whereas Georg's direct discourse in the dialogue is accompanied, or more accurately supplemented, by the continual presence of the narrator telling us what Georg is thinking and feeling. Thus his perspective is not confined to the first part, but rather remains present during the dialogue so that we can better judge the validity of the father's utterances. Again, we have only the father's words—no or almost no insight whatever into any thoughts or feelings complementary or supplementary to those words. But insofar as those words prove to be right, within the logic of the text, they take on the quality of *the* word, *the* law, *the* judgment, as opposed to what we will confirm to be Georg's travesty of language. (Here is one of those places where it is tempting to spin off into a symbolic interpretation of the text—the father's words are *the* word, the father has no name, thus the father is God the Father, which is substantiated by the maid then calling out "Jesus!" as Georg, the son, races past her and by the crucifixion tableau, just before his death, of Georg's

---

[*] "'You've come to me about this business, to talk it over with me'" (55)

body hanging vertically from the horizontal bridge, etc., etc.—but I think it is also one of those instances where the tendency to draw such extensive symbolic equivalences from a resolutely literal story is best restrained.)

My reading of the story, like the story itself, is in two main, one might almost say analogous parts: the first is concerned primarily with language, with *expression*, while the second will deal more with *repression*. Before we can consider the relativization and judging of Georg's perspective and of Georg himself, we need to know what exactly he does that eventually writes his death sentence. So let us turn to that first part of the story, where Georg has just finished writing his letter and at least *we* are as yet unsuspecting, having only his view of things.

Precious little actually happens in the first part of the story: Georg slowly and playfully folds the letter, he thinks about his correspondence while gazing out the window, and an acquaintance walking past Georg's window greets him. But, in its reproduction of Georg's thoughts, this first part nevertheless focuses intently on one major act, for Georg's writing itself—the rhetoric of his letter and its content—constitutes an act. What kind of act is it and what is at stake in this writing? I would say that the text already provides us with a clear answer to this question in the second paragraph. There Georg is reflecting on the difficult situation of his expatriate friend in Russia, and since we are already into limited omniscient narration at this point, if not free indirect discourse, we know that this is all what Georg thinks, but that it is of course not necessarily so. Georg's view is that his friend fled to Russia dissatisfied with his progress and prospects at home, that his business in St. Petersburg—unlike Georg's own, as we will later learn—is not doing so well. We have to remember that, even though we read the statement that the friend complains about his business during his ever rarer visits home, the narrative perspective makes that part of Georg's supposition, not a "fact." We learn further that the friend is getting sicker and sicker, that he has made no proper connection to the colony of expatriates there, and that he has "fast keinen gesellschaftlichen Verkehr" (27)[*] with "native families." Even without knowing the significance the word *Verkehr* will acquire at the end of the story, and then retroactively, this paragraph already makes it clear that *Verkehr*, which here signifies social intercourse, is one of the primary grounds of Georg's judgment of his friend's life and thus a main theme of the story. So we have to keep an eye out for anything that has to do with social intercourse. Put more generally, especially since the scene is a scene of *writing*, the theme is *communication*. Thus, *how*

---

[*] "almost no social intercourse" (50)

Georg communicates with his friend, what sort of social intercourse he has and maintains with him, is of central concern.

It does not take long to discover there is something not quite right about Georg's communication with the friend. In the next paragraph, Georg asks himself what one can write to such a person, with such problems, suggesting that any genuine communication would be misunderstood and taken as an insult or criticism. But we have to remember that this is all based on a view of the friend's life from Georg's perspective. And on this basis he spins a yarn about all the truly critical things one would have to write to him if one wanted to be upright and really do him a favor: tell him to come home, tell him to depend on his old friends back home, tell him that all he has attempted has been a failure, that he should give it up, come home, and let himself forever be viewed as a failure, as an "old child" who has to subject himself to his successful friends who stayed home. But then, according to Georg's perspective, even if he followed this advice, he might come home and not find his way or his friends, so would it not actually be best if he were just to stay away? Besides revealing an extraordinary tendency to control the life of the friend (as well as a healthy portion of vanity), this is in itself evidence of an attempt to forestall communication with him. And the conclusion Georg draws from all these imagined possible communications and their projected damage is that "Aus diesen Gründen konnte man ihm, wenn man noch überhaupt die briefliche Verbindung aufrecht erhalten wollte, *keine eigentlichen Mitteilungen machen*" (28; my emphasis).[*] Thus Georg has convinced himself that he can only communicate with his friend—"maintain an epistolary connection"—in that he does not communicate with him at all. Our first conclusion, then, about Georg's communication must be that it is "unreal," if you will—that, in the terms established by the story, he *lies*.

From here, with regard to the central theme of communication, things only get worse. We learn that over the last years—besides the death of his mother, which seems to be cause for him to hold a grudge against the friend for not having been sufficiently effusive in his letter of condolence—Georg, at least in his own view, has enjoyed considerable success in his business. But we also learn that the friend has no inkling of this success—"Der Freund aber hatte keine Ahnung von dieser Veränderung" (29)[†]—and thus that Georg has omitted from his letters news of some of the most important developments

---

[*] "For such reasons, supposing one wanted to maintain an epistolary connection at all, one could not send him any real news" (50–51)

[†] "But Georg's friend had no inkling of this change" (51)

in his life. In other words, that he has undermined the very notion of personal correspondence by not maintaining in his exchange of letters the more literal sense of correspondence that the word implies, even in its common usage. In still other words, that he has, by withholding crucial information, *falsified communication*. Georg seems to sense this, at least in a very minimal way, because the combination of limited omniscient narration and free indirect discourse gives us access to the excuses for it that he makes to himself: "Georg aber hatte keine Lust gehabt, dem Freund von seinen geschäftlichen Erfolgen zu schreiben, und hätte er es jetzt nachträglich getan, es hätte wirklich einen merkwürdigen Anschein gehabt" (29). [*]

The result of this falsification is further and more far-reaching falsification: "So beschränkte sich Georg darauf, dem Freund immer nur über bedeutungslose Vorfälle zu schreiben" (29). [†] We then see the extreme and comic effect of this false communication (funny except for the friend, since the joke is on him): "So geschah es Georg"—and note here that Georg sees this as having happened to him, perversely sees himself as a victim, even though he was its sole agent, and that he thus gives evidence of being in denial about his own subversion of communication—"So geschah es Georg, daß er dem Freund die Verlobung eines gleichgültigen Menschen mit einem ebenso gleichgültigen Mädchen dreimal in ziemlich weit auseinanderliegenden Briefen anzeigte, bis sich dann allerdings der Freund, ganz gegen Georgs Absicht, für diese Merkwürdigkeit zu interessieren begann" (29). [‡] The phrase "ganz gegen Georgs Absicht" [§] is the first explicit indication in the text that Georg does not have quite the control over his language that he would like to think he has. But more on that later. Indeed, one might read it just the other way around, concluding that this is a case of Georg lying to himself for appearances' sake and that this deflection of interest away from his own life and toward the life of people he doesn't care a jot about is precisely what he intended. Either way, what we discover here is that Georg creates for his friend a false image of his own reality, in that he covers up important information about his life, substituting it with information that is "gleichgültig," that means nothing to him.

---

[*] "But Georg had had no desire to write to his friend about his business success, and if he were to do it now, retrospectively, it would certainly have looked peculiar" (52)

[†] "Thus Georg confined himself to writing only about meaningless occurrences" (52)

[‡] "And so it happened to Georg that three times in fairly widely separated letters he told his friend about the engagement of an unimportant man to an equally unimportant girl, until indeed, quite contrary to his intentions, his friend began to show interest in this notable event" (52)

[§] "quite contrary to his intentions" (52)

Worse, though, is that he thereby separates the friend himself from this reality, undermining the very purpose of the communication that correspondence is meant to represent—namely, to maintain the at least vicarious integration into one's own life and concerns of the person with whom one corresponds, that is, to establish a verbal connection that substitutes for the missing geographical one.

We learn in the next paragraph what this false communication supplants, namely, conveying to his friend the news of his engagement to Miss Frieda Brandenfeld. So Georg's false communication is revealed as the direct suppression of true communication. Georg gives his fiancée all sorts of excuses for not informing the friend of his impending wedding, but insofar as these excuses are all based on his perspective and thus on his own imaginings about the friend's life, which, as we have seen, we have no reason to believe are reliable and some reason to see as disingenuous, the excuses constitute yet another false communication, a false communication with his fiancée.

Were it true that the friend is living in desolate isolation, then we would have to conclude that Georg has at the very least contributed to that isolation, if indeed he has not been instrumental in it, through his false communication. In that he has systematically distorted the reality of home, he has made his friend even more a foreigner. But now, one might object, Georg does sit down on this sunny spring morning in order finally to inform his friend of his engagement: "Und tatsächlich berichtete er seinem Freund in dem langen Brief ... die erfolgte Verlobung" (30),* the "tatsächlich" revealing just what a novelty it is for Georg to produce what we might consider genuine communication. The question, of course, especially since we are concerned here with the use of language and the nature of communication, is *how* he informs his friend. He tells him he has gotten engaged but suppresses details about his fiancée with the following rhetorical act of control, "'heute genüge Dir'" (30),† a phrase that should, by now, automatically activate our false communication antennae. And rightfully so, for just a few lines later we discover that, under the pretext of establishing a closer connection between the friend and home, Georg actually and actively isolates him even further: "'Ich weiß, es hält Dich vielerlei von einem Besuche bei uns zurück, wäre aber nicht gerade meine Hochzeit die richtige Gelegenheit, einmal alle Hindernisse über den Haufen zu werfen? Aber wie dies auch sein mag, handle ohne alle Rücksicht und nur

---

* "And indeed he did inform his friend, in the long letter, ... about his engagement" (53)

† "'for today let it be enough for you'" (53)

nach Deiner Wohlmeinung'" (30–31). Those final words are truly words after Georg's own heart, for *he* is the one who has always acted and continues
to act "ohne alle Rücksicht."[†] This invitation to his wedding is a rhetorically
nearly perfect plea for the friend to stay away; while appearing to encourage
his friend to get rid of all the "Hindernisse"[‡] to a visit home, Georg is rhetorically erecting precisely such "Hindernisse." He uninvites his friend in the very
act of inviting him.

Save a very short paragraph, that un-invitation, that use of communication for the purpose of further isolating his correspondent, is the final note in
the first part of the story. What the short paragraph provides is a kind of independent verification (coming from the omniscient narrator, not from Georg's
perspective) of what we have been seeing all along. With the letter in his hand,
Georg sits at his desk, facing the window, but he barely acknowledges an acquaintance who passes by the window and greets him. That window, given
the theme of communication that the first part of the story has so thoroughly
set into play, is a vehicle of communication between him and his surrounding
world. Hardly acknowledging the acquaintance's greeting reveals that Georg's
falsified communication in the letter he holds in his hand, and all the earlier
letters it represents, attenuates his own connection to the real world around
him. We might then project that what he does, as I wondered at the beginning
of my reading, that eventually writes his own death sentence is actually an
act of writing: writing such letters to a friend. It remains to be seen, of course,
why this should result in something so extreme as a death sentence.

The transitional paragraph to the second part of the story follows upon
this scene of non-communication, and this paragraph provides yet further
evidence of the degree to which genuine communication does not occur in
Georg's life. This paragraph at the hinge of the story is also one of the more
amazing bits of prose in German literature—amazing in general for its brilliant syntactical inscription of equivocation and specifically for its excessive
and vertiginous equivocation of ostensible communication:

> Endlich steckte er den Brief in die Tasche und ging aus seinem Zim-
> mer quer durch einen kleinen Gang in das Zimmer seines Vaters,

---

[*] "'I know there are many things that prevent you from visiting us, but would not
my wedding be precisely the right occasion to toss aside all obstacles for once? But
whatever the case may be, do only as seems good to you, without any consideration
for others'" (53)

[†] "without any consideration for others" (53)

[‡] "obstacles" (53)

in dem er schon seit Monaten nicht gewesen war. Es bestand auch
sonst keine Nötigung dazu, denn er verkehrte mit seinem Vater
ständig im Geschäft, das Mittagessen nahmen sie gleichzeitig in einem Speisehaus ein, abends versorgte sich zwar jeder nach Belieben,
doch saßen sie dann meistens, wenn nicht Georg, wie es am häu-
figsten geschah, mit Freunden beisammen war oder jetzt seine Braut
besuchte, noch ein Weilchen, jeder mit seiner Zeitung, im gemeinsa-
men Wohnzimmer. (31)[*]

Georg goes into his father's room, where he hasn't been for months, even
though they live together. There's no need for him to go into his father's room
(the use of the word "Nötigung,"[†] of course, also conveys the sense that communication and intersubjectivity intimidate Georg, or that he has to be coerced
into it)—there's no need, we learn, because he "verkehrt"[‡] constantly with his
father in the business. It is crucial that this word signifying interaction and
communication should appear at this juncture, for it thus structures the story
and its formal closure as well, in line with the bipartite structure with a hinge
we have already seen, in terms of communication/*Verkehr*—the *Verkehr* in
the second paragraph, the *Verkehr* here at the turning point of the story, and
the *Verkehr* in the last sentence of the text. That Georg and his father interact
constantly in the business is, as we shall see, one of those things the father
will draw seriously into doubt. Lunch they take "simultaneously"—notice not
"together"—in a restaurant, and in the evenings each takes care of himself as
he wishes, but most of the time they sit in the common living room for a little
while—again the essential word "together" is missing—except when, as most
often happens, Georg is with friends or, recently, visiting his fiancée. And on
what turn out to be those exceedingly rare occasions when they are actually
in each other's proximity, sitting in the same room, they don't talk, for each is
occupied with his own newspaper. Remembering, once again, that the narra-

---

[*] "At last he put the letter in his pocket and went out of his room across a small
hallway into his father's room, where he had not been for months. There was in fact
no requirement for him to go there, since he constantly interacted with his father in
their business and they took their midday meal simultaneously in a restaurant; in the
evening, it was true, each did as he pleased, yet even then, unless Georg— as mostly
happened— was with friends or, more recently, visiting his fiancée, they usually sat for
a while, each with his newspaper, in their common living room" (54)

[†] "requirement" or being forced to do something against one's will or pleasure—usually a legal term (54)

[‡] "interacts" (54)

tion here is limited omniscient, that is, that the narrator is telling things from Georg's perspective, the statement that there was no reason why he should have needed to enter his father's room, since they interact constantly, is thus another of Georg's lies, giving the illusion that there is communication where there is actually none.

At this point we can refine the differentiation of the monologic situation in the first part of the story from the dialogic one in the second part. As Georg's failure to respond to the greeting of the acquaintance passing by his window turns what should be a dialogue into a monologue, so too is the letter-writing of the first part of the story, which is of course inherently dialogic, rendered monologic by Georg's falsification of the communication that writing entails. Much as the description—essentially Georg's description—of his life together with his father renders communication non-communicative and interaction non-interactive.

On stepping into his father's room, however, Georg enters into a real dialogue where issues of importance are discussed, although he might prefer to avoid them, and questions are asked and answered, if only, sometimes, in his very attempt to avoid answering them. Georg's dialogue with his father provides, as I said, the context according to which the text, and we, judge the first part of the story and Georg himself.

At first it seems odd that Georg's father should prove to be the standard for judging Georg, since our first impressions of him could easily lead us to think he's just a little crazy. He sits in the dark and likes to keep his window closed; upon Georg's bringing up his friend and the letter, he immediately accuses his son of not telling the truth; and with no good reason apparent to the reader, at least not yet, he simply and bluntly questions the very existence of the friend to whom Georg has written: "'Hast du wirklich diesen Freund in Petersburg?'" (33)[*] and about a page later, "'Du hast keinen Freund in Petersburg. Du bist immer ein Spaßmacher gewesen und hast dich auch mir gegenüber nicht zurückgehalten'" (33).[†] What in the world is he talking about? we ask ourselves. We may have witnessed the falsification of communication that Georg perpetrates, but we had no reason to doubt the existence of the friend. Yet once the father makes these remarks, we begin thinking about them and about

---

[*] "'Do you really have this friend in St. Petersburg?'" (56)

[†] "'You have no friend in St. Petersburg. You've always been a leg-puller and you haven't even shrunk from pulling my leg'" (57)

Georg's veracity in general, beyond his letters. With such doubts planted, we
then begin to notice that there are many points in this dialogic scene where
Georg reveals a sense of guilt or guilty knowledge of his own actions. After
reprimanding his father for the darkness of his room and his closed window,
Georg's first action is to tell his father that he has now, "after all," announced
his engagement to the friend—thus revealing, by the by, that the father was
aware of Georg's failure to communicate properly with the friend—and to
pull the letter just a bit out of his jacket pocket, giving his father a glimpse of
it before letting it fall back into the pocket. In other words, he shows the letter
as if to prove to *himself* that he has done the right thing, but the nature of his
action also makes it seem as though his letter might be a dirty little secret, as
though his almost surreptitious action inadvertently reveals something surreptitious about the letter itself. And we do already have grounds to know
that this is closer to the mark and thus that Georg does have reason to feel
guilty about the letter, even if he is in denial about it. Further signs of a guilty
conscience are the embarrassment that overcomes Georg immediately upon
his father's questioning whether he "really [has] this friend in St. Petersburg"
and when, under the force of his father's accusations, Georg "stand in einem
Winkel, möglichst weit vom Vater" (36) * and we learn that "Vor einer langen
Weile hatte er sich fest entschlossen, alles vollkommen genau zu beobachten,
damit er nicht irgendwie auf Umwegen, von hinten her, von oben herab über-
rascht werden könne" (36);† this constitutes an acknowledgment of guilt, for
he cannot have such thoughts and have made such plans if he had not already
known, *before* he came into his father's room, that there is something he has
to protect himself from, that there is some attack to which he is vulnerable. A
final sign, for now, of Georg's guilty conscience comes when he exclaims to his
father, "'Du hast mir also aufgelauert!'" (38), ‡ and thereby actually *proves* his
own guilt, since he could not say his father was lying in wait for him if he did
not know that there was, indeed, something to lie in wait *for*.

All of these revelations of guilt on Georg's part attenuate our initial doubt
about the father, for they give us reason to suppose, at least, that his attacks on
his son's veracity and straightforwardness might actually have some reliable
foundation. When we examine those attacks, we gradually discover that the
father is *right* in his accusations. At first, there is just the hint that the father

---

* "shrinks into a corner, as far away from his father as possible" (60)
† "A long time ago he had firmly made up his mind to observe everything with
complete precision, so that he could not be surprised by any indirect attack, a pounce
from behind or above" (60)
‡ "'So you've been lying in wait for me!'" (62)

knows Georg is a deceiver, when he says, "'Aber es ist nichts, es ist ärger als nichts, wenn du jetzt nicht die volle Wahrheit sagst'" (32),* although at this point we still haven't sufficient reason to believe him and might add this to the evidence that he is a bit loony. But within less than a page, Georg more or less proves his father right. This happens when, instead of answering the apparently ridiculous question, "'Hast du wirklich diesen Freund in Petersburg?'" (32),† he stands up, embarrassed. Not only that, but he proceeds, in one of the more dramatic attempts to avoid answering a question one is likely to find, to deflect the question, first through a nonsensical non sequitur—"'Tausend Freunde ersetzen mir nicht meinen Vater'" (33)‡—that shows just how rattled he is by the question, then with a feigned concern for the father's well-being that takes the form of an attempt to control his father's life, "'Wir müssen da eine andere Lebensweise für dich einführen. Aber von Grund aus'" (33),§ then through an extended attack—you sit here in the dark, you don't eat properly, you don't get enough fresh air—leading first to the suggestion that Georg and his father switch rooms (an obvious attempt, of course, by the son to supplant the father) and culminating in Georg treating his father like a child: "'Komm, ich werde dir beim Ausziehn helfen'" (33).** *All* this to avoid answering that apparently ridiculous question, which, were it ridiculous, Georg would have simply answered by saying something like, "Don't be silly, of course I have this friend." When, after this extraordinary deflection of the question over the course of half a page, Georg actually gets around to addressing it, he ends up proving his father right. Georg says, "'Denk doch einmal nach, Vater … jetzt wird es bald drei Jahre her sein, da war ja mein Freund bei uns zu Besuch. Ich erinnere mich noch, daß du ihn nicht besonders gern hattest. Wenigstens zweimal habe ich ihn vor dir verleugnet, trotzdem er gerade bei mir im Zimmer saß'" (34).†† Some friend! And that is precisely the point. First of all, Georg says he remembers the father did not like him, but the text gives us reason to doubt the dependability of this memory, for a little later on we have not

---

* "'But it's nothing, it's worse than nothing, if you don't tell me the whole truth now'" (56)

† "'Do you really have this friend in St. Petersburg?'" (56)

‡ "'A thousand friends can't replace my father for me'" (56)

§ "'We'll have to make a change in your way of living. But a radical change'" (56)

** "'Come, I'll help you undress'" (57)

†† "'Just think about it, Father … it'll soon be three years ago that my friend came to visit us. I remember that you didn't like him very much. At least twice I disowned him in your presence, despite the fact that at those very moments he was sitting in my room'" (57)

only the father's claim that he maintains a close connection to the friend, but we also learn that Georg "immerfort [alles] vergaß" (37).[*] So what we are left with is that Georg at least twice (thankfully not three times, otherwise those who read the story as a religious allegory would be even more encouraged) disowned or denied the existence of his friend in the father's presence. Here we recall that the father never questioned the existence of the *person* to whom Georg has written a letter, but rather specifically asked the question whether and then denied that Georg has a "friend" in St. Petersburg. And what we learn through Georg's own admission (as we, of course, already implicitly learned by examining the nature of his communication with this person) is that this friend does not exist, at least not as a *friend* in any recognizable meaning of the word, for Georg's treatment of him, both in his correspondence and in disowning him repeatedly in front of the father, precludes friendship.

Given our understanding of the nature of Georg's use of language, of his falsified communication, we can then be certain that the father is more dependable, that he knows the truth, that he is *right* when he says that Georg has been deceiving the "friend" for so long—"Darum hast du ihn auch betrogen die ganzen Jahre lang"[†]—and when he remarks that Georg locks himself up in his office "'nur damit du deine falschen Briefchen nach Rußland schreiben kannst'" (35).[‡] "Deine falschen Briefchen": this statement finally provides incontrovertible *proof* that the father is right, and we know this because the first part of the story, the scene of Georg's writing, and our reading of it supply the independent verification of his claim. Georg's letters *are* "falsch." The text itself, and we as its readers, prove the father right.

According to the logic of the narrative, then, the father is the teller of truth. Once he has been revealed as such, we come to recognize the accuracy of his other seemingly odd tirades as well. For example, his claim that Georg is not nearly so successful in the business as he imagines, that he is basically finishing off deals his father had prepared and then taking credit for them, gains credibility once we know that he is right about Georg's abuse of communication. We can also say that the father is right about Georg wanting to cover him up—"'Du wolltest mich zudecken, das weiß ich, mein Früchtchen, aber zugedeckt bin ich noch nicht'" (35).[§] Georg—as he also proves when he suggests that he and his father switch rooms and when he treats his father like a child,

---

[*] "kept on forgetting everything" (61)

[†] "'That's why you've been deceiving him all these years'" (59)

[‡] "'just so that you can write your lying little letters to Russia'" (59)

[§] "'You wanted to cover me up, I know, my young sprig, but I'm far from being covered up yet'" (59)

offering to help him undress, carrying him to bed, and tucking him in—obviously wants to take his father's place, and his father recognizes this, even if Georg is not prepared to admit it. But he also need not admit it, for the text itself provides the proof that Georg longs for his father's ruin, wants him out of the way, when the limited omniscient narration gives us access to Georg's malevolent thoughts: "'Jetzt wird er sich vorbeugen', dachte Georg, 'wenn er fiele und zerschmetterte!' Dieses Wort durchzischte seinen Kopf" (36).[*]

When these thoughts course through Georg's head, we recognize that, perhaps through the stress of his confrontation with his father, he is losing his grip on reality even more so than before. He is losing his grip on language as well. Earlier, when writing his letters, even though their falsification of communication entailed a separation from reality, he nearly always had exceptional control of his language, the kind of control it takes to be able to deceive others successfully. Here at the end of the story, however, we see signs that he is losing that control—for example, when he cannot stop himself from calling his father a comedian, immediately recognizes the damage he has done and, too late, literally bites his tongue, punishing himself until the pain almost makes him collapse. Here his language once again does damage to others, but this time it is out of Georg's control, and in trying to regain control, he damages his own instrument of language. He doesn't regain that control, however, for one page later we find him making a totally irrelevant and nonsensical remark, just to himself, and believing it could help him to obliterate his father: upon the father's statement that he has Georg's customers "in his pocket," Georg says to himself, "'sogar im Hemd hat er Taschen!' … und glaubte, er könne ihn mit dieser Bemerkung in der ganzen Welt unmöglich machen" (37).[†] A few lines later, the father says that the friend "'weiß alles tausendmal besser,'"[‡] to which Georg replies "'Zehntausendmal,'"[§] thinking he can make fun of his father by saying so, but then realizing the deadly seriousness of what he has said, of having himself now proved his father right (37). This is a loss of control over language, where Georg's own language turns against him, betrays him; when he *wants* to lie, it becomes truth. Finally, Georg's father comments on his son's loss of control over his language; when Georg says, "'Du hast mir

---

[*] "Now he'll lean forward, thought Georg, if only he would fall and burst into pieces! These words went hissing through his head" (61)

[†] "'even in his shirt he has pockets!' … and believed that with this remark he could make him an impossible figure for all the world" (61)

[‡] "'knows everything a thousand times better'" (62)

[§] "'Ten thousand times!'" (62)

also aufgelauert!,'"[*] inadvertently revealing his guilty conscience, his father replies pityingly but also derisively, "'Das wolltest du wahrscheinlich früher sagen. Jetzt paßt es ja gar nicht mehr'" (38).[†] After this, Georg says only one more thing; just before letting himself fall from the bridge to his death, he says, and in its nonsensical, almost surreal quality, given the situation, the statement could be seen as the culmination of his loss of control over language: "'Liebe Eltern, ich habe euch doch immer geliebt'" (38).[‡] So Georg's language does not fit anymore, "paßt … nicht mehr." This is the result of his language—the writing of the letter and the thoughts surrounding it in the first part of the story—being put to the test in an intersubjective, dialogic context. As long as Georg was alone he could use language falsely and make it sound like the truth. But once he is confronted by his father, by an outside reference and perspective, the failure of his language to correspond to reality is revealed.

On the other hand, according to the logic of the narrative, the father is portrayed as the teller of truth, as the true communicator who has informed the friend of the true state of affairs: "'Er weiß doch alles, dummer Junge, er weiß doch alles! Ich schrieb ihm doch, weil du vergessen hast, mir das Schreibzeug wegzunehmen. Darum kommt er schon seit Jahren nicht, er weiß ja alles hundertmal besser als du selbst, deine Briefe zerknüllt er ungelesen in der linken Hand, während er in der Rechten meine Briefe zum Lesen sich vorhält'" (37).[§] Now the father is getting a bit too exercised here and himself going a bit far, since we do not have any reason to suspect, for example, that Georg is lying to himself when he reflects on the friend having begun to get interested in that inconsequential engagement Georg reported in three letters, although I suppose it is *possible* that the effects of his miscommunication are a product of Georg's imagination as well. What is most interesting, however, in what the father says here is the juxtaposition of left and right, of the sinister and the morally upright; through this juxtaposition the text—and not just the father, for there is nothing in the text to disprove his having such a close connection

---

[*] "'So you've been lying in wait for me!'" (62)

[†] "'You probably wanted to say that earlier on. Now it doesn't fit at all anymore'" (62)

[‡] "'Dear parents, I really have always loved you'" (63)

[§] "'He knows it already, you stupid boy, he knows it all! I've been writing to him, for you forgot to take my writing things away from me. That's why he hasn't been here for years. He knows everything a hundred times better than you do yourself; in his left hand he crumples your letters unread, while in his right hand he holds up my letters to read!'" (61–62)

with the friend—once more passes judgment on the nature of Georg's communication.

It is the father who explicitly passes judgment upon his son and sentences him to death by drowning, but it is the text that seeks to prove this judgment and sentence right and fair. The judgment is that his son was "actually" an innocent child, but that "more actually" he was a devilish human being. (Saying that one thing is "eigentlich" but another "noch eigentlicher" attributes a greater degree of truth to the latter, for *das Eigentliche* is the truth, while *das Uneigentliche* is metaphor or lie.) Now we could take or leave the father's judgment as we please, if it weren't for the fact that the text, just as it had proved the father right regarding the falsity of Georg's letter-writing, immediately proves him right in *this* judgment. For as Georg sails down the stairs to go out and throw himself from the bridge, he runs into the maid, and her response to him is to cry out "'Jesus!'" and to cover her face with her apron, that is, the conventional reaction of the religiously superstitious to seeing what they think is the *devil*—intoning the name of the savior and covering one's face to avoid seeing the face of evil. Thus, immediately following the father's judgment that Georg is a devilish human being, *the text has him appear as a devil*. And immediately upon being sentenced to death by drowning, *the text has Georg carry out the sentence*. The text itself thus gives the final proof of the father's justification in passing this judgment and this sentence. There could hardly be a more definitive proof of the propriety of the sentence, at least within the logic of the narrative.

In "Das Urteil," then, the figure who falsifies communication, who lies and thus undermines community, in that he subverts true social intercourse, *Verkehr*, with his friend, with the acquaintance who greets him, and with his father, is sentenced to die for having done so. And as Georg falls from the bridge, symbols of community and communication suddenly proliferate in this story that up until this point has rather studiously avoided symbols and metaphors. As Georg hangs from the bridge, his grasp growing weaker, he spies through the railing of the bridge a bus that will "übertönen [drown out]" his fall.[*] But this is not just any bus and it is not there without reason. The manner in which the story articulates the theme of communication forces us to conclude that the bus is there to replace, in the moment of Georg's death, Georg's abuse of language, his falsification of communication, with its own "language," if you will, with its own "tones." Its language is the language of community, the opposite of Georg's language, insofar as the bus

---

[*] "cover the noise of," literally "tone over" (63)

Kafka writes into his story is not described by the word that normally would have been used to describe a bus at that time. According to Trübners, common parlance would have referred to it simply as an *Omnibus* or an *Autobus*, the latter of which might have been more likely for Kafka, with his interest in new technologies. Kafka chose instead the full but rare designation, "Auto-omnibus." Why? The context I have articulated answers this question, I think: by using the word "Autoomnibus," the text calls attention precisely to the presence of community, which will drown out, so to speak, the representative of the subversion of community—to the *Auto-omnibus*, the *self-for-all* that will take Georg's place. Moreover, as he lets himself fall, "ein geradezu unendlicher Verkehr"[*] courses over the bridge. Thus Georg's language, which has broken down to the point of the pitiful statement in the previous line, "'Liebe Eltern, ich habe euch doch immer geliebt,'"[†] is replaced by that signifier of communication and community, *Verkehr*, the signifier of what, in his deceitful use of language, Georg had undermined.

The question, of course, is whether you or I would like to be part of the community Georg's father represents. For seen from another angle, one could almost say that Georg is a victim of this overbearing community, of this monolithic communication, indeed of the narrative itself and its closure, which establish the parameters for his judgment and (self-)execution. That doesn't seem quite fair. And as grotesque as Georg's subversion of community and falsification of communication may be, the person who condemns him for it also seems grotesque—just think of the father playing with Georg's watch chain or jumping up and down and finally collapsing on the bed, dead for all we know, in a paroxysm of self-righteous judgment.

As much as the establishment of an opposition of true and false communication is part of the story, so too are that grotesqueness and that lingering sense of unfairness. Accounting for them forces me beyond the bounds of the text, but in themselves, these aspects of the story already breach its highly articulated narrative closure. As does that little remark by the father, "'noch eigentlicher warst du ein teuflischer Mensch,'"[‡] which in the end severely attenuates his role as the speaker of truth, for in opening up the possibility of something that is "eigentlicher" than what is "eigentlich," that is thus more

---

[*] "an unending stream of traffic" (63)
[†] "'Dear parents, I really have always loved you'" (63)
[‡] "'even more actually you were a devilish human being'" (62)

true than what is true, the story introduces into its center—the language of truth—the possibility of *degrees of truth*, which in turn undermine the closure of *the* truth that grounds the closure of the story as a whole (in this connection we might think of how Nietzsche's "my truths" are his instrument of the subversion of "the" truth of Western philosophy). So it is necessary to take a step back from minute attention to the details of the story to consider the implications of my reading within the story's intellectual-historical context, but to do so in a manner that accords with and builds on what my reading has already told us about the text. The context I am referring to is the primary context of the *fin-de-siècle*, the one whose parameters are articulated by the texts of Nietzsche and Freud. I mentioned early on that my reading would concern itself centrally with questions of expression and repression. The hinge between the two parts of my reading may also be seen to reflect the hinge on which the two parts of the story swing—the hinge between the monologic and the dialogic—insofar as I shift here from what might be construed as a monologic reading, in its close attention to the inner logic of the narrative, to what in its intertextual and contextual references might be seen as a dialogic reading.

Re-reading the story with Nietzsche, which seems more than just appropriate, given the constant emphasis on truth and lie, we would then have to question the "truth" of the speaker of truth, the father, and also recognize that the rejection of the "liar," Georg, is an act of the moralistic herd. Indeed, morality is very much at issue here, since the title of the story is "The Judgment" and it deals throughout with questions of guilt, both spoken and unspoken. Re-reading Kafka with Freud, though perhaps not exactly as Kafka meant when, in remarking on influences, he jotted down "Freud of course," we can also hardly ignore that the story is one of a power struggle between son and father, where the son is trying, however unsuccessfully, to obtain power, but the father, the figure of the super-ego, the outside agent of repression, will not allow it. Instead, the father continues to effect repression in his son, sexually as well—for example, in trying to instill in Georg a feeling of shame over his supposedly prurient sexual interest in his fiancée ("'Weil sie die Röcke gehoben hat,' fing der Vater zu flöten an, 'weil sie die Röcke so gehoben hat, die widerliche Gans'" [36] [*]), a sexual interest that would be only normal for this grown young man.

Bringing in Nietzsche and Freud threatens to open up whole new worlds

---

[*] "'Because she lifted up her skirts,' his father began to flute, 'because she lifted her skirts like this, the disgusting creature'" (60)

of complexity, but here, too, I think we can get what we need for carrying my interpretation beyond the closure of the text by keeping it fairly simple, and brief as well. In his seminal text, "On Truth and Lie in an Extra-Moral Sense," Nietzsche undertakes a critique of the Western philosophical tradition by deconstructing the binary opposition of truth and lie that grounds it.[3] The critique is based, first of all, on a critique of language and a demonstration of its quality as a social convention and as a scene of power relations, its fundamental arbitrariness and non-referentiality, its extreme removal from the world of real experience—by being not just a *Bild* but an *Abbildung*, not just a representation but a re-representation, it is twice removed from that world—and its function as a system of dead metaphors, metaphors that we have forgotten are metaphors: "For what 'truth' will be from now on is fixed; a uniformly valid and binding terminology for things is invented and the legislation of language also enacts the first laws of truth ... the distinction between truth and lie arises. The liar uses the valid terms, the words, to make the unreal appear real ... He misuses established conventions ... When he does this in a selfish and damaging manner, society will no longer trust him and so it will exclude him from its presence" (247–48). Nietzsche asks "What is truth?" and answers: "a mobile army of metaphors, metonyms, anthropomorphisms ... Truths are illusions about which it has been forgotten that they *are* illusions ... [in order to exist] society [imposes] the obligation: to be truthful, i.e., to use the customary metaphors, or in moral terms, the obligation to lie according to an established convention" (250).

I think this is probably already enough, and it should not be too difficult to see where this takes us in terms of "Das Urteil." In the broadest terms, one might say that the text itself, in proving the father to be the speaker of truth, in extensively avoiding metaphor, and in simultaneously championing community and true communication, performs the kind of societal forgetting or denial of the metaphoricity of all language that Nietzsche describes. The story as a whole, however, just like the "truth-language" of the speaker of truth who invokes the law of "the actual [Eigentlichkeit]" in judging his son, is always already "non-actual [uneigentlich]," always already thoroughly metaphorical, always already a lie, simply because it is language, but also because it is, after all, a fictional narrative.

How, though, do Nietzsche's thoughts on language inform our reading of Kafka's story in more specific terms? Certainly the Freudian opposition of father and son is inextricably linked to the theme of communication. And of course we already know that it is language that is at issue in Georg's "false" communication. Reading with Nietzsche, we could then say that Georg fails to use language in a manner acceptable to society, that he does not meet that "obligation to lie according to an established convention," but rather lies only outside that convention. He uses, one might say manipulates, language however he, as an individual, thinks best. We are dealing, in other words, with what Nietzsche might call a moral economy of truth and lie, an economy in which the father represents truth and condemns his son as a liar, a moral economy in which Georg does not participate. And because he does not participate, he must be excluded from society.

That the story operates within such an economy is emphasized by Georg's father. He admonishes his son to tell the "whole truth," not to lie: "'es ist nichts, es ist ärger als nichts, wenn du mir jetzt nicht die volle Wahrheit sagst'" (32).* According to the father, the friend holds the father's letters in his (moral) right hand in order to read them, while Georg's letters are crumpled up, unread, in the (sinister) left hand. That is, the herd brands the divergent use of language as immoral, as evil, and rejects it. When, on the basis of Georg's falsification of communication and subversion of community, the father passes his judgment that Georg was an innocent child but a devilish human being—again, claiming truth for himself by invoking the truth of "Eigentlichkeit"—he is saying that Georg is devilish as a grown member of society, or, in Nietzsche's terms, the herd. The innocence he attributes to Georg as a child should recall to us a scene in that other seminal work of *fin-de-siècle* language critique, Hofmannsthal's "Ein Brief," where Lord Chandos's lament at having upbraided his daughter for lying reflects his crisis of expression, formulated here as the return of the repressed, the repressed being the child's failure to use language in the socially "standard" manner, or rather the child's use of language in a socially *non*-standard way. In other words, Georg's father would see his son as harmless and innocent were he using language as he does, but still as a child who does not yet have to be completely subject to the obligations society creates. Since he is grown up, however, he is expected to use language, appropriately, within the context of the herd. Because he does not, he is branded immoral, even evil ("teuflisch"), and must be excluded from society: thus the death sentence and thus, again but in a somewhat different light now, the *Autoomnibus* that drowns him out.

The problem with this, the perversity of it, is that it is the *father* himself who actually forces Georg to remain a child, in that he maintains his super-ego function, representing society and forever calling attention to the repression expected of Georg. We see this in his admonition to Georg to tell him the

---

* "'it's nothing, it's worse than nothing, if you don't tell me the whole truth now'" (56)

"whole truth," and throughout their dialogue he speaks not as one would to a grown son but as one would to a child. We see it, as well, in his ridiculing and trying to suppress Georg's sexual interest in his fiancée, thus attempting, one might say, to keep his son trapped in the period of latency. And in many senses, Georg *is* still a child. He still lives at home, even, it seems, in his childhood room. He can so little bear the thought of leaving his father that he intends to take him along to his new home. He sees his father as a giant of a man: "'mein Vater ist noch immer ein Riese'" (31). [*] He feels he has to show his father the letter he has written, as if he needed some kind of adult approval. And so on and so on. Finally, in the moment of his death, the text reinforces his childlike status—why else, given the fact that he is in the process of killing himself, would there be that exceedingly odd remark, issuing no less from the omniscient narrator, that "Er schwang sich über, als der ausgezeichnete Turner, der er in seinen Jugendjahren zum Stolz seiner Eltern gewesen war" (38)?! [†] The word "als" [‡] is the textual proof that in this moment he *is* that child. Not only this, but he then utters those words that seemed so nonsensical before, but that now make much more sense because they demonstrate that Georg is a child, and, moreover, a child who has still not accepted or come to terms with the death of his mother: "'Liebe Eltern, ich habe euch doch immer geliebt'" (38). [§] What all this shows is that Georg's father, even by the standard of his own moral code or economy, is *unjust* in his judgment and in condemning his son to death, for his son is still that child whom he, the father, will not allow to grow up.

The father's reference to gender and sexuality—Georg's sexual interest in his fiancée—is not accidental, nor is it just one of many other of his devices of ridicule and derision, for the moral economy of truth and lie that we have now seen the story as implicitly *criticizing* is intimately linked to questions of gender and sexuality. With a nod to Freud, this economy can be recast in terms of the normal and the abnormal, and to do so in connection with "Das Urteil" seems appropriate, for the father's criticism and judgment of Georg can easily be seen, now that we have examined that economy of truth and lie in Nietzschean terms, as a case of the father insisting on his role as the norm by which the son is judged and according to which Georg is abnormal.

---

[*] "'My father is still a giant of a man'" (54)

[†] "He swung himself over, as the distinguished gymnast he had once been in his youth, to his parents' pride" (63)

[‡] "as" (63)

[§] "'Dear parents, I really have always loved you'" (63)

   The role of the super-ego is, after all, the role of the *norm* and the socially *normal*. If we look to Freud's writings on sexuality and gender—primarily the "Three Essays on the Theory of Sexuality" of 1905 and the later essays on femininity—we discover the degree to which the notion of the normal is central to his theories, but at the same time gets him into trouble because of its very slipperiness and the prejudices it ultimately reveals. If we try to determine what the normal is in Freud, we initially run into some problems, because we find that it can be equated neither with a primitive state of nature nor with high civilization, since the former accounts for some "normal" behavioral manifestations only in young children and the latter, civilization, is eventually equated with illness, with neurosis. We have to consider the possibility that it is precisely neurosis—i.e., illness—that is "normal" in Freud's theory, but if the normal is the sick, then what is the abnormal? Is it a question of the degree of neurosis or of the differentiation between neurosis and psychosis? The latter seems plausible, but Freud does not say this is the case. The problem is precisely that Freud operates throughout on the basis of what he calls normal—the normal is always the implied given, the ground—but he never *defines* the normal. (We, of course, may with justification argue that it is a value-laden term, a moral category that is the product of Freud's own cultural stereotypes or prejudices, which is precisely what Freud is trying to get away from.) The problem lies, more specifically, in Freud's assumption of something called "normal" and his repeated attempt to establish it on the basis of the abnormal, a logical impossibility. But Freud must have had and obviously did have an idea of what he thought was normal; acting as if he were deriving it from the abnormal may have been disingenuous, but, at least in the case of children, it did have the positive effect of expanding the canon of the normal (and we might think here, again, of Georg and how the father finds much more acceptable in the child than in the grown man). Where Freud runs into his greatest problems is in using the notion of the normal in his differentiation of the sexes, and this is what will bring us back to Kafka's story, if somewhat obliquely, and perhaps justify my digression. In this differentiation, Freud has a very clear idea of what is normal, namely the boy, the man, the phallus. In one of his less stellar moments, Freud portrays the masculine as the norm from which the feminine diverges: he tells us "the little girl is a little man" because the clitoris is a stunted penis and she must repress knowledge of this castration, and he writes of what he calls "the boy's far superior equipment," concluding that fulfillment as a woman comes only through the acquisition of a penis in the form of a male child. The point of all this, for my purpose, is to recognize that the broader theoretical context of Kafka's text, a context he expressly acknowledges, includes this extreme inscription of the sexually and socially normal as the masculine. This is perhaps another way of explaining why the super-ego has to be the father, or rather that the super-ego function must be represented by the father.

Reading with Freud, then, we can say that the moral and linguistic economy of truth and lie as it is articulated by the text and represented by the father, that the discourse he advocates, which demands the repression of the non-conformist discourse of his son, is a specifically *phallic discourse*. Indeed, the story goes to some lengths to establish the father as the phallic authority, as the representation of a specifically phallic order. There is his suddenly jumping up erect, "aufrecht," in bed when he denies his loss of power and authority, when he denies that he is covered up, "zugedeckt" (35). Reading in this context we might even reach perhaps a little far and relate the stabbing gestures he makes with his "Zeigefinger"*—in order to make the point that he maintains control over the relations with the friend in St. Petersburg—to his phallic discourse (36). But the clearest and most emphatic revelation of the father's phallic power occurs soon after Georg enters his room. As Georg arrives, his father crosses the room to greet him; in doing so, his robe opens and Georg *immediately* remarks to himself that "mein Vater ist noch immer ein Riese" (31).† Some would say Georg is clearly responding to seeing his father's genitalia, others would use all sorts of arguments to disprove this, reminding us that later on we learn the father is wearing not one, but two pairs of underwear under his robe (34) and proposing that Georg, the young adult but still the child, is simply surprised that as an old man his father should still be so imposing a figure. To the latter arguments I would only say: nice try. If we wanted to get really technical, we could say that, if his father really is such a phallic giant, Georg could easily notice this through even two pairs of underwear, and even especially since one of those is of a jersey-like material ("Trikot") that might well cling to the body; moreover, Georg carries his father to bed, which would seem to indicate that he is not such a giant, relative to Georg, in the more conventional sense. But we need not get technical in this way, for the rhetoric of the passage itself, Georg's remark to himself in immediate and direct response to his father's robe opening up, is more than sufficient proof that he is recognizing, to borrow Freud's unfortunate phrase, his father's "superior equipment" and thus, metaphorically, his phallic power and authority.

---

* "pointing finger," i.e., "forefinger" (60)
† "My father is still a giant of a man" (54)

Given these Nietzschean and Freudian perspectives, we could explain Georg's death sentence differently than in my first reading: namely, *not* as an affirmation of the father's position and of the "truth," by now severely attenuated, that Georg deserves to die, but rather as the result of the repression demanded and exacted by the moral economy of truth and lie and thus as an implicit *critique of phallic discourse.* Insofar as that economy is a social one, we would then have to see the story as an indictment of society's destruction of the non-conforming individual, an indictment of that community the story set up as an ideal so that we could see how Georg subverted it. The death of Georg is to be "witnessed," we then recall, by the *Autoomnibus*, but a less favorable reading of that symbol of community, that "self-for-all," is now in order, for we can now say that Georg's (self-)execution occurs under the sign of the *Autoomnibus* as the forced subsumption of the individual into the herd.

The *Verkehr* that seems almost to push Georg down into the depths, to make him lose his grip on life, also calls for a somewhat modified reading now, for this intercourse—*Verkehr* signifying traffic, social intercourse, and sexual intercourse—is not only the social intercourse mentioned at the beginning of the story, but, specifically, a *phallic* social intercourse, the repressive phallic discourse of the father. Thus *Verkehr*, which through its strategic placement at the beginning, middle, and end of the story seemed to structure the closure of the text, through its multifarious signification actually breaches that closure.[4] And if we are to believe Kafka, it breaches it like the breaching of a dam, for Kafka said that when he wrote that last line about "ein geradezu unendlicher Verkehr"[*] coursing over the bridge, he was thinking of "a forceful ejaculation."

At this point, finally, we have to realize that we, the readers, are part of that herd that Georg's father represents, that we are also the target of critique, because, as I pointed out early on, the text succeeds in associating us with Georg's father by installing us alongside him as Georg's judges. The joke, in a sense, is on us. But it also is not. Because by the time—namely *now*—we are in a position to recognize this, we have already grown out of that role and understood the necessity of judging the father and what he represents, much more so than Georg. Still, in my second reading as much as in the first, on which it is necessarily if paradoxically predicated, we never, either as agents or as recipients, escape judgment.

---

[*] "an unending stream of traffic" (63)

Notes

1   It is the smothering of "Das Urteil" under the mass of the history of its recep-
    tion, including Kafka's own interpretation in his letters and diaries, that leads
    me to think a reading that excludes that reception and focuses almost entirely
    on the inner logic of the narrative itself—a simple reading, one might say—is
    in order. Of course, it would be silly to deny altogether the influence of Kafka
    scholarship on my reading of the text, given courses long ago in graduate school
    that occasionally dealt with Kafka and conversations over the years with friends
    and colleagues who also happen to be Kafka scholars. I can only say that I have
    not knowingly drawn on existing Kafka scholarship. Since completing the draft
    of this essay, however, I have benefited from insightful readings of it by Stuart
    Barnett, Michel Chaouli, and Richard Gray. I would like to thank them for their
    critical generosity.

2   Franz Kafka, *Die Erzählungen* (Frankfurt: Fischer, 1961), 27; *The Metamorphosis,
    In the Penal Colony, and Other Stories* (New York: Schocken, 1995), 49; in many
    cases the translations, which appear as footnotes, have been emended.

3   In *Friedrich Nietzsche on Rhetoric and Language*, ed. Sander Gilman, Carole
    Blair, and David J. Parent (New York: Oxford University Press, 1989).

4   *Verkehr* also signifies other things not addressed here, such as commerce.

Philosophical Exercises in Repetition: On Music, Humor, and Exile in Wittgenstein and Adorno

LYDIA GOEHR

In den finsteren Zeiten
wird da noch gesungen werden?
Ja! da wird gesungen werden von den finsteren Zeiten.
da wird gesungen werden von den finsteren Zeiten.

—"Spruch 1939," Hollywood Songbook, Bertolt Brecht/Hanns Eisler)

I.

"WHEN I CAME home I expected a surprise and there was no surprise for me, so of course I was surprised." So wrote Wittgenstein circa 1944.[1] Adorno and Horkheimer wrote of home the same year. Quoting Novalis, they spoke of philosophy as homesickness and of home as a place always sought. But worrying about the Nazi appeal to a natural homeland and of its justification through myth, they thought of a different natural home, one "wrested from" myth, they said, neither discovered nor returned to, but one sought in philosophy, travel, or in the exiled state "of having escaped."[2] This essay is about how philosophers have thought about seeking home through the exiling activity of philosophy.

This essay compares philosophy with two other activities with dynamic structures and important endings: humor and music. The comparison has a long history. Yet I juxtapose these themes primarily in the work of two modernists, Wittgenstein and Adorno. I focus less on independent thoughts about humor, music, or exile and more on how each contributes to modernist understandings of philosophy's dynamic form.

My initial motivation to juxtapose these themes came from reading those sections of the *Critique of Judgment* in which Kant establishes a formalist and non-conceptual model for both music and humor. There he gives us a clue about how we might think about the movement of thought—how we might think about something one way and then come to think about it differently. In this regard, his model connects to one often claimed advantage of exile, namely, that in the foreignness exile imposes, one comes to think differently about home. One way to think about how philosophy moves thought is in terms of how it brings a philosopher from a confused to a truthful place. Modernists sometimes call this truthful place "home."

Obviously philosophy aims to bring clarification at home by providing rational arguments, arguing us in and out of positions, and it matters what the content of these arguments is. However, some philosophers also pay attention to form, and even to the performance of their arguments, to show how the content is literally moved. Kant was less interested in performance than in form, yet he influenced the modernists. Of course the modernists had other precursors, and in the matter of philosophy's performance, Socrates has always been exemplary. So let us begin by recalling Socrates' proclamation in the *Phaedrus* that

> writing has this strange quality about it, which makes it really like painting: the painter's products stand before us quite as though they were alive; but if you question them, they maintain a solemn silence. So, too, with written words: you might think they spoke as if they made sense, but if you ask them anything about what they are saying, if you wish an explanation, they go on telling you the same thing, over and over forever.

Yet think by contrast, Socrates continues, of a discourse that is used with knowledge, or as "a living, animate discourse." And he draws this analogy: would a sensible farmer who cared about his seeds and wanted them to "yield him a good crop seriously plant it during the summer … and then take pleasure in the spectacle of a fine crop on the eighth day?" Or wouldn't he "make full use of scientific husbandry and plant it in suitable soil and be perfectly satisfied it if came to maturity in the eighth month?"[3] For Socrates, the farmer may serve as a model for the philosopher, the person who uses her knowledge and art in a suitable way, with good timing or with a good sense of the time that it takes to learn.

Taking the right time for learning is a process of coming to understand, and one aspect of coming to understand is that a change in thought occurs: we see something one way—presumably a mistaken way—then we come to see it another way—presumably a (more) correct way. Socrates' worry about philosophy's being written down is that the text will keep being read, as a painting will keep be seen, in the same, perhaps mistaken, way over and over again. But if, he says, the speech remains a living, animate discourse, the danger of repeated error is less threatening. I am interested in this danger. For although repetition is quite necessary in the process of learning, learning happens when we move beyond seeing the same thing "over and over" again and come to see it differently.

Both Wittgenstein and Adorno were concerned with the performance of their philosophical argument, and as part of that concern they focused on repetition. Both focused on the sort of differential repetition that captures the movement of a "living, breathing discourse," in which one comes to see "the same thing" differently. Someone who comes to understand a piece of music will, Wittgenstein once wrote, "listen differently … play differently, hum differently, talk differently."[4] Adorno could have written the same words, and in neither philosopher's case would the "difference" of which they spoke have been trivial. With all the rhetorical repetition he could muster, Adorno wrote: "The minimal differences from the ever-the-same" define "the difference concerning the totality." In these differences, in divergence itself, is our hope concentrated.[5] Just as relevantly he compared the "wretched fate" of memory and individuality to the joke that is "specifically committed to paper so that we can remember it."[6] Writing down a joke fixes a meaning as "ever-the-same" and renders redundant its performance in divergent contexts. He would also speak about musical recordings as presenting themselves as "already complete from the very first note." Performances nowadays, he said, sound like their own phonograph records.[7]

For both philosophers, repetition was conceived negatively and positively. Guided by the principle of eternal sameness, repetition can just mean doing the same thing over and over again. Here, it suggests the identikit production of copies or the following of rules "to the letter." Strictly speaking, under this form of repetition, the copies or acts produced are interchangeable; for their identity, each stands to the rules or model in exactly the same way. Think perhaps of Nelson Goodman's prescription for perfectly compliant musical performances that, logically speaking, are interchangeable.[8] We might well call this form of repetition uninspired, cold, or, with all the Socratic significance of this term, "unmusical." Repetition, conceived positively, is by contrast developmental, constructive, or generative; its guiding principle is difference or change. Here we might think of the rondo or sonata forms (say, Haydn's Joke Quartet in E♭, Op. 33), with their procedures of variation, interrupted or unconventional resolutions, and unexpected repetitions. Or we might think of musical performances standing to each other historically, thus producing a reception-history of a given work. Or we may think of the production of examples, which, following the same model or set of rules, exhibit between them evidence of learning, development, and musicality. In this case, we are interested not just in how well each example follows the rules or model, but also in the development and change that obtains between them. "In music," Wittgenstein writes:

> a variation on a theme could be imagined, which, phrased a bit differently, say, can be conceived as a completely different kind of variation of the theme. … Indeed what I mean is probably to be found absolutely always, when a repetition makes the theme appear in a quite different light.[9]

Developmental repetition is preferable to cold repetition, yet it cannot be articulated independently of its cold alternative. It persistently shows the cold threat of the "ever-the-same" on its other side as a regressive pattern we may fall into when we are not paying attention. Wittgenstein and Adorno both demonstrate this in their different performances of philosophical argument, how changing the way we think or see, or changing our attitude towards the world, requires that we persistently resist the lure of cold repetition. Wittgenstein once captured something of the special attentiveness we need in matters of understanding when he wrote: "We speak of understanding a sentence in the sense in which it can be replaced by another which says the same; but also in the sense in which it cannot be replaced by any other. (Any more than one musical theme can be replaced by another.)"[10]

Consider now the idea of exile seen from a double perspective: first, literally, in terms of two philosophers living abroad, away from home, by choice or force, or by the dire political necessity of a century with two world wars, and then, second, metaphysically or metaphorically as a condition of estrangement, unfamiliarity, and foreignness. Wittgenstein and Adorno both thought about both sorts of exile, although Adorno much more explicitly. What I find intriguing is how they both internalized their thoughts about exile or foreignness into the form of their philosophical argument and how they used musical models to do so. Both thought also about humor. Much in their philosophical arguments depended on triggering a change of attitude, yet they did not simply reject a false view and then positively offer a true view in its place. They tried to do more, actually to bring about the change of attitude itself. And this they did by focusing, as one would in music and humor, on the performance of their argument. Both employed techniques of estrangement and defamiliarization to break the power of (cold) sameness: in Wittgenstein's case, metaphysical illusions of deep or core essences, and in Adorno's case, ideological distortions of conformity and identity. Wittgenstein spoke of "the injustices of philosophy,"[11] Adorno of "damaged life."[12] Both used their philosophy to challenge the comforts of home, to throw into doubt what we take to be most familiar and self-evident. Both aimed to demonstrate the distinction between truth and deception, to contrast a false feeling of familiarity with a true one, to replace, they said, a false sense of home with a true sense.

Yet for all this similarity they ended up with different conceptions of home. Wittgenstein's philosophy led him to propose a conservative and harmonious home; Adorno's to a critical and dissonant home. Wittgenstein thought about happy endings; Adorno rejected them. The question I leave unanswered until the end is whether or not their different homes or endings could have been determined by philosophical form alone. If this is a project about philosophical formalism, then it is also about how far form can take you. This, and this is where we shall begin, is Kant's concern too.

II.

Many readers think Kant had nothing interesting to say about music. I think he had, especially if we read his comments on music as a prelude to those on humor. By connecting music to humor, he proposed an artistic formalism linked to the health of the body that corresponds, given the higher arts, to an aesthetic formalism linked to the health of the mind.

Kant classified the fine arts into those of word, gesture, and tone, and then, in more detail, into the arts of speech, under which he includes rhetoric and poetry; the formative arts, including painting and sculpture; and, at the bottom of the hierarchy, the arts of sensation, including the art of music. In his general scheme, the fine arts of beauty express aesthetic ideas, where those ideas, he wrote, are representations to the faculty of the imagination that induce in us thought but to which no definite thought attaches itself as adequate.[13] Here is one aspect of formalism, an abstraction that, partially because of the inadequacy, removes from aesthetic ideas a definite conceptual content. Yet aesthetic ideas can be analogically matched (in the formal play between the faculties of imagination, understanding, and reason) to cognitive and moral ideas and acquire high value for the mind thereby. However, some arts hardly even do this, and among them Kant includes instrumental music, "wallpaper music" or "fantasias" without text or program. A temporal and agreeable art, he wrote, instrumental music produces little more than pleasant and fleeting sensations through its patterns of tones. Here is another aspect of formalism, a formal play of patterned sensations that involves no more than this play. In this context, Kant concluded, music is best conceived as a *Tonspiel* classified alongside other kinds of play: the play of poker (*Glückspiel*) and the play of thought (*Gedankenspiel*). The play of thought is the display of wit, of humor. Though they excite the mind through the body, none of these plays has high mental or cognitive value, for though they play, say, with thought, Kant asserted, "*nothing in the end is thought.*" Henceforth Kant focused on music and humor. Poker, he said, obviously has an interest—winning and monetary gain.

Although in the end *nothing is thought*, music and humor still promote health and well-being. In explaining how, Kant stressed the temporal and formal nature of their play, the play, he said, of *changes*, because their point is not to communicate a thought or interest, but to bring about, through the oscillation of the body, a physical state of rest after its having been aroused. Although "nothing is thought," these arts enliven the mental faculties through the body, in music's case, through aural or sensorial stimulation, and in humor's case, through laughter, through the lively gratification that comes from the quickening oscillation of our diaphragms. Kant spoke of changes of sensation and of representation. Of music, he wrote first:

> But the affections of hope, fear, joy, anger, and derision here engage as play, as every moment they change their parts, and are so lively that, as by an internal motion, the whole vital function of the body seems to be furthered by the process—as is proved by a vivacity of the mind produced—although no one comes by anything by the way of profit or instruction.[14]

Then he moved on to humor. When we hear a joke something is presented to the understanding that at some point goes wrong or disappoints us. The frustrated expectation forces us to relinquish the understanding's control.

In response, our body slacks and our organs oscillate. Capturing the rhythm of the process itself, Kant wrote: "Laughter is an affection arising from an expectation that is strained [*gespannt*], and which suddenly reduces to nothing [*verschwindet plötzlich in nichts*]." As however our diaphragm is calmed and our understanding restored, we experience a peaceful state. And that is beneficial to our health.

Kant developmentally demonstrated his theory by telling *three*, and importantly three *interrelated*, jokes that would entertain us at a dinner party. (I think in fact he was the first to make explicit the philosophical import of the comedian's "Rule of Three.") So an Indian is sitting at an Englishman's dinner table in Surat and sees a bottle of ale opened and all the beer frothing and flowing out. The Indian is astonished and when the Englishman asks why, the Indian says: I am not astonished at how the beer gets out of the bottle, but how you ever managed to get it in? Kant said: "at this we laugh, and it gives us hearty pleasure." But, he added, we do not laugh at the Indian man's ignorance. We laugh only because our expectation was extended to the limit, and in being frustrated, dissolves into nothing, like a snapped violin string that vibrates until it dies. The second joke is about the heir to a wealthy fortune who in arranging an ostentatious funeral for his benefactor complained that the more money he gave the mourners to look sad, the more pleased they looked. Again the expectation is reduced to nothing. For we do not tell a story simply to state an untrue or reverse conclusion; that would not be funny. Rather, we laugh when the expectation of one ending is replaced by another ending, because that is what strains the expectation. We laugh at the absurdity of the logic. Consider if we said there was a man who grieved so much that his hair turned white in a single night. We would not laugh. However, if we said there was a man who grieved so much that his wig turned white, we would. We would laugh at the juxtaposition of the expectation with its straining. Kant added that jokes must have something in them capable of momentarily deceiving us. Let us call this feature the cognitively dissonant moment, the moment when we react to the formal play of thought less the thoughts themselves, when something in this play strikes us momentarily as having gone awry. Just consider how often (although it doesn't always work) we transpose the content of jokes from one cultural context to another, yet retain the form. The formal play alone stimulates the reaction.

For Kant, the problem with focusing on form is that it is hard to determine its importance beyond play. Is bodily health enough? As in his time so still in ours we keep asking what cognitive value music has. What do we get from experiencing pleasurable sensation or tonally moving forms? Similarly, we might ask what humor's cognitive value is if laughter ends, as Kant said, with nothing thought. ("Joke," we might ask to adapt Fontenelle's famous eighteenth-century question of the sonata, "what do you want of me?") However, I think these questions mislead insofar as they focus our attention on the process's outcome, not the process itself. As so focused, we fail to see how far humor and music may serve as models for thinking about how philosophical argument can trigger a change of thought. Yet these models work only if we emphasize the temporally structured processes of music and jokes, the complex patterns that enable cognitively dissonant moments to occur, independently of the question of achievement.[15] Had Kant focused more on music's form than on its material content of sensations, he would have seen, as later theorists did, that music too has its own patterns of expectation, frustration, and fulfillment. However, he does not, and therefore does not see, as others later do, that it is not only the humorous person, but the musical person too, who has a talent, as Kant put it, for entering a "topsy turvy world" or "a frame of mind in which everything is estimated on lines that go quite off the beaten track." Both following a piece of music and following a joke may serve as models for thinking about how philosophy can take us off the beaten track, since in none of these cases, as Kant observed, is moving off the beaten track moving into unstructured territory. On the contrary, these activities are all highly structured. However, as with all analogies, the Kantian one only goes so far, because, contrary to music and humor, we would not be satisfied with a philosophy that merely gave us bodily health or with a philosophical home in which "nothing is thought." But still, the form might have shown us something of considerable importance on the way.

III.

Influential on both Wittgenstein and Adorno, Freud was also concerned with process and cognitive dissonance, and what is useful for us in his account is the analogy he drew between the temporal structure of jokes and that of dream analysis. Freud emphasized both the presence and play of double meanings, of latent and manifest content, where, for example, an unexpected conclusion makes explicit what was latent at first in the formation of the expectation. Like Kant, Freud was concerned with the form of jokes, in how the formal play itself would provoke the laughter. To provoke that laughter would require the joke, as in dream analysis, to rearrange and move its content in an unexpected way.

Yet Freud introduced an element Kant did not, namely, the idea that when we hear a joke for the first time we laugh, but when we hear it repeated we don't. Addressing the topic of repetition, he wrote:

> Nor can children have their *pleasurable* experiences repeated often enough, and they are inexorable in their insistence that the repetition shall be an identical one. This character trait disappears later on. If a joke is heard for a second time it produces almost no effect; a theatrical production never creates so great an impression the second time as the first; indeed, it is hardly possible to persuade an adult who has very much enjoyed reading a book to re-read it immediately. Novelty is always the condition of enjoyment.[16]

Freud was probably right to say that identical repetition without a time lapse is not of great interest to adults who are (purportedly) freed from the basic repetition-compulsion, but surely a timely or fresh repetition of the same joke, play, or book can be. In his Preface to *The World as Will and Representation*, Schopenhauer remarked precisely on the necessity for readers to read his book twice for the reason that, first time around, you do not know the ending, and the second time you do, which means at least between the first and second reading your thinking through the argument would have changed. Freud likely would have acknowledged this had he been thinking here about the repeated pleasure we have from listening to a piece of music more than once, for we are bored neither by repeated hearings of the same music, nor even, if we know how to listen, by the same (identical) recording. It is not that listening to music caters to an infantile desire for mere repetition—though sometimes it does. Nor is it just that sometimes we hear something new in music and jokes in each rehearing. *Rather, it might just be that it is the formal structure of music itself that moves us over and over again, just as a joke provokes us to laugh at repeated hearings given the impact of its form's movement.* Recall that, for both Kant and Freud, it is not the outcome or ending of the joke that makes us laugh *per se*, but the absurdity of logic, the provocative juxtaposition of thoughts. *We laugh even when we know the punch line in advance, because we laugh not so much at where we get but at how we get there.* A good joke can jolt our sense of humor as a good piece of music can play to our musical sense—many times. (Of course, there are other kinds of jokes too.)

Let me see if I can demonstrate my point by letting you read a joke you have hopefully heard before and which has the added philosophical point of being a joke about repetition. Some say it is the oldest joke in the world, but it cannot be since it's a meta-joke—a joke about jokes, so presumably at least two other jokes existed before it.

> A passenger on a train watches in astonishment as an old man sitting opposite him keeps repeating the same pattern. First he mumbles some words to himself, smiles and then waves his hand dismissively—after a while the passenger asks the old man what he is doing and whether anything is wrong: Not at all, replies the old man, whenever I take a train I get bored—so I tell myself jokes which is why you saw me smiling. But why then do you keep waving your hand dismissively as if to brush the smile away? Oh that gesture! says the old man. It's to interrupt myself when I've heard the joke before.

Here's another version:

> When you tell a joke to a Russian peasant he laughs three times: when you tell the joke, when you explain it, and when he understands it, for a peasant loves to laugh. When you tell a joke to a landowner he laughs twice—when you tell the joke and when you explain it, for the landowner never really understands it. When you tell a joke to an army officer he laughs once, when you tell it, because he never lets you explain it and he never understands it. But when you tell a joke to a Jew, before you finish, he interrupts you. First, he tells you he's heard it before; second, that you're telling it wrong, and third, that he wants to tell you a better version.[17]

IV.

Wittgenstein, like Freud, was deeply interested in what it's like to get a joke. Often he drew comparisons to music, what it's like to understand a piece of music or express the pleasure one feels, or what it's like to have (or not to have) a musical sense. He didn't think that praising a work by saying "this is beautiful" made the point. Rather, he said, we show our understanding, our pleasure, when we return to the work over and over again.[18] What does it mean to show our understanding? In his *Remarks on the Philosophy of Psychology*, he asked us to think about "[t]he peculiar feeling that the recurrence of a [musical] refrain gives us." He continued:

> I should like to make a gesture. But the gesture isn't really at all char-
> acteristic precisely of the recurrence of a refrain. Perhaps I might
> find that a *phrase* characterizes the situation better; but it too would
> fail to explain why the refrain strikes one as a joke, why its recur-
> rence elicits a laugh or grin from me. If I could dance to the music,
> that would be my best way of expressing just *how* the refrain moves
> me. Certainly there couldn't be any better expression than that.—
>
> I might, for example, put the words "To repeat," before the re-
> frain. And that would certainly be apt; but it does not explain why
> the refrain makes a strongly comic impression on me. For I don't
> always laugh when a "To repeat" is appropriate.[19]

In this and other similar kinds of sentences, Wittgenstein wanted to expose
a philosophical error. When we try to account for our feeling of pleasure, of
understanding, or of recognition, it's mistaken to think there's any *depth explanation*—an extra act, intention, or image, or a gesture, phrase, or movement—that philosophically explains it. To exaggerate: the getting of a joke
requires no additional explanation other than getting the joke; understanding
a sentence has no extra act of understanding other than getting the point;
recognizing a face as familiar has no extra or external act of recognition. In
his *Philosophical Investigations* he wrote:

> Asked: "Did you recognize your desk when you entered your room
> this morning?"—I should no doubt say "Certainly!" And yet it
> would be misleading [for a philosopher] to say that an act of recog-
> nition had taken place. Of course the desk was not strange to me; I
> was not surprised to see it, as I should have been if another one had
> been standing there, or some unfamiliar kind of object.

And in the following remark:

> No one will say that every time I enter my room, my long-familiar
> surroundings, there is enacted a recognition of all that I see and
> have seen hundreds of times before.[20]

Wittgenstein thought that it sufficed philosophically to stay with, and on
the same level as, the experience itself, with the joke being told, the sentence
being uttered, with the face one recognizes. The point was not merely that the
experience elicits the response, but that in the experience itself resides all the

philosophical issues. So he wasn't suggesting that we just accept the experience as is: we do have to investigate it. He just thought the investigation should not consist of our searching for a depth explanation somehow behind the experience. Of course he wasn't denying the role of mundane explanations as, say, when we explain why someone understood this German sentence by pointing out that she was brought up in Germany. He was only denying that in a philosophical account one need move beyond the content of the utterances given or the experiences had in particular contexts of use. Philosophers, he complained, are always looking for some deep principle or essence that will explain what is meant by a particular utterance or experience. At most one can compare and contrast contexts; what one should not do is move beyond context altogether. One of the most serious metaphysical illusions to which philosophers succumb, he thus wrote, is thinking that "what is sublime, what is essential, … consists in … grasping one comprehensive essence."[21] Again, he was not denying the sublime, only a certain sort of metaphysical explanation.

In his *Lectures on Aesthetics*, Wittgenstein demonstrated how giving an example, and always more than one, is nearly always philosophically more plausible than seeking an essence or exact definition. Why? Again, because aesthetic responses, like some other responses, are not reducible to a single causal principle or to any other kind of scientific or exact explanation. Recall Kant's telling of three jokes and compare this to Wittgenstein's interest in the kind of response we have when we say "oh yes, now I see the point, now I understand, now I get it," where the idea is that having not initially seen something, we get the point at the third if not the second seeing, when, as he said, something *seems to* click into place. What he thought not possible was that empirical psychology could ever explain the nature of that response. To think it could, he said, would be "funny, very funny indeed."

> So two rabbis are sitting silently over a glass of tea—you know, says the first, life is like a glass of tea with sugar. A glass of tea with sugar? asks the other, How do you explain that? How should I know, says the first: What do you think I am, a philosopher?

The point being that only philosophers are tempted to seek an explanation for the meaning of life. And now Wittgenstein:

> You might call the explanation Freud gives a causal explanation. "If it is not causal, how do you know it's correct?" You say: "Yes, that's right." Freud transforms the joke into a different form which is rec-

ognized by us as an expression of the chain of ideas which led us from one end to another of a joke….

And then Wittgenstein points out that one thing we tend to say is that a certain kind of explanation "clicks" or "is the right one." But, he continues:

> Suppose someone said: "The tempo of that song will be all right when I can hear distinctly such and such." I have pointed to a phenomenon which, if it is the case, will make me satisfied…. We are again and again using this simile of something clicking and fitting, when really there is nothing that clicks or that fits anything…. People still have the [incorrect] idea that psychology is one day going to explain all our aesthetic judgments, and they mean experimental psychology. This is very funny—very funny indeed. There doesn't seem any connection between what psychologists do and any judgment about a work of art.[22]

What did it mean for Wittgenstein to get a joke, a melody, or indeed, a philosophical point? A transition or transfiguration that moves us from not getting it to getting it. And what could make the move? Rearranging the pieces or evidence in front of you. (Remember his love of chess games or his famous duck-rabbit example.) Wittgenstein thought the whole process quite difficult: it isn't easy to change the way you see.[23] The point is also that Wittgenstein thought the change could come with us all the time staying on the surface of things, with what was always and already in front of our eyes or, in his other terms, in "plain view." "The aspects of things that are most important for us are hidden," he wrote, "because of their simplicity and familiarity. (One is unable to notice something—because it is always before one's eyes.)"[24] Never, he wrote elsewhere, do we need to "penetrate to depths deeper than language itself reveals,"[25] for recall: "One of the greatest impediments for philosophy is the expectation of new, deep (unheard of) elucidations."[26]

In staying on the surface and denying depth explanation, Wittgenstein was not denying depth. Rather, precisely in the process of coming to understand the surface, the surface would acquire depth in all its penetrating "dimensions."[27] Wittgenstein once expressed a desire to use a part of Goethe's poem "Allerdings" as an epitaph to his *Philosophical Investigations*, although in the end he did not. What would have been his point? To demonstrate his formalism, that behind the philosophical expression, the experience itself, the arrangement of pieces, there is no bedrock or core meaning to be found.

However, *in* that expression, that experience or arrangement was all the depth of the world. Goethe's own phrase for this depth was "offenbares Geheimnis."

> I have heard this reiterated for 60 years,
> And cursed it on the quiet
> I tell myself a thousand times:
> Nature gives everything amply and gladly
> She has neither core
> Nor husk
> You just ask yourself
> Whether you are core or husk.[28]

In nearly all cases of showing what he meant for a surface to acquire depth, Wittgenstein provided aesthetic analogies, often with jokes and often with music. Here is an analogy with jokes that concerns depth:

> The problems arising through a misinterpretation of our forms of language have the character of depth. They are deep disquietudes; their roots are as deep in us as the form of our language and their significance is as great as the importance of our language. Let us ask ourselves: why do we feel a grammatical joke to be deep? (And that is what the depth of philosophy is).[29]

And now an analogy with music that demonstrates the formalism:

> The same strange illusion which we are under when we seem to seek the something which a face expresses whereas, in reality, we are giving ourselves up to the features before us—that same illusion possesses us even more strongly if repeating a tune to ourselves and letting it make its full impression on us, we say "This tune says something," and it is as though I had to find what it says. And yet I know that doesn't say anything such that I might express in words or pictures what it says. And if, recognizing this, I resign myself to saying "It just expresses a musical thought," this would mean no more than saying "It expresses itself."—"But surely when you play it you don't play it anyhow, you play it in a particular way ... Precisely, and that's all I can say about it....

Wittgenstein now provided his oft-quoted conclusion:

> What we call "understanding a sentence" has, in many cases, a much
> greater similarity to understanding a musical theme than we might
> be inclined to think . . . For understanding a sentence, we say, points
> to a reality outside the sentence. Whereas one might say "Under-
> standing a sentence means getting hold of its content; and the con-
> tent of the sentence *is in* the sentence" (my emphasis)[30]

Wittgenstein would further compare the case when one fails to read a
person's mood from his face (an example of what he called aspect blindness),
with the inability to hear, or with the failure to have a "musical ear." Or he
would compare reinterpreting a facial expression with reinterpreting a musical chord, "when we hear it as a modulation first into this, then into that key."[31]
Or he would compare one's recognizing something as familiar with one's
"immediately grasp[ing] a particular rhythm in the picture and stay[ing]
with it."[32]

Wittgenstein was not using such comparisons, metaphors and similes
merely as the content of his demonstration; he was also internalizing them
into its form. To write philosophy was to take us through the process of coming to see the point: actually to let its form move us from confusion to a new
"perspicuity" or "transparency."[33] There was, he was always telling us, no place
to look or to go beyond what comparisons, metaphors, similes—the sentences—say themselves. Through his repeated use of developmentally-repetitive
examples, "intermediate cases," and methodological pronouncements, all the
time he was *showing* us, or in his more narcissistic moments *showing* himself,
the depth of his own philosophy.

> I myself still find my way of philosophizing new, and it keeps strik-
> ing me so afresh, and that is why I have to repeat myself so often. It
> will have become part of the flesh and blood of a new generation
> and it will find the repetitions boring. For me they are necessary.[34]

Coming to see what Wittgenstein meant by the depth of the world we
come to see Wittgenstein as a figure of exile also, although in a paradoxical and deeply philosophical sense. I have already mentioned that the move
from not seeing to seeing, the process by which we come to understand, occurs within the form of experience, in rearranging the pieces of the surface to
find for them a new order, indeed, Wittgenstein says, the correct order. "The
philosophical problem is an awareness of disorder in our concepts, and can
be solved by ordering them."[35] However I have not yet emphasized that Witt-

genstein spoke of this process not only in terms of aesthetic response but also in a language of foreignness and defamiliarization. What, for him, was the common thread?—a commitment to "bumpy" juxtapositions of different yet comparable uses in different contexts, all in front of our eyes.[36] Hence Wittgenstein spoke many, many times of sending language out for a cleaning and bringing it home in order, or of decoding experiences of familiarity by sending them into foreign territories, or of what it was like to come to understand a word in a foreign language, and whether indeed such understanding was possible at all. Once he wrote: "Two people who are laughing together, at a joke perhaps. One of them has said certain somewhat unusual words & now they both break out into a sort of bleating [*Meckern*]. That might appear very bizarre to someone arriving among us from a quite different background. Whereas we find it quite *reasonable*."[37]

Yet, for all these excursions into foreign territory, Wittgenstein in one very specific sense moved nowhere. He traveled and lived for much of his life in a foreign land. But, as a philosopher, he stayed on the surface, with everything in plain view. Metaphorically, that meant he stayed at home. Indeed, he said, one did not need to go any further than home because home is where the confusion is. Adapting one of the most famous lines of exile: for Wittgenstein, wherever you are, you are home. Always his point was about doing philosophy: "For the ground keeps on giving us the illusory image of a greater depth, and when we seek to reach this, we keep finding ourselves on the old level."[38] If one did find oneself needing to go somewhere, he suggested only that we take a step into "the backgarden." "To go down into the depths you don't need to travel far,"[39] for the philosophical detective need never abandon his "immediate and accustomed environment."[40]

So, for what purpose all this philosophical travel that keeps us nonetheless at home? To change our attitude to the world, to transfigure our "way of looking at things." In this sense, the strangeness of exile was, for Wittgenstein, no more than the strangeness of doing philosophy. For familiar phenomena, he wrote, "don't strike us as remarkable until we put them in a strange light by philosophizing."[41]

Why the necessity for putting things in a strange light? Because language, home, and culture shroud the world in all sorts of illusions and deceptions that put us at odds with it, and philosophers should not further the deception. Linguistic or metaphysical error makes the philosopher unhappy. To remove the error is to see the world for what it is and this makes him happy. The change does not affect the world; no, as Wittgenstein said with his well-known quietism, it leaves "everything as it is."[42] It is the seeing of everything in its place that makes him happy. "The world of the happy man is a different one from that of the unhappy man," Wittgenstein famously wrote.[43] It is the attitudinal change that makes the difference. So the happy man is the man who stays home, having shed his seeing of its metaphysical error.

All films have happy endings, Wittgenstein said as he sat in Cambridge watching cowboy westerns. And what is a happy ending? No more than "feeling at home in what I see" and understanding aright that feeling of familiarity.[44] "In order to live happily," he wrote early on in his *Notebooks*, "I must be in agreement with the world. And that is what 'being happy' means."[45]

But did Wittgenstein ever reach happiness? That, for Wittgenstein, was the wrong question. For when he wrote that "[t]he truth can be spoken only by someone who is already at home in it," he once more told us not about the philosopher who had returned home but about the philosopher who had never left, about the philosopher who had found the right starting point from which to philosophize—at home. He did not want to say that we start with truth already in hand, rather that we have to start in the right or truthful place knowing how to proceed without metaphysical error or confusion, without losing our sense of humor. With whom would he contrast the philosopher who starts in this truthful place? Precisely the person who starts from the wrong place or, as he continued the sentence, "who still lives in untruthfulness, and does no more than reach towards it from within untruthfulness."[46]

Who was capable of losing their sense of humor? Those who had the wrong attitude to the world. Moving away from the kind of jokes that make us laugh to the sort of attitudinal humor that befits a deeper human melancholy, Wittgenstein now wrote:

> Humor is not a mood [*Stimmung*], but a way of looking at the world. So, if it's right to say that humor was eradicated in Nazi Germany, that does not mean that people were not in good spirits or anything of that sort, but something much deeper & more important.[47]

V.

In 1964, Adorno, back in Frankfurt since 1949 after his exile in America, recalled a meeting with Charlie Chaplin. "He once imitated me," he remembered with some pleasure, for

surely I am one of the few intellectuals to whom this happened and

to be able to account for it when it happened. Together with many
others we were invited to a villa in Malibu, on the coast outside
of Los Angeles. While Chaplin stood next to me, one of the guests
was taking his leave early. Unlike Chaplin, I extended my hand to
him a bit absent-mindedly, and, almost instantly, started violently
back. The man [Harold Russell] was one of the lead actors from *The
Best Years of Our Lives*, a film famous shortly after the war; he lost a
hand during the war, and in its place bore practicable claws made
of iron. When I shook his right hand and felt it return the pressure,
I was extremely startled, but sensed immediately that I could not
reveal my shock to the injured man at any price. In a split second
I transformed my frightened expression into an obliging grimace
that must have been far ghastlier. The actor had hardly moved away
when Chaplin was already playing the scene back. All the laughter
he brings about is so near to cruelty; solely in such proximity to cruelty does it find its legitimation and its element of the salvational.[48]

Adorno, like Wittgenstein, emphasized the transfiguration of response that
occurs in the dissonant moment of humor: laughter transfigured into, or
displaced by, cruelty, aggression, or malice, but embarrassment displaced by
relief and ease. In the story and in Adorno's telling, repetition or mimesis is
essential: the imitation of a man's gesture recorded and conveyed, and transfigured thereby.

Adorno's recollection of Chaplin was not his first. Yet the first, thirty
years earlier, before his exile, was not about recollection but prophesy, in fact
"Kierkegaard prophesying Chaplin." In this prophetic stance, repetition
changed too, from backward to forward motion. In 1930, Adorno wrote:

In *Repetition,* one of his earlier pseudonymous writings, Kierkegaard ... speaks ... of the old Friedrichstädter Theater in Berlin and
describes a comedian named Beckmann whose image evokes, with
the mild fidelity of a daguerreotype, that of the Chaplin who was to
come. The passage reads: "He is not only able to walk, but he is also
able to *come walking*. To come walking is something very distinctive,
and by means of this genius he also improvises the whole scenic setting. He is able not only to portray an itinerant craftsman; he is also
able to come walking like one and in such a way that one experiences everything, surveys the smiling hamlet from the dusty highway,
hears its quiet noise, sees the footpath that goes down by the village

pond when one turns off there by the blacksmith's—where one sees [Beckmann] walking along with his little bundle on his back, his stick in his hand, untroubled and undaunted. He can come walking onto the stage followed by street urchins whom one does not see."

"The one," Adorno continued,

who comes walking is Chaplin, who brushes against the world like a slow meteor even where he seems to be at rest; the imaginary landscape that he brings along is the meteor's aura, which gathers here in the quiet noise of the village into transparent peace, while he strolls on with the cane and hat that so become him. The invisible tail of street urchins is the comet's tail through which the earth cuts almost unawares. But when one recalls the scene in *The Gold Rush* where Chaplin, like a ghostly photograph in a lively film, comes walking into the gold mining town and disappears crawling into a cabin, it is as if his figure, suddenly recognized by Kierkegaard, populated the cityscape of 1840 like staffage; from this background the star only now has finally emerged.[49]

Under the pseudonym Constantin Constantius, Kierkegaard's own discussion in *Repetition* focused on his return from his native home to Berlin (once a home abroad), on the need to take something back that had been lost, on the need to return to a place that could not by recollection alone be envisaged (contra Wittgenstein) by sitting in his living room. He actually went back—to his home, to the theaters he had once frequented, to the performances recognized but not recognized—only to find that "there is no such thing as repetition," or at least that, if any sense can be made of it, repetition is not a going back—a repeat of sameness—but a forward motion, a future-directed realization of different world, a topsy-turvy world in which everything seems "out of tune." Kierkegaard's essay, not incidentally, is about all the themes of my essay: repetition, home, laughter, music, philosophy, and what makes a person happy. "Repetition and recollection are the same movement except in the opposite directions," he wrote to capture the doubleness of backward and forward motion, "for what is recollected has been, is repeated backwards, whereas repetition is recollected forward. Repetition, therefore, if it is possible, makes a person happy, whereas recollection makes him unhappy."[50]

When Adorno returned to Frankfurt after the war, he was returning home. His thoughts of return were nostalgic, sentimental, and self-serving. He spoke (actually he almost sang in the Schumannesque tones of his spoken voice) of doing philosophy once more in its essential language—German; of tasting venison with cream sauce; of feeling the gravel of the road beneath a car that did not yet, like American cars, have wheels that transmute the gravel into a smooth (disciplined) surface of sameness.[51] In a letter to his colleague Horkheimer he wrote of "Returning to Europe" as having

> taken hold of me with a force I cannot describe. And the beauty of Paris shines through the tatters of poverty more touchingly than ever before . . . What still exists here may be historically condemned, and it bears the traces of this clearly enough, but the *fact* that it still exists, the embodiment of temporal disparity, is part of the historical picture and allows a little hope that something humane is surviving in spite of everything.[52]

However, by internalizing the condition of exile into his philosophical writing, Adorno transmuted his nostalgia into critical, philosophical reflection. Instead of his thoughts being self-serving, they were written to "serve the self," to return the subject home. From where was the self returning? From a position of being lost or imprisoned in a mass of metaphysical confusion and ideological deception.

To open his final and unfinished masterpiece of 1969, *Aesthetic Theory*, Adorno declared for art what he had felt also on his return to Germany many years before: "It is self-evident that nothing concerning art is self-evident any more, not its inner life, not its relation to the world, not even its right to exist." Here it sounds as if Adorno was expressing regret that art no longer lives with its self-evidence. However, if we put term "Germany" in the place of "art" we also see a sense of relief. For self-evidence belongs *at best* to an enlightened world that once was but no longer is, but *at worst* to a world that, first time around, produced Auschwitz. Adorno could find little sense in being either merely resigned or merely ironic about art or Germany having come somehow to an end.

For Adorno, in contrast to Wittgenstein, the self that returned was not happy. As Wittgenstein said, the world of the happy man is different from that of the unhappy man. Yet happiness for Adorno was something transmuted into the deepest and most internalized subjective misery. Like Wittgenstein, Adorno was concerned with a metaphysical return home. Like Wittgenstein, the return meant seeing the proper condition of one's attitude to the world. However, at the opposite pole, the returned self was a self that would refuse oneness or agreement with the world and choose to stay rather in a condition of exile or resistance. Exile, Adorno wrote at the end of his recollection of "scientific experiences" in America, was deprovincializing. He was "induced no longer to regard as natural the conditions that had developed historically, like those in Europe: '*not to take things for granted*.'"[53] Exile, even after return, was still the place to be—the place where philosophical thinking starts and where in modernity it ends.

When Adorno internalized his exile or estranged subjectivity into philosophical form, he did so, as Wittgenstein did, under the influence of a Viennese modernism represented by figures such as Karl Kraus, Adolf Loos, and Arnold Schoenberg. All these modernists wanted to demonstrate a distinction in their re-conceptualizations of form, between the truthfulness of internal, logical form and "falsity" or "crime" of externally imposed (socially co-opted) ornament and style. Thus, Schoenberg, for example, spoke of a musical logic according to which a work is compositionally structured by an Idea [*Gedanke*], which is more or less (the relation is unclear) identical to a "tone row." The Gedanke is taken to replace the more traditional core or structuring principle of tonality. If a "core" or "center" is retained at all in the new compositional method, it is so under the formalist provision that it be understood entirely in terms of the ordering and arrangement of the tone row according to the "logical" rules of continuation. Schoenberg characteristically referred to these as the rules of developing variation. Any arrangement of the tone-row has equal status as each tone has in the row. Each tone is related to all others although not in virtue of an independent unifying principle. In describing this conceptual shift in the history of serial music, Adorno wrote exactly to the point: "Variations are no longer composed on themes: composition becomes variation in general, without a static theme."[54]

Adapting the shift to philosophical writing, the modernists focused on the logical or formal ordering of individual sentences. Compare Wittgenstein's techniques of surface juxtaposition and repetition of sentences and thoughts with Adorno's use of declarative sentences that are rarely connected by explicit connective terms. In his *Aesthetic Theory* he uses almost no "therefores." The formalist assertion here is that the sentences are connected implicitly or latently through the internal meaning of each thought itself: truthful form without the confusion of ornament, without the announcement of repetition, without, as in music, the declaration of recapitulation. Developing variation either in music and philosophy is about the structural (temporal and spatial) movement of thoughts.

For the modernists, form served jointly to sustain philosophical argument and cultural critique. Consider a typical sentence from Adorno from his critique of the culture industry: Radio promises freedom and individuality but in fact "turns all participants into listeners and authoritatively subjects them to broadcast programs which are all exactly the same."[55] The sameness gives them comfort they seek, but it is a false comfort. Identifying with the infantile aggression of "canned laughter" they do not notice the real humor and dignity emanating from what (if anything) is being said. They learn to respond entirely to technology's effects, to identify with exactly what they are being given. The habits formed fit far less their freedom than the comfortable identity they think they have achieved.

Adorno was concerned to break these habits, to break the spell of technology's form and effect. He thought that (Schoenberg's) music could help. Schoenberg's music was dissonant not only in its emancipated atonal form; it was also socially dissonant insofar as it had the potential to challenge musical listeners' most established habits just by flouting their expectations about what they thought music should be like. Such music would provoke cognitively dissonant moments just by forbidding the listeners a false comfort or the "culinary delights" of easy identification. What was the point of breaking the habits? To give listeners a glimpse of a freedom and dignity they were being promised but most denied. The culture industry, he famously wrote, speaks in untruth: the more it promises freedom, difference and individuality, the more it administers a kind of sameness, conformity, and identity. How does it break its promises? Through the play of form. We listen not to what we are not being told, only to what we are told; we do not recognize how the form of media or technology makes the dialectic of content possible, by presenting the content at the same time that it manipulates it.

Yet, if form was being used to mask truth, it could also be used to reveal it. For Adorno, dissonance was a mode of description pertaining not just to musical form itself but also to the socially antagonistic relation between music and listener. He spoke accordingly of the double character of the work of music in terms of its aesthetic form and social truth potential. The only point I want to stress here is that, in his view, the double character of music was transferable to philosophy: if music could challenge the listener through form, so philosophy could challenge the thinker through form. Adorno's aim was to write a dissonant philosophy in terms appropriate to philosophy. What was his purpose? To challenge a metaphysics of sameness that was giving philosophers a false sense of happiness in their philosophical homes.

Adorno made the potential of dissonance the point of most of his writings on music. But he also made it the point of his essays about the return to

Germany. The person, he asserted, who can adapt to exile is no different in conformist mentality from the person who can adapt to home. It was adaptation Adorno feared most. "All mass culture is fundamentally adaptation," the repetition of the selfsame, he argued in "The Schema of Mass Culture."[56] So when he returned home, he said he wanted to return to a home or a society that would not repeat itself. No repeat, he repeated at least six times in one essay, of Auschwitz. In another essay about return entitled "On the Question: 'What is German?,'" he admitted his desire to feel the identification with the familiar, but not if that entailed the repetition of disaster. He wanted return without repetition, or if repetition, then forward directed repetition without sameness. And what would prevent such disaster? Changing the way we were rationalizing the home in which we found ourselves.

However, Adorno was not content with a world in which the metaphysical resting place showed you that everything was in its place: this, for him, was just another conservative and potentially most dangerous illusion. "The viewer," he wrote,

> is supposed to be as incapable of looking suffering in the eye as he is of exercising thought. However, even more essential than transparent affirmation is the predetermined resolution in the "happy ending" of every tension whose purely apparent character is revealed by the ritual conclusion. Every specimen of mass culture in its very structure is as historical as the perfectly organized world of the future could wish it to be.[57]

Yet, like Wittgenstein, Adorno did think that desirable change was situated in the way we think. Adorno here appealed to something the experience of exile and return had taught him, namely, that "a sense of continuity and loyalty to one's own past is not the same as arrogance and obstinacy with regard to the person one happens to be, no matter how easily the former degenerates into the latter." For real loyalty demands not relinquishing oneself so that one may adapt, but developing a the sort of discriminating self where one is able to understand other people.[58]

He also spoke, repeatedly, of breaking the spell and fascination of Fascism by working through of the past. What did such a working through mean? He showed us: a *working* through was a *walking* through, a process of repeated steps and dissonant formal development that would break the spell of our most familiar rationalizations, the rationalizations that would allow us to continue to feel comfortable in a world that had once ended in Auschwitz.

What did he fear in the present? That the Fascist tendencies once manifest in the objective conditions of Nazi Germany were still present in the post-war conditions of democracy:

> I consider the survival of National Socialism *within* democracy to be potentially more menacing than the survival of fascist tendencies *against* democracy. Infiltration indicates something objective; ambiguous figures make their *comeback* and occupy positions of power for the sole reason that conditions favor them.[59]

Ambiguous figures making their "comeback" was an image that stood precisely at the opposite extreme, for Adorno, of the figure, Chaplin, who—still with humor—"comes walking."

The form of the essay of "The Meaning of Working through the Past" was designed to walk us step by step through our most optimistic rationalizations in order to break their spell. Dissonant tactics were used throughout; familiarity constantly transfigured into unease; juxtapositions of what it is easier to feel with what it is harder to feel. "One wants to break free of the past," Adorno wrote:

> rightly, because nothing at all can live in its shadow, and because there will be no end to the terror as long as guilt and violence are repaid with guilt and violence; wrongly, because the past that one would like to evade is still very much alive.[60]

We use euphemisms, he said, to make the terror of fascism less terrible; we distract ourselves by quarrelling about numbers; we argue that somehow the victims brought the terror upon themselves; we talk about getting on with the future; we say the Germans suffered too. Adorno's point was to show—mimetically—not the truth or falsity of such claims *per se*; but the way we create patterns of rationalizations to veil what frightens us most. We become convinced by such rationalizations. How do we come to see through them? By listening to what we say. By stating our beliefs coldly, repeating them, juxtaposing them, exaggerating them to create a different pattern such that if our beliefs are being held without thought, they will once again become food for thought. Adorno called this process doing philosophy or dialectics at the extreme. "I have exaggerated the somber side, following the maxim that only exaggeration per se today can be the medium of truth."[61]

Where do we arrive when our "walking-cure" is over, when the spell of our rationalizations is broken? Not immediately to a transformation of society's objective conditions—how could a walk through rationalizations do that?—but, like Wittgenstein, to a transformation of the subject, of the person taking the walk. "A working through of the past understood as enlightenment is essentially such a turn towards the subject, the reinforcement of a person's self-consciousness and hence also of his self."[62]

Adorno described this move from non-understanding to understanding, or from confusion to truthfulness, as a subjective enlightenment. In what did it consist? In the alteration of the unhappiness of unfreedom into the unhappiness of freedom, i.e., from the transformation of a subject who cannot resist the lure of familiarity that will suck him into an identity with a world that deceives him to a subject who critically resists his desire to feel comfortably at home in a world that is in danger. Adorno remained unhappy as free subject because he found a "wretched reality" in plain view. In "Education after Auschwitz," he wrote, under Freud's influence: "education must take seriously an idea in no wise unfamiliar to philosophy: that anxiety must not be repressed." What he meant was that, at best, true anxiety would replace a displaced anxiety for which we tend to seek the comfort of rationalizations.[63]

Still in Los Angeles, it seemed that Adorno thought the end really marked an end, and everything that would follow would be too late. With Horkheimer he wrote: "What Odysseus hears is without consequence for him; he is able only to nod his head as a sign to be set free from his bonds; but it is too late."[64] And yet, after his return, he saw the survival of the subject still to depend upon the work it did if not *in* the world, then at least in attitudinal relation to it. What does one do when it is too late? Accept nothing but the ironic possibility of cold repetition or write still of how the subject might restore itself? Neither option for Adorno was happy, although both were possible. That Adorno ended so many of his essays with an appeal for the return of self certainly plays a final chord of residual hopefulness in an otherwise most pessimistic picture. What does this show? At least a commitment to a notion of self that, in working through the deceptions with which the world confronted it, has not utterly despaired of seeking its home—even if, as I have argued, it was a search pursued in the perpetually exiled state of having escaped. But why this perpetually exiled state? Because, for Adorno, it was precisely the way not to isolate the subject from society, but, rather, to maintain its dialectical play with it. Exile may have been a distancing condition for the subject, but it was always a social condition through and through. Home, for Adorno, was no living room.

VI.

Seeking a home for the modern subject returns us in the best possible world to Kant's civilized dinner parties where the outcome of listening to music and to jokes leads to the restfulness, peace, and security of Enlightenment optimism. Or does it? Recall that with his own philosophical formalism, Kant told us about guests who laugh at jokes less because of their content, and more because of their dissonant form: the form of expectation, frustration, and resolution. We laugh, he said, at the dissonance in logic, the frustrated expectation that finally gets resolved. However Kant emphasized something else too, that although listening to music and laughing at jokes might tell us something about the form of experience, these particular forms of experience end in a place where "nothing is thought."

Let me adapt this Kantian limitation to the arguments of our philosophical modernists. If philosophical form internalizes Wittgenstein's and Adorno's conditions of exile or estrangement, as I have argued, it too runs the risk of ending in nothing thought. Yet both Wittgenstein and Adorno offer endings that seem to be about something thought. So what are we to think? Maybe that the outcome that gives Wittgenstein his happy ending and Adorno his miserable one may not, after all, be the outcome solely of form *per se*, but also reassertions of content, and invoking Freud again, reassertions of unconscious content. If the purpose of dissonant philosophical form, a form that refuses a core, is to leave space for a free and dynamically constituting subject, then the subject we find in this freedom might in the end be a divided or contradictory one. "The principle of individuality was always full of contradiction," Adorno wrote.[65] Hence, in this free space, we might find not only a *philosophical* subject with a critically thinking attitude, but also a *living* subject whose desires, nostalgias and sentiments have been left in place.

In other terms, the nostalgia and sentiment that lures the *living* subject home might not always be transmuted successfully by the *philosophical* subject who chooses to see his home differently. Certainly the endings often sound more like assertions of temperament than philosophical thoughts. "I don't mind what I eat," Wittgenstein famously once said, "so long as it's always the same thing." Would Adorno have said the same of his venison in cream sauce? But if one thinks now that a potentially unresolved ending betrays, and thus renders a failure, the philosopher's form, that would be to miss the point. Because the real failure of philosophical form wouldn't necessarily be one that left a space for an unresolved ending, but one precisely that did not leave such a space.

"The way things are," wrote Adorno to end one of his essays, "should not be the final word."[66] In regard to philosophy, even the happier Wittgenstein would have agreed. "It is as though I had lost my way and asked someone the way home. He says he will show me and walks along a nice smooth path. This suddenly comes to an end. And now my friend says: 'All you have to do now is find the rest of the way home from here.'"[67] The point is that, for both philosophers, "the rest of the way home" is just where all the "friction" and "rough ground" resides. For Wittgenstein it was the rough ground of philosophy; for Adorno, the rough ground also of politics. For Wittgenstein it was the sickness of philosophy, for Adorno the philosophical melancholia that never "returns" (but never say never) to health. If this is correct, then it is so independently of whether or not "the way things are" make for happy or unhappy endings.[68] The exiled German poet Erich Fried, influenced by Adorno and yet thinking about Wittgenstein, knew this only too well. Of doing philosophy at Oxford, he wrote in 1978:

> "Philosophy leaves everything the way it is"
>   Then upon the way it is depends the gravity of its crime in leaving everything the way it is.[69]

Notes

1   *Culture and Value*, ed. G. H. von Wright (Oxford: Blackwell, 1980), 52.

2   *Dialectic of Enlightenment*, trans. John Cumming (New York: Continuum, 1996), 78.

3   *Phaedrus*, 275–6, trans. W. C. Helmbold and W. G. Rabinowitz (New York: Bobbs-Merrill, 1956), 69–70.

4   *Culture and Value*, 80.

5   "Culture and Administration," in *The Culture Industry: Selected Essays on Mass Culture*, ed. J. M. Bernstein (London: Routledge, 1991), 113.

6   "The Schema of Mass Culture," in *The Culture Industry*, 75.

7   "On the Fetish-Character in Music and the Regression of Listening," in *The Essential Frankfurt School Reader*, trans. Andrew Arato and Eike Gebhardt (New York: Continuum, 1995), 284.

8   Goodman, *Languages of Art: An Approach to a Theory of Symbols* (London: Oxford University Press, 1969), 144ff.

9   *Remarks on the Philosophy of Psychology*, ed. G. E. M. Anscombe and G.H. von Wright, 1 (Oxford: Blackwell, 1980), 517.

10   *Philosophical Investigations*, ed. G. E. M. Anscombe and Rush Rhees, (Oxford: Blackwell, 1997), sec. 531, 143–4.

11   *Philosophical Occasions, 1912–1951*, ed. James C. Klagge and Alfred Nordmann (Indianapolis: Hackett, 1993), 180.

12   *Minima Moralia. Reflections from Damaged Life*, trans. E.F.N. Jephcott (London: Verso, 1978).

13   *The Critique of Judgment*, sec. 51–5.

14   *The Critique of Judgement*, trans. James Creed Meredith (Oxford: Clarendon, 1980), 198.

15   I am not saying that only the temporal arts contain such moments; only that they are exemplary in being able to display the changing patterns within cognitive development.

16   *Beyond the Pleasure Principle*, trans. and ed. James Strachey (New York: Norton, 1961), 42.

17   I have taken these versions from *The Big Book of Jewish Humor*, ed. William Novak and Moshe Waldoks (New York: Harper, 1981).

18   *Lectures on Aesthetics, Psychology and Religious Belief*, ed. Cyril Barrett (Oxford: Blackwell, 1966), 4.

19   *Remarks on the Philosophy of Psychology*, pt. 1, sec. 90, 19.

20   *Philosophical Investigations*, pt. 1, sec. 602–3, 157.

21   *Zettel*, ed. G. E. M. Anscombe and G.H. von Wright, 2nd edition (Oxford: Blackwell, 1967), sec. 444, 77.

22   *Lectures on Aesthetics*, 18–9.

23   *Culture and Value*, 55.

24   *Philosophical Investigations*, pt. 1, sec. 129, 50.

25   *Philosophical Grammar*, ed. Rush Rhees (Oxford: Blackwell, 1974), pt. 2, 283–4.

26   *Philosophical Occasions*, 178.

27   Cf. *Philosophical Investigations*, pt. 1, sec. 594, 55.

28   Quoted in B. R. Tilghman's *Wittgenstein, Ethics, and Aesthetics* (London: Macmillan, 1991), 116.

29   *Philosophical Investigations*, pt. 1, sec. 111, 47.

30   *The Blue and Brown Books: Preliminary Studies for the Philosophical Investigations*, (Oxford: Blackwell, 1969), 2nd ed., pt. 2, 166–7.

31   *Philosophical Investigations*, pt. 1, sec. 536, 144.

32   *Philosophical Grammar*, pt. 1, 79.

33   *Philosophical Occasions,* 177.

34   *Culture and Value,* 3.

35   *Philosophical Occasions,* 181.

36   On bumps, see *Philosophical Investigations,* pt. 1, 48.

37   *Culture and Value,* 88.

38   *Remarks on the Foundations of Mathematics,* ed. G.H. von Wright, G. E. M. Anscombe, and Rush Rhees (Oxford: Blackwell, 1978), revised 3rd edition, 333.

39   *Culture and Value,* 57.

40   *Remarks on the Philosophy of Psychology,* 1, pt. 1, sec. 361, 71.

41   *Philosophical Grammar,* sec. 120, 169.

42   *Philosophical Occasions,* 177.

43   *Tractatus,* 6.43.

44   *Philosophical Grammar,* pt. 1, 165.

45   *Notebooks, 1914–1916,* ed. G.H. von Wright and G. E. M. Anscombe (Oxford: Blackwell, 1979), 8.7.16, 75.

46   *Culture and Value,* 41.

47   *Culture and Value,* 88. Cf. Freud's remark on humor that "possesses a dignity which is wholly lacking, for instance, in jokes, for jokes either serve simply to obtain a yield of pleasure or place the yield of pleasure that has been obtained in the serve of aggression," (quoted in Simon Crichley's most insightful paper "Freud's Sense of Humour—or Why the Super-Ego is Your Amigo," a paper that treats Freud's little-known essay on humor, as opposed to his larger theory of jokes (ms.).

48   "Chaplin Times Two," trans. John Mackay, *The Yale Journal of Criticism,* 9, no. 1 (1996), 57–61.

49   loc. cit.

50   *Fear and Trembling. Repetition,* trans. Howard V. Hong and Edna H. Hong, *Kierkegaard's Writings,* 6 (Princeton: Princeton University Press, 1983), 132–76.

51   "Erika Mann und Theodor W. Adorno im Gespräch mit Adolf Frisé, January 29, 1958," in *Rückkehr in die Fremde? Remigranten und Rundfunk in Deutschland (1945–1955),* ed. Hans-Ulrich Wagner (Berlin: Vista, 2000).

52   Quoted by Rolf Wiggershaus, *The Frankfurt School: Its History, Theories, and Political Significance,* trans. Michael Robertson (Cambridge, MA: MIT Press, 1994), 403.

53   "Scientific Experiences of a European Scholar in America," *Critical Models: Interventions and Catchwords,* trans. Henry W. Pickford (New York: Columbia University Press, 1998), 239.

54 "The Prehistory of Serial Music," in *Sound Figures*, trans. Rodney Livingstone (Stanford: Stanford University Press, 1999), 59.

55 *Dialectic of Enlightenment*, 122

56 *The Culture Industry*, 58.

57 "The Schema of Mass Culture," 60.

58 "On the Question: 'What is German?'," *Critical Models*, 209–10.

59 "The Meaning of Working Through the Past," *Critical Models*, 90.

60 Ibid., 89.

61 Ibid., 99.

62 Ibid., 102.

63 *Critical Models*, 199.

64 *Dialectic of Enlightenment*, 34.

65 *Dialectic of Enlightenment*, 155.

66 "What is German?," 214.

67 *Culture and Value*, 53.

68 *Philosophical Investigations*, sec. 107.

69 *100 Poems without a Country*, trans. Stuart Hood (London: John Calder, 1990), 144. I am most grateful to many colleagues, students, and friends, notably to Danny Herwitz, Gregg Horowitz, and Ernst Osterkamp, but most especially to Steve Gerrard with whom I jointly conceived the Wittgensteinian side of this paper as he was writing his companion piece: "How not to do philosophy: Wittgenstein on mistakes of surface and depth."

The Anti-Hermeneutic Impulse:
Beyond Modernity or Beyond Modernism?

Production of Presence, Interspersed with Absence: a Modernist View on Music, Libretti, and Staging

HANS ULRICH GUMBRECHT

I CAN BY no means claim any particular competence in the field of the art-form opera, and even to present myself as a friend of the opera would be a hardly sustainable exaggeration. Nonetheless opera, as a special type of staging, belongs to the type of phenomena in which I am most interested in my academic work. For opera is one of those art forms and objects of reference for aesthetic experience which one would not do justice to by experiencing it and analyzing it exclusively within the dimension of meaning-production or meaning-identification—that is, through interpretation based on a style of philosophical reflection that we call hermeneutics. I am fascinated by the "other" of production and identification of meaning thus implicitly postulated, and I call it "production of presence," in which—as will be clarified in more detail—the aspect of spatiality in the concept of presence must be emphasized over that of temporality. If I am interested in presence as something different from meaning, that in no way means that I take meaning to be a bad thing, or think that eliminating or minimizing it—or even just avoiding it in academic work—would be a noble intellectual goal. Moreover, I of course admit that there can be no cultural phenomena (from any epoch or society) for which meaning components and presence components are not both constitutive, in various combinations. In opera this convergence of "production of meaning" and "production of presence" is just more clearly apparent than in other art forms, but it is by no means an exception either in terms of structure or in terms of medium.

As with all other cultural phenomena, it is true of opera that we gain a more complex view (in the old days we might have said that we see "in another light" or "with new eyes"), as soon as we take into account its presence component. In order to achieve precisely this goal, I will now try to recapitulate what is meant when we (ordinarily and in the context of leisure time) talk about staging. A more detailed (but still highly condensed) clarification of the typological difference between "meaning culture" and "presence culture"—as typological models—will follow, and will lead into a re-definition, from the point of view of presence culture, of some analytic concepts which are central for our context (sign, event, play, and theater). I will then make a short historical excursus into the era in which opera as we know it began to be differentiated from other art forms, an era when it became at the same time apparently embarrassing even to mention the components of presence culture. And finally I will discuss a specific concept of staging proposed by Carl Dahlhaus, seek criteria for good (and bad) staging, and propose that we imagine staging as an "accentuated present" ("auffaellige Gegenwart"), following an idea proposed by the philosopher Martin Seel. All of this will ultimately make it possible to ask what exactly "aesthetic" could mean in our current cultural situation—and perhaps also what it should mean.

II.

In modern Western culture (meaning nothing more here than post-medieval culture), it has become standard to expect that art should be a depiction, mimesis, mirror, representation of the world. Anything that does not fit into this schema is exiled and marginalized as an exception (that is, abstract art). We think of representation as the evocation of a spatially and/or temporally absent object of reference through something present, which we understand as a sign for the absent object (and its possible content/meaning). Thus the question arises of whether a sign adequately depicts this absent object, or whether it distorts or changes it (and one can of course identify the productive aspect of mimesis in such a change). In any case, as soon as this question appears, representation is bound to the dimension of meaning. Meaning here would be the consciousness that each completed depiction can be seen as the consequence of a choice between a multitude of alternative possible depictions.

What we call fiction seems for a moment to pose problems for this conception of depiction/representation, since after all, in fictions we do not think of any absent objects in the world to which the fiction refers. But in the case of fiction it has long become a generally accepted theoretical convention to fill this empty spot with the concept of imagination—which changes the question about meaning into a question about the relationship between imagination and fiction. Regardless of whether the depiction/representation refers to an object in the world or to a product of the imagination, however, within this conceptual framework we assume that stage productions function in the same way as books (and other complex linguistic signs)—the only difference being that in productions on a stage, the bodies present take on the role of signs.

An entirely different way of seeing opens up the minute we write the word "re-presentation" with a hyphen and think about its possible etymological meaning, namely as a making-present again. Such a re-presentation is not a representative for something permanently absent, but rather the production of the renewed presence of something existing which has been temporarily absent. This object, made present again, is thus not only synchronized with the observer's time of observation; it is also (and above all) present in the space of the observer—it is tangible for him. The question raised in the dimension of meaning regarding the (in)adequacy of the depiction of an absent object cannot arise here, since the object itself (the original, so to speak) is indeed made present again. Rather than a dimension of meaning, re-presentation produces present-ness as tangibility.

III.

If I now extend this difference between representation and re-presentation into two complex concepts that can stand for two types of culture, I do not assume thereby that either type could ever be purely concretized in any historical reality. Rather, as I already indicated, I assume, in the spirit of the (Max) Weberian tradition, that it is possible—and intellectually productive—to describe any culture and any (sufficiently complex) cultural phenomenon as a combination, however differently structured or proportioned, of elements of both types. One or the other cultural epoch, one or the other cultural phenomenon, might seem to be associated more strongly with one or the other side of our differentiation (e.g., music more with the production of presence/ books more with the production of meaning; medieval culture with the production of presence/seventeenth-century European culture with the production of meaning). What is crucial is simply that we rule out the possibility of any unambiguous identifications on this level.

We can present both of the types of culture envisaged here, that of meaning culture and that of presence culture, starting from two different premises of human self-reference. In meaning culture, humans understand themselves principally as consciousness (in the Cartesian manner: as a *res cogitans*, or as a subject), whereas in presence culture, the principal self-reference is as a body (*res extensa*). As subjects, humans in meaning culture think of themselves as eccentric *vis-à-vis* the world of things (of which they are observers). On the other hand, the body is a (non-eccentric) part of the cosmological order that presence culture understands the world of things to be. The subject interprets the world of things, in that it penetrates their material surfaces and identifies something immaterial, namely meaning, underneath. The body, as the self-reference of presence culture, on the other hand, fittingly inscribes itself into the rhythms and regularities of the world seen as cosmological order. In meaning culture, knowledge of the world is always knowledge produced by humans through acts of interpretation, whereas in presence culture, knowledge can only be obtained through transcendental revelation (if you want to avoid the dimension of transcendence, you could say with Heidegger, through "Being unconcealing itself").

In meaning culture, humans have the right—and sometimes the obligation—to reshape the world constantly through their actions. What we call motivations for action (or intentions) are indeed anticipatory images of a world changed through action. In presence culture, however, while humans may be able to make use of certain (revealed, unconcealed) laws of cosmology (in the form of magic formulas and the like), they cannot hope to ever change the course of the cosmos. Because time is necessary for putting intentions into effect, time is the dominant dimension of meaning culture. Conversely, presence culture is dominated by the dimension of space, since spaces are constituted around bodies—thus around the central human self-reference of presence culture. The (dominant) temporality of meaning culture is irreversible time, the time of an inevitably changing world, a time in which the past can never return, which is why it is available only to memory. In presence culture, however, time is reversible—and for precisely this reason magic and re-presentation (making present again) appear to be possible. Presence culture is constituted around rituals of making-present-again, of re-incarnation. The Eucharist, in the Catholic theological understanding, is an example of such a ritual. It was the central ritual of medieval culture—as a production of the real presence of a God, who was already supposed to have been present at

one point in the past as a tangible body on earth. As rituals of meaning culture, on the other hand, we could mention methods of consent formation: institutions (like parliaments) in which individual intentions directed towards
transforming the world could be reconciled with each other.

IV.

These binary distinctions may be somewhat obsessive, but as I indicated,
what I want to achieve with them is an alternative, on the side of presence
and re-presentation, to the dominant, *exclusive*, paradigm of interpretation,
semiotics, and hermeneutics, which is entirely unchallenged in humanities
departments. (Interpretation, semiotics, and hermeneutics, despite certain
intrinsic differences, converge at least insofar as they will address any culture
only as a meaning culture.) My initial strategy will be to defamiliarize a series of key concepts which ultimately—together with the canonized versions
thereof—should be taken to a higher level of descriptive complexity. The
Saussurian concept of the *sign*, for example, is defined as the unity of the difference between the *signifiant* and the *signifié* (between the material signifier
and the immaterial signified). From the perspective of presence culture, this
can be countered with, for example, the (of course much earlier) Aristotelian
concept of the sign. A sign, in the sense of Aristotle, would be the unity of
the difference between substance and form, where substance is that which
takes up space, and thus creates and maintains presence, whereas form allows
substance to be perceptible and differentiated at each moment (which means
that it makes substance capable of adopting a meaning, but not necessarily
meaningful). In this spirit, in a meaning culture, an *event* is quickly identified
as the unexpected *per se*; as that which does not correspond to the anticipations and implicit expectations of human intentions. For a presence culture,
the concept of the event cannot be defined as the contrast between intentions
and expectations (these play no role on the presence side of our typology).
Rather, an equivalent must be found within the dimension of an unchanging
cosmological regularity. One version of the concept of event in a presence
culture is synonymous with the concept of miracle: an exception to the cosmological laws—but granted and/or produced by God. What is interesting for
questions of staging is above all another revision, through which the concept
of event becomes independent of the dimension of the unexpected. Indeed,
the appearance of the expected also causes a moment of discontinuity which
we can call an event from the perspective of presence culture. In this sense the
moment of take-off, the moment in which the first note of a concert rings

out, is an event, even though everyone has been waiting for it, and at least among specialists its identity is no secret. Without the effect of such a take-off event—in other words, if it really were only a question of the novelty of the content—stage productions would quickly be exhausted through regular repetition.

From the point of view of meaning culture, we understand *plays* as interactions whose participants leave their everyday intentions outside when they enter into the play. This creates a contrast to the seriousness of everyday intentions as the characteristic of plays, and we associate this contrast with the concept of fiction. But it also creates the necessity of rules internal to the play, through which interactions in the play must be structured, since the participants after all have left their own intentions (which give them orientations for how to act) outside of the play. Theatricality and fictionality in this sense cannot arise in a presence culture, because presence cultures lack the contrasting foil of everyday seriousness based on intentions. If there were something like an equivalent to plays and fiction in presence culture, it would most likely be the production of inverted worlds (for example in Carnival) or of anti-worlds (imaginations of hell, for example, which the audiences of medieval passion plays reveled in). A similar argument can be developed for the concept of theater. There are no counterparts in presence culture to theater (as it is understood in meaning culture). In the centuries of our modern culture, which has been understood and constituted primarily as a meaning culture, theater has become the only form of literature which relies on bodies—instead of words, letters, books—as signifiers. It is precisely this function which creates the "as if" status of bodies on the modern stage—the physical presence of the actors' bodies is canceled, as it were, by their function as signs. For presence culture, on the other hand, there can be no theater in this sense, since embodiment (the structuring of a substance through form) is the norm, and by no means the cultural exception. In presence culture the body of the actor (but already this word is too modern; perhaps we should speak of the body of the medium) can become possessed by a spirit (the spirit of a dead person, of a demon, of a god) whom he helps to a renewed present-ness through his body—a present-ness, which in comparison to everyday presence can be experienced as more pronounced rather than as effaced.

V.

Before we now—against the grain of interpretation/semiotics/hermeneutics—sketch a picture of opera encompassing its presence elements, we should pose the question of how these elements can have so fully disappeared from our cultural consciousness that it would be at all possible to approach opera entirely through procedures of meaning. The answer is that components of presence culture have been seen as increasingly inappropriate (if not indeed simply embarrassing), since the time when the restructuring of human self-reference started towards the telos of Cartesianism, that is, towards an ontology in which the reality of human existence was made dependent solely on the ability to think. Since then (thus more or less since the age of the Reformation), doctrines like transubstantiation have become a nuisance for many theologians (even, although more or less secretly, for many Catholic theologians), while numerous other occurrences and phenomena that did not fall in line with the paradigm of meaning culture were, with increasing certainty, allocated the status of what we call special effects today. The fact that we still at least register such special effects proves that despite the dominance of meaning culture in modernity, elements of presence culture never entirely (as we could indeed say here) vanished from the scene. They exist within well-circumscribed enclaves which are either excluded from canonization and auraticization as high culture because they belong to presence culture (as in the case of sports), or are superimposed with discourses and practices of meaning culture and thus legitimated (as in the case of music or opera). The fact that the sound of a symphony has no meaning has not hindered music critics from interpreting and describing symphonies almost as if they were stories. It is true that there are grounds for assuming that this nearly linear process towards an ever-growing dominance of meaning culture over centuries has recently been derailed. Here indeed, the history of the notion of special effects (which obviously begins in the mid-twentieth century), could be just as revealing as the fact that certain aspects of performance have in recent years moved more intensely into the center of academic interests (and also into the artistic interests of directors).

In the context of these reflections, it seems to be a welcome historical confirmation that the Italian beginnings of the art-form opera go back to the late-sixteenth and the first half of the seventeenth centuries—thus to the decades where the kind of thinking emerged which would soon, in conjunction with the name Descartes, become a synonym for thinking per se. Philosophy was constructing itself on elevating meaning and the activity of the mind to the sole defining elements of human existence; modern theater—above all on the French stage (think of Corneille's late works and Racine's tragedies)—was becoming more speech- and meaning-laden than ever before or after; finally the convention of experiencing the big roles and characters of a play only as complex concepts (entirely independently of any specific actor's body) was getting underway. It was at this historical moment that forms of staging such as the *commedia dell'arte,* based entirely on body artistry, and the opera, started to appear. They may well have been the first compensations in light of the normalization of the Cartesian world view. The condition of possibility for the canonization and legitimation of these (compensatory?) genres is the overemphasis on the content and the plot in the *commedia dell'arte,* which was in reality never primarily about the illustration of a story, and—indeed from the beginning on—the overemphasis on the meaning of the libretto for opera (as if its music were entirely the formulation of a plot).

VI.

In a colloquium some fifteen years ago dedicated to "Libretto-Forschung," of all things, I witnessed the great Carl Dahlhaus provoking his own colleagues from musicology departments (and several literary critics) with the thesis that operas were not dramas between characters, but rather dramas whose dynamic emerged from the play between voices and notes—between soprano, tenor, mezzo-soprano, baritone, alto, and bass—and the instrumental sounds of the orchestra. The implicit revision therein of the reigning view of the relation between music and libretti fits perfectly with our reformulation of the concept of the sign in terms of presence culture. The physical reality of the voices and of the instrumental music now emerges as the substance of the opera, whereas the plot marked out by the libretto—but on a microscopic level also by each one of its words—appears as the form, as the condition of possibility for the substance of the voices and the music becoming discernable and fitting together as discernable elements of a complex structure. This view does not follow the common conception (which legitimates opera in modern culture) of a balance between the play and the music, a functional complementarity within which the music illustrates so to speak, the content given by the libretto. In contrast, Carl Dahlhaus' idea suggests a clear subordination of the plot to the music. It allows the form of the plot to appear as a structural condition of possibility for the epiphany of a musical substance in its full intensity.

Epiphany (and indeed, epiphany of form) is a concept I have experimented with in order to grasp and describe what fascinates the spectators of sports. In a successful play in sports, a form prevails against the constant danger of not succeeding, which is, here, the threat of entropy. This is, to be precise, a form which is embodied (in the fullest sense of the word) through the player, and moreover a form which only exists as a temporalized form (no individual moment, no photograph, can capture the form of a sports play). In sports, substance is always already given through the presence of the players on the field, and all the attention and suspense is focused on the possibility of a form emerging out of the interplay of the bodies present. In the case of opera, however, it is not substance but rather form which is always already given through the plot of the libretto. Thus the attention of the audience (but also of course the attention of the singers and the musicians) is directed towards the epiphany—or the emergence—of substance, in this specific case: towards the epiphany or emergence of the sound. Evening after evening the libretto will steadfastly guide the plot to a happy or an unhappy end. But whether the substance of the voices and the volume of the orchestra can meet the demands of the score—that is a question which, evening after evening, produces new events of presence.

VII.

What would then be—if we accept the idea of the epiphany of sonic substance as the center of opera—criteria under these conditions for successful (or failed) opera productions? Comparatively little—I am *not* saying nothing—would depend upon (and we should emphasize yet again: if we are ready to hear an opera under the premises specified here) whether the production succeeds in making the appearance of an overweight sixty-year-old tenor as a young lover plausible—especially if this singer has an impressive voice at his disposal. The effort of wringing scenic quality or perhaps psychological depths out of literarily third-rate libretti—think of the *Magic Flute*, *Fidelio*, or the *Meistersinger*—can readily be down-scaled. And the seemingly user-friendly gesture that allows a translation of the text sung (for example, in Italian) to accompany the action in supertitles runs the risk of distracting too much audience attention from the sound in favor of the content.

By contrast, what would be ideal—in the conception of opera from the perspective of presence culture—would be a production which supported, developed and (in the literal sense, for it is indeed a question of an articulation in space) brought out, based on the structural condition of its plot and its interpretation, the epiphany of the musical substance, the complexity and intensity of the interplay of voices and instruments. We know, for example, that it is important to fill the entire space of the stage and the opera house in order to achieve such effects. Likewise, it is obvious that the choreography of the bodies on stage is more important than the mimetic play of costumes,

gestures, and facial expressions. The entrances and exits of the various singers, the way their voices open up and fall silent, create strong event effects.
(This repertoire of forms of emergence and disappearance has been brought
to undreamt-of sophistication and mastery in Kabuki and No, the two classical staged forms of Japanese culture.) I hope we could go so far as to postulate
that not all special effects of light, color, and scenery need to be transformed
into symbols which interpret the plot of the libretto and the psyche of the
characters. For if the core of opera is substance—more precisely, the epiphany of a synesthesia of substances—then there certainly exists the danger of
diminishing the effect of these simultaneously elicited substances through a
surplus of semantic allocations and subordinations.

VIII.

The German philosopher Martin Seel has proposed to identify the forms that
we call staging as a specific case of the production of presence, namely as the
"production of an accentuated present." In reality, stage productions in the
true sense—thus, for example, stagings of opera performances—are exceptional in that they are centered on the production of events of emergence
and on the epiphany of substance or form, and therein lies their *raison d'être*.
On the other hand, while the staging of everyday interactions is admittedly
dependent on substances and forms (on bodies, on spatial delineations, on
gestures, that belong to specific roles and times), nevertheless such present-
nesses produce effects of presence only in passing, as inevitable by-products.
Many everyday interactions have controls at their disposal which make possible the bracketing of effects of present-ness (she cannot complain about the
ugly voice of her interlocutor; and he must not let it show that her miniskirt
fascinates him more than the business proposal she just presented).

But how do stagings manage to refer to their own present-ness such that
it becomes a accentuated present-ness? Above all (and indeed almost always)
because they have clearly marked starting elements and (normally somewhat
less clear) concluding gestures, by which they give themselves forms which set
them apart from the course of everyday interactions. The moment of silence
before the orchestra begins, for example, creates a discontinuity between
the everyday and the musical production. An especially high level of complexity and coordination of choreographed bodies, and an overarticulation
of individual body movements through rhythm are then further elements
that accentuate present-ness. This articulation of bodily movements through
rhythm emphasizes the present-ness of their substance. You do not walk on

the stage of an opera—you stride and you dance—just as the characters of the opera do not speak, but sing. These observations can be formulated as a paradox: while such procedures of articulation set the bodies on stage apart from their environments, they enable the intensification of their present-ness (the impression, finally, that they are tangible). Perhaps this is what the New Testament calls transfiguration, i.e., the conversion of a body, which intensifies its present-ness.

IX.

In the philosophical discussions of the twentieth century about the objects and effects that we associate with the word, "aesthetic," the dimension of presence has gained an increasing prominence. We are only today in the process of discovering what a constitutive role the dimension space, as the sphere in which objects become tangible, played in the work of Walter Benjamin, for example. If Martin Heidegger emphasizes that aesthetic experience brings into the clearing less the possibility and the force than precisely the event of the self-unconcealment of Being, then we must take into consideration that in this event of self-unconcealment not only a form appears, but a formed substance also always becomes present. Against privileging interpretation as the assignment of meaning, Jean-Luc Nancy has referred, in the debates of recent years, to art's connection to the "desire for the fulfillment of limits of perfect presence and perfect absence." And when Niklas Luhmann described aesthetic communication as the *one* type of communication in which perception, as well as meaning, can be communicated, his thought opened—this once—onto the mode of sensory (and not just sense-mediated) contact with the world of things.

I presuppose this tradition of philosophical aesthetics, still barely understood and certainly not yet fully elaborated, as the context for my proposal to look at the production of presence as the dominant component in the staging apparatus of opera. But what could it mean to speak of dominance in this context? The effects of presence in opera certainly cannot do without the contribution of the libretto which establishes form; without its meaning, that is, without interspersing presence with effects of absence through meaning. And we must therefore go even one step further and ask ourselves whether and why we should object to a mode of reception which concentrates on the plot of the libretto as the dominant component of opera. As soon as we pose this counterquestion, it becomes apparent that placing the dimension of presence in a position of dominance is the result of a polemical impulse, one which

reacts against the unquestioned other—opposite—dominance; the under-
questioned dominance of the dimension of meaning and of the hermeneutic
relation to the world. Aesthetic experience reveals situations of tension and
oscillation between perception and meaning, between the dimension of presence and the dimension of absence. It is trivial—but also unavoidable—to
remember that scarcely any other art form is so completely founded on this
oscillation and thrives on this tension as much as opera. In order for it to
display this complexity, what is called for above all in contemporary culture is
to strengthen the dimension of the production of presence, and moreover to
emphasize that the exceptional quality of opera lies in the dynamic it obtains
from the unresolvability of this tension. To transform it into a stable hierarchy
or a stable relationship of functional complementarity could be fatal—for
opera.

X.

But for which reason do I call the argument unfolded on the previous pages
a *modernist* view on opera, libretto, and staging? One answer to this question
has been implicit in my argumentation. If we can say that the invention of
opera as a form of staging occurred at a historical moment when the Cartesian style of early modern culture—that is, the unilateral privileging of a
self-reference centered on the spirit over a self-reference including the body
(and, with the body, substance)—provoked and produced a number of cultural forms that would compensate for such one-sidedness, then it is plausible
to claim that, paradoxically, opera is a specifically modern phenomenon. But
I would like to add a further, more complex perspective—a perspective based
on a different concept of modernity, a perspective, finally, which is capable
of shedding a new light on some of the critical discourses that dominate the
humanities today.

Following an intuition by Martin Heidegger, modern culture is not only
the culture that emphasizes the mind and temporality (while bracketing the
body and the dimension of space), but also the culture that obliges us to view
the world in general and art in particular as representations, in Heidegger's
own words, "as pictures" of something. Conversely then, seen from the artist's
side, art appears as the expression of something inside the artist. Music under these premises may be understood, for example, as the expression of the
human heart or of the artist's deepest feelings. Such a view puts music under the intellectual regime of interpretation and hermeneutics, and it might
even oblige us to find stories under music's "arrow of time," as Karol Berger

says—which is, I think, a highly problematic position from the angle of the aesthetics of music. For while it is of course possible (although by no means necessary) to imagine that a composer or a musician wanted to express something, music is definitely not a language that would allow us to find an intersubjectively plausible path back from expression (a chain of signifiers) to what is supposed to be expressed (the signified). In this sense at least, it is safe to say that music has no meaning.

But if the early modern habit of staging the world and art as a picture invariably confronts us with the frustrating suggestion to read and to find a meaning in music, how can it then be possible, from an epistemological point of view, to find another way back, a way back from the potential (but impossible) hermeneutics of music to an appreciation of music as the substance of sound, and of opera as the production of such substance in the form of epiphany? I believe that any modern view of music that is critical of its conception as expression is made possible by the high modernist moment of the early-twentieth century, the very historical moment which art history and literary history have long described as the crisis of representation. In art history and literary history, the critique of the claim of universality for representation and expression immediately led to a rediscovery of the sensual qualities of what had until then been exclusively seen as the signifiers. If in addition to this understanding of the legacy of high modernism we adopt the thesis of the German critic Karl Heinz Bohrer (according to which, ever since Charles Baudelaire the high modern crisis of representation went along with a new temporality of suddenness, that is, of a sudden appearance and vanishing of imperceptibly short moments of intensity), then we can even postulate a connection between the rediscovery of the sensual quality of music as substance of sound and the epiphanic form of its emergence and vanishing.

Seen from the side of some of their neighboring disciplines, therefore, it is somewhat surprising to observe that musicologists today are becoming increasingly eager to interpret music—when literary criticism and art criticism are beginning to develop serious alternatives to their grand hermeneutic traditions. But different disciplines may have different temporalities and therefore react in different ways to the different cascades of modernity.

Translated by Matthew Tiews

Cipher and Performance in Sternberg's *Dishonored*

CAROLYN ABBATE

MUSIC CAN MEAN many things—it all depends. Musical gestures are understood as signifiers when we consult intention, or reconstructed historical and cultural surroundings, or our own individual and accidental associations, or the emotional dictionaries set up by operas and movies, or caprice and fantasy, and they mean anything one person wishes, or nothing at all. Compared to discursive language, works in language, and any visual and representational art—this needs to be stressed again and again—music is uniquely indeterminate and unconstrained by shared cultural agreements about signification. Put another way, no one can *give the lie* to any individual claim about a particular meaning embodied in a melody or harmonic turn, in a composer's style, in the strangest musical moment at one extreme, or the most ordinary procedure or convention at the other.

When musical works are placed under hermeneutic domination, treated as texts subject to decryption, this indulges a deep desire for correspondence. Musical hermeneutics sees musical configurations as analogous to, or reflecting, giving voice to, giving rise to, representing, tracing, or embodying something else.[1] This is meant to be a happy situation, with music being also a supra-audible Other, and connected-ness and correspondence being perpetual virtues. Yet there is a dubious aspect to correspondence, an underside or bitter flavor that has gone unnoticed in most writing on music and meaning, for there are morbid corollaries to the respectable academic activity of "deciphering the specific social characteristics of music" (Adorno),[2] contingent nightmare scenarios at its far edge. Arriving at these scenarios says something important about hermeneutics.

To have faith in legible correspondences flowing between music and an Other, whether that Other is society, culture, a poetic text, someone's life story, subjectivity, visual art, philosophy, sexuality, or what you will, is to be profoundly operatic and cinematic in one's formation. More specifically, this faith is historically indebted to Richard Wagner and his *Gesamtkunstwerk* ideals, which have precipitated for more than a century as much into popular as into rarified intellectual culture, in powerful forms. Hermeneutics as an academic habit, the sociological program that reads cultural facts in musical configurations, the aesthetic position that embraces multi-media works as ideal, critical approval of modernist artists for transgressing single-art boundaries, all share a similar, distinct hope. They huddle under one umbrella.

Citing Wagner, the all-purpose demon umbrella, is nonetheless too quick and too easy—he can make anything dubious in a flash. I do want to spend time with the underside, not via Wagner or the aesthetics of correspondence in Romantic culture, but via Josef von Sternberg's *Dishonored* (1931), a Depression-era movie that presents music-and-something-else as irony and absurdity. This is not its only vote of no confidence: the movie harbors deep reservations about aesthetic association and synaesthesia, and thus dissents to certain modernist and Romantic ideals, with a warning signal about correspondences resembling those in contemporary literary texts, Rainer Maria Rilke's *Primal Sounds* (1919) for one.

The anti-synaesthesic position sees dystopian potential, even horror, both in hermeneutics as theoretical program and in media crossovers as aesthetic product, such modernist classics as Picasso's cubism becoming cubes in Satie.[3] This position goes very much against the grain, given that modernism has often been regarded as an inter-media high-water mark. As Daniel Albright sums up a majority view, synaesthesic or trans-sensory or cross-media collisions are modernism's meat and potatoes. There are, he writes,

> A number of highly charged modernist experiments in discovering how strongly the boundaries separating artistic media manage to repel transgression. In some cases the component media seem to pull apart; in other cases, they seem to work together. And in the cases where they draw together, the complete artwork seems to presuppose the existence of some indivisible center, casting out extensions of itself into the varied realms of music and painting and language, but itself simple and unitary … presupposing a deep concord among artistic media.[4]

Sternberg's *Dishonored* says no to "deep concord," by staging ills that might come of that ideal. *Dishonored* was made for the masses, in Hollywood, and is a popular text without regrets about its status, which is no invitation to treat its reservations as vulgar bibelots, to be appreciated and abandoned, nor to dismiss it as marginal *vis-à-vis* hegemonic high art or philosophical aesthetics. For one thing, the way in which *Dishonored* "says no" is not allegorical, and what is dubious about correspondence is not conveyed by the plot and nowhere described out loud. Doubts arise instead, to take one instance, in the machine—that is, in the film's technical apparatus as well as its evocations of technology. For this reason I want to juxtapose the movie with its techno-logic-historical context, right down to the acoustics of its original theatrical screenings in early 1931. Reconstructing the sensory constitution of a bygone theatrical experience is never an irrelevance, though it is a rarity. To say, for instance, that Albright's admirable work on modernism passes over contemporary performances, preferring to analyze "texts" in the abstract, is not to single it out as unusual or even to scold, but to suggest that the habit of ignoring the physical reality of actual performances is common.

My larger point, however, is that *Dishonored* exemplifies what one might call "vernacular philosophy"—a phrase that adapts a famous locution, "vernacular modernism," coined by film historian Miriam Hansen.[5] Hansen's purpose is to bring popular texts and "mass-consumed phenomena" into arenas where, it has sometimes been presumed, they were never meant to be and are unable to compete, since modernism should "encompass cultural practices that both articulated and mediated the experience of modernity."[6] Hollywood movies of the 1920s and 30s, she argues, make avant-garde moves and construct fluid new subjectivities in plain sight, with kitsch plots and bankable stars making it all easy on the eye. Such films have a "reflexive dimension in relation to modernity" that "may take cognitive, discursive, or narrativized forms but is crucially anchored in sensory experience and sensational affect."[7] The vernacular philosophy sketched in Sternberg's movie indeed has few narrativized manifestations, and one could say that it savages at least one academic-cognitive habit. But Hansen's conclusion, equally relevant here, is that arguments made in the vernacular are as urgent in those in high hegemonic texts—they are not to be mistaken for curiosities, without value or sustained relevance. To question the intellectual limitations inherent in focusing on music-as-work, to focus instead on performance and improvisation, to escape hermeneutic dystopias—these are only some of the possibilities Sternberg's movie suggests. These possibilities have value here and now, perhaps more than ever in an intellectual culture where decrypting musical works and celebrating music's alignment with a supra-audible Other has become a *non plus ultra*, in the worst case a bitter dead end.

But what is music's Other? An easy starting point: rephrase the question as a conundrum. What associations cling to a particular melody, and how does one go from those association to arrive at a point where one can decipher the melody and arrive at its import? This object lesson in "music and something else" brings *Dishonored* into an argument demonstrating the unsurprising truism that musical gestures assume and shed meanings as they travel through time and across national cultures. This simplest instance reminds us that while music can take on a specific supra-audible meaning, and thus be useful as a symbol in a mass medium, that same musical gesture is irrevocably slippery, gets connected to something new, and means something else entirely.

Three different movies, then, over almost seven decades of Hollywood time, in which the same melody corresponds to and invokes quite different Others. In the 1999 thriller *Payback*, small-time crook Porter (Mel Gibson) is shot and left for dead by his wife Lynn (Deborah Unger). He survives, and returns months later to confront her. But she is strung out on heroin, and he feels unexpected pity. After putting her to bed, sitting sadly at her side, he sees a music box on the bedside table and opens it up. Against some surreal music on the soundtrack, the music box plays the first phrase of "Donauwellen," the "Danube Waves" waltz by Rumanian composer Iosif Ivanovici, written in 1880. Then, Lynn reaches out in her stupor and closes the box with a bang.

Why "Danube Waves"? One explanation is that "Danube Waves" (Ex. 1, a basic version giving the A and B sections) is simply a typical music box piece.[8] More than typical: surveying catalogues for several Swiss music box manufacturers reveals that it is up there with "Lara's Theme from Dr. Zhivago." Ivanovici died in 1902, but his waltz had quite an afterlife in the annals of mechanically reproduced music. Like many popular Viennese waltzes, it was a favorite on the calliope. Before the 1920s—when gramophones marched into every bourgeois living room—"Danube Waves" was widely available on piano rolls. In the "Q.R.S. Word Roll no. 3730," an American player piano roll from 1913, the punches have words printed next to them, a text that can be sung along to the music. The melody has given rise to some lyrics about Vienna:

> (A) I'm dream-ing to-night of a place far a-way.
> In fan-cy I see one who means the world to me.

Example 1

(B) There on the Dan-ube with my Viennese,
Float-ing down-stream singing love mel-o-dies,
Lost as we were in our own mem-o-ries,
From wor-ry and care so free! (etc.)

So the music that ends up in the box in *Payback* has an acquired affinity for such devices, and a fairly long history in their company.

But for Americans of a certain generation, the "Danube Waves" melody comes with other lyrics, nothing to do with Vienna. The tune also appears in *The Jolson Story* (1946), a biopic based on the life of Al Jolson, in which Larry Parks plays Jolson and lip-synchs songs to his voice on the soundtrack. In the movie's most famous scene, Cantor Joelson (Ludwig Donath) encourages his son Al, unhappily married to a glamorous actress, to sing a song that was played long ago at Cantor Joelson's wedding. After some bantering about whose voice is better, Cantor Joelson intones the "Danube Waves" melody without words, giving it a Jewish-liturgical touch. Al Jolson responds by singing the waltz to these words:

> Oh, how we danced on the night we were wed,
> We vowed our true love, though a word wasn't said.
> The world was in bloom, there were stars in the skies,
> Except for the few that were there in your eyes.
> Dear, as I held you close in my arms
> Angels were singing a hymn to your charms.
> Two hearts gently beating, murmuring low
> "Darling, I love you so!"
> The night seemed to fade into blossoming dawn,
> The sun shone anew but the dance lingered on.
> Could we but recall that sweet moment sublime,
> We'd find that our love is unaltered by time.

When Cantor Joelson sings it, "Danube Waves" suddenly sounds Eastern, playing into Al Jolson's Old World identity and his Judaic musical roots. This was, in fact, not the first time "Danube Waves" had crossed into American Jewish culture; in 1914, the Hebrew Publishing Company issued an arrangement by Joseph M. Rumshinsky, "the Jewish Victor Herbert," the most popular Yiddish lyricist and composer of early-twentieth-century America.[9] Yet once one knows Al Jolson's words to what became a global hit in 1946 as "The Anniversary Song," another aspect of the music box in *Payback* is opened up. The melody from the music box brings unheard words in its wake. Sentiments about enduring marriage—"our love is unaltered by time"—are cruelly misplaced in the scene between Porter and his junkie wife, and that is why she slams the lid down when she hears this music. For her, it is not tinkling music-box sounds or even this melody per se, but the melody's supra-audible reference to marriage that has become unendurable.[10]

"Danube Waves" is a constant acoustic presence in *Dishonored*, and in this case the waltz edges closer to its origins, since the movie is set in Vienna during World War I. "Danube Waves" acts as a signature number for Marie Kolverer (the heroine, played by Marlene Dietrich), who is a war widow and genius musician turned prostitute. She is offered the chance to spy for the Austrian government as "Agent X-27." While undercover in Poland, she discovers and transmits the Russian army's secret invasion plans. But having fallen in love with her nemesis, a Russian officer named Lieutenant Kranau (Victor McLaughlin), her loyalties become divided. She saves him from the Austrians, and is executed by firing squad for her treason.

The waltz turns up in the first scene, when Marie brings a prospective client to her flat and the old gentleman takes a turn at her piano. He plays the waltz as Marie changes into her slippers, but stops when she comes over to the piano to watch him perform. Her comment on his abilities is dismissive: "Shall I drop in another coin?" The ensuing dialogue establishes an important point about her identity:

> (Offended): "Do I sound like a pianola?"
> (With a smile): "Almost."
> (Examining her piano music collection): "I suppose you are a great musician."
> (Still smiling): "No. But I do know something about music."

In 1931, the waltz card is being played in a different game. We are in Vienna. The Hinterhof flat is recreated right down to the porcelain stove, and a Viennese expatriate directs emigré actors, one of whom (Gustav von Seyffertitz) is also Viennese. "Danube Waves" as "Viennese" has thus disappeared into its surroundings, like a chameleon into foliage whose colors match its own. There is a symbolic value in play, but that value is no longer based on the work *per se*, instead involving *how* two different pianists perform the waltz. The old gentleman bashes through the score; every note is correct, but there is no breathing or variation in dynamics. He is a machine. Her musicianship becomes evident when she takes her turn. The old gentleman tries to convince her to spy against Austria. Being a good citizen, she calls the police and has him arrested. As he is marched away, she plays her version of the waltz.

What she plays is not just "Danube Waves" played by an expressive human being. It is a mad virtuoso excursus on "Danube Waves," something almost no longer recognizable as "Danube Waves," as far from the original as Liszt's fantasy on *Don Giovanni* is from the Mozartean source text. Marie's pianism refers to Liszt and his improvisations, and includes one hyper-virtuosic moment when she stops on the dominant ninth chord that introduces the B theme. This arrested sonority is the entry point for phalanxes of runs up the piano, too many of them. They take over; the waltz is lost, and technique and ornament as pure sound-object supplant it. This goes beyond Liszt to the enraged virtuosity of Maurice Ravel, the Ravel of *Tzigane* or the left-hand piano concerto. Marie, it turns out, habitually arrests the waltz at this point—in the movie's penultimate scene, she stops on the same dominant ninth chord.

These performances in *Dishonored* are invested with gender implications along predictable lines. The old gentleman is the chief of the Austrian Secret Service, and was testing Marie's patriotism before recruiting her. He is absolute in his politics. She has a habit of musical transgression. That her scandalous nature and her improvisational gifts are linked is made clear in a later scene where, now installed in a palazzo, Marie plays the "Moonlight" Sonata with impassioned tempo shifts and unwritten octave transpositions and other unique modifications. Lieutenant Kranau has slipped in to search her premises, and listens to her playing. Their first big love scene follows upon her musical performance, as if sexual attraction were the natural corollary of an unorthodox way with the Beethoven piano sonatas.

Yet the association between musical excess and feminine surplus is supplanted when the tension between inscription, work, and performance is delivered in different dosages, to different ends. And just as the "Danube Waves" waltz as it moves through the twentieth century and through three films acquires or loses cultural associations, or assumes and then shakes off different lyrics—has many different Others—so improvisation as a phenomenon in *Dishonored* comes to shoulder different burdens.

Who decided this should be? When it comes to film, to Hollywood films of this era, or to any film produced under great practical constraints and often under chaotic conditions, with improvisation on the set and technological parquetry in the final product, questions about intent and authorship are sometimes unanswerable—a happy thought. For if the questions are unanswerable, if films are collective and uncoordinated and accidental masterpieces, then one is freer to observe the results and less bound to brood over intent and the degree to which it should or should not control understanding. Yet the roles that performance and musical meaning play in the film are so large, and Sternberg's reputation as a latter-day Wagner policing every possible aspect of production is so well-entrenched—authorship counts more than usual in this film, in Sternberg's oeuvre in general. It cannot be whisked away.

Josef von Sternberg and Marlene Dietrich are Hollywood legends too familiar to require extensive commentary. Sternberg often suggested *a priori* pieces or requested particular songs for his films, and indeed *Dishonored* relies chiefly on diegetic music, the "Danube Waves" waltz, the "Moonlight"

Sonata, and some other ditties that Dietrich hand-synchs throughout the film. But there is one musical object made especially for the movie, which with some minimal non-diegetic soundtrack music is credited to Karl Hajos (1889–1950), a Paramount house composer. Born in Budapest, Hajos spent the earlier 1920s in Berlin, where he worked as a conductor and song composer.[11] He emigrated in the mid-twenties, and his collaborations with Sternberg began shortly thereafter. Over the course of his career Hajos composed music for over 180 films, the most famous being *Morocco* (1930, for which he wrote Marlene Dietrich's songs, "What Am I Bid for my Apple" and "Give Me the Man") and *Shanghai Express* (1932). Much of his work was subsequently done for westerns and horror films.[12]

What makes Hajos's pedigree interesting in light of the music he wrote for *Dishonored* is that he had high-modernist friends. When Bertold Brecht brought Paul Dessau to Hollywood in 1942, Hajos employed Dessau as an orchestrator at Paramount. When Detlef Sierck emigrated from Berlin to Los Angeles and became Douglas Sirk, Hajos wrote the score for his first American feature, *Hitler's Madman* (1943), a film about Reinhard Heydrich, twin to the more celebrated *Hitler's Hangman* of Brecht, Lang, and Eisler.[13] Loosely, then, in a way commonplace among emigré film composers, Hajos was connected to European musical nobility. His Austro-Hungarian roots on the other hand, his Jewish background (like Sternberg's), add mixed overtones to the nostalgic resonance of "Danube Waves" in *Dishonored*. Sternberg used a waltz that by virtue of its very waltz-ness, and perhaps even as a specific, recognized semiotic marker (witness the 1913 player piano roll), could be counted upon to spell Vienna for the mainstream American audience. While for him, for a part of that audience, through its elective affinity for sentimental Judaic melancholy (witness the 1914 Rumshinsky version), the melody may have alluded to another lost past as well.[14]

Hajos's original musical contribution to *Dishonored* appears late in the movie and its value as a locus for vernacular philosophy far outweighs either its aesthetic panache (minimal) or its actual airtime (relatively minor). Once Marie has been infiltrated into Poland, she uses music as a cipher to record the military secrets she has discovered. Disguised as a servant girl, she gets information from a Russian colonel by drinking him under the table. Once he passes out, she returns to her room and we see her writing something on paper, writing furiously and desperately. She is clearly writing down what she learned from the Russian colonel, but only when the camera focuses on her hand do we realize that she is encoding the invasion plans as a musical score, somehow translating the plans into musical code. The camera's eye is so close to the page that barely a measure of what she writes is visible within the frame. We can make out an already-written bass line; a treble line is being added below it (Fig. 1). But after writing down the final measure, the hand goes back to add accents and slurs, pausing for calculation (see Fig. 2).

Figure 1   *Figure 2*

These performance indications are clearly not superfluous. Are they an aspect of the cipher itself, or a disguise added to make the fake score look plausible to a suspicious observer? Not enough is clear—nor will it ever be as the code as a conceit just gets more and more nonsensical—to decide which might be true. The code defeats knowledge in the sense that its workings remain inexplicable, and this inexplicability must not be dismissed as a flaw, as if it were just screenplay ineptitude. The gesture of adding expressive markings, however, does have a point. As Marlene Dietrich's hand writes pitches and rhythms then makes a second track for expressive markings, her hand recapitulates the movie's opening gambit, the his-and-hers performances of "Danube Waves." The old gentleman played every note without fail and without anything more, but the second performance, Marie's virtuoso outcry, added tremendous expressive detail. These two performances have been irised down to their graphic quintessence, the notes alone set against the surplus of accents and slurs.

The cipher score is a wonderful cinematic morsel. But this aside, it is also worth lingering over as the entry point into the chimera of musical meaning. Putting pressure on this cipher puts pressure on a treasured belief, what one might even call a basic disciplinary assumption: that musical configurations themselves, structured sound itself, is legible as a product of social forces or cultural conditions. This is a hermeneutic faith whose morbid corollary the film exposes with a certain sardonic pleasure, with ironic attention to connection and correspondence as equivocal virtues.

What does the cipher score imply? Precise military information is translated into musical notation. Marie's score signifies human bodies and physical objects, their array in future time and space, invasion plans and their political fault lines, with a perfect match between musical inscription and practical meaning brokered by the mechanical secret of the cipher. These code-notes, one could say, give symbolic expression to a fantasy about music, to the "low" hermeneutic belief that just as musical works *encode* at the moment they are composed, so they can be *decoded* to yield meanings.[15] This is a brutally simple procedure, unlike anything a real individual with unique knowledge and memories might do on the "soft" side with the "Danube Waves" melody. Assigning meaning to the "Danube Waves" waltz as ironic signifier for wedded bliss in *Payback* demands specific cultural competence, familiarity with Al Jolson's "Anniversary Song." Getting from "Danube Waves" to "old Vienna" demands similarly complex negotiations, in which one may absorb competing carousel calliope factors, Al Jolson factors, cantorial overtones, or bad poetry about "the night we were wed" into a mental circus of signification. All such negotiations are inflected by intention and memory, mutable with time, and ephemeral.

With the cipher score, the process is reduced to an unchanging act of encryption and decryption, a culture-less process, and music's decipherability is proposed as straightforward fact, with musical configurations becoming an esoteric language. What must not go unnoticed is that this simple faith is hardly unknown to academia. To cite a single instance is not to imply rarity: "If we think about meaning in music and how it is produced, about music as a socially constructed discourse whose meanings are decipherable once we learn to interpret its rules and codes, we may find composers using music in special ways."[16] To multiply similar examples, where the vocabulary inclines to "code" or "deciphering" (Adorno's personal favorite) would serve no useful purpose. But even that is not the point. Even if mechanical deciphering—"low hermeneutics" at its worst—must be cordoned off from "soft" hermeneutics and its post-modern subtleties, cordoned off as a silly or debased or intentionalist variant, the two nonetheless differ in degree and execution, but not in kind. The richness of one, and the quasi-automatism of the other, does not obviate their kinship.

For even in exalted forms, musical hermeneutics involves certain suppressions and losses, unacknowledged, or accepted as fair trade. As Vladimir Jankélévitch put it, "to decipher who-knows-what cryptic message, to put a stethoscope on a canticle and to hear something else in every song, to interpret that which is heard as the allegory of a secret, incredible meaning:

these are the indelible traits of hermeneutics."[17] Like Formalism, hermeneutics attracts through metaphysical glamour, a promise that music as a drastic, physical event will be transcended when the abstraction we call "the work" is brought into play.[18] In a further retreat towards abstraction, matched in Formalism by the rush to paradigms, hermeneutic faith promises that this "work" is a medium giving access to histories, composers' psychological quirks, sexuality, consciousness, subjectivity, cultural tectonic shifts. The retreat towards abstraction arises from anxieties about music in performance.[19] But what I would add is that this retreat suggests how a supra-audible Other is becoming the true object of desire. Thus it would seem that real music, as a sensory phenomenon with physical effects, at times simply becomes boring. The cipher score satirizes musical meaning as semiosis—the correspondence between notes and their signifieds. Indirectly, however, this satire invokes performance as a sensual antithesis to the gnostic attitude that seeks a metaphysical Other in music.

Performance would nonetheless seem to be the one thing directly precluded by Marie's cipher score. She intends no actual realization, since the cipher is not really music but Russian offensives disguised as musical notation. Musical notation implies future unleashing as musical sound, but getting from Marie's cipher to the invasion plans entails decryption without the cooperation of the acoustic—her score is never meant to be played.

But saying that it is "never meant to be played" within the movie's fiction introduces a mysterious temptation to do so, without fully explaining this sense that such realizations are taboo. To appreciate the full flavor of that taboo, which is not just a historical element emotionally unavailable in the here-and-now, one must nonetheless consider several historical issues, the era of the movie's production, and that era's debates about inscription-realization technology. Marie's score bears a prohibition against being played and heard. To play such notation as real music, rather than deciphering it as military positions, would be to translate a physical trace in the wrong medium. If the cipher score per se satirizes a mechanical connection between message and medium, this taboo in turn demonizes mechanical relationships between graphic inscriptions and acoustic realizations.

Why? One could see such translation—reading an inscription with the wrong eye, so to speak—as mechanical synaesthesia, a mechanistic variant of experiments in inter-media transposition, which were hardly unknown to high modernism around World War I. As noted above, inter-media transposition nourished the modernist avant-garde, with "arts seeming endlessly impermeable," and refutation of that given being "motivated precisely" by the fall of so many walls.[20] Such experiments had positive virtues. Kandinsky's

Yellow Sounds, Walther Ruttman's films *Opus* (musical configurations made into abstract visual shapes) and *Berlin: Symphonie einer Grosstadt* (1927, traffic patterns suggesting musical forms) are familiar members of an extensive collective. In synaesthesic experimentation of this nature—this is a commonplace but needs to be emphasized—the translation is mediated by human intelligence, and much of the final product does not flow in any sense from the alien source of inspiration.

At issue here, however, are not artistic experiments but rather a technological degree zero. Film sound and phonographic technologies as mechanical processes also produce synaesthesic crossovers. Theirs, however, are several times more absolute and purely automatic. Synchronized sound, sound-on-film—the "photographic" recording technology that swept silent film away after 1927—involved sound visible to the naked eye on the physical soundtrack, since the recording medium for sound was a photographic trace of the electrical impulses from the receiving microphone (which were converted into light oscillations). The crossover between the acoustic and the visual is made evident to the senses by technology, which is a human product, yet is not itself inflected or changed by human intervention. What made sound-on-film so triumphantly successful was that it eliminated mismatches between sound and image that had plagued the many "portmanteau technologies" that preceded it.[21]

But its homogenizing effect was not merely technological. Synchronized sound also eliminated improvisation and variability in the musical background, as it did the ludic resistance to narrative that live silent-film music could engender, when the accompanist decided to satirize the film being shown. Indeed, as James Lastra has pointed out, the move towards technically secure synchronized sound was among other things the studios' way to exert total control over their product's meanings via the acoustic. As he puts it:

> In addition to the stress sound effects accompaniment placed upon the performers, and therefore their direct and discursive relationship with the audience, it simultaneously and problematically altered the nature of the cinematic commodity. Although film producers had been generally successful in consolidating their control over the product, sound accompaniment, more and more a part of standard exhibitions after 1907, remained an arena wherein individual exhibitors could alter the public's relation to the film.[22]

Once the acoustic became the optical, conjured back into being simultaneously with the projected image, film no longer required an accompanist's or a projectionist's artisan intervention into acoustic matters and centralized control became a reality. This is an important point, since the flawless correspondence between grapheme and resultant sound was not just a scientific desideratum. It became both the means to guide and limit understanding via music/sound, and the technological metaphor for that control. Its flawlessness was a sealed channel tantamount to those between master and slave, director and executor, work and performer, or the world and music, with the first always cutting the fissures, the second always the consequence, or what has been marked.

Indeed, the relationship between a scientific coup and a discourse of mastery and control may intimate some good reasons for reservations about "mechanical synaesthesia." If film sound technology simply normalized a physical match between optical and acoustic, and created music from squiggles, then why should there be a sense of "taboo" against such a crossover in the case of Marie's cipher score? Why not take inspiration from the optical-to-acoustic wizardry of the soundtrack? Take an inscription (which in this case neither reflects musical ideas nor results from actual physical sounds, but *resembles* those that do) and realize it acoustically to hear what it produces? Forging ahead with this experiment would speak both to sheer scientific glee, and to a psyche unperturbed by all those sealed channels, as by their dystopian force.

Endorsing the "why not" position, we in fact have Sternberg himself, fascinated by the enhanced control implied by optical-acoustic absolutes inherent in synchronized sound. Aspiring throughout his career to orchestrate all aspects of film production, he was transfixed in particular by an obscure form of material synaesthesia, so-called "tönende Handschrift" (resonant writing). "Tönende Handschrift" was the brainchild of Rudolf Pfenninger, a German sound engineer working in Munich in the 1920s and 30s. Through experimentation, Pfenninger determined the exact relationship between a given sound and its optical trace on the photographic soundtrack. Using these prototypes he could go backwards, in a laborious process where squiggles drawn as now-predictable graphemes for particular sounds were transferred via photography to the soundtrack, and played back. Squiggles became synthesized music, and the first truly synthetic speech.[23] The technique was publicized in Germany in 1929, while Sternberg was filming *The Blue Angel* in Berlin. News of a similar technology devised in England by physicist E.A. Humphries later appeared in an exclamatory report in the *New York Times* in February 1931.[24]

Sternberg claimed in his memoirs that he manipulated soundtracks *ex post facto* through an analogous process, by inking lines directly onto the sound sector of his master prints. A phantom voice was thus scratched into being:

> I have corrected faulty pronunciation and sibilants that disturbed
> me by the use of pen and ink on the sound track that runs sixteen
> [sic] frames away along the edge of the emulsion; and it was an-
> nounced some time ago that someone had succeeded in writing
> photostatic lines on the sound track that [when realized] resembled
> the sounds made by the human voice. Imagine producing human
> speech with pen and ink![25]

What status to accord this claim? It first appeared in slightly different form, in
a 1955 essay Sternberg published in *Film Culture*, alongside other rhapsodies
to automation and artificial life:

> Actors are usually tricked into a performance not too dissimilar
> from the process employed by Walt Disney or Edgar Bergen. In
> films we have a large assortment of actors with a variety of looks
> and talent, but they are as powerless to function alone as is the me-
> chanical dummy before he is placed on his master's lap and has the
> strings pulled that move head and jaw. I doubt many are intensely
> interested in the mechanism that moves an actual dummy, and it is
> possible that no one is interested in the strings which move the stars
> of our day, but I am going to discuss the strings anyway.[26]

The essay is striking for backstage revelations focused on film's artifice as a
mechanically assembled product. But what unleashes Sternberg's particular
relish is the human actor's helplessness in the grip of this process. As he says:
"I have myself replaced the voices of many actors with their own voices from
other scenes and in many cases have replaced their voices with the voices
of other actors, thereby using the voice of one man and the face of another.
Though this is not usual, it can always be done and is to be recommended."[27]

Whether or not Sternberg actually mastered the "resonant writing" technique, whether he really did manage to create synthesized speech, what remains as interesting as the claim itself is his attitude. He describes a monster,
film as something assembled from body parts ("the cutter ... can retain pieces
which make hands and legs look like slabs of blubber")[28] with living marionettes and non-human voices, yet does so without any apparent reservations
and no particular self-consciousness about his metaphorical field. That this
is typical in the history of technologies—clinical good cheer among practitioners is the first order of the day, and doubts come later, among poets—by
no means makes it less engrossing. The same antimony can define stages in a

philosophical demarche, as has been argued *vis-à-vis* Walter Benjamin, whose welcome mat for technology (the famous "Artwork" essay) gave way to disquiet over sensory estrangement and experiential blockades.[29] There are even pre-emptive strikes from the engineers, as in the anonymous article "The Conservation of Sound—A Technical Causerie," which appeared in 1933:

> Phenomena which would have caused our forefathers not so very long ago to shudder, and would have been attributed by them to witchcraft or some other devilish manipulations, are regarded by us today as a mere matter of course. Gramophone records, the radio, television—the discoveries and invention of science show a continuous, unbroken progression, to which we have grown so accustomed that we often no longer perceive its truly phantastic nature. Enrico Caruso's incomparable voice has been preserved for future generations, although the singer himself is long since dead. The sound film has fittingly completed the work thus begun by the gramophone record.[30]

Post-technological doubts, having been anticipated, are read back into the genealogy of the technology itself as pre-technological superstitions that science and reason subsequently and rightly erase.

In the case of synthetic voices, Sternberg's continued good cheer in 1955 is belated; it would have been so even in 1931. Thomas Levin points out that E.A. Humphries' 1931 synthetic sound demonstration produced "uncanny human speech" that indeed caused "shudders" in its enlightened modern listeners.[31] As Sternberg says, imagine! Good cheer would have been belated even in the nineteenth century, since a sense that mechanically reproduced speech is uncanny pre-dates Edison. "Media always already provide the appearance of specters," according to Friedrich Kittler, and the vocabulary of the necropolis never lags far behind.[32]

But if the graphemes in "tönende Handschrift" remain disquieting, if their realization as human speech seems to breach some prohibition against creating human sounds "out of nothing," these graphemes are still nowhere near as radical conceptually as Marie's cipher score in Sternberg's movie. Unlike Pfenninger's or Humphries' or Sternberg's marks on the soundtrack, the cipher score does not inscribe actual sound or actual musico-sonic ideas as means to the end of reproduction—the notation inscribes invasion plans, and its graphic form is a ruse.

So what speaks out against its realization? If everything cited so far provides only indirect explanations, then among Kittler's collected technological ghost stories, Rilke's *Primal Sound* stands out for being attuned to a specific prohibition that it cannot bring itself to elaborate. If it does not fully explain this taboo, does not tell us directly or exactly *why* objects like Marie's cipher score should be left in silence—in fact, breaking off just when that explanation might be forthcoming—then at least it sets out some limit values.

Rilke's essay is a minority report in the reception history of synaesthesia and inter-media experimentation in modernist art, dealing gingerly with such phenomena, associating them with a strictly mechanical process, gramophonic recording. *Primal Sound* starts with recollections of boyhood science experiments: how a primitive gramophone needle, reacting to musical noises, would trace a spiky line on wax. Now before Rilke sits a human skull, which he examines. His attention is caught by the coronal suture, the spiked juncture left where the plates of the skull grow together:

> The coronal suture in the skull (let us stop to consider) has—let us say—a certain resemblance to the deep line that the phonograph needle engraves in the rotating cylinder of the apparatus. What then if one fooled the needle, and, at the moment it was returning to its original position, directed it over a trace that did not originate in the graphic translation of a musical sound, but that was in and of itself natural—good, let us say it aloud: for example, what if one put the needle on the coronal suture? What would happen? A tone would be heard, a series of tones, music . . . Feelings—what are they? Disbelief, shame, terror, awe—yes, which, among all the possible feelings in this instance, prevents me from suggesting a name for the primal sound that would then come into the world?[33]

The coronal suture is a false grapheme whose resemblance to a phonographic trace is coincidental—one of nature's jokes, like the image of a city skyline on the wings of a moth. But if such accidental traces were to be realized as music, the consequences are unthinkable, and Rilke stops, unable to contemplate the sound "that would then *come into the world.*" Unleashing the non-acoustic grapheme as sound is wrong, an error whose magnitude he senses without its consequences being evident to reason.

Rilke's fear about letting certain sounds "come into the world" is perhaps a fear about what they might do once they got there. Sternberg's enthusiasm for scratching synthetic voices into film emulsions suggests on the other hand a readiness to move freely between acoustic graphemes and the unknown sounds they will engender, so it is not surprising that Rilke's prohibition is breached in *Dishonored*, and that the cipher score is played.

Lieutenant Kranau has been quartered at the same Polish border inn where Marie is working undercover. He sees through her disguise, captures her, and finds her score—"What do you call this masterpiece?" He asks Marie to play the score, saying, "I'll furnish the piano. And the audience! I wish I could read notes." She tries to fool him with a gypsy czardas, and he pushes her aside—"Let me play it for you!" As it turns out he can read notes very well, and his sight-reading of the cipher score (transcribed in Ex. 2) produces an

Example 2

Example 2 (continued)

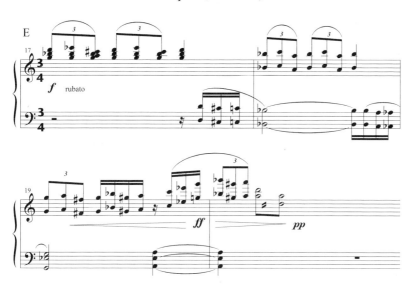

amazing audible joke. Put the needle on the coronal suture, play a fake score that encodes a Russian invasion, and you will get modernism itself, a little potpourri, some late Romantic piano concerto (part E), some parallel fifths in the bass that represent neo-primitivism (or maybe *The Rite of Spring*, part B), some generic atonality (parts A, D). And one passage where Lieutenant Kranau plays an octave in the bass, followed at a snail's pace by eight others whose grim footfalls mimic a serial gambit, the slowly exposed row (part C). "I don't know what this code means," snarls Victor McLaughlin (Fig. 3), "but I have an idea that each note might mean the death of a thousand soldiers!" When he finishes his performance, he burns the score with a Mephistophelean smile.

While the Dadaist conceit of automatic writing underpins this scene in which musical modernism is defined as radical parataxis (or as simple accident), this is not the only aesthetic judgment being made. As Lieutenant Kranau plays, Marie's eyes are shown in close-up, scanning from left to right (Fig. 4). Later the meaning of this activity becomes clear. Anticipating that he would destroy the score, she was memorizing his acoustic realization of the cipher, imprinting music on herself so the information will not be lost. Thus objectified as the wax tablet on which the acoustic etches its marks, Marie has lost her identity as improvisational sound source.

Figure 3   *Figure 4*

The cipher score thus is the site of two dangerous constrictions: as code, it represents an eternally legible union between music and meaning. Realized as a "work," its sound turns Marie into a mechanism. Nowhere—neither in the cipher with its rigid semiotics, nor in the process that converts inscription to sound and sound to body memory—is there an escape hatch. The discourse of control and manipulation via precise coordination, which is present in the studios' embrace of synchronized sound, and present in another form in Sternberg's "marionettes" and "ventriloquists' dummies" as in his praise for resonant writing, is thus given material expression in the movie.

But Lieutenant Kranau's line "each note might mean the death of a thousand soldiers" intimates a reason for Rilke's taboo. Lieutenant Kranau gives voice, of course, to a parody hermeneutics, where little humility is solicited in confronting a musical work, where the musical work has become code mechanism, stethoscope, seismograph.[34] What is at stake, when technology's metaphors and artifacts, their implications of objectivity and their aura, are mustered in arguments that musical works measure social phenomena, in legible patterns? Beyond parody, the line suggests a fantastic short circuit as well. What Lieutenant Kranau puts into words is not the safe musicological pastime, in which musical configurations are understood as representing say, soldiers' deaths, or post-Kantian subjectivity. The verb "to mean" has another connotation, "to cause" or "to lead to." Once Marie's cipher is unleashed into the acoustic, it is the modernist "work" and no longer the fake notation that has real meaning and consequences, and the morbid corollary of hermeneutic belief that becomes evident to the senses.

Before coming to this nadir, I want to note that one of the constrictions implied by the cipher score in *Dishonored* is dissolved quickly, and to note as well the manner of its defeat. After Lieutenant Kranau burns Marie's score, they spend a blissful night together, whereupon Marie manages to drug his wine and escape back to the Austrian lines. There she recreates the modernist potpourri from memory for some officers. As she plays, we see a second image superimposed: Marie's face and eyes in close-up from the earlier scene where Lieutenant Kranau played, where her moving eyes represented the inscriptive action of memory. And while playing, she also pauses four times (in part E), turning towards a desk behind her, grabbing a pen, and scribbling something hastily down, apparently reconstructing a graphic trace based on what she is pounding out (Fig. 5). Is she writing musical notation, or something else? That too has to wait, at least until other implications of this extraordinary scene are paid their due.

Figure 5   *Figure 6*

What is most immediately evident is that Marie the improviser, the old Marie is back, freed from the constriction that made her into immobile audience and recording device. Her modernist potpourri is different from the potpourri played by Lieutenant Kranau, and not just because he was sight reading (slowly at times) and she is playing fluently, not just because, as with the his-and-hers "Danube Waves," she plays with a passion that was absent before. Motifs are slightly altered, virtuoso embellishments and lavish harmonies have been added, and the separate parts of the potpourri are re-ordered and in some cases repeated (with part B entirely omitted).

Then, just as her performance approaches its end, there is an acoustic bleed-through from this scene to the next. Her tremolo open fifths elide into an orchestrated version of those tremolos on the soundtrack and a battle montage begins with images of rolling tanks superimposed on infantrymen, who run and fall stricken in agony (Fig. 6). This is the first non-diegetic music heard in the movie, and it extends the potpourri beyond the two prototypes (Lieutenant Kranau's and Marie's) by bringing back the nine-note bass figure (part C), repeating it three times with strings and winds doing glissandi above, fading finally into the clacking staccato of telegraphs for the next scene.

Asking what the effect of this orchestral music is, what it sounds like, and what fantasy may be expressed by the precise manner of its birth, is not just an aesthetic inquiry. On one hand, once music from the potpourri passes into the inter-space between the diegetic world and the audience, it becomes conventional soundtrack music for catastrophes: full of augmented harmonies, with sinister brass shouting out the now-familiar bass figure, and weird strings in the background. The paratactic lurches and mechanical repetitions, which appear so odd in Lieutenant Kranau's and Marie's versions, are far less evident now even though the musical configurations themselves have not changed, due to a complicated psychological sleight-of-hand. Harping on a single figure by repeating and transposing it seems less irritating when accompanied by a complicated visual ballet, because music fades into second place in soliciting an aesthetic judgement. Indeed, the music as something put together from small building blocks in succession is analogous to this ballet in one sense, since what one sees also passes from one image to another, superimposing them in succession. The orchestration decks out paratactic thinness and repetition in richer sonorities, thus excusing them a little. The bare piano can make no excuses. And, of course, cinema audiences here and now, at the turn of the twenty-first century, are accustomed to putting soundtrack music, musical slips and pieces, into a hopper with visual delights and making a coherent experience of the whole.

But while this excerpt from the modernist potpourri may seem suddenly more banal for all these reasons, this banality by no means disfigures the vernacular philosophy that comes into presence at precisely this point.

That some music is pushed across the border between phenomenal and noumenal (an old operatic trick) is not remarkable *per se*, though commingling the two was less common in the early years of synchronized sound than it is now. What matters here is the exact manner and preparation. When the music jumps from Marlene Dietrich's piano playing to the tanks and dying men, the passage from diegetic to non-diegetic sound fulfills a dreadful possibility. Watching the battle montage, hearing the bleed-through from real piano to phantasmic orchestra, remembering the strange statement that notes "mean" death, you are encouraged to experience a hallucination. It is as if the brass section's bellowing were pushing the tanks forward, and the winds' glissandi were hurrying the soldiers into harm's way. In a few desolate moments, every note, every sound, music configurations themselves have caused "the death of a thousand soldiers." It is as if the modernist potpourri were actually producing this destruction. By analogy with Rilke's *Primal Sounds*, it would be as if real music, actual tones, were always and everywhere cutting fissures into unborn human skulls.

Dishonored's little hallucinated wrong-ness (unlike Rilke's) is not something described in words or allegorized by plot, but is instead a phenomenal element that exists between musical gesture and verbal and visual representation, mediated by technology. In fact, shifts in film projection technology around 1930–31 made the scene more spectral then than it can seem seventy-odd years later. In synchronous sound's earliest years, roughly 1927–1931, the distinction between realistic sound and non-diegetic music was maintained in individual movie theaters by speaker placement, as Rick Altman has pointed out. Projectionists "needed to know the sound track like an orchestral conductor," in order to switch from a high speaker pointed down for source sound (dialogue, sound effects, diegetic music) to a low speaker pointed up for non-diegetic music, a speaker position that mimicked an opera orchestra's—in the pit. But this arrangement was cumbersome, and was outmoded by winter 1930–31 when mixing separate tracks became technologically feasible.[35] Henceforth, until much later, all sound came from one locus.

It is worth pausing over this historical turn, trying to imagine the ways in which acoustic perception in the theater, along with the musical epistemology it had supported, was upended by the new technology. Audiences accustomed to opera, to accompanied silent film or synchronized-sound film on switched speakers, had always heard orchestral music apart or away from the diegetic world's own strictly separate acoustic space. Sounds were segregated. What happened to audience sensoria when noumenal music suddenly migrated, to share the acoustic space of the diegetic world, where it had never been before? If that music conveyed knowledge—as music in opera or film has always done—would the knowledge seem more apropos, or just less transcendent? Perception is historical, and lost perceptual effects can be partially recovered. Until audiences got inured to the new situation, was there an uncanny interim in 1930–31, when the ear was not yet numb and when the idea of unreal music "coming into the world" (to echo Rilke) suddenly had actual physical meaning—disembodied orchestral music moved up into the space of the screen—and thus a still-disquieting acoustic tangibility? *Dishonored* was filmed in winter 1930–31 at the point of the turn, and in some sense consummates the breached border that technology just that moment had set before its makers.

But sensing wrong-ness goes beyond this historical-technological point, to one that is more abstract.

Consider some truisms about non-diegetic soundtrack music. By implying that music is somehow *a priori* to events it forces into being, the battle montage turns the literal production of film music on its head. In practice, films give rise to non-diegetic musical scores in the late stages of production.

A film composer's role is to take in what is seen and said, and to produce something that in varying degrees across the spectrum between extremes amplifies and underscores the narrative, ironically and perversely does something contradictory, interacts, inter-cuts. Whichever direction is chosen, the composer's basic marching orders have been delivered beforehand.

The epistemological rhetoric of film music transfers the common genetic order of film-music production into the works themselves. As in opera, it is not just that non-diegetic music is largely brought in *ex post facto*, designed and/or integrated after the dramatic fact. Such music also is taken to function within the finished product—like operatic music—as commentary or enhancement or revelation (through leitmotifs or expressive surplus or anempathic irony) in relation to the fiction embodied in what is seen, in the characters' emotions as given voice in their speech. As one strand in a multi-media phenomenon it does not literally come later in time. Yet it is understood as consequent nonetheless, tumbling from the fictional world and coming knowledgeably in its wake, murmuring what we should believe or feel and completing that world in some way. The modernist potpourri in the battle montage is rhetorically and epistemologically the opposite: it has been woven into a hallucination that noumenal music is causing things to happen within the fiction.

Like all generalizations, these are to be hedged with reservations and exceptions. The idea that non-diegetic music comes "after" a fictional world that it augments is nonetheless a pervasive natural force in writing on film music. Kathryn Kalinak finds its roots in ideological "assumptions of visual ascendancy and aural subordination" that pervade classical film theory, from Eisenstein to Arnheim, Krakauer, and Balázs, and beyond.[36] James Buhler accepts this "natural force" in less defensive terms: "The signifying capabilities of [film] music help mystify the diegetic world by rendering its inner properties apparent to us."[37] The epistemological habit remains, whether the music in question is parallel on the one hand, or contrapuntal or anempathic on the other, whether the musical score "fits" narrative moods and actions "like a glove" or is deliberately at odds with them.[38] The habit remains even beyond this classic distinction—getting rid of the distinction leaves the habit intact. Meticulous attention is paid to leitmotif, sonic aides, mysterious musical auras, and ironic mismatches, rightly understood as musical clarifications or (thus the post-classic argument) as both reading and being read by speech and image, as both interpreting and producing an effect. Non-diegetic music "has been seen to be a form of fiction that parallels the narrative," according to Royal S. Brown, and film praxis encourages the audience to equate "diegetic [music] with 'reality' and non-diegetic with 'unreality'" as well as myth, omniscience, or control.[39] I would put this a different way. Musical gestures may well act within the film totality Claudia Gorbman describes as an expressive synergy,[40] but so long as they are non-diegetic, their action is an allocution, and its object is our perceptions and beliefs. In the sense that movies encourage this assumption (as Brown points out) it is irreproachable.

As soon as one self-consciously inverts the natural habit, one sees just how perverse the inversion can be. Consider some plausible interpretations of Bernard Hermann's famous violin shrieks for *Psycho*, first heard in the shower scene. The violin shrieks have been regarded as a secret clue—their screeching bird sounds point to Norman Bates, who has a raptor nose and favors stuffed-bird decor.[41] But in another reading, they are surrogates for a sound absent from the diegesis, since we see that Marion is screaming but cannot hear her.[42] Or, they could be a sort of Greek chorus, giving voice to our terror, which may well be unarticulated. Or, their crazed, violent sound reflects Norman Bates' psychotic mentality.[43] Or they are upsetting atonal music that both corresponds to and gives rise to a very upsetting moment.[44] Or, perhaps they inspire musings on whether matching atonal violin screams to violent death is ideologically regressive, or not. Or whether displeasure is valuable. All these suggestions are unexceptionable proposals that non-diegetic music mediates between the spectator-listener and the diegetic world. Soundtrack music may create an emotional temperature within the audience, but not in the fictional characters—they have enough emotional temperature on their own, and it is theirs that the music recreates or clarifies or flattens or satirizes for us. Leitmotifs may tell the audience about a fictional character's memories or premonitions, or his or her nostalgia, or may tell the audience something the characters do not know, adding a wonderful surplus, but are not made to appear to produce memory or premonition or nostalgia or knowledge within those characters.

But what if *Psycho*'s violin shrieks were understood as analogous to the modernist potpourri in *Dishonored*? Then you would need to consider a genuinely disturbing impossibility. It is not Norman Bates' fury that drives his murderous hand. Instead, it would seem that loud violin shrieks, no longer an allocutionary sign with no real presence in his world, have come into his world and forced his hand to descend. Music barred from the fictional world would nonetheless appear to inhabit that world and change it, though not because that music is literally, physically present, somehow diegetic after all. Insofar as violin shrieks would seem to induce something within the fiction, to be unheard and yet move mountains, they would invade that fiction as a transgressor that has slipped in, not phenomenally perceptible within but at its work nonetheless. The difference between *Psycho* and *Dishonored* is that *Psycho* gives its audience no formal or narrative or technical reasons to believe that this fantasy is so, where the piano-to-battle montage in *Dishonored* makes it hard to think otherwise.

In *Dishonored*, the bleed-through to the battle scene labors in this direction, to create the illusion that noumenal orchestral music precedes the disastrous actions that it seems to have called into being. The relationship between musical sound and an external reality flows not from human events or human consciousness or ideology *into* a musical idea, but *backwards* from musical sounds into the world.

And the idea that this might happen, the wish that it could, can be pathological. Is there a musical work that has the power to cut lines into our skulls, to manipulate objects in our world, a work that is literally compelling, turning us into automata, engendering our actions or beliefs, or killing us in the end? Should we wish for such things? As Karlheinz Stockhausen suggested in what has become his most notorious metaphor, was it a great symphony, carefully rehearsed, that brought down the World Trade Center on September 11, 2001?[45] The general claim that music is the legible trace of a world that it also constructs is a jovial staple in musical hermeneutics—as one latter-day founder (Jacques Attali) puts it, "sound matter [is] the herald of society," and "sounds and their arrangements fashion societies."[46] But is that idea harmless? Always a good thing? *Dishonored* has music that is grounded in the world delivering fatal charges.

The fantasy articulated in *Dishonored*'s piano-to-battle montage thus sounds the warning note found in Rilke's *Primal Sounds*, and completes the reasoning that Rilke left suspended in his essay. There are graphemes that should never be realized as sound, and cross-media transpositions that should never take place. But the reason for the taboo is that such music could have the power to create us, to manipulate our world, to cause harm. Thus postulating music's legible connection to the world at one extreme, carried out in a fantastic elaboration, has nightmare implications at the other.

Whenever the cipher score creates constrictions, they act like little alarms that anticipate the battle montage's disastrous musical charge. In every case, whether large or small, there is trouble in correspondences or concords between inscription and the body, code and meaning, notation and realization. The cipher score has something to say about being converted to a recording medium in any process that imprints music on the body, since its acoustic realization immobilizes the heroine. When Marlene Dietrich takes in the cipher's realization, she becomes a passive substance that absorbs musical shocks, and is remade. The cipher score has something to say about what notation as inscription does to performers as the body it acts upon, since notation cranks Lieutenant Kranau into motion, as a sight-reader laboring to replicate every note without error. Performing music becomes dispassionate slavery. Playing something read or memorized is always parroting and repetition, no matter how expressionist one's stage manner may be, and Marie is heroic for breaking this constriction, not by playing the right notes passionately, but by improvising notes that are not there. This signifies escape.

What the cipher score skewers most cruelly, however, qua musical code for Russian Offensives, is a discourse that at once envisions musical works as legible in their minutest details as social or cultural or biographical traces, and dreams its dreams about music re-shaping the world. Via the film's representations of inscription, via Lieutenant Kranau's priceless snarl, musical hermeneutics gets aligned with correspondence on the side of the devil: with mechanism, enslavement, and, finally, with the violence wrought by a musical work that reaches its hand into the world. The cipher score embodies a belief in musical works as media for concealed meanings that can be extracted. And this belief is staged as a series of smooth passages from the enciphered to the deciphered and back again, from black marks to an acoustic realization that in turn lays traces back into a woman's body, leaving no time for escape, no corridor in which improvisational verve can survive, and in the battle sequence, leaving nothing alive.

So it seems important that *Dishonored* releases music from grounding and legibility, and pulls the rug out from under that idea both before and after the battle montage that stages its macabre logical end. This philosophical swerve has been there all along, everywhere in the movie, hidden in plain sight. To explain how it works, one must rewind several times, and end up again at Marie's virtuoso performance of the modernist potpourri. Like her performance of "Danube Waves," what she does with the potpourri dismantles the notion of a stable musical work, as it does the hermeneutics symbolized by the cipher score.

Think seriously about Marie's musical code, remembering the intimation that this "code" in fact grows more and more nonsensical as the movie goes on. The only time the actual notation can be read—as we see it written out—what we glimpse in fact bears no relation to the music Lieutenant Kranau plays at the piano later on, when he is supposedly reproducing this score. The on-screen notation, in other words, is simply musical notation as *mysterium*, the universal confounding sign.

In the scene where she reconstructs the potpourri, Marie turns to write things down. Another loose end: what does she write down? As she plays and then writes furiously on her paper the urge to laugh is very strong, and this laughter is a symptom that marks her writing as ludicrous. Given the few seconds she scribbles, she cannot be transcribing the music she has just played. She writes too quickly to be copying out elaborate military intelligence. In those microseconds of scrawl, nothing could be set down except scrawl itself. Her writing is, then, simply the motion of writing. Just as the notation is mysterium, this is an arabesque.

And, finally, an observation that takes the logic of the plot as given: if military data could be thus instantly and efficaciously translated from musical sound *remembered so easily*, then why did the notation need to be written down in the first place? Why not simply keep an acoustic vehicle corresponding to the notation in your head?

All of these things are unanswerable and left as such, because Sternberg is not making logical ends meet but presenting the audience with a series of fabulous absurdities, easy to see, not even minimally concealed from the eye and ear. Vernacular modernism in cinema (to repeat Miriam Hansen's point) exists outside scenarios or narrative logic, being at home rather in the sensorial matrices woven by technology and apparatus—this is equally true for vernacular philosophy.

Thus the historicity of perception once again counts, though it is by no means certain whether a hypothetical contemporary audience—if such a monolith existed—would always and in every case have seen every fabulous absurdity. It is not easy to say whether, seventy-odd years later, a present-day spectator is likely to be sharper. What one can say, however, is that Sternberg's stylization and narrative illogic were as famous as they were both despised and celebrated in the 1930s—he was Sternberg the "great anarchist," "emphasizing the externals of film mechanics in a most inarticulate manner," whose plots are obviously contrived and "false."[47] And add that the fabulous absurdities in *Dishonored* are forms of luxury and artifice, and that they set everyone free. Notation does not match realization; Marie's virtuoso potpourri does not match an original that is in any case an ontological phantom—the non-existent phantom that both her performance and Lieutenant Kranau's therefore cannot reproduce. Her implausible swerves from piano to paper stage writing that cannot match what it purports to record. The same Sternberg who thrived on control and manipulation and wrote so eloquently about them produces this marvelous fête, in which again and again what had seemed to be coupled and connected falls apart. Marlene Dietrich's hands only casually mime real piano playing, sometimes failing the mark of what is heard on the soundtrack by several octaves or beats. At one truly magical juncture, she holds a cigarette with her left hand while the piano left-hand part continues audibly for just a second.

Such rare insouciance! Sound gets detached from everything visible or concrete that might have accrued to it: notation, visual image, and human hands, from the very idea of a stable work, the automatic physical trace. And thus the vernacular philosophy whose opening proposition was the battle montage's nightmare comes to an unexpectedly hopeful conclusion. When the idea that a musical code encrypts military information is thus exploded by the cinematic apparatus, the explosion takes along a correlative, the belief that musical works trace social phenomena in decipherable ways. And when an automatism that allows no escape routes between inscription and realization is thus dismantled the pathological specter of music coming into the world and causing death is dispersed as well.

Dishonored makes an ontological proposition that the musical "work" exists neither as an abstraction nor as a score, only as a performance. What remains and what counts is sheer verve, the intensity of the performance, and the physical freedom of Marlene Dietrich's movements against the immobility of her audience. These things are not absurd. An earlier and perhaps predictable association between feminine wiles and improvisational impulses has evaporated, and a more abstract, even ethical dimension has arisen to supplant it. Within the plot that ethical dimension has to do with Marie's navigation through her conflicting allegiances, her allowing Lieutenant Kranau to escape from the Austrians after he is captured. On trial for this treason, she says only "perhaps I—loved him," the sole and suicidal explanation she offers. As rhapsodist, she has realized that she is not ready to survive the strictures of nationalism, let alone any coming totalitarian regime.

For this reason, Sternberg's intimations of Franz Liszt in his heroine's musical persona are significant, down to the trick of smoking while performing (Fig. 7).[48] Liszt is one last Austro-Hungarian particle that floats into the film. Yet, like "Danube Waves," "Liszt" does not primarily serve as Imperial window-dressing. Liszt wrote variations and rhapsodies on *a priori* pieces, which reflect his practice of spontaneous improvisation. Yet his original compositions are also unstable; their many published versions represent his penchant for in-concert paraphrase.[49] "Liszt" is thus not the Czardas prince but rather the virtuoso, the memory of radical destabilization and musical surplus, of performed etudes that are transcendent and ephemeral and not subject to capture by graphic trace.

Figure 7   *Figure 8*

Liszt could appear prominently in an alternative account of musical modernism, in a challenge to Second Vienna School musical habits and its claims to modernism's only respectable musical antecedents, and only proper artistic consequences. Liszt anticipated the modernism in which the dialectic of dissonance and consonance is less important than games with open works and found objects, with the radical potential of technique and virtuosity—the modernism of Paris more than Vienna. Yet there is still more to Liszt, for reasons that made him central to Jankélévitch's moral philosophy. Jankélévitch saw Liszt's music-making as a model for reflection upon ethical dilemmas. There is a narrow corridor between spiritual automatism, in which one follows a script (whether ethical, musical, or otherwise), and caprice or chaotic irresponsibility, and it is represented by Liszt's improvisations. You cannot plan to occupy this corridor—the moral ideal is accessible through verve, by proceeding where the path is uncertain.[50]

Such moral heroism belongs to the human genus, and the final performance of "Danube Waves" in *Dishonored* brings it back into play. On the eve of her execution, Marie spends the night playing the waltz. She freezes, as she had before, on the dominant ninth chord that introduces the waltz's second theme, and repeats the chord several times, turning to check for the sunrise at the window as she does (Fig. 8).

The stammer and the repetitions incorporate Marie into the realm of mechanism, as a marionette with the hiccups—"automaton" is their supra-audible Other. But no, the hammering of the chord is prefiguring, in slow motion, the drum-roll that will announce Marie's death a few minutes down the line. Like her monitoring the sunrise, it refers ahead.

But no, the stammer and the drum-roll are a spill into the sonic avant-garde. The drum-roll goes on and on (like a skipped needle or arrested CD), and its reverberations seem almost as long. Sternberg had to fight for this in the final scene, and he was convinced that his insistence on an unusual sound effect earned the movie (and Paramount) the first-ever Oscar for sound production.[51] If a kind of violent sonic anger has thus grown out of the waltz, it replaces the virtuosity that had once arisen at the same place, out of the same chord and the same pause for breath.

No again, the arrested chord is something else, not a terminus and not a nihilistic sign. Marlene Dietrich is contemplating the chord, the entry point for rare virtuosity when she first played the waltz. She is remembering what used to be there. She has gone on in imagination, to transcendent etudes that will never now "come into the world."

And, as Sternberg never tired of pointing out, it is not she who is dishonored. Paramount forced that title on him, and he was angry about it. Like *La traviata*, the title reminds you that the heroine is a prostitute, lest you come to admire her too much. His preferred title was the heroine's professional cognomen: *X-27*.[52] But the truly dishonored are those who refuse the uncertainties that she sustains so well, in the narrow corridor where the brief instant of improvisation is not mischief, but evidence of life.

Notes

1 For a critique of musical hermeneutics, which asks what might be involved in treating music as performance, see Abbate, "Music—Drastic or Gnostic?" *Critical Inquiry* 30, no. 3 (Spring 2004), 505–36.

2 Theodor W. Adorno, *Introduction to the Sociology of Music*, trans. E.B. Ashton (New York: Continuum, 1976), 62.

3 Daniel Albright, "Metaphors for Cubes in Satie's Music," in his *Untwisting the Serpent: Modernism in Music, Literature, and Other Arts* (Chicago and London: University of Chicago Press, 2000), 206–7.

4 Ibid., 6.

5 Mirian Hansen, "The Mass Production of the Senses: Classical Cinema as Vernacular Modernism," originally in *Modernism/Modernity* 6, no.2 (1999): 59–77; reprinted (and here cited) in Christine Gledhill and Linda Williams, eds., *Reinventing Film Studies* (New York: Oxford University Press, 2000), 332–350.

6 Ibid., 333.

7 Ibid., 343.

8 The waltz had appeared in music box disk form as early as 1896 (cf. Regina Music Disk no. 4010).

9 "Waves of the Danube," arrangement by J.M. Rumshinsky (New York: Hebrew

Publishing Co., 1914). On Rumshinsky's career see Mark Slobin *Tenement Songs* (Urbana: University of Illinois Press, 1982), 11–14 and 36–47. Rumshinsky's life, as Slobin points out, was one prototype for the fictional "Jakie Rabinowitz" of *The Jazz Singer* (the choir boy who becomes a popular-music success). And, as Slobin observes, Al Jolson belonged to Rumshinsky's generation and cultural milieu; the two were well acquainted.

10 One last cinematic incarnation: Bollywood star Raj Kapoor plays it on his violin in *Barsaat* (*Rain*, in Hindi, 1949), where it seems to stand for sheer intensity of feeling; he played it in several other films as well. Whether the melody in the later 1940s, in Bombay, was already "The Anniversary Song," and what complex cross-cultural metamorphoses are represented by Raj Kapoor's obsession with the tune, must remain open questions.

11 In Berlin he made recordings for Homocord; cf. Homocord B251, featuring Siegfried Arno singing operetta, with the orchestra conducted by Hajos.

12 See William Rosar, "Music for the Monsters: Universal Pictures' Horror Film Scores of the Thirties," *U. S. Library of Congress Quarterly Journal* 40, no.4 (1983), 390–421.

13 Gerd Gemünden, "Brecht in Hollywood: *Hangmen Also Die* and the anti-Nazi Film," *The Drama Review* 43, no. 4 (1999), 65–76.

14 Sternberg mentions the "Danube Waves" in his reminiscences about childhood in Vienna; see Josef von Sternberg, *Fun in a Chinese Laundry* (New York: Mac-Millan, 1965), 8–9, "mine was every crevice of the vast amusement park [the Prater in Vienna], the like of which never again existed . . . hundreds of shooting galleries, Punch and Judy and the inevitable Satan puppet, chalk-faced clowns in their dominos, boats sliding from a high point down into the water with a great splash, leather-faced dummies that groaned when slapped . . . a glass maze from which the delighted customers stumbled with black eyes and gashed heads, hypnotists who practiced levitation and passed hoops around the dormant females swaying five feet from where they ought to have been, and the central figure of a huge Chinese mandarin with drooping mustaches longer than the tail of a horse revolving on a merry-go-round to the tune of Ivanovici's *Donauwellen*—what more could I have asked?"

15 "Low hermeneutics" sees social meanings as inscribed in musical texts at the moment of their creation, remaining legible in semi-permanent ways thereafter. "Soft hermeneutics" acknowledges that nothing is immanent in the work, that music unleashes associations in the listening subject, which may correspond in part to the historically pedigreed reactions of some hypothetical past listener, as reconstructed through investigative zeal. But soft inevitably shades into low.

16 Elizabeth Wood, "Lesbian Fugue: Ethel Smyth's Contrapuntal Arts," in Ruth Solie, ed., *Musicology and Difference* (Berkeley and Los Angeles: University of California Press, 1993), 164. For more on the discourse of cryptograms in musicology, see Abbate, "Drastic or Gnostic," 524–29.

17 Vladimir Jankélévitch, *Music and the Ineffable*, 11.

18 Music in this regard constitutes "presence as event," a presence "capable of touching, and even of hitting us," and hence a "presence and an absence that constitute movement and are *counter to representation*," as described by Hans Ulrich Gumbrecht in his "Form without Matter versus Form as Event," *MLN* 11 (1996), 578–92 (citation, 586).

19 Abbate, "Drastic or Gnostic," 513–514, 530.

20 Albright, *Untwisting the Serpent*, 6–7.

21 James Lastra describes these alternatives in *Sound Technology and the American Cinema: Perception, Representation, Modernity* (New York: Columbia University Press, 2000), 101–102.

22 Ibid., 104

23 On the pre-history of synthetic speech in cinema see Thomas Y. Levin, "'Töne aus dem Nichts': Rudolf Pfenninger und die Archäologie des synthetischen Tons," in Thomas Macho and Sigrid Weigel, eds., *Zur Medien-und Technikgeschichte der Stimme* (Berlin: Akademie Verlag, 2001), 313–355.

24 Levin, "Töne aus dem Nichts," 313.

25 *Fun in a Chinese Laundry*, 100–101.

26 Essay originally in *Film Culture* 1, no.5–6 (1955); reprinted in Andrew Sarris, *Interviews with Film Directors* (New York: Bobbs Merrill, 1967), 413–27; citation 417–18. The passage on "tönende Handschrift" reads: "I have corrected faulty diction and exaggerated sibilants by using pen and ink on the sound track that runs with the film; and it has been announced that someone had succeeded in writing on the sound track markings so skillfully resembling the photostatic image of words that, when projected, the human language was heard. Imagine writing the sound of a human language with pen and ink—or changing the human language not only with pen and ink, but with the slightest twist of a dial or alteration of speed raising or lowering the pitch of a voice." (420).

27 Ibid., 419

28 Ibid.

29 As described by Miriam Hansen, "Benjamin and Cinema: Not a One-Way Street," *Critical Inquiry* 25, no.2 (1999): 306–343. See especially 310–13, where Hansen describes Benjamin's search for an "alternative reception of technology" that would be neither naively optimistic nor revert to pessimism and crypto-nostalgia.

30 See *The Picturegoer's Who's Who and Encyclopedia of the Screen Today*, (London: Odhams Press, 1933), 502–3 (citation 502).

31 "Töne aus dem Nichts," 316.

32 Kittler, *Gramophone. Film. Typewriter*, translated with an introduction by Geoffrey Winthrop-Young and Michael Wutz (Stanford: Stanford University Press, 1999), 12.

33 "Die Kronen-Naht des Schädels (was nun zunächst zu untersuchen wäre) hat—
    nehmen wirs an—eine gewisse Ähnlichkeit mit der dicht gewundenen Linie,
    die der Stift eines Phonographen in den empfangenden rotierenden Zylinder
    des Apparates eingräbt. Wie nun, wenn man diesen Stift täuschte und ihn, wo er
    zurückzuleiten hat, über eine Spur lenkte, die nicht aus der graphischen Über-
    setzung eines Tones stammte, sondern ein an sich und natürlich Bestehendes—,
    gut: sprechen wirs nur aus: eben (z. B.) die Kronen-Naht wäre—: Was würde
    geschehen?—Ein Ton müßte entstehen, eine Ton-Folge, eine Musik . . . Gefühle
    - welche? Ungläubigkeit, Scheu, Furcht, Ehrfurcht—: ja, welches nur von allen
    hier möglichen Gefühlen verhindert mich, einen Namen vorzuschlagen für das
    Ur-Geräusch,welches da zur Welt kommen sollte." On Rilke's essay see Kittler,
    Gramophone. Film. Typewriter, 38–45.

34 The "seismograph" metaphor, famously, from Theodor W. Adorno, "Schubert,"
    originally in *Die Musik* 21 (1928), republished Rolf Tiedemann, ed., *Gesammelte
    Schriften* 17 [=*Musikalische Schriften* IV] (Frankfurt-am-Main: Suhrkamp Ver-
    lag, 1982], 18–33. "In unregelmässigen Zügen, einem Seismographen gleich, hat
    Schubert's Musik die Botschaft von der qualitativen Veränderung des Menschen
    notiert . . . wir können sie nicht lesen; aber dem schwindenden, überfluteten
    Auge hält sie vor die Chiffren der endlichen Versöhnung" (33). ["In irregular
    jerks, like a seismograph, Schubert's music transcribes a qualititative change in
    humankind . . . we cannot read it, but it sets ciphers of the reconciliation that
    will finally come in front of our failing, tear-filled eyes."]

35 See Altman, "Sound Space," in Altman, ed., *Sound Theory/Sound Practice* (Lon-
    don and New York: Routledge, 1992), 47–48.

36 Kalinak, *Settling the Score: Music and the Classical Hollywood Film* (Madison:
    University of Wisconsin Press, 1992), 24–28.

37 See his "*Star Wars*, Music and Myth," in James Buhler, Caryl Flynn, and Da-
    vid Neumeyer, eds., *Music and Cinema* (Middletown, CT: Wesleyan University
    Press, 2000), 33–57 (citation, 43); Buhler is summarizing an analogous premise
    about music's position as interpreter of diegetic narrative—hence, between fic-
    tion and spectator—in Caryl Flinn's *Strains of Utopia: Gender, Nostalgia, and
    Hollywood Film* (Princeton: Princeton University Press, 1992).

38 The phrase "fit like a glove" is Max Steiner's, as quoted by David Neumeyer, with
    Caryl Flinn and James Buhler, in their "Introduction," *Music and Cinema*, 15; see
    also 15–17 on the binarism of "synchronous" and "autonomous" music. Neu-
    meyer et al. point out that the classic "issue of synchronization and counter-
    point," historically of such importance, has tended to be re-inscribed in present
    academic praxis. There are critics who read films as aesthetic objects—hence
    focusing on the product as a whole and integrating its musical parts with its
    other parts ("synchronous"). There are those who concentrate on the ideol-
    ogy of film and therefore maintain an ironic distance from the aesthetic object
    ("counterpoint"), preferring to "disrupt . . . apparently closed texts" (16).

39 Royal S. Brown, *Undertones and Overtones* (Berkeley and Los Angeles: Univer-
    sity of California Press, 1994), 84.

40 Claudia Gorbman, *Unheard Melodies: Narrative Film Music* (Bloomington: Indiana University Press, 1987), 30.

41 Louis Gianetti, *Understanding the Movies* (Englewood Cliffs, NJ: Prentice-Hall, 1972), 156: "In several scenes of Hitchcock's *Psycho*, Bernard Hermann's score—consisting entirely of strings—suggests shrill bird noises. This motif is used as a form of characterization. A shy and appealing young man (Anthony Perkins) is associated with birds early on in the film. He stuffs birds as a hobby, and his own features are rather intense and hawk-like. During a brutal murder sequence, the soundtrack throbs with screeching bird music. The audience assumes the murderer is the boy's mother, but birds have been associated with him, not her."

42 David Bordwell and Kristin Thompson, *Film Art: An Introduction*, 3rd edition (New York: McGraw-Hill, 1990), 248: "In *Psycho*, when a woman screams, we expect to hear a human voice and instead hear screaming violins."

43 Royal S. Brown, *Undertones and Overtones*, 165, argues that Hitchcock's disturbed males are discursively aligned with spooky non-diegetic music, especially in *Vertigo* and *Psycho*. He makes the astute observation that while in *Vertigo* there is ordinary diegetic music, reminding us that music is not just a signifier of psychosis, *Psycho* is quite different: "Since *Psycho* has no diegetic music to somewhat rationalize music's very presence in the film, the non-diegetic music gets an even stronger weighing-in on the side of the irrational. It is as if Norman hears only this 'unseen' score." The metaphor of Norman's "hearing" the score, which is so striking, remains nonetheless metaphorical, since the music is read as translating his madness into musical form, thus bringing it home to the audience.

44 David A. Cook, *A History of Narrative Film* (New York and London: W. W. Norton, 1981), 302, "the sequence is perfectly complemented by the shrieking staccato violins of Bernard Hermann's edgy score."

45 Stockhausen's press conference of 16 September 2001 in the Hotel Atlantic, Hamburg, "Also—was da geschehen ist, ist natürlich—jetzt müssen Sie alle ihr Gehirn umstellen—das größtmögliche Kunstwerk was es je gegeben hat, dass also Geister in einem Akt etwas vollbringen, was wir in der Musik nie träumen könnten, dass Leute zehn Jahre üben wie verrückt, total fanatisch für ein Konzert und dann sterben. Das ist das größte Kunstwerk, was es überhaupt gibt für den ganzen Kosmos. Stellen sie sich das doch vor, was da passiert ist, das sind Leute, die sind so konzentriert auf das, auf die eine Aufführung und dann werden 5000 Leute in die Auferstehung gejagt in einem Moment. Das könnte ich nicht. Dagegen sind wir gar nichts als Komponisten." ["What happened there is, is of course—you all have to rearrange your brains now—the greatest work of art ever, ok, that free spirits bring about, in a single act, that which we in music cannot dream of, that people practice like madmen for ten years, like total fanatics, for a concert, and then die. That is the greatest work of art there is, in the whole universe. Imagine what happened: there are people that are incredibly concentrated on this one thing, on this one performance, and then in a single moment five thousand are hustled into the sweet hereafter. I could

not do that. Compared to that, we composers are nothing."] A transcript of the interview, broadcast on Norddeutscher Rundfunk, is available at http://www. kerzel.de/mulinks.htm

46   Attali, *Noise: The Political Economy of Music*, trans. Brian Massumi (Minneapolis: University of Minnesota Press, 1985), 5, 6. The sentiment is a perennial in musical hermeneutics, a signature tune. As Richard Leppert re-states it, "Music … has always been a strong force in society, not only as it reflects and reacts to social forces but also as it helps shape society and its culture"; see his "Music, Domestic Life, and Cultural Chauvinism," in Richard Leppert and Susan Mc-Clary, eds., *Music and Society* (Cambridge: Cambridge University Press, 1987), 102.

47   Louis Chavance, *Le cas Josef von Sternberg*, in *La Revue de Cinéma* 2, no.12 (1930), 3–14, reprinted in Peter Baxter, ed., *Sternberg* (London: BFI Publications, 1980), 16–20 (citation 19). B.G. Braver-Mann, "Josef von Sternberg," in *Experimental Cinema* 1, no.5 (1934), 17–21, reprinted in *Sternberg*, 28–34 (citations 30, 31). Even Chavance, assessing Sternberg in glowing terms, felt that in Sternberg's case "the scenario has no importance for him" (17).

48   A propos Liszt and smoking, see the account by Jules Laurens, cited by Charles Rosen, *The Romantic Generation* (Cambridge: Harvard University Press, 1995), 510: "Lighting a cigar which passed at moments from his lips to his fingers, executing with ten fingers the part written for organ pedals, and indulging in other *tours de force* and prestidigitation, he was prodigious."

49   As Rosen writes (ibid., 499): "Here there [has been] a critical failure to recognize an extraordinary form of originality. The new versions of the Transcendental Etudes are not revisions but concert paraphrases of the old, and their art lies in the technique of transformation."

50   See his essay "De l'improvisation," in *Liszt: Rhapsodie et improvisation* (Paris: Flammarion, 1998), 107–73, in particular the sections "L'État de grâce et l'état de verve" (121–27) and "L'homme en verve" (164–73).

51   *Fun in a Chinese Laundry*, 258.

52   Ibid., 257.

Notes on Contributors

Notes on Contributors

CAROLYN ABBATE's books include *Unsung Voices* (1991), which appears in French as *Voix hors chant* (2004), and *In Search of Opera* (2001). She has translated Jean-Jacques Nattiez's *Sémiologie générale et musicologie* (Music and Discourse, 1990) and Vladimir Jankélévitch's *La musique et l'ineffable* (Music and the Ineffable, 2003). Author of essays on the operas of Wagner, Debussy, and Mozart, as well as on the aesthetics and philosophy of music, film, performance, and music technology, she has received awards from the Guggenheim Foundation and the National Endowment for the Humanities, and has been a fellow of the Wissenschaftskolleg, Berlin. She appears frequently on the Metropolitan Opera Broadcasts, and has worked as an assistant for dramaturgy at the Metropolitan Opera.

KAROL BERGER, a music historian, is Osgood Hooker Professor in Fine Arts at Stanford University. His *Musica Ficta* (Cambridge University Press, 1987) received the Otto Kinkeldey Award of the American Musicological Society. His most recent book is *A Theory of Art* (Oxford University Press, 2000).

HORST BREDEKAMP studied art history, archaeology, philosophy and sociology in Kiel, Munich, Berlin, and Marburg, where he received his PhD in 1974. After having worked at the Museum of Sculpture in Frankfurt/Main (1974–76) he became Assistant Professor and, after 1982, Professor of Art History at the University of Hamburg. Since 1993 he has taught art history at Humboldt University, Berlin, and in 2003 was named Permanent Fellow of the Wissenschaftskolleg, Berlin. He has published on iconoclasm, medieval sculpture, Renaissance and Mannerism, political iconography, museology and new media.

PETER BURGARD is Professor of German at Harvard University. He studied at The Johns Hopkins University (BA) and at the Universities of Cologne, Bonn, and Virginia (MA, PhD). He teaches Goethe, Nietzsche, Freud, early modern cultural history, baroque art and literature, and the culture of *fin-de-siècle* Austria and Germany. In addition to essays on Caravaggio, Opitz, Gryphius, Goethe, Herder, Lessing, Nietzsche, Mann, Adorno, Ibsen, Miller, and Warhol, he is the author of *Idioms of Uncertainty: Goethe and the Essay* and editor of *Nietzsche and the Feminine* and *Barock: Neue Sichtweisen einer Epoche*. His current project is a book entitled *Towards an Aesthetic of the Baroque*.

SCOTT BURNHAM holds graduate degrees in music composition (Yale '82) and in music theory and analysis (Brandeis, '88). His 1988 PhD dissertation was on the nineteenth-century German music theorist A.B. Marx. In 1988–89, he taught in the Music Department at SUNY-Stony Brook; since then, he has taught at Princeton University (Associate Professor in 1995; Professor in 2000; Chair of Department in 2000). He has written articles and essays on a variety of subjects, including the history of tonal theory, Beethoven reception, Mozart opera, and aspects of analysis and criticism. His book-length projects include *Beethoven Hero* (1995); *Beethoven and His World* (2000), a collection of essays he co-edited with Michael P. Steinberg; A. B. Marx, *Musical Form in the Age of Beethoven* (1997), selected writings by Marx that he translated and edited; and the forthcoming *Beethoven*, a spin-off volume of the lengthy *New Grove Encyclopedia* article on Beethoven that he revised and co-authored with the original authors Joseph Kerman and Alan Tyson. He is currently working on a critical study of the instrumental music of Schubert and Mozart, for which he has received fellowships from the National Humanities Center and the Guggenheim Foundation.

HERMANN DANUSER is Chair of the Music Department at Humboldt University, Berlin. He is a prolific author and leading scholar on nineteenth- and twentieth-century music and has published important works on Wagner, Mahler, twentieth-century music, music theory, aesthetics, and historiology, and the history of interpretation and hermeneutics. Recent articles include "Between Enlightenment and Romanticism in Music History: 'First Viennese Modernism' and the Delayed Nineteenth Century" in *19th-Century Music* (2001–02) and "Die 'erste Wiener Moderne' als historiographische Alternative zur 'Wiener Klassik'" in *Wiener Klassik: Ein musikgeschichtlicher Begriff in Diskussion*, ed. Gernot Gruber (2002).

LYDIA GOEHR is Professor of Philosophy at Columbia University. She specializes in aesthetics, critical theory, exile theory, and especially the philosophy of music. She is the author of *The Imaginary Museum of Musical Works, an Essay in the Philosophy of Music* (1992) and *The Quest for Voice* (1998), a book of essays on philosophy, politics, and music with a focus on Richard Wagner. She is the author of numerous articles and reviews, including an entry for the philosophy of music for the *New Grove Dictionary* (2002), and essays on Adorno, Merleau Ponty and Danto on the relation of art to politics. She is the recipient of numerous fellowships from, and visiting Professorships at, the Guggenheim Foundation, Getty Research Institute, Mellon Foundation, N.E.H., and

Wissenschaftskolleg, Berlin, Warburg Haus, and University of California at Berkeley as the Visiting Ernest Bloch Professor. She is currently writing two thematically similar books, one on the relation between philosophy and music in the work of Adorno, and the other, *Lonely Composers and Solitary Thinkers*, on the history of the relation between philosophy and music (1750–1950) as investigated through the famous quarrels between philosophers and composers. She is the co-author of the forthcoming *The Don Giovanni Moment: On the philosophical and literary legacy of an Opera*.

HANS ULRICH GUMBRECHT is the Albert Guérard Professor of Literature at Stanford University. Among his books on literary theory and literary and cultural history are *Eine Geschichte der spanischen Literatur* (1990), *Making Sense in Life and Literature* (Minnesota University Press, 1992), *In 1926—Living at the Edge of Time* (Harvard University Press, 1998), and *The Powers of Philology* (University of Illinois Press, 2003). He is an editor of the forthcoming *New Harvard History of German Literature* and a regular contributor to the *Frankfurter Allgemeine Zeitung, Neue Zürcher Zeitung, Folha de São Paulo*, and *Merkur—Zeitschrift für europäisches Denken*. Since 1998 he has been a Fellow of the American Academy of Arts & Sciences. In 2004 he received an honorary PhD from the Université de Montréal.

KLAUS KROPFINGER has been Professor of Musicology at the Freie University of Berlin and at the University of Kassel. His main field of research is music history and aesthetics from the Middle Ages through the twentieth century, with special emphasis on reception theory and the interrelationship of the arts. His most recent publications are *Beethoven* (Bärenreiter/Metzler, 2001; Italian version, 2004); "Wagners triadische Zeitbeschwörung," in *Der Raum Bayreuth. Ein Auftrag aus der Zukunft*, Frankfurt am Main 2002, 70–93; "Denn was schwer ist, ist auch schön, gut, gross," *Bonner Beethoven-Studien* 3, 2003; Italian version, *Musica/Realtà* 72, 2003.

DAVID LEWIN (1933–2003) held the Walter W. Naumburg professorship at Harvard. Professor Lewin was a Guggenheim Foundation Fellow in 1983–1984, and held a residency at the Rockefeller Foundation Study and Conference Center at Bellagio, Italy. He was awarded honorary degrees by the University of Chicago (1995) and the New England Conservatory of Music (2000). He was a member of the American Academy of Arts and Sciences, 1985–1988; life member, 2000. A symposium in his honor on the Schoenberg string quartets was held at Harvard University in 1998. His main work included numerous compositions and many publications in the field of music theory such as *Generalized Form and Transformation* (New Haven, 1987); and *Musical Form and Transformation* (New Haven, 1993), which won the ASCAP-Deems Taylor Award. He also wrote many articles in *Journal of Music Theory, Perspectives of New Music, Music Perception, 19th-Century Music*, and other journals.

ANTHONY NEWCOMB is currently Professor of Music and Italian Studies and Chair of Music at University of California at Berkeley. He has recently stepped down as Dean of Arts and Humanities at Berkeley, then as Chair of Art History. He holds an AB from the University of California at Berkeley (1962) and a PhD from Princeton (1969). He taught at Harvard from 1968–73 before moving to Berkeley. He has held Fulbright, Woodrow Wilson, Martha B. Rockefeller, Guggenheim, and NEH research Fellowships. He was elected to the American Academy of Arts and Sciences in 1992. His particular areas of specialization are: Italian secular music, both vocal and instrumental, 1540–1640; German vocal and instrumental music, ca. 1815–1915; and the interaction between musical and verbal and conceptual meanings in both periods.

KAREN PAINTER, Associate Professor of Music at Harvard University, specializes in musical aesthetics, ideology, and intellectual history. Trained at Yale and Columbia Universities, she taught at Dartmouth before joining the Harvard faculty in 1997. She is the editor of *Mahler and His World* (2002) and *Late Thoughts*, on music and art history, co-edited with Thomas Crow (the Getty Institute, forthcoming). She is completing *Symphonic aspirations. German ideology and musical thought, 1900–45*, for Harvard University Press. Other publications explore various musical repertories in connection with bourgeois culture in the early-nineteenth century, socialism in the early-twentieth, and Jewish identity and anti-Semitism in the early-twentieth. She has written on the role of Mozart in cultural and intellectual history in the early- and mid-nineteenth centuries, as part of a larger project on Mozart myths.

JUDITH RYAN received her BA from Sydney University, Australia, and her PhD from the University of Münster, Germany. Before coming to Harvard, she taught for many years at Smith College. Her teaching and research interests are nineteenth- and twentieth-century literature, especially poetry and the novel. She is the author of *Umschlag und Verwandlung*, a book on Rilke's poetry; *The Uncompleted Past*, which treats postwar German novels; *The Vanishing Subject*, which traces the relation of literature to empiricist psychology, and *Rilke, Modernism and Poetic Tradition*, a study of Rilke's intertextual relations. She has also written articles on such authors as Franz Kafka, Paul Celan, Christa Wolf, and Günter Grass. Professor Ryan teaches courses on German lyric poetry, postwar German literature, modernism, and on the postmodern novel.

ANNE C. SHREFFLER studied at the New England Conservatory, receiving the B.Mus. in flute performance and M.Mus. in music theory, followed by doctoral studies at Harvard University. She has published widely on Webern, including a book, *Webern and the Lyric Impulse: Songs and Fragments on Poems by Georg Trakl* (Oxford University Press, 1994) as well as many articles. Her current research interests include music and politics, American music, the historiography of twentieth-century music, composers in emigration, and contemporary opera. She taught at the University of Basel in Switzerland from 1994 until 2003 and is currently the James Edward Ditson Professor of Music at Harvard University.

LEO TREITLER is Distinguished Professor of Music Emeritus, the Graduate Center, The City University of New York. He has had numerous teaching assignments in the U.S., Europe, and The People's Republic of China. He studied at Princeton (PhD, 1966) and the University of Chicago (MA, 1957). His publications include studies of music in the Middle Ages, music criticism, theory of musicology (historiography, epistemology, language), and the philosophy of music.

MARTIN WARNKE teaches at the University of Hamburg, Germany. His books include *Peter Paul Rubens* (Barron's, 1980); *The Court Artist* (Cambridge University Press, 1988); and *Political Landscape* (Harvard University Press, 1995).

HENRI ZERNER is a Professor of History of Art and Architecture at Harvard and former curator at the Fogg Art Museum. He is the author of *Romanticism and Realism* (Viking, 1983) with Charles Rosen, and, most recently, of *Renaissance Art in France* (Flammarion, 2004).

Index

Index